THE LITERARY CRITICISM OF JOHN RUSKIN

THE LITERARY CRITICISM
of
JOHN RUSKIN

SELECTED, EDITED, AND
WITH AN INTRODUCTION BY
HAROLD BLOOM

A DA CAPO PAPERBACK

Library of Congress Cataloging in Publication Data

Ruskin, John, 1819-1900.
The literary criticism of John Ruskin.

(A Da Capo paperback)
Reprint. Originally published: Garden City, N.Y.: Doubleday, c1965.
Bibliography: p.
Includes index.
1. Literature—History and criticism. 2. English literature—History and criticism. 3. Aesthetics.
I. Bloom, Harold. II. Title.
PR5252.B6 1987 820′.9 86-32996
ISBN 0-306-80294-5 (pbk.)

This Da Capo Press paperback edition of *The Literary Criticism of John Ruskin* is an unabridged republication of the edition published in Garden City, NY in 1965. It is reprinted by arrangement with Doubleday & Co., Inc.

Published by Da Capo Press, Inc.
A Subsidiary of Plenum Publishing Corporation
233 Spring Street, New York, N.Y. 10013

Manufactured in the United States of America

CONTENTS

INTRODUCTION

—But there's a Tree, of many, one,
A single Field which I have looked upon,
Both of them speak of something that is gone:
The Pansy at my feet
Doth the same tale repeat:
Whither is fled the visionary gleam?
Where is it now, the glory and the dream?

1

Ruskin was born in London, on February 8, 1819, in the same year that Queen Victoria was born. His father, John James Ruskin, the son of a bankrupt, self-slain Edinburgh wine merchant, had prospered in partnership with the Domecq sherry vineyards, and aspired to raise himself out of his lower middle class position, though he was forced to put aside artistic and literary interests while he made his fortune. Ruskin's mother, Margaret Cox, was John James Ruskin's cousin, and had waited nine years to marry him, while he made his way in London. Energetic and shrewd as John James Ruskin was, he appears to have been a weaker character than his fiercely Evangelical wife, whose rigid nature dominated the formative years of her only child's life, and who clearly was responsible for the psychic malforming that made John Ruskin's emotional life a succession of disasters. Margaret Ruskin, before her son's birth, dedicated him to the service of God, intending him for the ministry. Nature intended otherwise, and made even of the infant Ruskin an aesthetic visionary, fascinated by the world of form and color. The world of language was revealed to the child, between the ages of four and fourteen, by daily

Bible readings with his mother. That ten-year march and countermarch through the Book made Ruskin as Bible-soaked a writer as Milton or Blake, and formed the ultimate basis for the characteristic Ruskinian prose style, with its ornate and opulent diction, prophetic rhythm, and extraordinary emotional range.

Ruskin had the misfortune to be a child prodigy, as forced a one as John Stuart Mill. A poet at seven, educated largely at home, scarcely allowed friends, brooded over by a sternly loving mother and a totally indulgent and admiring father, Ruskin was ruined before his thirteenth birthday. He was ruined, one qualifies, in terms of his fully human potential, but not at all in regard to the unique gift that was his, and that his peculiar upbringing did much to nourish.

On his thirteenth birthday, Ruskin received the present of a copy of Samuel Rogers' long poem *Italy*, richly illustrated with steel engravings, including twenty-five plates from drawings by J. M. W. Turner. Immediately captured by Turner, Ruskin was to become an artist under this influence, but his painting like his poetry finally proved marginal, and the lasting effect of Turner was to confirm a critical gift of genius. As a critic of all the arts and of society, Ruskin became, and still remains, a unique figure in the European cultural tradition. This uniqueness was finally a uniqueness of sensibility, and cannot be understood apart from the history of sensibility.

The natural world Ruskin saw was half-created by his Romantic vision, a vision for which his personal sensibility provided the beginnings, but in which his great and essential teachers were Wordsworth and Turner, the dominant figures in the poetry and painting of their generation. Like Shelley before him, Ruskin was haunted throughout his life by Wordsworth's great *Ode: Intimations of Immortality from Recollections of Earliest Childhood.* The fundamental experience of the Ode, and of *Tintern Abbey,* is at one with the central and decisive experiences of Ruskin's life. Attempting to describe the unifying element in

Ruskin's complex religious development, Derrick Leon, perhaps unintentionally, paraphrased *Tintern Abbey:*

> Ruskin's real communion, throughout his life, was the communion of the artist and poet: his *panis supersubstantialis* those rare moments of fully awakened consciousness when the mind is detached and deliberately at rest; when the usual egotism of being is deliberately suppressed, and the emotional faculties, cleansed of all human desire and sorrow, respond in serenity and joy to the mystery and beauty of the external world.

In his old age, Ruskin looked back at his essential character as a child, and recognized again his affinity to Turner, Wordsworth, and Shelley, though he did not hesitate to give the preference to himself, the failed poet, over those who had succeeded:

> I was different, be it once more said, from other children even of my own type, not so much in the actual nature of the feeling, but in the mixture of it. I had, in my little clay pitcher, vialfuls, as it were, of Wordsworth's reverence, Shelley's sensitiveness, Turner's accuracy, all in one. A snowdrop was to me, as to Wordsworth, part of the Sermon on the mount; but I never should have written sonnets to the celandine, because it is of a coarse, yellow and imperfect form. With Shelley, I loved blue sky and blue eyes, but never in the least confused the heavens with my own poor little Psychidion. And the reverence and passion were alike kept in their places by the constructive Turnerian element; and I did not weary myself in wishing that a daisy could see the beauty of its shadow, but in trying to draw the shadow rightly, myself.

This self-congratulatory paragraph tells us why Wordsworth and Shelley were poets, and Ruskin only a critic, albeit a great one. Reverence, sensitiveness, and accuracy, taken together, are the theological virtues for criticism, but the combination can thwart creation. Ruskin, at the age of nine, was a better poet than Ruskin at twenty, when he won the Newdigate Prize at Oxford. At nine, Ruskin wrote good Wordsworthian verse, better perhaps than Wordsworth was writing in 1828:

> Skiddaw, upon thy heights the sun shines bright,
> But only for a moment; then gives place
> Unto a playful cloud which on thy brow
> Sports wantonly,—then floats away in air,—
> Throwing its shadow on thy towering height;
> And, darkening for a moment thy green side,
> But adds unto its beauty, as it makes
> The sun more bright when it again appears.

But, by 1839, Ruskin's imagination had not the patience to wait upon the restraints of verse. He knew the truth, or many divisions of it, and he sought the prophet's style in which to deliver it. Fortunately, the truth always remained a poet's truth, and relied on the sources of visionary experience, known to Ruskin from his childhood on, and confirmed in him by his discovery of the visual equivalent in Turner's work.

Ruskin's life, from the revelation of Turner on to his disastrous marriage, was a continuous process of self-discovery, assured and "organic" in its development. Foreign tours, with his parents, encouraged his passion for close observation of nature, for the study of geology and botany, and for incessant sketching and versifying. Even his unreciprocated first love, for Adele Domecq, daughter of his father's business partner, created no more disturbance than could be quieted by an outpouring of much pseudo-Byronic verse. The closeness of the family-circle was not affected by his studies at Christ Church, Oxford, from January 1837 on, as Mrs. Ruskin imperturbably settled in that city and required her son to appear for tea every evening, with Ruskin's father hastening to join them from London every weekend. Despite the family presence, Ruskin had a successful career at Oxford, composing his first book, *The Poetry of Architecture,* while still an undergraduate. But an attack of tuberculosis delayed his taking a degree, and sent him abroad instead, creating the circumstances that altered his career. His return to the Vale of Chamouni, his confronting again the sight of the sublimity of Mont Blanc, renewed the sense of exaltation he had first encountered at the same spot when he was fifteen. The visionary dialectic of Wordsworth's *Tintern Abbey* was renewed in Ruskin, and prepared him for a climactic return to Chamouni in August 1842. In *that* moment of renewal, as Wordsworthian a "spot of time" as any in *The Prelude, Modern Painters,* volume I, had its genesis. Ruskin returned to England, gave up all plans of taking orders, and devoted himself to vindicating the genius of Turner's Romantic landscape art, on principles grounded in the critic's own visionary experience.

By the time Ruskin had to seek healing consolation through another return to Chamouni, in 1854, his critical reputation was established, and his personal life was fairly well set towards destruction. He had published the second volume of *Modern Painters, The Seven Lamps of Architecture,* and *The Stones of Venice,* and he had married Euphemia Gray in 1848 with motives that have puzzled the best of his biographers. The marriage was not consummated, and was annulled in 1854, after the lady fled back to her parents. She married the Pre-Raphaelite painter Millais, whom Ruskin had befriended and patronized, and the entire affair soon passed out of the realm of scandal. Ruskin himself remained reticent on the matter (his marriage is not mentioned in his autobiography, *Praeterita*) and devoted himself more passionately to his work, which increasingly moved from art criticism to social prophecy. As the friend of Rossetti, Carlyle, and the Brownings, as the foremost expositor of the visual arts ever to appear in Great Britain, and as a prose poet of extraordinary power who took the whole concern of man as his subject, Ruskin appeared to have realized himself during the years from 1854 to 1860. Volumes three and four of *Modern Painters* came out in 1856, eliciting from

George Eliot the definitive comment: "He is strongly akin to the sublimest part of Wordsworth." By 1860, Ruskin ought to have been at the supreme point of his development, and in a sense he was, but not in terms of continuity, for by 1860 he was at the turning, and entered into what was at once his great decade and his tragedy.

In 1860, Ruskin stood forth as a prophet fully armed in *Unto This Last,* his most eloquent and vital book. The central experiences of his life had led him beyond Wordsworth's quietism, and returned him to the Biblical origins of his vision. The "theoretic faculty" of man, our ability to enter into the state of aesthetic contemplation depicted in *Tintern Abbey,* had now to issue in the Hebraic and Protestant impulse to free all men towards finding the way to individual vision, to an enjoyment of the sense of something more divinely interfused. Eloquent as he always was, Ruskin rose to the heights of his rhetorical power in *Unto This Last.* If there is a kernel passage in his work, it is the one that climaxes:

> *There is no wealth but Life*—Life, including all its powers of love, of joy, and of admiration. That country is the richest which nourishes the greatest number of noble and happy human beings.

This is the moral force behind the apocalyptic yearnings of the fifth and final volume of *Modern Painters,* also published in 1860. A fully perceptive reader in that year might have seen Ruskin as being poised on the threshold of a creative period akin to the great years granted to a whole tradition of English poetic visionaries before him. The expectation would not have been altogether disappointed by Ruskin's works in the sixties, particularly by the sequence of *Munera Pulveris* (1863), *Sesame and Lilies* (1865), and *The Queen of the Air* (1869), but the decade essentially was one of brilliant decline, and two decades of writing after it showed the decline more consistently, until there came the final, intermittent brilliance of *Praeterita,* after which Ruskin had to be silent.

Part of the cause of this downward movement is found clearly enough by an examination of Ruskin's life from 1860 on. In that year Ruskin, already forty, met Rose La Touche, not yet ten, and their extraordinary love began. By 1860 Ruskin had no religious belief in any orthodox sense, having become intellectually agnostic, though his temperament remained a deeply Evangelical one. Rose was, at ten, something of a religious fanatic, and she evidenced already the tortured sensibility that was to result in the illness (at least partly mental) that killed her when she was twenty-five. Despite all the obvious barriers—of differences in age and belief, of the strong opposition of Rose's mother (who, perhaps unconsciously, seems to have desired Ruskin for herself)—Ruskin proposed marriage to Rose on her seventeenth birthday. Ambiguously, Rose delayed her answer for over a year, until correspondence between Ruskin's former wife and Mrs. La Touche revealed the supposed fact of his impotence. There followed a complex cycle of estrangements and reconciliations, concluding with a final reconciliation in 1874, by which time Rose's mental illness had become extreme. With her death, in 1875, Ruskin's long decline commenced. He became involved in spiritualism, and began to identify the memory of Rose with Dante's Beatrice and with St. Ursula. One sympathetic biographer called the Ruskin of the late 1870s a morbid prig, and he was not far wrong. By 1878, Ruskin believed himself to have failed, in love and work alike, and with this sour belief came the onset of his own mental illness. He had been Slade Professor of Fine Art at Oxford since 1868, but the controversy with Whistler and subsequent trial, in 1877, caused him to resign that influential forum. He resumed the chair in 1883, but resigned again when it became clear he could no longer lecture coherently. Thenceforward he lived under what he termed the Storm Cloud, and his whole existence took on the beauty and terror of nightmare, haunted by the Evil One, who had intercepted all his desires, and who plagued him now in the shapes of peacock and cat. From this terror Ruskin partly rescued himself by a Wordsworthian return to childhood, celebrated by the writing of *Praeterita*. He returned also to a kind of religious belief, though he continued to hate the notion of justification by faith, and seems in his last days to have been more Catholic than Protestant in his outlook. In a final twilight period of deep peace alternating with total alienation from reality, Ruskin lived out his last days, dying on January 20, 1900.

2

There are three major areas of Ruskin's achievement: art, social, and literary criticism, and this volume is wholly devoted to only one of the three, being a companion to my colleague Robert L. Herbert's *The Art Criticism of John Ruskin*. There are many anthologies that emphasize Ruskin's social criticism, and several that attempt to give a picture of the whole man, or of his achievement as a prose stylist. I have allowed myself a broad interpretation of "literary criticism" in editing this volume, since Ruskin is very much an anticipatory critic in regard to some schools of literary criticism in our own time. Ruskin is one of the first, if not indeed the first, "myth" or "archetypal" critic, or more properly he is the linking and transitional figure between allegorical critics of the elder, Renaissance kind, and those of the newer variety, like Northrop Frye, or like W. B. Yeats in his criticism. Even if he did not have this unique historical position, Ruskin would stand as one of the handful of major literary critics in nineteenth-century England, though his importance has been obscured by misapprehensions about his work. Most histories of literary criticism tag Ruskin as a "moral" critic which is true only in Ruskin's own terms, but not at all in conventional ones. An Oxford lecture delivered by him in 1870 makes clear the special sense in which Ruskin insists upon the morality of art:

> You must first have the right moral state, or you cannot have art. But when the art is once obtained, its reflected action enhances and completes the moral state out of which it arose, and, above all, communicates the exultation to other minds which are already morally capable of the like. For instance take the art of singing, and the simplest perfect master of it—the skylark. From him you may learn what it is to sing for joy. You must get the moral state first, the pure gladness, then give it finished expression, and it is perfected in itself, and made communicable to others capable of such joy. Accuracy in proportion to the rightness of the cause, and purity of the emotion, is the possibility of fine art. You cannot paint or sing yourself into being good men; you must be good men before you can either paint or sing, and then the colour and sound will complete in you all that is best . . .

In this passage the "right moral state" and "being good men" are phrases that suggest conventional moral attitudes, yet the only moral state mentioned is that of the skylark, "the pure gladness." Behind Ruskin's passage are Wordsworth and Shelley, both in their skylark poems, and in their insistence upon the poet's joy and on poems as necessarily recording the best and happiest moments of the happiest and best minds. Ruskin's literary theory is primarily a Wordsworthian one, and as such it shows a family resemblance to all such theories down to Wallace Stevens, with his eloquent, Paterian insistence that "the morality of the poet's radiant and productive atmosphere is the morality of the right sensation." Ruskin's morality, as a critical theorist, is a morality of aesthetic contemplation, like the morality of *Tintern Abbey*. It is not, in content, an Evangelical morality, though its fervor stamps it as a displaced version of Evangelicism. Ruskin's literary criticism has an explicit moral purpose, as Wordsworth's poetry does also, yet the purpose no more disfigures the criticism than it does the poetry. To understand Ruskin's criticism we need to study not only the pattern of Ruskin's life and career, but also the radical version of Romanticism his entire sensibility incarnated. Literary criticism rarely communicates the critic's own *experience* of literature, but in Ruskin's hands it very nearly always does, and in doing so touches upon the incommunicable. Ruskin did not believe that the imagination could create truth, but he did believe that it was the crucial faculty for the communication and interpretation of truth. Though Ruskin's judgment as a critic was fairly unsteady (he once declared Mrs. Browning's *Aurora Leigh* to be the greatest poem in the language), his central aesthetic experience was so powerful as to make him an almost miraculous medium for the truth of imagination to work through in order to reach sensibilities less uniquely organized than his own. In this respect, as in so many others, he resembles Wordsworth. Thus, speaking of Gothic as being representative of our universal childhood, Ruskin observes that all men:

> look back to the days of childhood as of greatest happiness, because those were the days of greatest wonder, greatest simplicity, and most vigorous imagination. And the whole difference between a man of genius and other men . . . is that the first remains in great part a child, seeing with the large eyes of children, in perpetual wonder, not conscious of much knowledge,—conscious, rather, of infinite ignorance, and yet infinite power; a fountain of eternal admiration, delight, and creative force within him, meeting the ocean of visible and governable things around him.

If this is the source of creative imagination, it follows tragically but pragmatically that the workings of the mature imagination must be compensatory, for the story of art must be one in which gain can come only through loss, and the subsequent memory of the glorious time preceding loss. This pattern is familiar to every reader of Wordsworth, and is nowhere more eloquently expressed than it is by Ruskin. In a letter (September 28, 1847) written to Walter Brown, once his tutor at Christ Church, Ruskin states the central experience of his life in phrases directly borrowed from the *Intimations* Ode:

> . . . there was a time when the sight of a steep hill covered with pines cutting against blue sky, would have touched me with an emotion inexpressible, which, in the endeavour to communicate in its truth and intensity, I must have sought for all kinds of far-off, wild, and dreamy images. Now I can look at such a slope with coolness, and observation of *fact.* I see that it slopes at twenty or twenty-five degrees; I know the pines are spruce fir—'Pinus nigra'—of such and such a formation; the soil, thus, and thus; the day fine and the sky blue. All this I can at once communicate in so many words, and this is all which is necessarily seen. But it is not all the truth: there is something else to be seen there, which I cannot see but in a certain condition of mind, nor can I make anyone else see it, but by putting him into that condition, and my endeavour in description would be, not to detail the facts of the scene, but by any means whatsoever to put my hearer's mind into the same ferment as my mind . . .

Ruskin's activity as a critic of all the arts, of society, and of nature, is a quest to fulfill that "endeavour in description." What makes him a tragic critic (if so odd a phrase may be allowed) is his post-Wordsworthian and post-Turnerian sense of reality. In reply to Walter Brown's Wordsworthian statement of recompense for a loss of primal delight in nature, Ruskin wrote a letter (November 27, 1847) which is an epilogue to the *Intimations* Ode:

> . . . You say, in losing the delight I once had in nature I am coming down more to fellowship with others. Yes, but I feel it a fellowship of blindness. I may be able to get hold of people's hands better in the dark, but of what use is that, when I have no

> where to lead them but into the ditch? Surely, devoid of these imaginations and impressions, the world becomes a mere board-and-lodging house. The sea by whose side I am writing was once to me a friend, companion, master, teacher; now it is *salt water*, and salt water only. Is this an increase or a withdrawal of *truth?* I did not before lose hold or sight of the fact of its being salt water; I could consider it so, if I chose; my perceiving and feeling it to be more than this was a possession of higher *truth*, which did not interfere with my hold of the physical one.

This sense of loss haunts Ruskin's criticism, until at last it becomes the apocalyptic desire of his later works, from *Modern Painters* V (1860) on to *Praeterita* (1885–89). Kenneth Clark has said, very accurately, that Ruskin was by nature an impressionist, to which one can add that an apocalyptic impressionist is a very strange being; it is difficult to conceive of Revelation as Proust would have written it, yet that is what the prophetic Ruskin gives us. Ruskin remained true to Wordsworth and Turner in being interested primarily in *appearances*, and in taking those appearances as final realities. Yet Wordsworth learned how to evade the apocalyptic element even in the sublime modes of poetry, and Turner, like Keats, thought the earth and the sun to be enough. If there is a central meaning to Ruskin's great change about 1860, it is that his movement from description to prophecy refused to abandon the external world or the arts that he had learned to scrutinize so accurately. Instead Ruskin demanded more from both nature and art than even he had asked earlier, and so made more terrible the process of loss his sensibility had made inevitable. The Ruskin of the Storm Cloud is what Wordsworth would have been, had he allowed his characteristic dialectic of love between man and nature to survive, unchanged, the crisis of 1805, out of which *Peele Castle* was written as palinode.

This is the terrible pathos of Ruskin's art as a critic, that no one else has had so intense an intimation of loss within the imaginative experience itself. Remembering the vision that was his as a child, Ruskin could say that "for me, the Alps and their people were alike beautiful in their snow, and their humanity; and I wanted, neither for them nor myself, sight of any thrones in heaven but the rocks, or of any spirits in heaven but the clouds." This primary humanism never left Ruskin, as it did finally leave the older Wordsworth. What preserved it in Ruskin was the greater purity of his own Wordsworthianism; like the poet John Clare, he excelled Wordsworth as a visionary, and *saw* constantly what the greater poet could see only by glimpses:

> . . . My entire delight was in observing without being myself noticed,—if I could have been invisible, all the better. I was absolutely interested in men and their ways, as I was interested in marmots and chamois, in tomtits and trout. If only they would stay still and let me look at them, and not get into their holes and up their heights! The living inhabitation of the world—the grazing and nesting in it,—the spiritual power of the air, the rocks, the waters, to be in the midst of it, and rejoice and wonder at it, and help it if I could,—happier if it needed no help of mine,—this was the essential love *of Nature* in me, this the root of all that I have usefully become, and the light of all that I have rightly learned.

If we call Ruskin's view of nature or of the self a mythical one, we need to qualify the classification, as Ruskin scarcely believed his view of either to be the product of his own creative powers. Wordsworth, and most of the Romantics after him, sought continuity between the earlier and the future self even at the expense of present time; Wordsworth indeed is mute in the face of nature at the living moment. Ruskin, like Blake, celebrated the pulsation of an artery, the flash of apprehension in which the poet's work is done. And, again like Blake, Ruskin placed his emphasis on *seeing* as the special mark of imagination. For Ruskin, unlike Wordsworth, the deepest imaginative effects are connected with the finite phenomena of nature, and the minute particulars of artistic detail. Wordsworth valued most highly in poetry "those passages where things are lost in each other, and limits vanish," but Ruskin, regarding art or nature, never ceased to see firm, determinate outlines, and every subtlety of detail. Ruskin, unlike Wordsworth, would not sacrifice either the landscape or the moment to the quest for continuity. Wordsworth's rewards for such sacrifices were immense, as Ruskin well knew, for no other writer has felt or made others feel so great a sense of the renewal of the past in the present, through the renovating influence of nature. Ruskin was an extraordinary psychologist, though a largely involuntary one, and did not believe that the therapy for an individual consciousness could come largely through a pursuit of after-images. Yet he wished to believe this, frequently wrote in the Wordsworthian mode, and achieved his final, autobiographical vision and last broken intervals of lucidity primarily through following Wordsworth's example, by tracing the growth of his own imagination. If Ruskin became one of the ruins of Romanticism, and even one of its victims, he became also one of its unique masters, who could justify asserting that "the greatest thing a human soul ever does in this world is to see something, and tell what it saw in a plain way. Hundreds of people can talk for one who can think, but thousands can think for one who can see. To see clearly is poetry, prophecy and religion all in one." Yet to see clearly was finally no salvation for Ruskin, but only gave him a maddening sense of loss, in the self and in nature alike.

3

Ruskin never gave up insisting that all art, literature included, was worship, but this insistence does not make him either a "religious" or a "moral" critic of literature. Though he moved in outward religion from Evangelical Protestantism to agnostic naturalism and on finally to a private version of primitive Catholicism, Ruskin's pragmatic religion always remained a Wordsworthian "natural piety," in which aesthetic and spiritual experience were not to be distinguished from one another. Ruskin's literary taste was formed by the King James Bible, more than any other reading, and therefore from the start he associated expressive and devotional values. In this also he stands with the great Romantics, whose theories of the Imagination are all displaced, radical Protestant accounts of the nakedness of the soul before God.

Ruskin's own theory of the Imagination is clearly derived from Coleridge's, and it has been argued that all Ruskin adds to his master's account is a multiplication of unnecessary entities. I have begun this volume of selections, after giving Ruskin's comments on Coleridge and Wordsworth, and his view of poetic knowledge, by a generous portion of Ruskin's writings on the Imagination, because Ruskin does add to Coleridge's theory a confidence in the autonomy of the imagination that Coleridge himself never possessed. Indeed it is Coleridge whose criticism is distorted by the claims of conventional morality and institutional religion, and not Ruskin. Ruskin could not have written "that it has pleased Providence, that the divine truths of religion should have been revealed to us *in the form of* poetry" (italics mine) or that "an undevout poet is mad: in the strict sense of the word, an undevout poet is an impossibility." Because he lacked Coleridge's doubts, Ruskin allowed himself to elaborate upon Coleridge's categories, there being no point at which he felt the imagination had to yield to a higher or more assured faculty. If these elaborations have failed to be influential, they yet remain interesting in themselves and indicate where a less inhibited Romantic theory of Imagination may still quarry for its materials.

Fundamentally Ruskin favored two groups of poets, those like Dante, Spenser, Milton, and Wordsworth who dealt in detail with the whole destiny of man, from creation to apocalypse, and those he had loved in his own youth, like Scott and Byron. A good part of this volume is necessarily devoted to these two groups. It is in the first that Ruskin's great strength as a critic lies, since he is given to special pleading for his childhood favorites. But there is an honorable place for special pleading in criticism, if it is done with the eloquent passion and exquisite discrimination of a Ruskin.

It is in his examination of the larger outlines of the structure of literature that Ruskin appears today to have been a major critical innovator. Because of his intimate knowledge of Biblical and Classical iconology, and of Dante, Spenser, and Milton as the heirs of such iconology, Ruskin arrived at a comprehensive theory of literature, which he never made fully explicit but which is evident throughout his criticism. One major assumption of this theory is that all great poetry whatsoever is allegorical; and that what it allegorizes is a fundamental myth of universal man, his fall from Paradise and his quest for a revelation that would restore him to Paradise. This myth is clearest in the Ruskin of the 1860s, who is most heavily represented in this volume, since I have included all of *The Queen of the Air*, and about half of *Sesame and Lilies*.

Though it is an obsession in the later Ruskin, a consciousness of this myth was always present in his criticism, since he relied from the start on a Wordsworthian experience of paradisal intimations within a wholly natural context. The Wordsworthian principle of continuity and dialectic of love between man and nature were generalized by the older Ruskin into the universal figures he had encountered in his early journeys from Genesis to Revelation. The symbols of *Modern Painters* V, *Munera Pulveris, Sesame and Lilies,* and *The Queen of the Air* are primarily Biblical ones, even when Ruskin investigates the many guises of Athena in the elaborate mythologizings of *The Queen of the Air*. The Garden of Eden, the Serpent or Dragon, the unfallen maiden who replaces Mother Eve and becomes the prime hope of salvation; these are for Ruskin the principal figures in a mythopoeic fantasia of his own, which is almost too available for psychoanalytical reduction, of the kind to which Ruskin is generally subjected in our time. When, in *The Queen of the Air,* this fantasia is mixed with extraordinary excursions into botany, political economy, and primordial folklore, the result demands a reader more exuberant than most Ruskin scholars have been.

The Queen of the Air, in one of its aspects, resembles some works of Elizabethan mythography like Henry Reynolds' *Mythomystes,* but an even closer parallel can be found in Blake's poetry and prose. Like Ruskin, Blake counterpoints both Classical and Biblical myth against an imaginative story of his own, which in itself is a deliberate modification of Milton's accounts of Fall and Redemption. Ruskin does not seem to invent "Giant Forms" or titanic personages, as Blake does, but he invents and explores states-of-being in a manner very similar to Blake's, though he does not give them Blake's kind of categorical names. Ruskin's Athena is finally a goddess of his own creation, and as such she is one of the major myth-makings of the Victorian age.

Ruskin's earlier, and more Wordsworthian literary criticism, is dominated by the problem of landscape, in the same way that his later criticism centers on typological figures of redemption. *Modern Painters* III (1856) contains Ruskin's principal achievement as a literary critic before he entered upon his own mythical phase, but it is an achievement that has been misunderstood, partly because Ruskin's famous formulation of the Pathetic Fallacy has been misinterpreted. The theory of the Pathetic Fallacy is a searching criticism of Romanticism from within, for the sake of saving the Romantic program of humanizing nature from extinction through excessive self-indulgence. Ruskin is the first writer within the Romantic tradition to have realized the high spiritual price that had to be paid for Wordsworthianism, the human loss that accompanied the "abundant recompense" celebrated in *Tintern Abbey.*

Ruskin was, more so even than most artists and critics, a kind of natural phenomenologist, to use a term now in fashion, or simply, a man to whom things spoke, and who spent his life describing "the ordinary, proper, and true appearances of things to us." Ruskin knew that, as man and artist, his debts and affinities were to what he called the second order of poets, the "Reflective or Perceptive" group (Wordsworth, Keats, Tennyson) and not to the first order, the "Creative" group (Shakespeare, Homer, Dante). Ruskin's purpose in expounding the Pathetic Fallacy, which characterizes the second order, is not to discredit the Wordsworthian kind of poetry, but to indicate its crucial limitation, which he knew himself to share.

Wordsworth and his followers present states of mind that "produce in us a falseness in all our impressions of external things." A. H. R. Ball, the most sympathetic student of Ruskin's literary criticism, was convinced that the theory of the Pathetic Fallacy contradicted Ruskin's own imaginative theory, which may be true, but the contradiction, if it exists, is only a seeming one. Ruskin understood that Romantic poetry, and its imaginative theory, were grounded upon the Pathetic Fallacy, the imputation of life to the object-world. To believe that there is the one life only, within us and abroad, was to heal the Enlightenment's split in consciousness between adverting mind and the universe of things, but at the price that the intuitive phenomenologist in Ruskin understood and resented. The myth of continuity, in Wordsworth and in his followers, Ruskin included, is the result of a homogeneity of sense-experience, which can result only from reduction. The psychiatrist J. H. Van den Berg, in his fascinating study, *Metabletica*, traces this reduction to Descartes, who saw objects as localized space, extensiveness. Wordsworth's quest was to find a way out of all dualisms, Cartesian included, but ironically Wordsworth and his school followed Descartes, unknowingly, in reducing the present to an elaborated past, and making the future also only a consequence of the past. Ruskin's formulation of the Pathetic Fallacy is a profound protest against nineteenth-century homogeneities, particularly landscape homogeneities. It is perhaps sour wit, but it seems true to remark that Wordsworth could see only landscapes that he had seen before, and that no landscape became visible to him that he had not first estranged from himself.

Ruskin's protest is against this estrangement of things, and against the Romantic delight in seeing a reduction, and then elevating that reduction to the ecstasy of enforced humanization. Van den Berg remarks somberly that the Romantic inner self became necessary when contacts between man and the external world became less valued. Ruskin's rejection of Romantic mythopoeia as the Pathetic Fallacy shows a similar distrust of Wordsworthian self-consciousness, but the later Ruskin put such distrust aside, and became the major Romantic myth-maker of the Victorian era. The aesthetic tragedy of Ruskin is that works like *Sesame and Lilies* and *The Queen of the Air* are giant Pathetic Fallacies, but the mingled grandeur and ruin of those books only make them still more representative of post-Romantic art, and its central dilemma. Ruskin may yet seem the major and most original critic that Romanticism has produced, as well as one of its most celebrated avatars.

BIBLIOGRAPHICAL NOTE

The best book yet written on Ruskin is Derrick Leon's *Ruskin the Great Victorian* (London, 1949), a superb biography. Frederic Harrison's *John Ruskin* (London, 1902), in the English Men of Letters series, remains the best short study. A. H. R. Ball's *Ruskin as Literary Critic: Selections* (Cambridge, England, 1928) is the only anthology, prior to this one, devoted wholly to Ruskin's literary criticism. Many of my selections have coincided, necessarily, with those in that volume, but I have attempted to give greater emphasis to what Ruskin wrote from 1860 on.

I have collated the text of all my selections with the great edition of Ruskin, the *Library Edition, The Works of John Ruskin,* edited by E. T. Cook and Alexander Wedderburn, published in London from 1903–10 by George Allen. The firm of George Allen and Unwin, Ltd. retains the copyright for unpublished Ruskin materials.

The arrangement of this volume is chronological, the dates of first editions being given in the Table of Contents. The headings and subheadings are not Ruskin's, but are derived from him, wherever possible. I have retained the paragraph numbering of the Library Edition for convenience of reference. Ruskin's own footnotes are indicated by asterisks, and by daggers, when there are more than one to a page. The numbered footnotes are a selection from those of Cook and Wedderburn, sometimes modified or shortened, and generally identify the sources of Ruskin's more important literary allusions.

I am grateful to A. Dwight Culler for his kindness in reading my Introduction, and advising me upon it.

H. B.

Yale University, January 1965

THE LITERARY CRITICISM OF JOHN RUSKIN

COLERIDGE AND WORDSWORTH

I love Coleridge, and I believe I know nearly every line of both the *Ancient Mariner* and *Christabel*—not to speak of the *Three Graves* and the *Hymn in Chamouni,* and the *Dejection,* and I am very willing to allow that he has more imagination than Wordsworth, and more of the real poet. But after all Coleridge is nothing more than an intellectual opium-eater—a man of many crude though lovely thoughts—of confused though brilliant imagination, liable to much error—error even of the heart, very sensual in many of his ideas of pleasure—indolent to a degree, and evidently and always thinking without discipline; letting the fine brains which God gave him work themselves irregularly and without end or object—and carry him whither they will. Wordsworth has a grand, consistent, perfectly disciplined, all grasping intellect—for which nothing is too small, nothing too great, arranging everything in due relations, divinely pure in its conceptions of pleasure, majestic in the equanimity of its benevolence—intense as white fire with chastised feeling. Coleridge may be the greater poet, but surely it admits of no question which is the greater *man.* Wordsworth often appears to want *energy* because he has so much *judgment,* and because he never enunciates any truth but with full views of many points which diminish the extent of its application, while Coleridge and others say more boldly what they see more partially. I believe Coleridge has very little moral influence on the world; his writings are those of a benevolent man in a fever. Wordsworth may be trusted as a guide in everything, he feels nothing but what we ought all to feel—what every mind in pure moral health *must* feel, he says nothing but what we all ought to believe—what all strong intellects *must* believe. He has written some things trifling, some verses which might be omitted—but none to be *regretted.*

Letter to Rev. Walter Brown, 1843.

POETIC KNOWLEDGE

Every kind of knowledge may be sought from ignoble motives, and for ignoble ends; and in those who so possess it, it is ignoble knowledge; while the very same knowledge is in another mind an attainment of the highest dignity, and conveying the greatest blessing. This is the difference between the mere botanist's knowledge of plants, and the great poet's or painter's knowledge of them. The one notes their distinctions for the sake of swelling his herbarium, the other, that he may render them vehicles of expression and emotion. The one counts the stamens, and affixes a name, and is content; the other observes every character of the plant's colour and form; considering each of its attributes as an element of expression, he seizes on its lines of grace or energy, rigidity or repose; notes the feebleness or the vigour, the serenity or tremulousness of its hues; observes its local habits, its love or fear of peculiar places, its nourishment or destruction by particular influences; he associates it in his mind with all the features of the situations it inhabits, and the ministering agencies necessary to its support. Thenceforward the flower is to him a living creature, with histories written on its leaves, and passions breathing in its motion. Its occurrence in his picture is no mere point of colour, no meaningless spark of light. It is a voice rising from the earth, a new chord of the mind's music, a necessary note in the harmony of his picture, contributing alike to its tenderness and its dignity, nor less to its loveliness than its truth.

Modern Painters, vol. 1, Preface, par. 30.

THE IMAGINATIVE FACULTY

Unfortunately, the works of metaphysicians will afford us in this most interesting inquiry, no aid whatsoever. They who are constantly endeavouring to fathom and explain the essence of the faculties of mind, are sure in the end, to lose sight of all that cannot be explained (though it may be defined and felt); and because, as I shall presently show, the essence of the Imaginative faculty is utterly mysterious and inexplicable, and to be recognized in its results only, or in the negative results of its absence, the metaphysicians, as far as I am acquainted with their works miss it altogether, and never reach higher than a definition of Fancy by a false name.

What I understand by Fancy will presently appear, not that I contend for nomenclature, but only for distinction between two mental faculties, by whatever name they be called; one the source of all that is great in the poetic arts, the other merely decorative and entertaining; but which are often confounded together, and which have so much in common as to render strict definition of either difficult.

Dugald Stewart's meagre definition may serve us for a starting point. "Imagination", he says, "includes conception or simple apprehension, which enables us to form a notion of those former objects of perception or of knowledge, out of which we are to make a selection; abstraction, which separates the selected materials from the qualities and circumstances which are connected with them in nature; and judgment or taste, which selects the materials and directs their combination. To these powers we may add that particular habit of association to which I formerly gave the name of Fancy, as it is this which presents to our choice all the different materials which are subservient to the efforts of imagination, and which may therefore be considered as forming the ground-work of poetical genius."[1]

(By Fancy in this passage, we find on referring to the chapter treating of it, that nothing more is meant than the rapid occurrence of ideas of sense to the mind.)

Now, in this definition, the very point and purpose of all the inquiry is missed. We are told that judgment or taste "directs the combination". In order that anything may be directed, an end must be previously determined; what is the faculty that determines this end? and of what frame and make, how boned and fleshed, how conceived or seen, is the end itself? Bare judgment or taste, cannot approve of what has no existence; and yet by Dugald Stewart's definition we are left to their catering among a host of conceptions, to produce a combination which, as they work for, they must see and approve before it exists. This power of prophecy is the very essence of the whole matter, and it is just that inexplicable part which the metaphysician misses.

As might be expected from his misunderstanding of the faculty he has given an instance entirely nugatory.[2] It would be difficult to find in Milton a passage in which less power of imagination was shown, than the description of

[1] *Philosophy of Human Mind,* Part I, ch. VIII.

[2] He continues thus: "To illustrate these observations, let us consider the steps by which Milton must have proceeded, in creating his imaginary garden of Eden. When he first proposed to himself that subject of description, it is reasonable to suppose that a variety of the most striking scenes which he had seen, crowded into his mind. The association of ideas suggested them, and the power of conception placed each of them before him with all its beauties and imperfections. In every natural scene, if we destine it for any particular purpose, there are defects and redundancies, which art may sometimes, but cannot always correct. But the power of Imagination is unlimited. She can create and annihilate, and dispose at pleasure, her woods, her rocks, and her rivers. Milton, accordingly, would not copy his Eden from any one scene, but would select from each the features which were most eminently beautiful. The power of abstraction enabled him to make the separation, and taste directed him in the selection."

Eden, if, as I suppose, this be the passage meant, at the beginning of the fourth book, where I can find three expressions only in which this power is shown; the "*burnished* with golden rind, hung amiable", of the Hesperian fruit, the "*lays forth* her purple grape" of the vine, and the "*fringed* bank with myrtle crowned" of the lake: and these are not what Stewart meant, but only that accumulation of bowers, groves, lawns, and hillocks, which is not imagination at all, but composition, and that of the commonest kind. Hence, if we take any passage in which there is real imagination, we shall find Stewart's hypothesis not only inefficient and obscure, but utterly inapplicable.

Take one or two at random.

On the other side,
Incensed with indignation, Satan stood
Unterrified, and like a comet burned,
That fires the length of Ophiuchus huge
In the arctic sky, and from his horrid hair
Shakes pestilence and war.[3]

(Note that the word incensed is to be taken in its literal and material sense, set on fire.) What taste or judgment was it that directed this combination? or is there nothing more than taste or judgment here?

Ten paces huge
He back recoiled; the tenth on bended knee
His massy spear upstaid; as if on earth
Winds under ground, or waters forcing way,
Sidelong had pushed a mountain from his seat,
Half-sunk with all his pines.[4]

Together both, ere the high lawns appeared
Under the opening eyelids of the morn,
We drove afield, and both together heard
What time the grey-fly winds her *sultry* horn.[5]

[3] *Par. Lost,* II, 707.
[4] *Par. Lost,* VI, 193.
[5] *Lycidas,* 25.

Missing thee, I walk unseen
On the dry smooth-shaven green,
To behold the wandering moon,
Riding near her highest noon,
Like one that had been led astray
Through the heaven's wide pathless way;
And oft, *as if her head she bowed,*
Stooping through a fleecy cloud.[6]

It is evident that Stewart's explanation utterly fails in all these instances; for there is in them no "combination" whatsoever, but a particular mode of regarding the qualities or appearances of a single thing, illustrated and conveyed to us by the image of another; and the act of imagination, observe, is not the selection of this image, but the mode of regarding the object.

But the metaphysician's definition fails yet more utterly, when we look at the imagination neither as regarding, nor combining, but as penetrating,

My gracious silence, hail!
Wouldst thou have laugh'd, had I come coffin'd home,
That weep'st to see me triumph? Ah, my dear,
Such eyes the widows in Corioli wear,
And mothers that lack sons.[7]

How did Shakespeare *know* that Virgilia could not speak?

This knowledge, this intuitive and penetrative perception, is still one of the forms, the highest, of imagination, but there is no combination of images here.

We find, then, that the Imagination has three totally distinct functions. It combines, and by combination creates new forms; but the secret principle of this combination has not been shown by the analysts. Again, it treats, or regards, both the simple images and its own combinations in peculiar ways; and, thirdly, it penetrates, analyzes, and reaches truths by no other faculty discoverable. These its

[6] *Il Penseroso,* 65.
[7] *Coriolanus,* II, i.

three functions, I shall endeavour to illustrate, but not in this order: the most logical mode of treatment would be to follow the order in which commonly the mind works; that is, penetrating first, combining next, and treating or regarding, finally; but this arrangement would be inconvenient, because the acts of penetration and of regard are so closely connected, and so like in their relations to other mental acts, that I wish to examine them consecutively; and the rather, because they have to do with higher subject matter than the mere act of combination, whose distinctive nature, that property which makes it imagination and not composition, it will, I think, be best to explain at setting out, as we easily may, in subjects familiar and material. I shall therefore examine the Imaginative faculty in these three forms; first, as Combining or Associative; secondly, as Analytic or Penetrative; thirdly, as Regardant or Contemplative.

Modern Painters, vol. II, sec. II, ch. i, pars. 2–6.

THE IMAGINATION ASSOCIATIVE

(*a*) *COMPOSITION*

We will suppose a man to retain such clear image of a large number of the material things he has seen, as to be able to set down any of them on paper, with perfect fidelity and absolute memory of their most minute features. In thus setting them down on paper, he works, I suppose, exactly as he would work from nature, only copying the remembered image in his mind, instead of the real thing. He is, therefore, still nothing more than a copyist. There is no exercise of imagination in this whatsoever.

But over these images, vivid and distinct as nature herself, he has a command which over nature he has not. He can summon any that he chooses; and if, therefore, any group of them which he received from nature be not altogether to his mind, he is at liberty to remove some of the component images, add others foreign, and re-arrange the whole.

Let us suppose, for instance, that he has perfect knowledge of the forms of the Aiguilles Verte and Argentière, and of the great glacier between them at the upper extremity of the valley of Chamonix. The forms of the mountains please him, but the presence of the glacier suits not his purpose. He removes the glacier, sets the mountains farther apart, and introduces between them part of the valley of the Rhone.

This is composition, and is what Dugald Stewart mistook for imagination, in the kingdom of which noble faculty it has no part nor lot.

The essential acts of Composition, properly so called, are the following. The mind which desires the new feature summons up before it those images which it supposes to be the kind wanted; of these it takes the one which it supposes to be fittest, and tries it; if it will not answer, it tries another, until it has obtained such an association as pleases it.

In this operation, if it be of little sensibility, it regards only the absolute beauty or value of the images brought before it; and takes that or those which it thinks fairest or most interesting, without any regard to their sympathy with those for whose company they are destined. Of this kind is all vulgar composition; the "Mulino" of Claude, being a characteristic example.

If the mind be of higher feeling, it will look to the sympathy or contrast of the features, to their likeness or dissimilarity: it will take, as it thinks best, features resembling or discordant; and if, when it has put them together, it be not satisfied, it will repeat the process on the features themselves, cutting away one part and putting in another; so working more and more delicately down to the lowest details, until by dint of experiment, of repeated trials and shiftings, and constant reference to principles (as that two lines must not mimic one another, that one mass must not be equal to another), etc., it has mortised together a satisfactory result.

This process will be more and more rapid and effective, in proportion to the artist's powers of conception and association, these in their turn depending on his knowledge and experience. The distinctness of his powers of conception will give value, point, and truth to every fragment that he draws from memory. His powers of association, and his knowledge of nature, will pour out before him, in greater or less number and appositeness, the images from which to choose. His experience guides him to quick discernment in the combination, when made, of the parts that are offensive and require change.

The most elevated power of mind of all these, is that of association, by which images apposite or resemblant, or of whatever kind wanted, are called up quickly and in multitudes. When this power is very brilliant, it is called Fancy; not that this is the only meaning of the word Fancy; but it is the meaning of it in relation to that function of the imagination which we are here considering; for fancy has three functions; one subordinate to each of the three functions of the imagination.

Great differences of power are manifested among artists in this respect; some having hosts of distinct images always at their command, and rapidly discerning resemblance or contrast; others having few images, and obscure, at their disposal, nor readily governing those they have.

Where the powers of fancy are very brilliant, the picture becomes highly interesting; if her images are systematically and rightly combined, and truthfully rendered, it will become even impressive and instructive; if wittily and curiously combined, it will be captivating and entertaining.

But all this time the imagination has not once shown itself. All this (except the gift of fancy) may be taught; all this is easily comprehended and analyzed; but imagination is neither to be taught, nor by any efforts to be attained, nor by any acuteness of discernment dissected or analyzed.

Modern Painters, vol. II, sec. II, ch. ii, pars. 2–6.

(*b*) *MANIFESTATION*

It has been said that in composition the mind can only take cognizance of likeness or dissimilarity, or of abstract beauty among the ideas it brings together. But neither likeness nor dissimilarity secures harmony. We saw in the Chapter on Unity that likeness destroyed harmony or unity of membership; and that difference did not necessarily secure it, but only that particular *imperfection* in each of the harmonizing parts which can only be supplied by its fellow part. If, therefore, the combination made is to be harmonious, the artist must induce in each of its component parts (suppose two only, for simplicity's sake), such imperfection as that the other shall put it right. If one of them be perfect by itself, the other will be an excrescence. Both must be faulty when separate, and each corrected by the presence of the other. If he can accomplish this, the result will be beautiful; it will be a whole, an organized body with dependent members;—he is an inventor. If not, let his separate features be as beautiful, as apposite, or as resemblant as they may, they form no whole. They are two members glued together. He is only a carpenter and joiner.

Now, the conceivable imperfections of any single feature are infinite. It is impossible, therefore, to fix upon a form of imperfection in the one, and try with this all the forms of imperfection of the other until one fits; but the two imperfections must be co-relatively and simultaneously conceived.

This is Imagination, properly so called; imagination associative, the grandest mechanical power that the human intelligence possesses, and one which will appear more and more marvellous the longer we consider it. By its operation, two ideas are chosen out of an infinite mass (for it evidently matters not whether the imperfections be conceived out of the infinite number conceivable, or selected out of a number recollected), two ideas which are *separately wrong,* which together shall be right, and of whose unity, therefore, the idea must be formed at the instant they are seized, as it is only in that unity that either is good, and therefore only the *conception of that unity can prompt the preference.*

Modern Painters, vol. II, sec. II, ch. ii, pars. 6–7.

(*c*) *GRASP AND DIGNITY*

A powerfully imaginative mind seizes and combines at the same instant, not only two, but all the important ideas of its poem or picture; and while it works with any one of them, it is at the same instant working with and modifying all in their relations to it, never losing sight of their bearings on each other; as the motion of a snake's body goes through all parts at once, and its volition acts at the same instant in coils that go contrary ways.

This faculty is indeed something that looks as if man were made after the image of God. It is inconceivable, admirable, altogether divine; and yet, wonderful as it may seem, it is palpably evident that no less an operation is necessary for the production of any great work: for, by the definition of Unity of Membership (the essential characteristic of greatness), not only certain couples or groups of parts, but *all* the parts of a noble work must be separately imperfect; each must imply, and ask for all the rest, and the glory of every one of them must consist in its relation to the rest; neither while so much as one is wanting can any be right. And it is evidently impossible to conceive, in each separate feature, a certain want or wrongness which can only be corrected by the other features of the picture (not by one or two merely, but by all), unless, together with the want, we conceive also of what is wanted, that is, of all the rest of the work or picture.

Modern Painters, vol. II, sec. II, ch. ii, par. 9.

(*d*) *TESTS OF IMAGINATION*

The Imaginative artist owns no laws. He defies all restraint, and cuts down all hedges. There is nothing within the limits of natural possibility that he dares not do, or that he allows the necessity of doing. The laws of nature he knows; these are to him no restraint. They are his own nature. All other laws or limits he sets at utter defiance; his journey is over an untrodden and pathless plain. But he sees his end over the waste from the first, and goes straight at it; never losing sight of it, nor throwing away a step. Nothing can stop him, nothing turn him aside; falcons and lynxes are of slow and uncertain sight compared with his. He saw his tree, trunk, boughs, foliage and all, from the first moment; not only the tree, but the sky behind it; not only that tree or sky, but all the other great features of his picture: by what intense power of instantaneous selection and amalgamation cannot be explained, but by this it may be proved and tested; that, if we examine the tree of the unimaginative painter, we shall find that on removing any part or parts of it, though the rest will indeed suffer, as being deprived of the proper development of a tree, and as involving a blank space that wants occupation, yet the portions left are not made discordant or disagreeable. They are absolutely and in themselves as valuable as they can be; every stem is a perfect stem, and every twig a graceful twig, or at least as perfect and as graceful as they were before the removal of the rest. But if we try the same experiment on the imaginative painter's work, and break off the merest stem or twig of it, it all goes to pieces like a Prince Rupert's drop. There is not so much as a seed of it but it lies on the tree's life, like the grain upon the tongue of Chaucer's sainted child.[8] Take it away, and the boughs will sing to us no longer. All is dead and cold.

[8] *The Prioresses Tale,* line 1852.

This then is the first sign of the presence of real imagination as opposed to composition. But here is another not less important.

We have seen that as each part is selected and fitted by the unimaginative painter, he renders it, in itself, as beautiful as he is able. If it be ugly it remains so; he is incapable of correcting it by the *addition of another ugliness*, and therefore he chooses all his features as fair as they may be (at least if his object be beauty). But a small proportion only of the ideas he has at his disposal will reach his standard of absolute beauty. The others will be of no use to him: and among those which he permits himself to use, there will be so marked a family likeness that he will be more and more cramped, as his picture advances, for want of material, and tormented by multiplying resemblances, unless disguised by some artifice of light and shade or other forced difference; and with all the differences he can imagine, his tree will yet show a sameness and sickening repetition in all its parts, and all his trees will be like one another, except so far as one leans east and another west, one is broadest at the top and another at the bottom: while through all this insipid repetition, the means by which he forces contrast, dark boughs opposed to light, rugged to smooth, etc., will be painfully evident, to the utter destruction of all dignity and repose. The imaginative work is necessarily the absolute opposite of all this. As all its parts are imperfect, and as there is an unlimited supply of imperfection (for the ways in which things may be wrong are infinite), the imagination is never at a loss, nor ever likely to repeat itself; nothing comes amiss to it; but whatever rude matter it receives, it instantly so arranges that it comes right; all things fall into their place, and appear in that place perfect, useful, and evidently not to be spared; so that of its combinations there is endless variety, and every intractable and seemingly unavailable fragment that we give to it, is instantly turned to some brilliant use, and made the nucleus of a new group of glory; however poor or common the gift, it will be thankful for it, treasure it up, and pay in gold; and it has that life in it and fire, that wherever it passes, among the dead bones and dust of things, behold! a shaking, and the bones come together bone to his bone.

And now we find what noble sympathy and unity there are between the Imaginative and Theoretic faculties. Both agree in this, that they reject nothing, and are thankful for all; but the Theoretic faculty takes out of everything that which is beautiful, while the Imaginative faculty takes hold of the very imperfections which the Theoretic rejects; and, by means of these angles and roughnesses, it joints and bolts the separate stones into a mighty temple, wherein the Theoretic faculty, in its turn, does deepest homage. Thus sympathetic in their desires, harmoniously diverse in their operation, each working for the other with what the other needs not, all things external to man are by one or other turned to good.

Modern Painters, vol. II, sec. II, ch. ii, pars. 13–16.

(*e*) *NATURE AND TRUTH*

There remains but one question to be determined relating to this faculty; what operation, namely, supposing it possessed in high degree, it has or ought to have in the artist's treatment of natural scenery?

I have just said that nature is always imaginative, but it does not follow that her imagination is always of high subject, or that the imagination of all the parts is of a like and sympathetic kind; the boughs of every bramble bush are imaginatively arranged, so are those of every oak and cedar; but it does not follow that there is imaginative sympathy between bramble and cedar. There are few natural scenes whose harmonies are not conceivably improvable either by banishment of some discordant point, or by addition of some sympathetic one; it constantly happens that there is a profuseness too great to be comprehended, or an inequality in the pitch, meaning, and intensity of different parts. The imagination will banish all that is extraneous; it will seize out of the many threads of different feeling which nature has suffered to become entangled, one only; and where that seems thin and likely to break, it will spin it stouter, and in doing this, it never knots, but weaves in the new thread; so that all its work looks as pure and true as nature itself, and cannot be guessed from it but by its exceeding simplicity (*known* from it, it cannot be); so that herein we find another test of the imaginative work, that it looks always as if it had been gathered straight from nature, whereas the unimaginative shows its joints and knots, and is visibly composition.

And here, then, we arrive at an important conclusion (though one somewhat contrary to the positions commonly held on the subject), namely, that if anything looks unnatural, there can be no imagination in it (at least not associative). We frequently hear works that have no truth in them, justified or elevated on the score of being imaginative. Let it be understood once for all, that imagination never deigns to touch anything but truth; and though it does not follow that where there is the appearance of truth, there has been imaginative operation, of this we may be assured, that where there is appearance of falsehood, the imagination has had no hand.

Modern Painters, vol. II, sec. II, ch. ii, pars. 21–22.

(*f*) *FINAL TESTS*

The final tests, therefore, of the work of Associative imagination are, its intense simplicity, its perfect harmony, and its absolute truth. It may be a harmony, majestic or humble, abrupt or prolonged, but it is always a governed and perfect whole; evidencing in all its relations the weight, prevalence, and universal dominion of an awful inexplicable Power; a chastising, animating, and disposing Mind.

Modern Painters, vol. II, sec. II, ch. ii, par. 22.

THE IMAGINATION PENETRATIVE

(*a*) *IMAGINATION AND FANCY*

Thus far we have been defining that combining operation of the Imagination, which appears to be in a sort mechanical, yet takes place in the same inexplicable modes, whatever be the order of conception submitted to it, though I choose to illustrate it by its dealings with mere matter before taking cognizance of any nobler subjects of imagery. We must now examine the dealing of the Imagination with its separate conceptions, and endeavour to understand, not only its principles of selection, but its modes of apprehension with respect to what it selects.

When Milton's Satan first "rears from off the pool his mighty stature", the image of leviathan before suggested not being yet abandoned, the effect of the fire-wave is described as of the upheaved monster on the ocean stream:

> On each hand the flames
> Driven backward, slope their pointing spires, and, rolled
> In billows, leave i' the midst a horrid vale.[9]

And then follows a fiercely restless piece of volcanic imagery:

> As when the force
> Of subterranean wind transports a hill
> Torn from Pelorus, or the shattered side
> Of thundering Ætna, whose combustible
> And fuelled entrails thence conceiving fire,
> Sublimed with mineral fury, aid the winds,
> And leave a singëd bottom all involved
> With stench and smoke: such resting found the sole
> Of unblest feet.

[9] *Par. Lost*, I, 222.

Yet I think all this is too far detailed, and deals too much with externals: we feel rather the form of the fire-waves than their fury; we walk upon them too securely; and the fuel, sublimation, smoke, and singeing seem to me images only of partial combustion; they vary and extend the conception, but they lower the thermometer. Look back, if you will, and add to the description the glimmering of the livid flames; the sulphurous hail and red lightning; yet all together, however they overwhelm us with horror, fail of making us thoroughly, unendurably *hot.* The essence of intense flame has not been given. Now hear Dante:

> Feriami 'l Sole in su l' omero destro,
> Che già raggiando tutto l' Occidente
> *Mutava in bianco aspetto di cilestro.*
> Ed io facea *con l' ombra più rovente*
> *Parer la fiamma.*[10]

That is a slight touch; he has not gone to Ætna or Pelorus for fuel; but we shall not soon recover from it, he has taken our breath away, and leaves us gasping. No smoke nor cinders there. Pure white, hurtling, formless flame; very fire crystal, we cannot make spires nor waves of it, nor divide it, nor walk on it; there is no question about singeing soles of feet. It is lambent annihilation.

Such is always the mode in which the highest imaginative faculty seizes its materials. It never stops at crusts or ashes, or outward images of any kind; it ploughs them all aside, and plunges into the very central fiery heart; nothing else will content its spirituality; whatever semblances and various outward shows and phases its subject may possess go for nothing; it gets within all fence, cuts down to the root, and drinks the very vital sap of that it deals with: once therein, it is at liberty to throw up what new

[10] *Purg.* XXVI, 4. Cary translates:

> The sun
> Now all the western clime irradiate changed
> From azure tinct to white; and, as I passed,
> My passing shadow made the umbered flame
> Burn ruddier.

shoots it will, so always that the true juice and sap be in them, and to prune and twist them at its pleasure, and bring them to fairer fruit than grew on the old tree; but all this pruning and twisting is work that it likes not, and often does ill; its function and gift are the getting at the root, its nature and dignity depend on its holding things always by the heart. Take its hand from off the beating of that, and it will prophesy no longer; it looks not in the eyes, it judges not by the voice, it describes not by outward features; all that it affirms, judges, or describes, it affirms, from within.

It may seem to the reader that I am incorrect in calling this penetrating possession-taking faculty Imagination. Be it so; the name is of little consequence; the faculty itself, called by what name we will, I insist upon as the highest intellectual power of man. There is no reasoning in it; it works not by algebra, nor by integral calculus; it is a piercing pholas-like mind's tongue, that works and tastes into the very rock heart; no matter what be the subject submitted to it, substance or spirit; all is alike divided asunder, joint and marrow, whatever utmost truth, life, principle it has, laid bare, and that which has no truth, life, nor principle, dissipated into its original smoke at a touch. The whispers at men's ears it lifts into visible angels. Vials that have lain sealed in the deep sea a thousand years it unseals, and brings out of them Genii.[11]

Every great conception of poet or painter is held and treated by this faculty. Every character that is so much as touched by men like Æschylus, Homer, Dante, or Shakespeare, is by them held by the heart; and every circumstance or sentence of their being, speaking, or seeming, is seized by process from within, and is referred to that inner secret spring of which the hold is never lost for an instant: so that every sentence, as it has been thought out from the heart, opens for us a way down to the heart, leads us to the centre, and then leaves us to gather what more we may. It is the Open Sesame of a huge, obscure, endless cave, with inexhaustible treasure of pure gold scattered in it: the

[11] *Arab. Nights,* ch. ii (Lane).

wandering about and gathering the pieces may be left to any of us, all can accomplish that; but the first opening of that invisible door in the rock is of the imagination only.

Hence there is in every word set down by the imaginative mind an awful under-current of meaning, and evidence and shadow upon it of the deep places out of which it has come. It is often obscure, often half-told; for he who wrote it, in his clear seeing of the things beneath, may have been impatient of detailed interpretation: but, if we choose to dwell upon it and trace it, it will lead us always securely back to that metropolis of the soul's dominion from which we may follow out all the ways and tracks to its farthest coasts.

I think the "Quel giorno più non vi leggemmo avante"[12] of Francesca di Rimini, and the "He has no children" of Macduff,[13] are as fine instances as can be given; but the sign and mark of it are visible on every line of the four great men above instanced.

The unimaginative writer on the other hand, as he has never pierced to the heart, so he can never touch it. If he has to paint a passion, he remembers the external signs of it, he collects expressions of it from other writers, he searches for similes, he composes, exaggerates, heaps term on term, figure on figure, till we groan beneath the cold disjointed heap; but it is all faggot and no fire; the life breath is not in it; his passion has the form of the leviathan, but it never makes the deep boil; he fastens us all at anchor in the scaly rind of it; our sympathies remain as idle as a painted ship upon a painted ocean.

And that virtue of originality that men so strain after is not newness, as they vainly think (there is nothing new), it is only genuineness; it all depends on this single glorious faculty of getting to the spring of things and working out from that; it is the coolness, and clearness, and deliciousness of the water fresh from the fountain head, opposed to the thick, hot, unrefreshing drainage from other men's meadows.

12 "That day we read no farther": *Inferno,* v, 138.
13 *Macbeth,* IV, iii.

This freshness, however, is not to be taken for an infallible sign of imagination, inasmuch as it results also from a vivid operation of fancy, whose parallel function to this division of the imaginative faculty it is here necessary to distinguish.

I believe it will be found that the entirely unimaginative mind *sees* nothing of the object it has to dwell upon or describe, and is therefore utterly unable, as it is blind itself, to set anything before the eyes of the reader.

The fancy sees the outside, and is able to give a portrait of the outside, clear, brilliant, and full of detail.

The imagination sees the heart and inner nature, and makes them felt, but is often obscure, mysterious, and interrupted, in its giving of outer detail.

Take an instance. A writer with neither imagination nor fancy, describing a fair lip, does not see it, but thinks about it, and about what is said of it, and calls it well turned, or rosy, or delicate, or lovely, or afflicts us with some other quenching and chilling epithet. Now hear Fancy speak:

> Her lips were red, and one was thin,
> Compared with that was next her chin,
> Some bee had stung it newly.[14]

The real, red, bright being of the lip is there in a moment. But it is all outside; no expression yet, no mind. Let us go a step farther with Warner, of Fair Rosamond struck by Eleanor:

> With that she dashed her on the lips
> So dyëd double red;
> Hard was the heart that gave the blow,
> Soft were those lips that bled.[15]

The tenderness of mind begins to mingle with the outside colour, the Imagination is seen in its awakening. Next Shelley:

[14] Quoted from Sir J. Suckling in Leigh Hunt's *Imagination and Fancy.*

[15] Quoted from William Warner, in Leigh Hunt.

Lamp of life, thy lips are burning
  Through the veil that seems to hide them,
As the radiant lines of morning
  Through thin clouds ere they divide them.[16]

There dawns the entire soul in that morning; yet we may stop if we choose at the image still external, at the crimson clouds. The imagination is contemplative rather than penetrative. Last, hear Hamlet:

> Here hung those lips that I have kissed, I know not how oft. Where be your gibes now, your gambols, your songs, your flashes of merriment that were wont to set the table on a roar?[17]

There is the essence of lip, and the full power of the imagination.

Again, compare Milton's flowers in *Lycidas* with Perdita's. In Milton it happens, I think, generally, and in the case before us most certainly, that the imagination is mixed and broken with fancy, and so the strength of the imagery is part of iron and part of clay:

Bring the rathe primrose, that forsaken dies,	*Imagination.*
The tufted crow-toe and pale jessamine,	*Nugatory.*
The white pink, and the pansy freaked with jet,	*Fancy.*
The glowing violet,	*Imagination.*
The musk rose, and the well-attired woodbine,	*Fancy,* vulgar.
With cowslips wan that hang the pensive head,	*Imagination.*
And every flower that sad embroidery wears.	*Mixed.*

Then hear Perdita:

[16] *Prometheus Unbound,* II, v, 54.
[17] *Hamlet,* v, i, 181.

O Proserpina,
For the flowers now, that, frighted, thou let'st fall
From Dis's waggon! daffodils,
That come before the swallow dares, and take
The winds of March with beauty; violets, dim,
But sweeter than the lids of Juno's eyes,
Or Cytherea's breath; pale primroses,
That die unmarried, ere they can behold
Bright Phœbus in his strength, a malady
Most incident to maids.[18]

Observe how the imagination in these last lines goes into the very inmost soul of every flower, after having touched them all at first with that heavenly timidness, the shadow of Proserpine's, and gilded them with celestial gathering, and never stops on their spots, or their bodily shape; while Milton sticks in the stains upon them, and puts us off with that unhappy freak of jet in the very flower that, without this bit of paper-staining, would have been the most precious to us of all. "There is pansies, that's for thoughts."[19]

So, I believe, it will be found throughout the operation of the fancy, that it has to do with the outsides of things, and is content therewith; of this there can be no doubt in such passages as that description of Mab so often given as an illustration of it,[20] and many other instances will be found in Leigh Hunt's work already referred to. Only some embarrassment is caused by passages in which Fancy is seizing the outward signs of emotion, understanding them as such, and yet, in pursuance of her proper function, taking for her share, and for that which she chooses to dwell upon, the outside sign rather than the emotion. Note in *Macbeth* that brilliant instance:

Where the Norweyan banners flout the sky,
And fan our people cold.[21]

[18] *Winter's Tale,* IV, iii.
[19] *Hamlet,* IV, v.
[20] *Romeo and Juliet,* I, iv.
[21] Act I, Sc. ii, line 51.

The outward shiver and coldness of fear is seized on, and irregularly but admirably attributed by the fancy to the drift of the banners. Compare Solomon's Song, where the imagination stays not at the outside, but dwells on the fearful emotion itself:

> Who is she that looketh forth as the morning; fair as the moon, clear as the sun, and terrible as an army with banners?

Now, if these be the prevailing characteristics of the two faculties, it is evident that certain other collateral differences will result from them. Fancy, as she stays at the externals, can never feel. She is one of the hardest-hearted of the intellectual faculties, or rather one of the most purely and simply intellectual. She cannot be made serious, no edgetools but she will play with. Whereas the Imagination is in all things the reverse. She cannot be but serious; she sees too far, too darkly, too solemnly, too earnestly ever to smile. There is something in the heart of everything, if we can reach it, that we shall not be inclined to laugh at. And thus there is reciprocal action between the intensity of moral feeling and the power of imagination; for, on the one hand, those who have keenest sympathy are those who look closest and pierce deepest, and hold securest; and on the other, those who have so pierced and seen the melancholy deeps of things are filled with the most intense passion and gentleness of sympathy. Hence, I suppose that the powers of the imagination may always be tested by accompanying tenderness of emotion; and thus, as Byron said,[22] there is no tenderness like Dante's, neither any intensity nor seriousness like his, such seriousness that it is incapable of perceiving that which is commonplace or ridiculous, but fuses all down into its own white-hot fire. And, on the other hand, I suppose the chief bar to the action of imagination, and stop to all greatness in this present age of ours, is its mean and

[22] Byron's *Diary*, Jan. 29, 1821.

shallow love of jest; so that if there be in any good and lofty work a flaw, failing, or undipped vulnerable part, where sarcasm may stick or stay, it is caught at, and pointed at, and buzzed about, and fixed upon, and stung into, as a recent wound is by flies; and nothing is ever taken seriously or as it was meant, but always, if it may be, turned the wrong way, and misunderstood; and while this is so, there is not, nor cannot be, any hope of achievement of high things; men dare not open their hearts to us, if we are to broil them on a thorn-fire.

This, then, is one essential difference between imagination and fancy; and another is like it and resultant from it, that the imagination being at the heart of things, poises herself there, and is still, quiet, and brooding, comprehending all around her with her fixed look; but the fancy staying at the outside of things, cannot see them all at once; but runs hither and thither, and round and about to see more and more, bounding merrily from point to point, and glittering here and there, but necessarily always settling, if she settle at all, on a point only, never embracing the whole. And from these single points she can strike out analogies and catch resemblances, which, so far as the point she looks at is concerned, are true, but would be false, if she could see through to the other side. This, however, she cares not to do; the point of contact is enough for her, and even if there be a gap left between the two things and they do not quite touch, she will spring from one to the other like an electric spark, and be seen brightest in her leaping.

Now these differences between the imagination and the fancy hold, not only in the way they lay hold of separate conceptions, but even in the points they occupy of time; for the fancy loves to run hither and thither in time, and to follow long chains of circumstances from link to link; but the imagination, if it may, gets hold of a moment or link in the middle that implies all the rest, and fastens there. Hence Fuseli's aphorism: "Invention never suffers the action to expire, nor the spectator's fancy to consume itself in preparation, or stagnate into repose. It neither begins from the egg, nor coldly gathers the remains."

Modern Painters, vol. II, sec. II, ch. iii, pars. 1–12.

(*b*) *INTUITIVE PERCEPTION OF ULTIMATE TRUTH*

Now, in all these instances, let it be observed—for it is to that end alone that I have been arguing all along—that the virtue of the Imagination is its reaching, by intuition and intensity of gaze (not by reasoning, but by its authoritative opening and revealing power), a more essential truth than is seen at the surface of things. I repeat that it matters not whether the reader is willing to call this faculty Imagination or not; I do not care about the name; but I would be understood when I speak of imagination hereafter, to mean this, the base of whose authority and being is its perpetual thirst for truth and purpose to be true. It has no food, no delight, no care, no perception, except of truth; it is for ever looking under masks, and burning up mists; no fairness of form, no majesty of seeming will satisfy it; the first condition of its existence is incapability of being deceived; and though it sometimes dwells upon and substantiates the fictions of fancy, yet its own operation is to trace to their farthest limit the true laws and likelihoods even of the fictitious creation.

Modern Painters, vol. II, sec. II, ch. iii, par. 29.

THE IMAGINATION CONTEMPLATIVE

We have, in the two preceding chapters, arrived at definite conclusions respecting the power and essence of the imaginative faculty. In these two acts of penetration and combination, its separating and characteristic attributes are entirely developed; it remains for us only to observe a certain habit or mode of operation in which it frequently delights, and by which it addresses itself to our perceptions more forcibly, and asserts its presence more distinctly than in those mighty but more secret workings wherein its life consists.

In our examination of the combining imagination, we chose to assume the first or simple conception to be as clear in the absence as in the presence of the object of it. This, I suppose, is, in point of fact, never the case, nor is an approximation to such distinctness of conception always a characteristic of the imaginative mind. Many persons have thorough and felicitous power of drawing from memory, yet never originate a thought, nor excite an emotion.

The form in which conception actually occurs to ordinary minds appears to derive value and preciousness from indefiniteness; for there is an unfailing charm in the memory and anticipation of things beautiful, more sunny and spiritual than attaches to their presence; for with their presence it is possible to be sated, and even wearied, but with the imagination of them never; in so far that it needs some self-discipline to prevent the mind from falling into a morbid condition of dissatisfaction with all that it immediately possesses, and continual longing for things absent: and yet I think this charm is not justly to be attributed to the mere vagueness and uncertainty of the conception, except thus far, that of objects whose substantial presence was painful, the sublimity and impressiveness, if there were any, are retained in the conception, while the sensual offensiveness is withdrawn; thus circumstances of horror may be safely touched in verbal description, and for a time dwelt upon by the mind as often by Homer and Spenser (by the latter frequently with too much grossness), which could not for a moment be regarded or tolerated in their reality, or on canvas; and besides this mellowing and softening operation on those it retains, the conceptive faculty has the power of letting go many of them altogether out of its groups of ideas, and retaining only those where the "meminisse juvabit"[23] will apply; and in this way the entire group of memories becomes altogether delightful. But of those parts of anything which are in themselves beautiful, I think the indistinctness no benefit, but that the brighter they are the better; and that the peculiar charm we feel in conception results from its grasp and blending of ideas, rather than from their obscurity; for we do not usually recall, as we have seen, one part at a time only of a pleasant scene, one moment only of a happy day; but together with each single object we summon up a kind of crowded and involved shadowing forth of all the other glories with which it was associated, and into every moment we concentrate an epitome of the day; and it will happen frequently that even when the visible objects or actual circumstances are not in detail remembered, the feeling and joy of them are obtained we know not how or whence: and so, with a kind of conceptive burning-glass, we bend the sunshine of all the day, and the fulness of all the scene upon every point that we successively seize; and this together with more vivid action of Fancy, for I think that the wilful and playful seizures of the points that suit her purpose, and help her springing, whereby she is distinguished from simple conception, take place more easily and actively with the memory of things than in presence of them. But, however this be, and I confess that there is much that I cannot satisfactorily to myself unravel with respect to the nature of simple conception, it is evident that this agreeableness, whatever it be, is not by art attainable, for all art is, in some sort, realization; it may be the realization of obscurity or indefiniteness, but still it must differ from the mere *conception* of obscurity and indefiniteness; so that whatever emotions depend absolutely on imperfectness of conception, as the horror of Milton's Death, cannot be rendered by art; for art can only lay hold of things which have shape, and destroys by its touch the fearfulness or pleasurableness of those which "shape have none".[24]

23 Vergil, *Aeneid,* I, 203.
24 *Par. Lost,* II, 667.

But on this indistinctness of conception, itself comparatively valueless and unaffecting, is based the operation of the Imaginative faculty with which we are at present concerned, and in which its glory is consummated; whereby, depriving the subject of material and bodily shape, and regarding such of its qualities only as it chooses for particular purpose, it forges these qualities together in such groups and forms as it desires, and gives to their abstract being consistency and reality, by striking them as it were with the die of an image belonging to other matter, which stroke having once received, they pass current at once in the peculiar conjunction and for the peculiar value desired.

Thus, in the description of Satan, "and like a comet burned," the bodily shape of the angel is destroyed, the inflaming of the formless spirit is alone regarded; and this, and his power of evil, associated in one fearful and abstract conception, are stamped to give them distinctness and permanence with the image of the comet, "That fires the length of Ophiuchus huge." Yet this could not be done, but that the image of the comet itself is in a measure indistinct, capable of awful expansion, and full of threatening and fear. Again, in his fall, the imagination gathers up the thunder, the resistance, the massy prostration, separates them from the external form, and binds them together by the help of that image of the mountain half sunk; which again would be unfit but for its own indistinctness, and for that glorious addition "with all his pines", whereby a vitality and spear-like hostility are communicated to its falling form; and the fall is marked as not utter subversion, but sinking only, the pines remaining in their uprightness and unity, and threatening of darkness upon the descended precipice; and again, in that yet more noble passage at the close of the fourth book, where almost every operation of the contemplative imagination is concentrated; the angelic squadron first gathered into one burning mass by the single expression "sharpening in mooned horns", then told out in their unity and multitude and stooped hostility, by the image of the wind upon the corn;

Satan endowed with god-like strength and endurance in that mighty line, "Like Teneriff or Atlas, unremoved", with infinitude of size the next instant, and with all the vagueness and terribleness of spiritual power, by the "Horrour plumed", and the "*what seemed* both spear and shield".[25]

The third function of Fancy, already spoken of as subordinate to this of the Imagination, is the highest of which she is capable; like the Imagination, she beholds in the things submitted to her treatment things different from the actual; but the suggestions she follows are not in their nature essential in the object contemplated; and the images resulting, instead of illustrating, may lead the mind away from it, and change the current of contemplative feeling: for, as in her operation parallel to Imagination penetrative we saw her dwelling upon external features, while the nobler sister faculty entered within; so now, when both, from what they see and know in their immediate object, are conjuring up images illustrative or elevatory of it, the Fancy necessarily summons those of mere external relationship, and therefore of unaffecting influence; while the Imagination, by every ghost she raises, tells tales about the prison house, and therefore never loses her power over the heart, nor her unity of emotion. On the other hand, the regardant or contemplative action of Fancy is in this different from, and in this nobler than, that mere seizing and likeness-catching operation we saw in her before; that, when contemplative, she verily believes in the truth of the vision she has summoned, loses sight of actuality, and beholds the new and spiritual image faithfully and even seriously; whereas, before, she summoned no spiritual image, but merely caught the vivid actuality, or the curious resemblance of the real object; not that these two operations are separate, for the Fancy passes gradually from mere vivid sight of reality, and witty suggestion of likeness, to a ghostly sight of what is unreal; and through this, in proportion as she begins to feel, she rises towards and partakes of Imagination itself; for Imag-

25 Vide *Par. Lost,* IV, 979–990.

ination and Fancy are continually united, and it is necessary, when they are so, carefully to distinguish the feelingless part which is Fancy's, from the sentient part which is Imagination's. Let us take a few instances. Here is Fancy, first, very beautiful, in her simple capacity of likeness-catching:

> To-day we purpose—ay, this hour we mount,
> To spur three leagues towards the Apennine.
> Come down, we pray thee, ere the *hot sun count*
> *His dewy rosary* on the eglantine.[26]

Seizing on the outside resemblances of bead form, and on the slipping from their threading bough one by one, the fancy is content to lose the heart of the thing, the solemnity of prayer: or perhaps I do the glorious poet wrong in saying this, for the sense of a sun worship and orison in beginning its race, may have been in his mind; and so far as it was so, the passage is imaginative and not fanciful. But that which most readers would accept from it, is the mere flash of the external image, in whose truth the Fancy herself does not yet believe, and therefore is not yet contemplative. Here, however, is Fancy believing in the images she creates:

> It feeds the quick growth of the serpent-vine,
> And the dark linked ivy tangling wild,
> And budding, blown, or odour-faded blooms,
> Which *star the winds with points of coloured light*
> As they rain through them; and *bright golden globes*
> *Of fruit suspended in their own green heaven.*[27]

It is not, observe, a mere likeness that is caught here; but the flowers and fruit are entirely deprived by the fancy of their material existence, and contemplated by her seriously and faithfully as stars and worlds; yet it is only external likeness that she catches; she forces the resemblance, and lowers the dignity of the adopted image.

[26] Keats, *Isabella*, XXIV.
[27] Shelley, *Prometheus*, III, 3.

Next take two delicious stanzas of Fancy regardant (believing in her creations), followed by one of heavenly imagination, from Wordsworth's address to the daisy:

A Nun demure—of lowly port;
Or sprightly maiden, of Love's court,
In thy simplicity the sport
Of all temptations.
A queen in crown of rubies drest,
A starveling in a scanty vest,
Are all, as seems to suit thee best—
Thy appellations.

I see thee glittering from afar—
And then thou art a pretty star;
Not quite so fair as many are
In heaven above thee!
Yet like a star, with glittering crest,
Self-poised in air thou seem'st to rest;—
May peace come never to his nest
Who shall reprove thee!

Bright flower! for by that name at last,
When all my reveries are past,
I call thee, and to that cleave fast,
Sweet silent creature!
That breath'st with me, in sun and air,
Do thou, as thou art wont, repair
My heart with gladness, and a share
Of thy meek nature!

Observe how spiritual, yet how wandering and playful, the fancy is in the first two stanzas, and how far she flies from the matter in hand; never stopping to brood on the character of any one of the images she summons, and yet for a moment truly seeing and believing in them all; while in the last stanza the imagination returns with its deep feeling to the heart of the flower, and "*cleaves fast*" to that. Compare the operation of the Imagination in Coleridge, on one of the most trifling objects that could possibly have been submitted to its action:

The thin blue flame
Lies on my low-burnt fire, and quivers not:
Only that film which fluttered on the grate
Still flutters there, the sole unquiet thing.
Methinks its motion in this hush of nature
Gives it dim sympathies with me, who live,
Making it a companionable form,
Whose puny flaps and freaks the idling spirit
By its own moods interprets, everywhere
Echo or mirror seeking of itself,
And makes a toy of thought.[28]

Lastly, observe the sweet operation of Fancy regardant, in the following well-known passage from Scott, where both her beholding and transforming powers are seen in their simplicity:

The rocky summits, split and rent,
Formed turret, dome or battlement,
Or seemed fantastically set
With cupola or minaret.
Nor were these earth-born castles bare,
Nor lacked they many a banner fair,
For, from their shivered brows displayed,
Far o'er th' unfathomable glade,
All twinkling with the dew-drop sheen,
The briar-rose fell, in streamers green,
And creeping shrubs of thousand dyes
Waved in the west wind's summer sighs.[29]

Let the reader refer to this passage, with its pretty tremulous conclusion above the pine tree, "where glistening streamers waved and danced", and then compare with it the following, where the Imagination operates on a scene nearly similar:

[28] *Frost at Midnight.*
[29] *The Lady of the Lake,* I, xi.

Grey rocks did peep from the spare moss, and stemmed
The struggling brook; tall spires of windlestrae
Threw their thin shadows down the rugged slope,
And nought but gnarled roots of ancient pines,
Branchless and blasted, clenched, with grasping roots,
Th' unwilling soil. . . . .
. . . A gradual change was here,
Yet ghastly. For, *as fast years flow away,*
The smooth brow gathers, and the hair grows thin
And white; and, where irradiate dewy eyes
Had shone, gleam stony orbs;—so from his steps
Bright flowers departed, and the beautiful shade
Of the green groves, with all their odorous winds
And musical motions. . . . .
. . . .
. . . . Where the pass extends
Its stony jaws, the abrupt mountain breaks,
And seems with its accumulated crags
To overhang the world; for wide expand
Beneath the wan stars, and descending moon,
Islanded seas, blue mountains, mighty streams,
Dim tracts and vast, robed in the lustrous gloom
Of leaden-coloured even, and fiery hills
Mingling their flames with twilight, on the verge
Of the remote horizon. The near scene,
In naked and severe simplicity,
Made contrast with the universe. A pine
Rock-rooted, stretch'd athwart the vacancy
Its swinging boughs, to each *inconstant blast*
Yielding one only response at each pause,
In most familiar cadence, with the howl,
The thunder, and the hiss of *homeless* streams,
Mingling its solemn song.[30]

In this last passage, the mind never departs from its solemn possession of the solitary scene, the Imagination only giving weight, meaning, and strange human sympathies to all its sights and sounds.

[30] Shelley, *Alastor,* 527.

In that from Scott* the Fancy, led away by the outside resemblance of floating form and hue to the banners, loses the feeling and possession of the scene, and places herself in circumstances of character completely opposite to the quietness and grandeur of the natural objects; this would have been unjustifiable, but that the resemblance occurs to the mind of the monarch, rather than to that of the poet; and it is that which, of all others, would have been the most likely to occur at the time; from this point of view it has high imaginative propriety. Of the same fanciful character is that transformation of the tree trunks into dragons noticed before in Turner's Jason; and in the same way this becomes imaginative, as it exhibits the effect of Fear in disposing to morbid perception. Compare with it the real and high action of the Imagination on the same matter in Wordsworth's *Yew trees* (perhaps the most vigorous and solemn bit of forest landscape ever painted):—

> Each particular trunk a growth
> Of intertwisted fibres serpentine,
> Up-coiling and inveterately convolved,
> *Nor uninformed with Phantasy, and looks*
> *That threaten the profane.*

It is too long to quote, but the reader should refer to it: let him note especially, if painter, that pure touch of colour, "By sheddings from the pining umbrage tinged."

I have been led perhaps into too great detail in illus-

* Let it not be supposed that I mean to compare the sickly dreaming of Shelley over clouds and waves, with the masculine and magnificent grasp of men and things which we find in Scott; it only happens that these two passages are more illustrative, by the likeness of the scenery they treat, than any others I could have opposed, and that Shelley is peculiarly distinguished by the faculty of Contemplative imagination. Scott's healthy and truthful feeling would not allow him to represent the benighted hunter, provoked by loss of game, horse, and way at once, as indulging in any more exalted flights of imagination than those naturally consequent on the contrast between the night's lodging he expected, and that which befitted him.

trating these points; but I think it is of no small importance to prove how in all cases the Imagination is based upon, and appeals to, a deep heart feeling; and how faithful and earnest it is in contemplation of the subject-matter, never losing sight of it, nor disguising it, but depriving it of extraneous and material accidents, and regarding it in its disembodied essence.

Modern Painters, vol. II, sec. II, ch. iv, pars. 1–7.

DANTE

In reading Dante, this mode of reasoning from contraries is a great help, for his philosophy of the vices is the only one which admits of classification; his descriptions of virtue, while they include the ordinary formal divisions, are far too profound and extended to be brought under definition. Every line of the *Paradiso* is full of the most exquisite and spiritual expressions of Christian truth; and that poem is only less read than the *Inferno* because it requires far greater attention, and, perhaps, for its full enjoyment, a holier heart.

His system in the *Inferno* is briefly this. The whole nether world is divided into seven circles, deep within deep, in each of which, according to its depth, severer punishment is inflicted. These seven circles, reckoning them downwards, are thus allotted:

1. To those who have lived virtuously, but knew not Christ.
2. To Lust.
3. To Gluttony.
4. To Avarice and Extravagance.
5. To Anger and *Sorrow*.
6. To Heresy.
7. To Violence and Fraud.

This seventh circle is divided into two parts; of which the first, reserved for those who have been guilty of Violence, is again divided into three, apportioned severally to those who have committed, or desired to commit, violence against their neighbours, against themselves, or against God.

The lowest hell, reserved for the punishment of Fraud, is itself divided into ten circles, wherein are severally punished the sins of,—

1. Betraying women.
2. Flattery.
3. Simony.
4. False prophecy.
5. Peculation.
6. Hypocrisy.
7. Theft.
8. False counsel.
9. Schism and Imposture.
10. Treachery to those who repose entire trust in the traitor.

There is, perhaps, nothing more notable in this most interesting system than the profound truth couched under the attachment of so terrible a penalty to sadness or sorrow. It is true that Idleness does not elsewhere appear in the scheme, and is evidently intended to be included in the guilt of sadness by the word "accidioso"; but the main meaning of the poet is to mark the duty of rejoicing in God, according both to St. Paul's command, and Isaiah's promise, "Thou meetest him that rejoiceth and worketh righteousness."[1] I do not know words that might with more benefit be borne with us, and set in our hearts momentarily against the minor regrets and rebelliousnesses of life, than these simple ones:

Tristi fummo
Nel aer dolce, che del sol s' allegra,
Or ci attristiam, nella belletta negra.

We once were sad,
In the sweet air, made gladsome by the sun,
Now in these murky settlings are we sad.[2] CARY.

The virtue usually opposed to this vice of sullenness is Alacritas, uniting the sense of activity and cheerfulness. Spenser has cheerfulness simply, in his description, never enough to be loved or praised, of the virtues of Woman-

[1] *Isa.* lxiv, 5.
[2] *Inferno,* VII, 121.

hood; first feminineness or womanhood in speciality; then,—

Next to her sate goodly Shamefastnesse,
Ne ever durst her eyes from ground upreare,
Ne ever once did looke up from her desse,[3]
As if some blame of evill she did feare
That in her cheekes made roses oft appeare:
And her against sweet Cherefulnesse was placed,
Whose eyes, like twinkling stars in evening cleare,
Were deckt with smyles that all sad humours chaced.

And next to her sate sober Modestie,
Holding her hand upon her gentle hart;
And her against, sate comely Curtesie,
That unto every person knew her part;
And her before was seated overthwart
Soft Silence, and submisse Obedience,
Both linckt together never to dispart.[4]

Another notable point in Dante's system is the intensity of uttermost punishment given to treason, the peculiar sin of Italy, and that to which, at this day, she attributes her own misery with her own lips. An Italian, questioned as to the causes of the failure of the campaign of 1848, always makes one answer, "We were betrayed"; and the most melancholy feature of the present state of Italy is principally this, that she does not see that, of all causes to which failure might be attributed, this is at once the most disgraceful, and the most hopeless. In fact, Dante seems to me to have written almost prophetically, for the instruction of modern Italy, and chiefly so in the sixth canto of the *Purgatorio.*

Hitherto we have been considering the system of the *Inferno* only. That of the *Purgatorio* is much simpler, it being divided into seven districts, in which the souls are severally purified from the sins of Pride, Envy, Wrath,

[3] "Desse", seat.
[4] *Faërie Queene,* IV, X, 50.

Indifference, Avarice, Gluttony, and Lust;[5] the poet thus implying in opposition, and describing in various instances, the seven virtues of Humility, Kindness,* Patience, Zeal, Poverty, Abstinence, and Chastity, as adjuncts of the Christian character, in which it may occasionally fail, while the essential group of the three theological and four cardinal virtues are represented as in direct attendance on the chariot of the Deity; and all the sins of Christians are in the seventeenth canto traced to the deficiency or aberration of Affection.

The system of Spenser is unfinished, and exceedingly complicated, the same vices and virtues occurring under different forms in different places, in order to show their different relations to each other. The peculiar superiority of his system is in its exquisite setting forth of Chastity under the figure of Britomart; not monkish chastity, but that of the purest Love. In completeness of personification no one can approach him; not even in Dante do I remember anything quite so great as the description of the Captain of the Lusts of the Flesh:

> As pale and wan as ashes was his looke;
> His body lean and meagre as a rake;
> And skin all withered like a dryed rooke;
> Thereto as cold and drery as a snake;
> That seemed to tremble evermore, and quake:
> *All in a canvas thin he was bedight,*
> *And girded with a belt of twisted brake:*
> Upon his head he wore an helmet light,
> Made of a dead mans skull.

* Usually called Charity: but this virtue in its full sense is one of the attendant spirits by the Throne; the Kindness here meant is Charity with a special object; or Friendship and Kindness, as opposed to Envy, which has always, in like manner, a special object. Hence the love of Orestes and Pylades is given as an instance of the virtue of Friendship; and the Virgin's, "They have no wine", at Cana, of general kindness and sympathy with others' pleasure.

[5] Vide Cantos x–xxv.

He rides upon a tiger, and in his hand is a bow, bent;

> And many arrows under his right side,
> Headed with flint, and fethers bloody dide.[6]

The horror and the truth of this are beyond everything that I know, out of the pages of Inspiration. Note the heading of the arrows with flint, because sharper and more subtle in the edge than steel, and because steel might consume away with rust, but flint not; and consider in the whole description how the wasting away of body and soul together, and the *coldness* of the heart, which unholy fire has consumed into ashes, and the loss of all power, and the kindling of all terrible impatience, and the implanting of thorny and inextricable griefs, are set forth by the various images, the belt of brake, the tiger steed, and the *light* helmet, girding the head with death.

Stones of Venice, vol. II, ch. viii, pars. 57–62.

THE GROTESQUE (1)

The superstitions which represented the devil as assuming various contemptible forms or disguises in order to accomplish his purposes aided this gradual degradation of conception, and directed the study of the workman to the most strange and ugly conditions of animal form, until at last, even in the most serious subjects, the fiends are oftener ludicrous than terrible. Nor, indeed, is this altogether avoidable, for it is not possible to express intense wickedness without some condition of degradation. Malice, subtlety, and pride, in their extreme, cannot be written upon noble forms; and I am aware of no effort to represent the Satanic mind in the angelic form which has succeeded in painting. Milton succeeds only because he separately describes the movements of the mind, and therefore leaves

[6] *Faërie Queene,* II, XI, 21.

himself at liberty to make the form heroic; but that form is never distinct enough to be painted. Dante, who will not leave even external forms obscure, degrades them before he can feel them to be demoniacal; so also John Bunyan: both of them, I think, having firmer faith than Milton's in their own creations, and deeper insight into the nature of sin. Milton makes his fiends too noble, and misses the foulness, inconstancy, and fury of wickedness. His Satan possesses some virtues, not the less virtues for being applied to evil purpose. Courage, resolution, patience, deliberation in council, this latter being eminently a wise and holy character, as opposed to the "Insania" of excessive sin: and all this, if not a shallow and false, is a smoothed and artistical, conception. On the other hand, I have always felt that there was a peculiar grandeur in the indescribable ungovernable fury of Dante's fiends, ever shortening its own powers, and disappointing its own purposes; the deaf, blind, speechless, unspeakable rage, fierce as the lightning, but erring from its mark or turning senselessly against itself, and still further debased by foulness of form and action. Something is indeed to be allowed for the rude feelings of the time, but I believe all such men as Dante are sent into the world at the time when they can do their work best; and that, it being appointed for him to give to mankind the most vigorous realisation possible both of Hell and Heaven, he was born both in the country and at the time which furnished the most stern opposition of Horror and Beauty, and permitted it to be written in the clearest terms. And, therefore, though there are passages in the *Inferno* which it would be impossible for any poet now to write, I look upon it as all the more perfect for them. For there can be no question but that one characteristic of excessive vice is indecency, a general baseness in its thoughts and acts concerning the body[1], and that the full portraiture of it cannot be given without marking, and that in the strongest lines, this tendency to corporeal degradation; which, in the time of Dante, could be done

[1] Let the reader examine, with especial reference to this subject, the general character of the language of Iago.

frankly, but cannot now. And, therefore, I think the twenty-first and twenty-second books of the *Inferno* the most perfect portraitures of fiendish nature which we possess; and, at the same time, in their mingling of the extreme of horror (for it seems to me that the silent swiftness of the first demon, "con l' ali aperte e sovra i pie leggiero",[2] cannot be surpassed in dreadfulness) with ludicrous actions and images, they present the most perfect instances with which I am acquainted of the terrible grotesque. But the whole of the *Inferno* is full of this grotesque, as well as the *Faërie Queene;* and these two poems, together with the works of Albert Dürer, will enable the reader to study it in its noblest forms, without reference to Gothic cathedrals.

Now, just as there are base and noble conditions of the apathetic grotesque, so also are there of this satirical grotesque. The condition which might be mistaken for it is that above described as resulting from the malice of men given to pleasure, and in which the grossness and foulness are in the workman as much as in his subject, so that he chooses to represent vice and disease rather than virtue and beauty, having his chief delight in contemplating them; though he still mocks at them with such dull wit as may be in him, because, as Young has said most truly,

'Tis not in folly not to scorn a fool.[3]

Now it is easy to distinguish this grotesque from its noble counterpart, by merely observing whether any forms of beauty or dignity are mingled with it or not; for, of course, the noble grotesque is only employed by its master for good purposes, and to contrast with beauty: but the base workman cannot conceive anything but what is base; and there will be no loveliness in any part of his work, or, at the best, a loveliness measured by line and rule, and dependent on legal shapes of feature. But, without resorting to this test, and merely by examining the ugly gro-

[2] *Inferno,* XXI, 33: "With wings outstretched, and feet of nimblest tread."

[3] *Night Thoughts,* i, 416.

tesque itself, it will be found that, if it belongs to the base school, there will be, first, no Horror in it; secondly, no Nature in it; and, thirdly, no Mercy in it.

I say, first, no Horror. For the base soul has no fear of sin, and no hatred of it: and, however it may strive to make its work terrible, there will be no genuineness in the fear; the utmost it can do will be to make its work disgusting.

Secondly, there will be no Nature in it. It appears to be one of the ends proposed by Providence in the appointment of the forms of the brute creation, that the various vices to which mankind are liable should be severally expressed in them so distinctly and clearly as that men could not but understand the lesson; while yet these conditions of vice might, in the inferior animal, be observed without the disgust and hatred which the same vices would excite, if seen in men, and might be associated with features of interest which would otherwise attract and reward contemplation. Thus, ferocity, cunning, sloth, discontent, gluttony, uncleanness, and cruelty are seen, each in its extreme, in various animals; and are so vigorously expressed, that, when men desire to indicate the same vices in connection with human forms, they can do it no better than by borrowing here and there the features of animals. And when the workman is thus led to the contemplation of the animal kingdom, finding therein the expressions of vice which he needs, associated with power, and nobleness, and freedom from disease, if his mind be of right tone he becomes interested in this new study; and all noble grotesque is, therefore, full of the most admirable rendering of animal character. But the ignoble workman is capable of no interest of this kind; and, being too dull to appreciate, and too idle to execute, the subtle and wonderful lines on which the expression of the lower animal depends, he contents himself with vulgar exaggeration, and leaves his work as false as it is monstrous, a mass of blunt malice and obscene ignorance.

Lastly, there will be no Mercy in it. Wherever the satire of the noble grotesque fixes upon human nature, it does so with much sorrow mingled amidst its indignation: in its highest forms there is an infinite tenderness, like that of the fool in Lear; and even in its more heedless or bitter sarcasm, it never loses sight altogether of the better nature of what it attacks, nor refuses to acknowledge its redeeming or pardonable features. But the ignoble grotesque has no pity: it rejoices in iniquity, and exists only to slander.

I have not space to follow out the various forms of transition which exist between the two extremes of great and base in the satirical grotesque. The reader must always remember, that although there is an infinite distance between the best and worst, in this kind the interval is filled by endless conditions more or less inclining to the evil or the good; impurity and malice stealing gradually into the nobler forms, and invention and wit elevating the lower, according to the countless minglings of the elements of the human soul.

Ungovernableness of the imagination. The reader is always to keep in mind that if the objects of horror in which the terrible grotesque finds its materials, were contemplated in their true light, and with the entire energy of the soul, they would cease to be grotesque, and become altogether sublime; and that therefore it is some shortening of the power, or the will, of contemplation, and some consequent distortion of the terrible image in which the grotesqueness consists. Now this distortion takes place, it was above asserted, in three ways: either through apathy, satire, or ungovernableness of imagination. It is this last cause of the grotesque which we have finally to consider; namely, the error and wildness of the mental impressions, caused by fear operating upon strong powers of imagination, or by the failure of the human faculties in the endeavour to grasp the highest truths.

The grotesque which comes to all men in a disturbed dream is the most intelligible example of this kind, but also the most ignoble; the imagination, in this instance, being entirely deprived of all aid from reason, and incapable of self-government. I believe, however, that the noblest forms of imaginative power are also in some sort ungovernable, and have in them something of the character of dreams; so that the vision, of whatever kind, comes uncalled, and will not submit itself to the seer, but conquers him, and forces him to speak as a prophet, having no power over his words or thoughts. Only, if the whole man be trained perfectly, and his mind calm, consistent, and powerful, the vision which comes to him is seen as in a perfect mirror, serenely, and in consistence with the rational powers; but if the mind be imperfect and ill trained, the vision is seen as in a broken mirror, with strange distortions and discrepancies, all the passions of the heart breathing upon it in cross ripples, till hardly a trace of it remains unbroken. So that, strictly speaking, the imagination is never governed; it is always the ruling and Divine power: and the rest of the man is to it only as an instrument which it sounds, or a tablet on which it writes; clearly and sublimely if the wax be smooth and the strings true, grotesquely and wildly if they are stained and broken. And thus the *Iliad*, the *Inferno*, the *Pilgrim's Progress*, the *Faërie Queene*, are all of them true dreams; only the sleep of the men to whom they came was the deep, living sleep which God sends, with a sacredness in it, as of death, the revealer of secrets.

Now, observe in this matter, carefully, the difference between a dim mirror and a distorted one; and do not blame me for pressing the analogy too far, for it will enable me to explain my meaning every way more clearly. Most men's minds are dim mirrors, in which all truth is seen, as St. Paul tells us, darkly.[4] This is the fault most common and most fatal; dulness of the heart and mistiness of sight, increasing to utter hardness and blindness; Satan breathing upon the glass, so that if we do not sweep the mist laboriously away, it will take no image. But, even so far as we are able to do this, we have still the distortion to fear, yet not to the same extent, for we can in some sort allow for the distortion of an image, if only we can see it

[4] 1 *Cor.* xiii, 12.

clearly. And the fallen human soul, at its best, must be as a diminishing glass, and that a broken one, to the mighty truths of the universe round it; and the wider the scope of its glance, and the vaster the truths into which it obtains an insight, the more fantastic their distortion is likely to be, as the winds and vapours trouble the field of the telescope most when it reaches farthest.

Now, so far as the truth is seen by the imagination in its wholeness and quietness, the vision is sublime; but so far as it is narrowed and broken by the inconsistencies of the human capacity, it becomes grotesque: and it would seem to be rare that any very exalted truth should be impressed on the imagination without some grotesqueness in its aspect, proportioned to the degree of *diminution of breadth* in the grasp which is given of it. Nearly all the dreams recorded in the Bible,–Jacob's, Joseph's, Pharaoh's, Nebuchadnezzar's,–are grotesques; and nearly the whole of the accessory scenery in the books of Ezekiel and the Apocalypse. Thus, Jacob's dream revealed to him the ministry of angels; but because this ministry could not be seen or understood by him in its fulness, it was narrowed to him into a ladder between heaven and earth, which was a grotesque. Joseph's two dreams were evidently intended to be signs of the steadfastness of the Divine purpose towards him, by possessing the clearness of special prophecy; yet were couched in such imagery, as not to inform him prematurely of his destiny, and only to be understood after their fulfilment. The sun, and moon, and stars were at the period, and are indeed throughout the Bible, the symbols of high authority. It was not revealed to Joseph that he should be lord over all Egypt; but the representation of his family by symbols of the most magnificent dominion, and yet as subject to him, must have been afterwards felt by him as a distinctly prophetic indication of his own supreme power. It was not revealed to him that the occasion of his brethren's special humiliation before him should be their coming to buy corn; but when the event took place, must he not have felt that there was prophetic purpose in the form of the sheaves of wheat which first imaged forth their subjection to him? And these two images of the sun doing obeisance, and the sheaves bowing down,—narrowed and imperfect intimations of great truth which yet could not be otherwise conveyed,—are both grotesques. The kine of Pharaoh eating each other, the gold and clay of Nebuchadnezzar's image, the four beasts full of eyes, and other imagery of Ezekiel and the Apocalypse, are grotesques of the same kind, on which I need not further insist.

Stones of Venice, vol. III, sec. III, pars. 53–62.

From what we have seen to be its nature, we must, I think, be led to one most important conclusion; that wherever the human mind is healthy and vigorous in all its proportions, great in imagination and emotion no less than in intellect, and not overborne by an undue or hardened pre-eminence of the mere reasoning faculties, there the grotesque will exist in full energy. And, accordingly, I believe that there is no test of greatness in periods, nations, or men, more sure than the development, among them or in them, of a noble grotesque; and no test of comparative smallness or limitation, of one kind or another, more sure than the absence of grotesque invention, or incapability of understanding it. I think that the central man of all the world, as representing in perfect balance the imaginative, moral, and intellectual faculties, all at their highest, is Dante; and in him the grotesque reaches at once the most distinct and the most noble development to which it was ever brought in the human mind. The two other greatest men whom Italy has produced, Michael Angelo and Tintoret, show the same element in no less original strength, but oppressed in the one by his science, and in both by the spirit of the age in which they lived; never, however, absent even in Michael Angelo, but stealing forth continually in a strange and spectral way, lurking in folds of raiment and knots of wild hair, and mountainous confusions of craggy limb and cloudy drapery; and, in Tintoret, ruling the entire conceptions of his greatest works to such a degree that they are an enigma or an offence, even to this day, to all the petty disciples of a formal criticism. Of the grotesque in our own Shakespeare I need hardly speak, nor of its intolerableness to his French critics; nor of that of Æschylus and Homer, as opposed to the lower Greek writers; and so I believe it will be found, at all periods, in all minds of the first order.

Stones of Venice, vol. III, sec. III, par. 67.

THEOLOGY OF SPENSER

The following analysis of the first book of the *Faërie Queene* may be interesting to readers who have been in the habit of reading the noble poem too hastily to connect its parts completely together, and may perhaps induce them to more careful study of the rest of the poem.

The Redcrosse Knight is Holiness,—the "Pietas" of St. Mark's, the "Devotio" of Orcagna,—meaning, I think, in general, Reverence and Godly Fear.

This Virtue, in the opening of the book, has Truth (or Una) at its side, but presently enters the Wandering Wood, and encounters the serpent Error; that is to say, Error in her universal form, the first enemy of Reverence and Holiness; and more especially Error as founded on learning; for when Holiness strangles her,

"Her vomit *full of bookes and papers was,*
With loathly frogs and toades, which eyes did lacke."

Having vanquished this first open and palpable form of Error, as Reverence and Religion must always vanquish it, the Knight encounters Hypocrisy, or Archimagus: Holiness cannot detect Hypocrisy, but believes him, and goes home with him; whereupon, Hypocrisy succeeds in separating Holiness from Truth; and the Knight (Holiness) and

Lady (Truth) go forth separately from the house of Archimagus.

Now observe; the moment Godly Fear, or Holiness, is separated from Truth, he meets Infidelity, or the Knight Sans Foy; Infidelity having Falsehood, or Duessa, riding behind him. The instant the Redcrosse Knight is aware of the attack of Infidelity, he

> "Gan fairly couch his speare, and towards ride."

He vanquishes and slays Infidelity; but is deceived by his companion, Falsehood, and takes her for his lady: thus showing the condition of Religion, when, after being attacked by Doubt, and remaining victorious, it is nevertheless seduced, by any form of Falsehood, to pay reverence where it ought not. This, then, is the first fortune of Godly Fear separated from Truth. The poet then returns to Truth, separated from Godly Fear. She is immediately attended by a lion, or Violence, which makes her dreaded wherever she comes; and when she enters the mart of superstition, this Lion tears Kirkrapine in pieces: showing how Truth, separated from Godliness, does indeed put an end to the abuses of supersition, but does so violently and desperately. She then meets again with Hypocrisy, whom she mistakes for her own lord, or Godly Fear, and travels a little way under his guardianship (Hypocrisy thus not unfrequently appearing to defend the Truth), until they are both met by Lawlessness, or the Knight Sans Loy, whom Hypocrisy cannot resist. Lawlessness overthrows Hypocrisy, and seizes upon Truth, first slaying her lion attendant: showing that the first aim of licence is to destroy the force and authority of Truth. Sans Loy then takes Truth captive, and bears her away. Now this Lawlessness is the "unrighteousness," or "adikia," of St. Paul; and his bearing Truth away captive is a type of those "who hold the truth in unrighteousness,"[1]—that is to say, generally, of men who, knowing what is true, make the truth give way to their own purposes, or use it only to forward them,

[1] Romans i. 18.

as is the case with so many of the popular leaders of the present day. Una is then delivered from Sans Loy by the satyrs, to show that Nature, in the end, must work out the deliverance of the truth, although, where it has been captive to Lawlessness, that deliverance can only be obtained through Savageness, and a return to barbarism. Una is then taken from among the satyrs by Satyrane, the son of a satyr and a "lady myld, fair Thyamis" (typifying the early steps of renewed civilization, and its rough and hardy character, "nousled up in life and manners wilde"), who meeting again with Sans Loy, enters instantly into rough and prolonged combat with him: showing how the early organization of a hardy nation must be wrought out through much discouragement from Lawlessness. This contest the poet leaving for the time undecided, returns to trace the adventures of the Redcrosse Knight, or Godly Fear, who, having vanquished Infidelity, presently is led by Falsehood to the house of Pride: thus showing how religion, separated from truth, is first tempted by doubts of God, and then by the pride of life. The description of this house of Pride is one of the most elaborate and noble pieces in the poem; and here we begin to get at the proposed system of Virtues and Vices. For Pride, as Queen, has six other vices yoked in her chariot; namely, first, Idleness, then Gluttony, Lust, Avarice, Envy, and Anger, all driven on by "Sathan, with a smarting whip in hand." From these lower vices and their company, Godly Fear, though lodging in the house of Pride, holds aloof; but he is challenged, and has a hard battle to fight with Sans Joy, the brother of Sans Foy: showing, that though he has conquered Infidelity, and does not give himself up to the allurements of Pride, he is yet exposed, so long as he dwells in her house, to distress of mind and loss of his accustomed rejoicing before God. He, however, having partly conquered Despondency, or Sans Joy, Falsehood goes down to Hades, in order to obtain drugs to maintain the power or life of Despondency; but, meantime, the Knight leaves the house of Pride: Falsehood pursues and overtakes him, and finds him by a fountain side, of which the waters are

> "Dull and slow,
> And all that drinke thereof do faint and feeble grow."

Of which the meaning is, that Godly Fear, after passing through the house of Pride, is exposed to drowsiness and feebleness of watch; as, after Peter's boast, came Peter's sleeping, from weakness of the flesh, and then, last of all, Peter's fall. And so it follows, for the Redcrosse Knight, being overcome with faintness by drinking of the fountain, is thereupon attacked by the giant Orgoglio, overcome, and thrown by him into a dungeon. This Orgoglio is Orgueil, or Carnal Pride; not the pride of life, spiritual and subtle, but the common and vulgar pride in the power of this world: and his throwing the Redcrosse Knight into a dungeon is a type of the captivity of true religion under the temporal power of corrupt churches, more especially of the Church of Rome; and of its gradually wasting away in unknown places, while Carnal Pride has the preeminence over all things. That Spenser means especially the pride of the Papacy, is shown by the 16th stanza of the book; for there the giant Orgoglio is said to have taken Duessa, or Falsehood, for his "deare," and to have set upon her head a triple crown, and endowed her with royal majesty, and made her to ride upon a seven-headed beast.

In the meantime, the dwarf, the attendant of the Redcrosse Knight, takes his arms, and finding Una, tells her of the captivity of her lord. Una, in the midst of her mourning, meets Prince Arthur, in whom, as Spenser himself tells us, is set forth generally Magnificence; but who, as is shown by the choice of the hero's name, is more especially the magnificence, or literally, "great doing," of the kingdom of England. This power of England, going forth with Truth, attacks Orgoglio, or the Pride of Papacy, slays him; strips Duessa, or Falsehood, naked; and liberates the Redcrosse Knight. The magnificent and well-known description of Despair follows, by whom the Redcrosse Knight is hard bested, on account of his past errors and captivity, and is only saved by Truth, who, perceiving him to be still feeble, brings him to the house of Cœlia, called, in the argument of the canto, Holiness, but properly, Heavenly Grace, the mother of the Virtues. Her "three daughters, well upbrought," are Faith, Hope, and Charity. Her porter is Humility; because Humility opens the door of Heavenly Grace. Zeal and Reverence are her chamberlains, introducing the new-comers to her presence; her groom, or servant, is Obedience; and her physician, Patience. Under the commands of Charity, the matron Mercy rules over her hospital, under whose care the Knight is healed of his sickness; and it is to be especially noticed how much importance Spenser, though never ceasing to chastise all hypocrisies and mere observances of form, attaches to true and faithful *penance* in effecting this cure. Having his strength restored to him, the Knight is trusted to the guidance of Mercy, who, leading him forth by a narrow and thorny way, first instructs him in the seven works of Mercy, and then leads him to the hill of Heavenly Contemplation; whence, having a sight of the New Jerusalem, as Christian of the Delectable Mountains, he goes forth to the final victory over Satan, the old serpent, with which the book closes.

Stones of Venice, appendix, 2.

POETRY AND NATURE

I am writing at a window which commands a view of the head of the Lake of Geneva; and as I look up from my paper, to consider this point, I see, beyond it, a blue breadth of softly moving water, and the outline of the mountains above Chillon, bathed in morning mist. The first verses which naturally come into my mind are—

> A thousand feet in depth below
> The massy waters meet and flow;
> So far the fathom line was sent
> From Chillon's snow-white battlement.[1]

Let us see in what manner this poetical statement is distinguished from a historical one.

It is distinguished from a truly historical statement, first, in being simply false. The water under the castle of Chillon is not a thousand feet deep, nor anything like it. Herein, certainly, these lines fulfil Reynolds's first requirement in poetry, "that it should be inattentive to literal truth and minute exactness in detail". In order, however, to make our comparison more closely in other points, let us assume that what is stated is indeed a fact, and that it was to be recorded, first historically, and then poetically.

Historically stating it, then, we should say: "The lake was sounded from the walls of the castle of Chillon, and found to be a thousand feet deep."

Now, if Reynolds be right in his idea of the difference between history and poetry, we shall find that Byron leaves out of this statement certain *un*necessary details, and retains only the invariable,—that is to say, the points which the Lake of Geneva and Castle of Chillon have in common with all other lakes and castles.

Let us hear, therefore.

[1] Byron: *Prisoner of Chillon,* VI.

A thousand feet in depth below.

"Below?" Here is, at all events, a word added (instead of anything being taken away); invariable, certainly in the case of lakes, but not absolutely necessary.

The massy waters meet and flow.

"Massy!" why massy? Because deep water is heavy. The word is a good word, but it is assuredly an added detail, and expresses a character, not which the Lake of Geneva has in common with all other lakes, but which it has in distinction from those which are narrow, or shallow. "Meet and flow." Why meet and flow? Partly to make up a rhyme; partly to tell us that the waters are forceful as well as massy, and changeful as well as deep. Observe, a farther addition of details, and of details more or less peculiar to the spot, or, according to Reynolds's definition, of "heavy matter, retarding the progress of the imagination".

So far the fathom line was sent.

Why fathom line? All lines for sounding are not fathom lines. If the lake was ever sounded from Chillon, it was probably sounded in metres, not fathoms. This is an addition of another particular detail, in which the only compliance with Reynolds's requirement is, that there is some chance of its being an inaccurate one.

From Chillon's snow-white battlement.

Why snow-white? Because castle battlements are not usually snow-white. This is another added detail, and a detail quite peculiar to Chillon, and therefore exactly the most striking word in the whole passage.

"Battlement!" why battlement? Because all walls have not battlements, and the addition of the term marks the castle to be not merely a prison, but a fortress.

This is a curious result. Instead of finding, as we expected, the poetry distinguished from the history by the omission of details, we find it consist entirely in the *addi-*

tion of details; and instead of being characterised by regard only of the invariable, we find its whole power to consist in the clear expression of what is singular and particular!

Modern Painters, vol. III, ch. i, pars. 8–9.

It is evident, therefore, that our author has entangled himself in some grave fallacy, by introducing this idea of invariableness as forming a distinction between poetical and historical art. What the fallacy is, we shall discover as we proceed; but as an invading army should not leave an untaken fortress in its rear, we must not go on with our inquiry into the views of Reynolds until we have settled satisfactorily the question already suggested to us, in what the essence of poetical treatment really consists. For though, as we have seen, it certainly involves the addition of specific details, it cannot be simply that addition which turns the history into poetry. For it is perfectly possible to add any number of details to a historical statement, and to make it more prosaic with every added word. As, for instance, "The lake was sounded out of a flat-bottomed boat, near the crab-tree at the corner of the kitchen-garden, and was found to be a thousand feet nine inches deep, with a muddy bottom." It thus appears that it is not the multiplication of details which constitutes poetry; nor their subtraction which constitutes history, but that there must be something either in the nature of the details themselves, or the method of using them, which invests them with poetical power or historical propriety.

It seems to me, and may seem to the reader, strange that we should need to ask the question, "What is poetry?" Here is a word we have been using all our lives, and, I suppose, with a very distinct idea attached to it; and when I am now called upon to give a definition of this idea, I find myself at a pause. What is more singular, I do not at present recollect hearing the question often asked, though surely it is a very natural one; and I never recollect hearing it answered, or even attempted to be answered. In general, people shelter themselves under metaphors, and while we hear poetry described as an utterance of the soul, an effusion of Divinity, or voice of nature, or in other terms equally elevated and obscure, we never attain anything like a definite explanation of the character which actually distinguishes it from prose.

I come, after some embarrassment, to the conclusion, that poetry is "the suggestion, by the imagination, of noble grounds for the noble emotions". I mean, by the noble emotions, those four principal sacred passions—Love, Veneration, Admiration, and Joy (this latter especially, if unselfish); and their opposites—Hatred, Indignation (or Scorn), Horror, and Grief,—this last, when unselfish, becoming Compassion. These passions in their various combinations constitute what is called "poetical feeling", when they are felt on noble grounds, that is, on great and true grounds. Indignation, for instance, is a poetical feeling, if excited by serious injury; but it is not a poetical feeling if entertained on being cheated out of a small sum of money. It is very possible the manner of the cheat may have been such as to justify considerable indignation; but the feeling is nevertheless not poetical unless the grounds of it be large as well as just. In like manner, energetic admiration may be excited in certain minds by a display of fireworks, or a street of handsome shops; but the feeling is not poetical, because the grounds of it are false, and therefore ignoble. There is in reality nothing to deserve admiration either in the firing of packets of gunpowder, or in the display of the stocks of warehouses. But admiration excited by the budding of a flower is a poetical feeling, because it is impossible that this manifestation of spiritual power and vital beauty can ever be enough admired.

Farther, it is necessary to the existence of poetry that the grounds of these feelings should be *furnished by the imagination.* Poetical feeling, that is to say, mere noble emotion, is not poetry. It is happily inherent in all human nature deserving the name, and is found often to be purest in the least sophisticated. But the power of assembling, by *the help of the imagination,* such images as will excite these feelings, is the power of the poet or literally of the "Maker".

Now this power of exciting the emotions depends of course on the richness of the imagination, and on its choice of those images which, in combination, will be most effective, or, for the particular work to be done, most fit. And it is altogether impossible for a writer not endowed with invention to conceive what tools a true poet will make use of, or in what way he will apply them, or what unexpected results he will bring out by them; so that it is vain to say that the details of poetry ought to possess, or ever do possess, any *definite* character. Generally speaking, poetry runs into finer and more delicate details than prose; but the details are not poetical because they are more delicate, but because they are employed so as to bring out an affecting result. For instance, no one but a true poet would have thought of exciting our pity for a bereaved father by describing his way of locking the door of his house:

> Perhaps to himself at that moment he said,
> The key I must take, for my Ellen is dead;
> But of this in my ears not a word did he speak,
> And he went to the chase with a tear on his cheek.[2]

In like manner, in painting, it is altogether impossible to say beforehand what details a great painter may make poetical by his use of them to excite noble emotions: and we shall, therefore, find that a painting is to be classed in the great or inferior schools, not according to the kind of details which it represents, but according to the uses for which it employs them.

It is only farther to be noticed, that infinite confusion has been introduced into this subject by the careless and illogical custom of opposing painting to poetry, instead of regarding poetry as consisting in a noble use, whether of colours or words. Painting is properly to be opposed to

[2] Wordsworth: *The Childless Father.*

speaking or *writing,* but not to *poetry*. Both painting and speaking are methods of expression. Poetry is the employment of either for the noblest purposes.

This question being thus far determined, we may proceed with our paper in the *Idler*.

> It is very difficult to determine the exact degree of enthusiasm that the arts of painting and poetry may admit. There may, perhaps, be too great indulgence as well as too great a restraint of imagination; if the one produces incoherent monsters, the other produces what is full as bad, lifeless insipidity. An intimate knowledge of the passions, and good sense, but not common sense, must at last determine its limits. It has been thought, and I believe with reason, that Michael Angelo sometimes transgressed those limits; and, I think, I have seen figures of him of which it was very difficult to determine whether they were in the highest degree sublime or extremely ridiculous. Such faults may be said to be the ebullitions of genius; but at least he had this merit, that he never was insipid, and whatever passion his works may excite, they will always escape contempt.
>
> What I have had under consideration is the sublimest style, particularly that of Michael Angelo, the Homer of painting. Other kinds may admit of this naturalness, which of the lowest kind is the chief merit; but in painting, as in poetry, the highest style has the least of common nature.

From this passage we gather three important indications of the supposed nature of the Great Style. That it is the work of men in a state of enthusiasm. That it is like the writing of Homer; and that it has as little as possible of "common nature" in it.

First, it is produced by men in a state of enthusiasm. That is, by men who feel *strongly* and *nobly;* for we do not call a strong feeling of envy, jealousy, or ambition, enthusiasm. That is, therefore, by men who feel poetically. This much we may admit, I think, with perfect safety. Great art is produced by men who feel acutely and nobly; and it is in some sort an expression of this personal feeling. We can easily conceive that there may be a sufficiently marked distinction between such art, and that which is produced by men who do not feel at all, but who reproduce, though ever so accurately, yet coldly, like human mirrors, the scenes which pass before their eyes.

Secondly, Great Art is like the writing of Homer, and this chiefly because it has little of "common nature" in it. We are not clearly informed what is meant by common nature in this passage. Homer seems to describe a great deal of what is common:—cookery, for instance, very carefully in all its processes.[3] I suppose the passage in the *Iliad* which, on the whole, has excited most admiration, is that which describes a wife's sorrow at parting from her husband, and a child's fright at its father's helmet;[4] and I hope, at least, the former feeling may be considered "common nature". But the true greatness of Homer's style is, doubtless, held by our author to consist in his imaginations of things not only uncommon but impossible (such as spirits in brazen armour, or monsters with heads of men and bodies of beasts), and in his occasional delineations of the human character and form in their utmost, or heroic, strength and beauty. We gather then, on the whole, that a painter in the Great Style must be enthusiastic, or full of emotion, and must paint the human form in its utmost strength and beauty, and perhaps certain impossible forms besides, liable by persons not in an equally enthusiastic state of mind to be looked upon as in some degree absurd. This I presume to be Reynolds's meaning, and to be all that he intends us to gather from his comparison of the Great Style with the writings of Homer. But if that comparison be a just one in all respects, surely two other corollaries ought to be drawn from it, namely,—first, that these Heroic or Impossible images are to be mingled with others very unheroic and very possible; and, secondly, that in

[3] *Iliad*, I, 463.
[4] *Iliad*, VI, 468.

the representation of the Heroic or Impossible forms, the greatest care must be taken in *finishing the details,* so that a painter must not be satisfied with painting well the countenance and the body of his hero, but ought to spend the greatest part of his time (as Homer the greatest number of verses) in elaborating the sculptured pattern on his shield.

Modern Painters, vol. III, ch. i, pars. 11–18.

THE GROTESQUE (2)

A fine grotesque is the expression, in a moment, by a series of symbols thrown together in bold and fearless connection, of truths which it would have taken a long time to express in any verbal way, and of which the connection is left for the beholder to work out for himself; the gaps, left or overleaped by the haste of the imagination, forming the grotesque character.

For instance, Spenser desires to tell us, (1) that envy is the most untamable and unappeasable of the passions, not to be soothed by any kindness; (2) that with continual labour it invents evil thoughts out of its own heart; (3) that even in this, its power of doing harm is partly hindered by the decaying and corrupting nature of the evil it lives in; (4) that it looks every way, and that whatever it sees is altered and discoloured by its own nature; (5) which discolouring, however, is to it a veil, or disgraceful dress, in the sight of others; (6) and that it never is free from the most bitter suffering, (7) which cramps all its acts and movements, enfolding and crushing it while it torments. All this it has required a somewhat long and languid sentence for me to say in unsymbolical terms,—not, by the way, that they *are* unsymbolical altogether, for I have been forced, whether I would or not, to use *some* figurative words; but even with this help the sentence is long and tiresome, and does not with any vigour represent the truth. It would take some prolonged enforcement of each sentence to make it felt, in ordinary ways of talking. But Spenser puts it all into a grotesque, and it is done shortly and at once, so that we feel it fully, and see it, and never forget it. I have numbered above the statements which had to be made. I now number them with the same numbers, as they occur in the several pieces of the grotesque:—

And next to him malicious Envy rode
(1) Upon a ravenous wolfe, and (2, 3) still did chaw
Between his cankred[1] teeth a venemous tode,
That all the poison ran about his jaw.
(4, 5) All in a kirtle of discolourd say
He clothed was, y-paynted full of eies;
(6) And in his bosome secretly there lay
An hatefull snake, the which his taile uptyes
(7) In many folds, and mortall sting implyes.[2]

There is the whole thing in nine lines; or, rather in one image, which will hardly occupy any room at all on the mind's shelves, but can be lifted out, whole, whenever we want it. All noble grotesques are concentrations of this kind, and the noblest convey truths which nothing else could convey; and not only so, but convey them, in minor cases with a delightfulness,—in the higher instances with an awfulness,—which no mere utterance of the symbolised truth would have possessed, but which belongs to the effort of the mind to unweave the riddle, or to the sense it has of there being an infinite power and meaning in the thing seen, beyond all that is apparent therein, giving the highest sublimity even to the most trivial object so presented and so contemplated.

"Jeremiah, what seest thou?"
"I see a seething pot; and the face thereof is toward
the north.

[1] Cankred—because he cannot then bite hard.
[2] *Faërie Queene*, I, iv, 30.

Out of the north an evil shall break forth upon all the
inhabitants of the land."[3]

And thus in all ages and among all nations, grotesque idealism has been the element through which the most appalling and eventful truth has been wisely conveyed, from the most sublime words of true Revelation, to the "ἀλλ' ὅτ' ἂν ἡμίονος βασιλεύς", etc., of the oracles,[4] and the more or less doubtful teaching of dreams; and so down to ordinary poetry. No element of imagination has a wider range, a more magnificent use, or so colossal a grasp of sacred truth.

Modern Painters, vol. III, ch. viii, pars. 4–5.

THE PATHETIC FALLACY

Now, therefore, putting these tiresome and absurd words quite out of our way, we may go on at our ease to examine the point in question,—namely, the difference between the ordinary, proper, and true appearances of things to us; and the extraordinary, or false appearances, when we are under the influence of emotion, or contemplative fancy; false appearances, I say, as being entirely unconnected with any real power or character in the object, and only imputed to it by us.

For instance—

The spendthrift crocus, bursting through the mould
Naked and shivering, with his cup of gold.[1]

This is very beautiful, and yet very untrue. The crocus is not a spendthrift, but a hardy plant; its yellow is not gold, but saffron. How is it that we enjoy so much the

[3] *Jeremiah,* i, 13.
[4] Herodotus, I, 55.
[1] O. W. Holmes, *Astraea.*

having it put into our heads that it is anything else than a plain crocus?

It is an important question. For, throughout our past reasonings about art, we have always found that nothing could be good or useful, or ultimately pleasurable, which was untrue. But here is something pleasurable in written poetry which is nevertheless *un*true. And what is more, if we think over our favourite poetry, we shall find it full of this kind of fallacy, and that we like it all the more for being so.

It will appear also, on consideration of the matter, that this fallacy is of two principal kinds. Either, as in this case of the crocus, it is the fallacy of wilful fancy, which involves no real expectation that it will be believed; or else it is a fallacy caused by an excited state of the feelings, making us, for the time, more or less irrational. Of the cheating of the fancy we shall have to speak presently; but, in this chapter, I want to examine the nature of the other error, that which the mind admits when affected strongly by emotion. Thus, for instance, in *Alton Locke*,—

> They rowed her in across the rolling foam—
> The cruel, crawling foam.

The foam is not cruel, neither does it crawl. The state of mind which attributes to it these characters of a living creature is one in which the reason is unhinged by grief. All violent feelings have the same effect. They produce in us a falseness in all our impressions of external things, which I would generally characterize as the "pathetic fallacy".

Now we are in the habit of considering this fallacy as eminently a character of poetical description, and the temper of mind in which we allow it, as one eminently poetical, because passionate. But I believe, if we look well into the matter, that we shall find the greatest poets do not often admit this kind of falseness,—that it is only the second order of poets who much delight in it.*

* I admit two orders of poets, but no third; and by these two orders I mean the Creative (Shakespeare, Homer, Dante), and

Thus, when Dante describes the spirits falling from the bank of Acheron "as dead leaves flutter from a bough",[2] he gives the most perfect image possible of their utter lightness, feebleness, passiveness, and scattering agony of despair, without, however, for an instant losing his own clear perception that *these* are souls, and *those* are leaves; he makes no confusion of one with the other. But when Coleridge speaks of

> The one red leaf, the last of its clan,
> That dances as often as dance it can,[3]

he has a morbid, that is to say, a so far false, idea about the leaf; he fancies a life in it, and will, which there are not; confuses its powerlessness with choice, its fading death with merriment, and the wind that shakes it with music. Here, however, there is some beauty, even in the morbid passage; but take an instance in Homer and Pope. Without the knowledge of Ulysses, Elpenor, his youngest follower, has fallen from an upper chamber in the Circean palace, and has been left dead, unmissed by his leader or companions, in the haste of their departure. They cross the sea to the Cimmerian land; and Ulysses summons the shades from Tartarus. The first which appears is that of the lost Elpenor. Ulysses, amazed, and in exactly the spirit of bitter and terrified lightness which is seen in Hamlet,[4] addresses the spirit with the simple, startled words:—

> Elpenor? How camest thou under the shadowy darkness?
> Hast thou come faster on foot than I in my black ship?[5]

Reflective or Perceptive (Wordsworth, Keats, Tennyson). But both of these must be *first*-rate in their range, though their range is different; and with poetry second-rate in *quality* no one ought to be allowed to trouble mankind.

---

[2] *Inferno*, III, 112.

[3] *Christabel*, pt. I.

[4] "Well said, old mole! can'st work i' the ground so fast?" (I, v.)

[5] *Odyssey*, XI, 56.

Which Pope renders thus:—

O, say, what angry power Elpenor led
To glide in shades, and wander with the dead?
How could thy soul, by realms and seas disjoined,
Outfly the nimble sail, and leave the lagging wind?

I sincerely hope the reader finds no pleasure here, either in the nimbleness of the sail, or the laziness of the wind! And yet how is it that these conceits are so painful now, when they have been pleasant to us in the other instances?

For a very simple reason. They are not a *pathetic* fallacy at all, for they are put into the mouth of the wrong passion —a passion which never could possibly have spoken them— agonized curiosity. Ulysses wants to know the facts of the matter; and the very last thing his mind could do at the moment would be to pause, or suggest in anywise what was *not* a fact. The delay in the first three lines, and conceit in the last, jar upon us instantly like the most frightful discord in music. No poet of true imaginative power could possibly have written the passage.*

Therefore we see that the spirit of truth must guide us in some sort, even in our enjoyment of fallacy. Coleridge's fallacy has no discord in it, but Pope's has set our teeth on edge. Without farther questioning, I will endeavour to state the main bearings of this matter.

The temperament which admits the pathetic fallacy, is, as I said above, that of a mind and body in some sort too weak to deal fully with what is before them or upon them; borne away, or over-clouded, or over-dazzled by emotion;

* It is worth while comparing the way a similar question is put by the exquisite sincerity of Keats:—

"He wept, and his bright tears
Went trickling down the golden bow he held.
Thus, with half-shut, suffused eyes, he stood;
While from beneath some cumb'rous boughs hard by,
With solemn step, an awful goddess came.
And there was purport in her looks for him,
Which he with eager guess began to read:
Perplexed the while, melodiously he said,
'How cam'st thou over the unfooted sea?' " (*Hyperion*, III.)

and it is a more or less noble state, according to the force of the emotion which has induced it. For it is no credit to a man that he is not morbid or inaccurate in his perceptions, when he has no strength of feeling to warp them; and it is in general a sign of higher capacity and stand in the ranks of being, that the emotions should be strong enough to vanquish, partly, the intellect, and make it believe what they choose. But it is still a grander condition when the intellect also rises, till it is strong enough to assert its rule against, or together with, the utmost efforts of the passions; and the whole man stands in an iron glow, white hot, perhaps, but still strong, and in no wise evaporating; even if he melts, losing none of his weight.

So, then, we have the three ranks: the man who perceives rightly, because he does not feel, and to whom the primrose is very accurately the primrose, because he does not love it. Then, secondly, the man who perceives wrongly, because he feels, and to whom the primrose is anything else than a primrose: a star, or a sun, or a fairy's shield, or a forsaken maiden. And then, lastly, there is the man who perceives rightly in spite of his feelings, and to whom the primrose is for ever nothing else than itself—a little flower apprehended in the very plain and leafy fact of it, whatever and how many soever the associations and passions may be, that crowd around it. And, in general, these three classes may be rated in comparative order, as the men who are not poets at all, and the poets of the second order, and the poets of the first; only however great a man may be, there are always some subjects which *ought* to throw him off his balance; some, by which his poor human capacity of thought should be conquered, and brought into the inaccurate and vague state of perception, so that the language of the highest inspiration becomes broken, obscure, and wild in metaphor, resembling that of the weaker man, overborne by weaker things.

And thus, in full, there are four classes: the men who feel nothing, and therefore see truly; the men who feel strongly, think weakly, and see untruly (second order of poets); the men who feel strongly, think strongly, and see truly (first order of poets); and the men who, strong as human creatures can be, are yet submitted to influences stronger than they, and see in a sort untruly, because what they see is inconceivably above them. This last is the usual condition of prophetic inspiration.

I separate these classes, in order that their character may be clearly understood; but of course they are united each to the other by imperceptible transitions, and the same mind, according to the influences to which it is subjected, passes at different times into the various states. Still, the difference between the great and less man is, on the whole, chiefly in this point of *alterability*. That is to say, the one knows too much, and perceives and feels too much of the past and future, and of all things beside and around that which immediately affects him, to be in anywise shaken by it. His mind is made up; his thoughts have an accustomed current; his ways are steadfast; it is not this or that new sight which will at once unbalance him. He is tender to impression at the surface, like a rock with deep moss upon it; but there is too much mass of him to be moved. The smaller man, with the same degree of sensibility, is at once carried off his feet; he wants to do something he did not want to do before; he views all the universe in a new light through his tears; he is gay or enthusiastic, melancholy or passionate, as things come and go to him. Therefore the high creative poet might even be thought, to a great extent, impassive (as shallow people think Dante stern), receiving indeed all feelings to the full, but having a great centre of reflection and knowledge in which he stands serene, and watches the feeling, as it were, from far off.

Dante, in his most intense moods, has entire command of himself, and can look around calmly, at all moments, for the image or the word that will best tell what he sees to the upper or lower world. But Keats and Tennyson, and the poets of the second order, are generally themselves subdued by the feelings under which they write, or, at least, write as choosing to be so; and therefore admit certain expressions and modes of thought which are in some sort diseased or false.

Now so long as we see that the *feeling* is true, we pardon, or are even pleased by, the confessed fallacy of sight which it induces: we are pleased, for instance, with those lines of Kingsley's, above quoted, not because they fallaciously describe foam, but because they faithfully describe sorrow. But the moment the mind of the speaker becomes cold, that moment every such expression becomes untrue, as being for ever untrue in the external facts. And there is no greater baseness in literature than the habit of using these metaphorical expressions in cold blood. An inspired writer, in full impetuosity of passion, may speak wisely and truly of "raging waves of the sea foaming out their own shame";[6] but it is only the basest writer who cannot speak of the sea without talking of "raging waves", "remorseless floods", "ravenous billows", etc.; and it is one of the signs of the highest power in a writer to check all such habits of thought, and to keep his eyes fixed firmly on the *pure fact*, out of which if any feeling comes to him or his reader, he knows it must be a true one.

To keep to the waves, I forget who it is who represents a man in despair, desiring that his body may be cast into the sea,

Whose changing mound, and foam that passed away,
Might mock the eye that questioned where I lay.

Observe, there is not a single false, or even overcharged, expression. "Mound" of the sea wave is perfectly simple and true; "changing" is as familiar as may be; "foam that passed away", strictly literal; and the whole line descriptive of the reality with a degree of accuracy which I know not any other verse, in the range of poetry, that altogether equals. For most people have not a distinct idea of the clumsiness and massiveness of a large wave. The word "wave" is used too generally of ripples and breakers, and bendings in light drapery or grass: it does not by itself convey a perfect image. But the word "mound" is heavy,

[6] *Jude*, 13.

large, dark, definite; there is no mistaking the kind of wave meant, nor missing the sight of it. Then the term "changing" has a peculiar force also. Most people think of waves as rising and falling. But if they look at the sea carefully, they will perceive that the waves do not rise and fall. They change. Change both place and form, but they do not fall; one wave goes on, and on, and still on; now lower, now higher, now tossing its mane like a horse, now building itself together like a wall, now shaking, now steady, but still the same wave, till at last it seems struck by something, and changes, one knows not how,—becomes another wave.

The close of the line insists on this image, and paints it still more perfectly,—"foam that passed away". Not merely melting, disappearing, but passing on, out of sight, on the career of the wave. Then, having put the absolute ocean fact as far as he may before our eyes, the poet leaves us to feel about it as we may, and to trace for ourselves the opposite fact,—the image of the green mounds that do not change, and the white and written stones that do not pass away; and thence to follow out also the associated images of the calm life with the quiet grave, and the despairing life with the fading foam:—

Let no man move his bones.
As for Samaria, her king is cut off like the foam upon
the water.[7]

But nothing of this is actually told or pointed out, and the expressions, as they stand, are perfectly severe and accurate, utterly uninfluenced by the firmly governed emotion of the writer. Even the word "mock" is hardly an exception, as it may stand merely for "deceive" or "defeat", without implying any impersonation of the waves.

It may be well, perhaps, to give one or two more instances to show the peculiar dignity possessed by all passages which thus limit their expression to the pure fact, and leave the hearer to gather what he can from it. Here is a notable one from the *Iliad*. Helen, looking from the

[7] 2 *Kings*, xxiii, 18; *Hosea*, x, 7.

Scæan gate of Troy over the Grecian host, and telling Priam the names of its captains, says at last:—

> I see all the other dark-eyed Greeks; but two I cannot see,—Castor and Pollux,—whom one mother bore with me. Have they not followed from fair Lacedæmon, or have they indeed come in their sea-wandering ships, but now will not enter into the battle of men, fearing the shame and the scorn that is in Me?

Then Homer:

> So she spoke. But them, already, the life-giving earth possessed, there in Lacedæmon, in the dear fatherland.[8]

Note, here, the high poetical truth carried to the extreme. The poet has to speak of the earth in sadness, but he will not let that sadness affect or change his thoughts of it. No; though Castor and Pollux be dead, yet the earth is our mother still, fruitful, life-giving. These are the facts of the thing. I see nothing else than these. Make what you will of them.

Take another very notable instance from Casimir de la Vigne's terrible ballad, "La Toilette de Constance." I must quote a few lines out of it here and there, to enable the reader who has not the book by him, to understand its close.

> Vite, Anna, vite; au miroir
> Plus vite, Anna. L'heure s'avance,
> Et je vais au bal ce soir
> Chez l'ambassadeur de France.

> Y pensez-vous, ils sont fanés, ces nœuds,
> Ils sont d'hier, mon Dieu, comme tout passe!
> Que du réseau qui retient mes cheveux
> Les glands d'azur retombent avec grâce.

[8] *Iliad*, III, 243.

Plus haut! Plus bas! Vous ne comprenez rien!
  Que sur mon front ce saphir étincelle:
Vous me piquez, maladroite. Ah, c'est bien,
  Bien,—chère Anna! Je t'aime, je suis belle.

Celui qu'en vain je voudrais oublier
  (Anna, ma robe) il y sera, j'espère.
(Ah, fi, profane, est-ce là mon collier?
  Quoi! ces grains d'or bénits par le Saint-Père!)
Il y sera; Dieu, s'il pressait ma main,
  En y pensant, à peine je respire;
Père Anselmo doit m'entendre demain,
  Comment ferai-je, Anna, pour tout lui dire?

Vite, un coup d'œil au miroir,
  Le dernier. ——J'ai l'assurance
Qu'on va m'adorer ce soir
  Chez l'ambassadeur de France.

Près du foyer, Constance s'admirait.
  Dieu! sur sa robe il vole une étincelle!
Au feu. Courez! Quand l'espoir l'enivrait
  Tout perdre ainsi! Quoi! Mourir,—et si belle!

L'horrible feu ronge avec volupté
  Ses bras, son sein, et l'entoure, et s'élève,
Et sans pitié dévore sa beauté,
  Ses dix-huit ans, hélas, et son doux rêve!

Adieu, bal, plaisir, amour!
  On disait, Pauvre Constance!
Et on dansait, jusqu'au jour,
  Chez l'ambassadeur de France.[9]

Yes, that is the fact of it. Right or wrong, the poet does not say. What you may think about it, he does not know. He has nothing to do with that. There lie the ashes of the dead girl in her chamber. There they danced, till the morning, at the Ambassador's of France. Make what you will of it.

If the reader will look through the ballad, of which I

[9] *Œuvres Posthumes—Derniers Chants.*

have quoted only about the third part, he will find that there is not, from beginning to end of it, a single poetical (so called) expression, except in one stanza. The girl speaks as simple prose as may be; there is not a word she would not have actually used as she was dressing. The poet stands by, impassive as a statue, recording her words just as they come. At last the doom seizes her, and in the very presence of death, for an instant, his own emotions conquer him. He records no longer the facts only, but the facts as they seem to him. The fire gnaws with *voluptuousness—without pity*. It is soon past. The fate is fixed for ever; and he retires into his pale and crystalline atmosphere of truth. He closes all with the calm veracity,

They said, "Poor Constance!"

Now in this there is the exact type of the consummate poetical temperament. For, be it clearly and constantly remembered, that the greatness of a poet depends upon the two faculties, acuteness of feeling, and command of it. A poet is great, first in proportion to the strength of his passion, and then, that strength being granted, in proportion to his government of it; there being, however, always a point beyond which it would be inhuman and monstrous if he pushed this government, and, therefore, a point at which all feverish and wild fancy becomes just and true. Thus the destruction of the kingdom of Assyria cannot be contemplated firmly by a prophet of Israel. The fact is too great, too wonderful. It overthrows him, dashes him into a confused element of dreams. All the world is, to his stunned thought, full of strange voices. "Yea, the fir-trees rejoice at thee, and the cedars of Lebanon, saying, 'Since thou art gone down to the grave, no feller is come up against us.'"[10] So, still more, the thought of the presence of Deity cannot be borne without this great astonishment. "The mountains and the hills shall break forth before you into singing, and all the trees of the field shall clap their hands."[11]

[10] *Isaiah,* xiv, 8.
[11] *Isaiah,* lv, 12.

But by how much this feeling is noble when it is justified by the strength of its cause, by so much it is ignoble when there is not cause enough for it; and beyond all other ignobleness is the mere affectation of it, in hardness of heart. Simply bad writing may almost always, as above noticed, be known by its adoption of these fanciful metaphorical expressions as a sort of current coin; yet there is even a worse, at least a more harmful condition of writing than this, in which such expressions are not ignorantly and feelinglessly caught up, but, by some master, skilful in handling, yet insincere, deliberately wrought out with chill and studied fancy; as if we should try to make an old lava stream look red-hot again, by covering it with dead leaves, or white-hot, with hoar-frost.

When Young is lost in veneration, as he dwells on the character of a truly good and holy man, he permits himself for a moment to be overborne by the feeling so far as to exclaim—

> Where shall I find him? angels, tell me where.
> You know him; he is near you; point him out.
> Shall I see glories beaming from his brow,
> Or trace his footsteps by the rising flowers?[12]

This emotion has a worthy cause, and is thus true and right. But now hear the cold-hearted Pope say to a shepherd girl—

> Where'er you walk, cool gales shall fan the glade;
> Trees, where you sit, shall crowd into a shade;
> Your praise the birds shall chant in every grove,
> And winds shall waft it to the powers above.
> But would you sing, and rival Orpheus' strain,
> The wondering forests soon should dance again;
> The moving mountains hear the powerful call,
> And headlong streams hang, listening, in their fall.[13]

This is not, nor could it for a moment be mistaken for, the language of passion. It is simple falsehood, uttered by

[12] *Night Thoughts*, II, 345.
[13] *Pastorals: Summer, or Alexis.*

hypocrisy; definite absurdity, rooted in affectation, and coldly asserted in the teeth of nature and fact. Passion will indeed go far in deceiving itself; but it must be a strong passion, not the simple wish of a lover to tempt his mistress to sing. Compare a very closely parallel passage in Wordsworth, in which the lover has lost his mistress:

Three years had Barbara in her grave been laid,
When thus his moan he made:—

"Oh, move, thou cottage, from behind yon oak,
  Or let the ancient tree uprooted lie,
That in some other way yon smoke
  May mount into the sky.
If still behind yon pine-tree's ragged bough,
  Headlong, the waterfall must come,
  Oh, let it, then, be dumb—
Be anything, sweet stream, but that which thou art now."[14]

Here is a cottage to be moved, if not a mountain, and a water-fall to be silent, if it is not to hang listening: but with what different relation to the mind that contemplates them! Here, in the extremity of its agony, the soul cries out wildly for relief, which at the same moment it partly knows to be impossible, but partly believes possible, in a vague impression that a miracle *might* be wrought to give relief even to a less sore distress,—that nature is kind, and God is kind, and that grief is strong: it knows not well what *is* possible to such grief. To silence a stream, to move a cottage wall,—one might think it could do as much as that!

I believe these instances are enough to illustrate the main point I insist upon respecting the pathetic fallacy, —that so far as it *is* a fallacy, it is always the sign of a morbid state of mind, and comparatively of a weak one. Even in the most inspired prophet it is a sign of the incapacity of his human sight or thought to bear what has been revealed to it. In ordinary poetry, if it is found in the thoughts of the poet himself, it is at once a sign of his be-

[14] " 'Tis said, that some have died for love. . . ."

longing to the inferior school; if in the thoughts of the characters imagined by him, it is right or wrong according to the genuineness of the emotion from which it springs; always, however, implying necessarily *some* degree of weakness in the character.

Take two most exquisite instances from master hands. The Jessy of Shenstone, and the Ellen of Wordsworth, have both been betrayed and deserted. Jessy, in the course of her most touching complaint, says:

If through the garden's flowery tribes I stray,
  Where bloom the jasmines that could once allure,
"Hope not to find delight in us", they say,
  "For we are spotless, Jessy; we are pure."

Compare with this some of the words of Ellen:

"Ah, why", said Ellen, sighing to herself,
"Why do not words, and kiss, and solemn pledge,
And nature, that is kind in woman's breast,
And reason, that in man is wise and good,
And fear of Him who is a righteous Judge,—
Why do not these prevail for human life,
To keep two hearts together, that began
Their springtime with one love, and that have need
Of mutual pity and forgiveness sweet
To grant, or be received; while that poor bird—
O, come and hear him! Thou who hast to me
Been faithless, hear him;—though a lowly creature,
One of God's simple children that yet know not
The Universal Parent, *how* he sings!
As if he wished the firmament of heaven
Should listen, and give back to him the voice
Of his triumphant constancy and love;
The proclamation that he makes, how far
His darkness doth transcend our fickle light."[15]

The perfection of both these passages, as far as regards truth and tenderness of imagination in the two poets, is

[15] *Excursion,* VI.

quite insuperable. But of the two characters imagined, Jessy is weaker than Ellen, exactly in so far as something appears to her to be in nature which is not. The flowers do not really reproach her. God meant them to comfort her, not to taunt her; they would do so if she saw them rightly.

Ellen, on the other hand, is quite above the slightest erring emotion. There is not the barest film of fallacy in all her thoughts. She reasons as calmly as if she did not feel. And, although the singing of the bird suggests to her the idea of its desiring to be heard in heaven, she does not for an instant admit any veracity in the thought. "As if", she says,—"I know he means nothing of the kind; but it does verily seem as if." The reader will find, by examining the rest of the poem, that Ellen's character is throughout consistent in this clear though passionate strength.*

It then being, I hope, now made clear to the reader in all respects that the pathetic fallacy is powerful only so far as it is pathetic, feeble so far as it is fallacious, and, therefore, that the dominion of Truth is entire, over this, as over every other natural and just state of the human mind, we may go on to the subject for the dealing with which this prefatory inquiry became necessary; and why necessary, we shall see forthwith.

Modern Painters, vol. III, ch. xii, pars. 4–15.

* I cannot quit this subject without giving two more instances, both exquisite, of the pathetic fallacy, which I have just come upon, in *Maud:*

"For a great speculation had fail'd;
And ever he mutter'd and madden'd, and ever wann'd with despair;
And out he walk'd, when the wind like a broken worldling wail'd,
And the *flying gold of the ruin'd woodlands drove thro' the air.*"

"There has fallen a splendid tear
From the passion-flower at the gate.
The red rose cries, 'She is near, she is near!'
And the white rose weeps, 'She is late.'
The larkspur listens, 'I hear, I hear!'
And the lily whispers, 'I wait.'"

THE LANDSCAPE OF LITERATURE

1. PATHETIC FALLACY

My reason for asking the reader to give so much of his time to the examination of the pathetic fallacy was, that, whether in literature or in art, he will find it eminently characteristic of the modern mind; and in the landscape, whether of literature or art, he will also find the modern painter endeavouring to express something which he, as a living creature, imagines in the lifeless object, while the classical and mediæval painters were content with expressing the unimaginary and actual qualities of the object itself. It will be observed that, according to the principle stated long ago, I use the words painter and poet quite indifferently, including in our inquiry the landscape of literature, as well as that of painting; and this the more because the spirit of classical landscape has hardly been expressed in any other way than by words.

Taking, therefore, this wide field, it is surely a very notable circumstance, to begin with, that this pathetic fallacy is eminently characteristic of modern painting. For instance, Keats, describing a wave breaking out at sea, says of it—

> Down whose green back the short-lived foam, all hoar,
> Bursts gradual, with a wayward indolence.[1]

That is quite perfect, as an example of the modern manner. The idea of the peculiar action with which foam rolls down a long, large wave could not have been given by any other words so well as by this "wayward indolence". But Homer would never have written, never thought of, such words. He could not by any possibility have lost

[1] *Endymion*, II, 350.

sight of the great fact that the wave, from the beginning to the end of it, do what it might, was still nothing else than salt water; and that salt water could not be either wayward or indolent. He will call the waves "over-roofed", "full-charged", "monstrous", "compact-black", "dark-clear", "violet-coloured", "wine-coloured", and so on. But every one of these epithets is descriptive of pure physical nature. "Over-roofed" is the term he invariably uses of anything—rock, house, or wave—that nods over at the brow; the other terms need no explanation; they are as accurate and intense in truth as words can be, but they never show the slightest feeling of anything animated in the ocean. Black or clear, monstrous or violet-coloured, cold salt water it is always, and nothing but that.

"Well, but the modern writer, by his admission of the tinge of fallacy, has given an idea of something in the action of the wave which Homer could not, and surely, therefore, has made a step in advance? Also there appears to be a degree of sympathy and feeling in the one writer, which there is not in the other; and as it has been received for a first principle that writers are great in proportion to the intensity of their feelings, and Homer seems to have no feelings about the sea but that it is black and deep, surely in this respect also the modern writer is the greater?"

Stay a moment. Homer *had* some feeling about the sea; a faith in the animation of it much stronger than Keats's. But all this sense of something living in it, he separates in his mind into a great abstract image of a Sea Power. He never says the waves rage, or the waves are idle. But he says there is somewhat in, and greater than, the waves, which rages, and is idle, and *that* he calls a god.

Modern Painters, vol. III, ch. xiii, pars. 1–3.

2. *GREEK LANDSCAPE*

Such being their general idea of the gods, we can now easily understand the habitual tone of their feelings towards what was beautiful in nature. With us, observe, the idea of the Divinity is apt to get separated from the life of nature; and imagining our God upon a cloudy throne, far above the earth, and not in the flowers or waters, we approach those visible things with a theory that they are dead, governed by physical laws, and so forth. But coming to them, we find the theory fail; that they are not dead; that, say what we choose about them, the instinctive sense of their being alive is too strong for us; and in scorn of all physical law, the wilful fountain sings, and the kindly flowers rejoice. And then, puzzled, and yet happy; pleased, and yet ashamed of being so; accepting sympathy from nature, which we do not believe it gives, and giving sympathy to nature, which we do not believe it receives,—mixing, besides, all manner of purposeful play and conceit with these involuntary fellowships,—we fall necessarily into the curious web of hesitating sentiment, pathetic fallacy, and wandering fancy, which form a great part of our modern view of nature. But the Greek never removed his god out of nature at all; never attempted for a moment to contradict his instinctive sense that God was everywhere. "The tree *is* glad", said he, "I know it is; I can cut it down: no matter, there was a nymph in it". "The water *does* sing", said he; "I can dry it up; but no matter, there was a naiad in it." But in thus clearly defining his belief, observe, he threw it entirely into a human form, and gave his faith to nothing but the image of his own humanity. What sympathy and fellowship he had, were always for the spirit *in* the stream, not for the stream; always for the dryad *in* the wood, not for the wood. Content with this human sympathy, he approached the actual waves and woody fibres with no sympathy at all. The spirit that ruled them, he received as a plain fact. Them, also, ruled and material, he received as plain facts; they, without their spirit, were dead enough. A rose was good for scent, and a stream for sound and coolness; for the rest, one was no more than leaves, the other no more than water; he could not make anything else of them; and the divine power, which was involved in their existence, having been all distilled away by him into an independent Flora or Thetis, the poor leaves or waves were left, in mere cold corporealness, to make the most of their being discernibly red and soft, clear and wet, and unacknowledged in any other power whatsoever.

Then, observe farther, the Greeks lived in the midst of the most beautiful nature, and were as familiar with blue sea, clear air, and sweet outlines of mountain, as we are with brick walls, black smoke, and level fields. This perfect familiarity rendered all such scenes of natural beauty unexciting, if not indifferent to them, by lulling and over-wearying the imagination as far as it was concerned with such things; but there was another kind of beauty which they found it required effort to obtain, and which, when thoroughly obtained, seemed more glorious than any of this wild loveliness—the beauty of the human countenance and form. This, they perceived, could only be reached by continual exercise of virtue; and it was in Heaven's sight, and theirs, all the more beautiful because it needed this self-denial to obtain it. So they set themselves to reach this, and having gained it, gave it their principal thoughts, and set it off with beautiful dress as best they might. But making this their object, they were obliged to pass their lives in simple exercise and disciplined employments. Living wholesomely, giving themselves no fever fits, either by fasting or over-eating, constantly in the open air, and full of animal spirit and physical power, they became incapable of every morbid condition of mental emotion. Unhappy love, disappointed ambition, spiritual despondency, or any other disturbing sensation, had little power over the well-braced nerves, and healthy flow of the blood; and what bitterness might yet fasten on them was soon boxed or raced out of a boy, and spun or woven out of a girl, or danced out of both. They had indeed their sorrows, true and deep, but still, more like children's sorrows than ours, whether bursting into open cry of pain, or hid with shuddering under the veil, still passing over the soul as clouds do over heaven, not sullying it, not mingling with it;—darkening it perhaps long or utterly, but still not becoming one with it, and for the most part passing away in dashing rain of tears, and leaving the man unchanged: in nowise affecting, as our sorrow does, the whole tone of his thought and imagination thenceforward.

How far our melancholy may be deeper and wider than theirs in its roots and view, and therefore nobler, we shall consider presently; but at all events, they had the advantage of us in being entirely free from all those dim and feverish sensations which result from unhealthy state of the body. I believe that a large amount of the dreamy and sentimental sadness, tendency to reverie, and general patheticalness of modern life results merely from derangement of stomach; holding to the Greek life the same relation that the feverish night of an adult does to a child's sleep.

Farther. The human beauty, which, whether in its bodily being or in imagined divinity, had become, for the reasons we have seen, the principal object of culture and sympathy to these Greeks, was, in its perfection, eminently orderly, symmetrical, and tender. Hence, contemplating it constantly in this state, they could not but feel a proportionate fear of all that was disorderly, unbalanced, and rugged. Having trained their stoutest soldiers into a strength so delicate and lovely, that their white flesh, with their blood upon it, should look like ivory stained with purple[2]; and having always around them, in the motion and majesty of this beauty, enough for the full employment of their imagination, they shrank with dread or hatred from all the ruggedness of lower nature,—from the wrinkled forest bark, the jagged hill-crest, and irregular, inorganic storm of sky; looking to these for the most part as adverse powers, and taking pleasure only in such portions of the lower world as were at once conducive to the rest and health of the human frame, and in harmony with the laws of its gentler beauty.

Modern Painters, vol. III, ch. xiii, pars. 13–15.

[2] *Iliad*, IV, 141.

3. *HOMER*

(*a*) *The Landscape of Comfort*

Thus, as far as I recollect, without a single exception, every Homeric landscape, intended to be beautiful, is composed of a fountain, a meadow, and a shady grove. This ideal is very interestingly marked, as intended for a perfect one, in the fifth book of the *Odyssey;* when Mercury himself stops for a moment, though on a message, to look at a landscape "which even an immortal might be gladdened to behold."[3] This landscape consists of a cave covered with a running vine, all blooming into grapes, and surrounded by a grove of alder, poplar, and sweet-smelling cypress. Four fountains of white (foaming) water, springing *in succession* (mark the orderliness), and close to one another, flow away in different directions, through a meadow full of violets and parsley (parsley, to mark its moisture, being elsewhere called "marsh-nourished", and associated with the lotus[4]); the air is perfumed not only by these violets and by the sweet cypress, but by Calypso's fire of finely chopped cedar wood, which sends a smoke, as of incense, through the island; Calypso herself is singing; and finally, upon the trees are resting, or roosting, owls, hawks, and "long-tongued sea-crows". Whether these last are considered as a part of the ideal landscape, as marine singing-birds, I know not; but the approval of Mercury appears to be elicited chiefly by the fountains and violet meadow.

Now the notable things in this description are, first, the evident subservience of the whole landscape to human comfort, to the foot, the taste, or the smell; and, secondly, that throughout the passage there is not a single figurative word expressive of the things being in any wise other than plain grass, fruit, or flower. I have used the term "spring"

[3] *Odyssey,* v, 58.
[4] *Iliad,* II, 776.

of the fountains, because, without doubt, Homer means that they sprang forth brightly, having their source at the foot of the rocks (as copious fountains nearly always have); but Homer does not say "spring", he says simply flow, and uses only one word for "growing softly", or "richly", of the tall trees, the vine, and the violets. There is, however, some expression of sympathy with the sea-birds; he speaks of them in precisely the same terms, as in other places of naval nations, saying they "have care of the works of the sea".[5]

If we glance through the references to pleasant landscape which occur in other parts of the *Odyssey*, we shall always be struck by this quiet subjection of their every feature to human service, and by the excessive similarity in the scenes. Perhaps the spot intended, after this, to be most perfect, may be the garden of Alcinous,[6] where the principal ideas are, still more definitely, order, symmetry, and fruitfulness; the beds being duly ranged between rows of vines, which, as well as the pear, apple, and fig-trees, bear fruit continually, some grapes being yet sour, while others are getting black; there are plenty of "*orderly* square beds of herbs", chiefly leeks, and two fountains, one running through the garden, and one under the pavement of the palace, to a reservoir for the citizens. Ulysses, pausing to contemplate this scene, is described nearly in the same terms as Mercury pausing to contemplate the wilder meadow; and it is interesting to observe, that, in spite of all Homer's love of symmetry, the god's admiration is excited by the free fountains, wild violets, and wandering vine; but the mortal's, by the vines in rows, the leeks in beds, and the fountains in pipes.

Modern Painters, vol. III, ch. xiii, pars. 16–18.

(*b*) *Leaves and Corn*

But to return more definitely to our Homeric landscape. When it is perfect, we have, as in the above instances, the

5 *Odyssey,* v, 67.
6 *Odyssey,* VII, 112.

foliage and meadows together; when imperfect, it is always either the foliage or the meadow; pre-eminently the meadow, or arable field. Thus, meadows of asphodel are prepared for the happier dead; and even Orion, a hunter among the mountains in his lifetime, pursues the ghosts of beasts in these asphodel meadows after death.[7] So the sirens sing in a meadow;[8] and throughout the *Odyssey* there is a general tendency to the depreciation of poor Ithaca, because it is rocky, and only fit for goats, and has "no meadows";[9] for which reason Telemachus refuses Atrides's present of horses, congratulating the Spartan king at the same time on ruling over a plain which has "plenty of lotus in it, and rushes", with corn and barley. Note this constant dwelling on the marsh plants, or, at least, those which grow in flat and well-irrigated land, or beside streams: when Scamander, for instance, is restrained by Vulcan, Homer says, very sorrowfully, that "all his lotus, and reeds, and rushes were burnt";[10] and thus Ulysses, after being shipwrecked and nearly drowned, and beaten about the sea for many days and nights, on raft and mast, at last getting ashore at the mouth of a large river, casts himself down first upon its *rushes,* and then, in thankfulness, kisses the "corn-giving land", as most opposed, in his heart, to the fruitless and devouring sea.[11]

In this same passage, also, we find some peculiar expressions of the delight which the Greeks had in trees; for, when Ulysses first comes in sight of land, which gladdens him, "as the reviving of a father from his sickness gladdens his children", it is not merely the sight of the land itself which gives him such pleasure, but of the "land and *wood*".[12] Homer never throws away any words, at least in such a place as this; and what in another poet would have

[7] *Odyssey,* XI, 571; XXIV, 13. The couch of Ceres, with Homer's usual faithfulness, is made of a *ploughed* field, v, 127.

[8] *Odyssey,* XII, 45.

[9] *Odyssey,* IV, 601.

[10] *Iliad,* XXI, 351.

[11] *Odyssey,* v, 398.

[12] *Odyssey,* v, 395.

been merely the filling up of the deficient line with an otherwise useless word, is in him the expression of the general Greek sense, that land of any kind was in nowise grateful or acceptable till there was *wood* upon it (or corn; but the corn, in the flats, could not be seen so far as the black masses of forest on the hillsides), and that, as in being rushy and corn-giving, the low land, so in being woody, the high land was most grateful to the mind of the man who for days and nights had been wearied on the engulphing sea. And this general idea of wood and corn, as the types of the fatness of the whole earth, is beautifully marked in another place of the *Odyssey*,[13] where the sailors in a desert island, having no flour of corn to offer as a meat offering with their sacrifices, take the leaves of the trees, and scatter them over the burnt offering instead.

But still, every expression of the pleasure which Ulysses has in this landing and resting, contains uninterruptedly the reference to the utility and sensible pleasantness of all things, not to their beauty. After his first grateful kiss given to the corn-growing land, he considers immediately how he is to pass the night; for some minutes hesitating whether it will be best to expose himself to the misty chill from the river, or run the risk of wild beasts in the wood. He decides for the wood, and finds in it a bower formed by a sweet and a wild olive-tree, interlacing their branches, or—perhaps more accurately translating Homer's intensely graphic expression—"changing their branches with each other" (it is very curious how often, in an entanglement of wood, one supposes the branches to belong to the wrong trees) and forming a roof penetrated by neither rain, sun, nor wind. Under this bower Ulysses collects the "*vain* (or *frustrate*) outpouring of the dead leaves"—another exquisite expression, used elsewhere of useless grief or shedding of tears;—and, having got enough together, makes his bed of them, and goes to sleep, having covered himself up with them, "as embers are covered up with ashes".[14]

13 *Odyssey*, XII, 357.
14 *Odyssey*, V, 481.

Nothing can possibly be more intensely possessive of the *facts* than this whole passage; the sense of utter deadness and emptiness, and frustrate fall in the leaves; of dormant life in the human body,—the fire, and heroism, and strength of it, lulled under the dead brown heap, as embers under ashes, and the knitting of interchanged and close strength of living boughs above. But there is not the smallest apparent sense of there being *beauty* elsewhere than in the human being. The wreathed wood is admired simply as being a perfect roof for it; the fallen leaves only as being a perfect bed for it; and there is literally no more excitement of emotion in Homer, as he describes them, nor does he expect us to be more excited or touched by hearing about them, than if he had been telling us how the chambermaid at the Bull aired the four-poster, and put on two extra blankets.

Modern Painters, vol. III, ch. xiii, pars. 21–23.

(*c*) *Rocks and Caves*

Now, exactly this same contemplation of subservience to human use makes the Greek take some pleasure in *rocks,* when they assume one particular form, but one only—that of a *cave.* They are evidently quite frightful things to him under any other condition, and most of all if they are rough and jagged; but if smooth, looking "sculptured",[15] like the sides of a ship, and forming a cave or shelter for him, he begins to think them endurable. Hence, associating the ideas of rich and sheltering wood, sea, becalmed and made useful as a port by projecting promontories of rock, and smoothed caves or grottoes in the rocks themselves, we get the pleasantest idea which the Greek could form of a landscape, next to a marsh with poplars in it; not, indeed, if possible, ever to be without these last; thus, in commending the Cyclops' country as one possessed of every perfection, Homer first says: "They have soft *marshy* meadows near the sea, and good, rich, crumbling,

[15] *Iliad,* II, 88.

ploughing-land, giving fine deep crops, and vines always giving fruit"; then, "a port so quiet, that they have no need of cables in it; and at the head of the port, a beautiful clear spring just *under a cave* and *aspen poplars all round it*."[16]

This, it will be seen, is very nearly Homer's usual "ideal"; but, going into the middle of the island, Ulysses comes on a rougher and less agreeable bit, though still fulfilling certain required conditions of endurableness; a "cave shaded with laurels", which, having no poplars about it, is, however, meant to be somewhat frightful, and only fit to be inhabited by a Cyclops.[17] So in the country of the Læstrygons, Homer, preparing his reader gradually for something very disagreeable, represents the rocks as bare and "exposed to the sun"; only with some smooth and slippery roads over them, by which the trucks bring down wood from the higher hills. Any one familiar with Swiss slopes of hills must remember how often he has descended, sometimes faster than was altogether intentional, by these same slippery woodman's truck roads.

And thus, in general, whenever the landscape is intended to be lovely, it verges towards the ploughed lands and poplars; or, at worst, to *woody* rocks; but, if intended to be painful, the rocks are bare and "sharp". This last epithet, constantly used by Homer for mountains, does not altogether correspond, in Greek, to the English term, nor is it intended merely to characterize the sharp mountain summits; for it never would be applied simply to the edge or point of a sword, but signifies rather "harsh", "bitter", or "painful", being applied habitually to fate, death, and in *Od.* II, 333, to a halter; and, as expressive of general objectionableness and unpleasantness, to all high, dangerous, or peaked mountains, as the Maleian promontory (a much-dreaded one), the crest of Parnassus, the Tereian mountain, and a grim or untoward, though, by keeping off the force of the sea, protective, rock at the mouth of the

[16] *Odyssey*, IX, 132, etc.
[17] *Odyssey*, IX, 183.

Jardanus; as well as habitually to inaccessible or impregnable fortresses built on heights.

In all this I cannot too strongly mark the utter absence of any trace of the feeling for what we call the picturesque, and the constant dwelling of the writer's mind on what was available, pleasant, or useful; his ideas respecting all landscape being not uncharacteristically summed, finally, by Pallas herself; when, meeting Ulysses, who after his long wandering does not recognize his own country, and meaning to describe it as politely and soothingly as possible, she says:[18]—"This Ithaca of ours is, indeed, a rough country enough, and not good for driving in; but, still, things might be worse: it has plenty of corn, and good wine, and *always rain,* and soft nourishing dew, and it has good feeding for goats and oxen, and all manner of wood, and springs fit to drink at all the year round."

It may indeed be thought that I am assuming too hastily that this was the general view of the Greeks respecting landscape, because it was Homer's. But I believe the true mind of a nation, at any period, is always best ascertainable by examining that of its greatest men; and that simpler and truer results will be attainable for us by simply comparing Homer, Dante, and Walter Scott, than by attempting (what my limits must have rendered absurdly inadequate, and in which, also, both my time and knowledge must have failed me) an analysis of the landscape in the range of contemporary literature. All that I can do is to state the general impression which has been made upon me by my desultory reading, and to mark accurately the grounds for this impression, in the works of the greatest men. Now it is quite true that in others of the Greeks, especially in Æschylus and Aristophanes, there is infinitely more of modern feeling, of pathetic fallacy, love of picturesque or beautiful form, and other such elements, than there is in Homer; but then these appear to me just the parts of them which were not Greek, the elements of their minds by which (as one division of the human race

[18] *Odyssey,* XIII, 236, etc.

always must be with subsequent ones) they are connected with the mediævals and moderns. And without doubt, in his influence over future mankind, Homer is eminently the Greek of Greeks: if I were to associate any one with him it would be Herodotus, and I believe all I have said of the Homeric landscape will be found equally true of the Herodotean, as assuredly it will be of the Platonic;—the contempt, which Plato sometimes expresses by the mouth of Socrates, for the country in general, except so far as it is shady, and has cicadas and running streams to make pleasant noises in it, being almost ludicrous. But Homer is the great type, and the more notable one because of his influence on Virgil, and, through him, on Dante, and all the after ages: and, in like manner, if we can get the abstract of mediæval landscape out of Dante, it will serve us as well as if we had read all the songs of the troubadours, and help us to the farther changes in derivative temper, down to all modern time.

Modern Painters, vol. III, ch. xiii, pars. 24–27.

4. MEDIEVAL LANDSCAPE

(a) The Great Change

In our examination of the spirit of classical landscape, we were obliged to confine ourselves to what is left to us in written description. Some interesting results might indeed have been obtained by examining the Egyptian and Ninevite landscape sculpture, but in nowise conclusive enough to be worth the pains of the inquiry; for the landscape of sculpture is necessarily confined in range, and usually inexpressive of the complete feelings of the workman, being introduced rather to explain the place and circumstances of events, than for its own sake. In the Middle Ages, however, the case is widely different. We have written landscape, sculptured landscape, and painted landscape, all bearing united testimony to the tone of the national mind in almost every remarkable locality of Europe.

That testimony, taken in its breadth, is very curiously conclusive. It marks the mediæval mind as agreeing altogether with the ancients, in holding that flat land, brooks, and groves of aspens, compose the pleasant places of the earth, and that rocks and mountains are, for inhabitation, altogether to be reprobated and detested; but as disagreeing with the classical mind totally in this other most important respect, that the pleasant flat land is never a ploughed field, nor a rich lotus meadow good for pasture, but *garden* ground covered with flowers, and divided by fragrant hedges, with a castle in the middle of it. The aspens are delighted in, not because they are good for "coach-making men"[19] to make cart-wheels of, but because they are shady and graceful; and the fruit-trees, covered with delicious fruit, especially apple and orange, occupy still more important positions in the scenery. Singing-birds—not "sea-crows",[20] but nightingales—perch on every bough: and the ideal occupation of mankind is not to cultivate either the garden or the meadow, but to gather roses and eat oranges in the one, and ride out hawking over the other.

Finally, mountain scenery, though considered as disagreeable for general inhabitation, is always introduced as being proper to meditate in, or to encourage communion with higher beings; and in the ideal landscape of daily life, mountains are considered agreeable things enough, so that they be far enough away.

In this great change there are three vital points to be noticed.

The first, the disdain of agricultural pursuits by the nobility; a fatal change, and one gradually bringing about the ruin of that nobility. It is expressed in the mediæval landscape by the eminently pleasurable and horticultural character of everything; by the fences, hedges, castle

[19] *Iliad,* IV, 485.
[20] *Odyssey,* V, 66.

walls, and masses of useless, but lovely flowers, especially roses. The knights and ladies are represented always as singing, or making love, in these pleasant places. The idea of setting an old knight, like Laertes (whatever his state of fallen fortune), "with thick gloves on to keep his hands from the thorns",[21] to prune a row of vines, would have been regarded as the most monstrous violation of the decencies of life; and a senator, once detected in the home employments of Cincinnatus, could, I suppose, thenceforward hardly have appeared in society.

The second vital point is the evidence of a more sentimental enjoyment of external nature. A Greek, wishing really to enjoy himself, shut himself into a beautiful atrium, with an excellent dinner, and a society of philosophical or musical friends. But a mediæval knight went into his pleasance, to gather roses and hear the birds sing; or rode out hunting or hawking. His evening feast, though riotous enough sometimes, was not the height of his day's enjoyment; and if the attractions of the world are to be shown typically to him, as opposed to the horrors of death, they are never represented by a full feast in a chamber, but by a delicate dessert in an orange grove, with musicians under the trees; or a ride on a May morning, hawk on fist.

This change is evidently a healthy, and a very interesting one.

The third vital point is the marked sense that this hawking and apple-eating are not altogether right; that there is something else to be done in the world than that; and that the mountains, as opposed to the pleasant garden-ground, are places where that other something may best be learned;—which is evidently a piece of infinite and new respect for the mountains, and another healthy change in the tone of the human heart.

Modern Painters, vol. III, ch. xiv, pars. 1–5.

[21] *Odyssey,* XXIV, 340.

(*b*) *Summary*

Now, assembling all these different sources of the peculiar mediæval feeling towards nature in one view, we have:

1st. Love of the garden instead of love of the farm, leading to a sentimental contemplation of nature, instead of a practical and agricultural one.

2nd. Loss of sense of actual Divine presence, leading to fancies, of fallacious animation, in herbs, flowers, clouds, etc.

3rd. Perpetual, and more or less undisturbed, companionship with wild nature.

4th. Apprehension of demoniacal and angelic presence among mountains, leading to a reverent dread of them.

5th. Principalness of delight in human beauty, leading to comparative contempt of natural objects.

6th. Consequent love of order, light, intelligibility, and symmetry, leading to dislike of the wildness, darkness, and mystery of nature.

7th. Inaccuracy of observance of nature, induced by the habitual practice of change on its forms.

From these mingled elements, we should necessarily expect to find resulting, as the characteristic of mediæval landscape art, compared with Greek, a far higher sentiment about it, and affection for it, more or less subdued by still greater respect for the loveliness of man, and therefore subordinated entirely to human interests; mingled with curious traces of terror, piety, or superstition, and cramped by various formalisms,—some wise and necessary, some feeble, and some exhibiting needless ignorance and inaccuracy.

Modern Painters, vol. III, ch. xiv, par. 15.

(*c*) *Dante*

The thing that must first strike us in this respect, as we turn our thoughts to the poem,[22] is, unquestionably, the *formality* of its landscape.

Milton's effort, in all that he tells us of his Inferno, is to make it indefinite; Dante, to make it *definite*. Both, indeed, describe it as entered through gates; but, within the gate, all is wild and fenceless with Milton, having indeed its four rivers,—the last vestige of the mediæval tradition,—but rivers which flow through a waste of mountain and moorland, and by "many a frozen, many a fiery Alp".[23] But Dante's Inferno is accurately separated into circles drawn with well-pointed compasses; mapped and properly surveyed in every direction, trenched in a thoroughly good style of engineering from depth to depth, and divided in the "*accurate* middle" (dritto mezzo)[24] of its deepest abyss, into a concentric series of ten moats and embankments, like those about a castle, with bridges from each embankment to the next; precisely in the manner of those bridges over Hiddekel and Euphrates, which Mr Macaulay thinks so innocently designed, apparently not aware that he is also laughing at Dante. These larger fosses are of rock, and the bridges also; but as he goes farther into detail, Dante tells us of various minor fosses and embankments, in which he anxiously points out to us not only the formality, but the neatness and perfectness, of the stonework. For instance, in describing the river Phlegethon, he tells us that it was "paved with stone at the bottom, and at the sides, and *over the edges of the sides*",[25] just as the water is at the baths of Bulicame; and for fear we should think this embankment at all *larger* than it really was, Dante adds, carefully, that it was made just like the embankments of Ghent or Bruges against the sea, or

[22] *Divina Commedia.*

[23] *Par. Lost,* II, 620; *Inferno,* III, 1–11.

[24] *Inferno,* XI, 16 *seq.;* XVIII, 1 *seq.*

[25] *Inferno,* XIV, 79.

those in Lombardy which bank the Brenta, only "not so high, nor so wide", as any of these. And besides the trenches, we have two well-built castles; one, like Ecbatana, with seven circuits of wall (and surrounded by a fair stream), wherein the great poets and sages of antiquity live; and another, a great fortified city with walls of iron, red-hot, and a deep fosse round it, and full of "grave citizens",—the city of Dis.

Now, whether this be in what we moderns call "good taste", or not, I do not mean just now to inquire—Dante having nothing to do with taste, but with the facts of what he had seen; only, so far as the imaginative faculty of the two poets is concerned, note that Milton's vagueness is not the sign of imagination, but of its absence, so far as it is significative in the matter. For it does not follow, because Milton did not map out his Inferno as Dante did, that he *could* not have done so if he had chosen; only, it was the easier and less imaginative process to leave it vague than to define it. Imagination is always the seeing and asserting faculty; that which obscures or conceals may be judgment, or feeling, but not invention. The invention, whether good or bad, is in the accurate engineering, not in the fog and uncertainty.

When we pass with Dante from the Inferno to Purgatory, we have indeed more light and air, but no more liberty; being now confined on various ledges cut into a mountain side, with a precipice on one hand and a vertical wall on the other; and, lest here also we should make any mistake about magnitudes, we are told that the ledges were eighteen feet wide,[26] and that the ascent from one to the other was by steps, made like those which go up from Florence to the church of San Miniato.[27]

Lastly, though in the Paradise there is perfect freedom and infinity of space, though for trenches we have planets, and for cornices constellations, yet there is more cadence, procession, and order among the redeemed souls than any others; they fly, so as to describe letters and sentences in

[26] "Three times the length of the human body."—*Purg.* x, 24.
[27] *Purg.* XII, 93.

the air, and rest in circles, like rainbows, or determinate figures, as of a cross and an eagle; in which certain of the more glorified natures are so arranged as to form the eye of the bird, while those most highly blessed are arranged with their white crowds in leaflets, so as to form the image of a white rose in the midst of heaven.

Thus, throughout the poem, I conceive that the first striking character of its scenery is intense definition; precisely the reflection of that definiteness which we have already traced in pictorial art. But the second point which seems noteworthy is, that the flat ground and embanked trenches are reserved for the Inferno: and that the entire territory of the Purgatory is a mountain, thus marking the sense of that purifying and perfecting influence in mountains which we saw the mediæval mind was so ready to suggest. The same general idea is indicated at the very commencement of the poem, in which Dante is overwhelmed by fear and sorrow in passing through a dark forest, but revives on seeing the sun touch the top of a hill, afterwards called by Virgil "the pleasant mount—the cause and source of all delight."[28]

While, however, we find this greater honour paid to mountains, I think we may perceive a much greater dread and dislike of woods. We saw that Homer seemed to attach a pleasant idea, for the most part, to forests; regarding them as sources of wealth and places of shelter; and we find constantly an idea of sacredness attached to them, as being haunted especially by the gods; so that even the wood which surrounds the house of Circe is spoken of as a sacred thicket,[29] or rather, as a sacred glade, or labyrinth of glades (of the particular word used I shall have more to say presently); and so the wood is sought as a kindly shelter by Ulysses, in spite of its wild beasts; and evidently regarded with great affection by Sophocles, for, in a passage[30] which is always regarded by readers of Greek tragedy with peculiar pleasure, the aged and blind

[28] *Inferno*, I, 73.
[29] *Odyssey*, X, 275.
[30] *Œd. Col.*, 668–711.

Œdipus, brought to rest in "the sweetest resting-place" in all the neighbourhood of Athens, has the spot described to him as haunted perpetually by nightingales, which sing "in the green glades and in the dark ivy, and in the thousand-fruited, sunless, and windless thickets of the god" (Bacchus); the idea of the complete shelter from wind and sun being here, as with Ulysses, the uppermost one. After this come the usual staples of landscape,—narcissus, crocus, plenty of rain, olive trees; and last, and the greatest boast of all,—"it is a good country for horses, and conveniently by the sea"; but the prominence and pleasantness of the thick wood in the thoughts of the writer are very notable; whereas to Dante the idea of a forest is exceedingly repulsive, so that, as just noticed, in the opening of his poem, he cannot express a general despair about life more strongly than by saying he was lost in a wood so savage and terrible, that "even to think or speak of it is distress,—it was so bitter,—it was something next door to death";[31] and one of the saddest scenes in all the Inferno is in a forest, of which the trees are haunted by lost souls: while (with only one exception[32]), whenever the country is to be beautiful, we find ourselves coming out into open air and open meadows.[33]

It is quite true that this is partly a characteristic, not merely of Dante, or of mediæval writers, but of *southern* writers; for the simple reason that the forest, being with them higher upon the hills, and more out of the way than in the north, was generally a type of lonely and savage places; while in England, the "greenwood", coming up to the very walls of the towns, it was possible to be "merry in the good greenwood",[34] in a sense which an Italian could not have understood. Hence Chaucer, Spenser, and Shakespeare send their favourites perpetually to the woods for pleasure or meditation; and trust their tender Canace, or Rosalind, or Helena, or Silvia, or Belphœbe, where Dante

[31] *Inferno,* I, 1–7.
[32] *Purg.* XXVIII.
[33] Vide *Inferno,* IV, 111.
[34] *The Lady of the Lake,* IV, 12.

would have sent no one but a condemned spirit. Nevertheless, there is always traceable in the mediæval mind a dread of thick foliage, which was not present to that of a Greek; so that, even in the north, we have our sorrowful "children in the wood", and black huntsmen of the Hartz forests, and such other wood terrors; the principal reason for the difference being that a Greek, being by no means given to travelling, regarded his woods as so much valuable property; and if he ever went into them for pleasure, expected to meet one or two gods in the course of his walk, but no banditti; while a mediæval, much more of a solitary traveller, and expecting to meet with no gods in the thickets, but only with thieves, or a hostile ambush, or a bear, besides a great deal of troublesome ground for his horse, and a very serious chance, next to a certainty, of losing his way, naturally kept in the open ground as long as he could, and regarded the forests, in general, with anything but an eye of favour.

Modern Painters, vol. III, ch. xiv, pars. 29–33.

(*d*) *Natural Hue*

The Greek sense of colour seems to have been so comparatively dim and uncertain; that it is almost impossible to ascertain what the real idea was which they attached to any word alluding to hue: and above all, colour, though pleasant to their eyes, as to those of all human beings, seems never to have been impressive to their feelings. They liked purple, on the whole, the best; but there was no sense of cheerfulness or pleasantness in one colour, and gloom in another, such as the mediævals had.

For instance, when Achilles goes, in great anger and sorrow, to complain to Thetis of the scorn done him by Agamemnon, the sea appears to him "wine-coloured".[35] One might think this meant that the sea looked dark and reddish-purple to him, in a kind of sympathy with his anger. But we turn to the passage of Sophocles, which has

[35] *Iliad*, I, 350.

been above quoted,—a passage peculiarly intended to express peace and rest,—and we find that the birds sing among "wine-coloured" ivy.[36] The uncertainty of conception of the hue itself, and entire absence of expressive character in the word, could hardly be more clearly manifested.

Again: I said the Greek liked purple, as a general source of enjoyment, better than any other colour. So he did; and so all healthy persons who have eye for colour, and are unprejudiced about it, do; and will to the end of time, for a reason presently to be noted. But so far was this instinctive preference for purple from giving, in the Greek mind, any consistently cheerful or sacred association to the colour, that Homer constantly calls death "purple death".[37]

Again: in the passage of Sophocles, so often spoken of, I said there was some difficulty respecting a word often translated "thickets". I believe, myself, it means glades; literally, "going places" in the woods,—that is to say, places where, either naturally or by force, the trees separate, so as to give some accessible avenue. Now, Sophocles tells us the birds sang in these "*green* going places"[38]; and we take up the expression gratefully, thinking the old Greek perceived and enjoyed, as we do, the sweet fall of the eminently *green* light through the leaves when they are a little thinner than in the heart of the wood. But we turn to the tragedy of Ajax, and are much shaken in our conclusion about the meaning of the word, when we are told that the body of Ajax is to lie unburied, and be eaten by sea-birds on the "*green* sand".[39] The formation, geologically distinguished by that title, was certainly not known to Sophocles; and the only conclusion which, it seems to me, we can come to under the circumstances,—assuming Ariel's[40] authority as to the colour of pretty sand,

[36] *Œd. Col.*, 674.
[37] Vide *Iliad*, v, 83.
[38] *Œd. Col.*, 673.
[39] *Ajax*, 1064.
[40] "Come unto these *yellow* sands."

and the ancient mariner's (or, rather, his hearer's[41]) as to the colour of ugly sand, to be conclusive,—is that Sophocles really did not know green from yellow or brown.

Now, without going out of the terrestrial paradise, in which Dante last left us, we shall be able at once to compare with this Greek incertitude the precision of the mediæval eye for colour. Some three arrow flights farther up into the wood we come to a tall tree, which is at first barren, but, after some little time, visibly opens into flowers, of a colour "less than that of roses, but more than that of violets".[42]

It certainly would not be possible, in words, to come nearer to the *definition* of the exact hue which Dante meant—that of the apple-blossom. Had he employed any simple colour-phrase, as a "pale pink", or "violet-pink", or any other such combined expression, he still could not have completely got at the delicacy of the hue; he might perhaps have indicated its kind, but not its tenderness; but by taking the rose-leaf as the type of the delicate red, and then enfeebling this with the violet grey, he gets, as closely as language can carry him, to the complete rendering of the vision, though it is evidently felt by him to be in its perfect beauty ineffable; and rightly so felt, for of all lovely things which grace the spring time in our fair temperate zone, I am not sure but this blossoming of the apple-tree is the fairest. At all events, I find it associated in my mind with four other kinds of colour, certainly principal among the gifts of the northern earth, namely:

1st. Bell gentians growing close together, mixed with lilies of the valley, on the Jura pastures.

2nd. Alpine roses with dew upon them, under low rays of morning sunshine, touching the tops of the flowers.

3rd. Bell heather in mass, in full light, at sunset.

4th. White narcissus (red-centred) in mass, on the Vevay pastures, in sunshine after rain.

41 "And thou art long, and lank, and *brown*,
As is the ribbed sea sand."

42 *Purg*. XXXII, 58.

And I know not where in the group to place the wreaths of apple-blossoms in the Vevay orchards, with the far-off blue of the lake of Geneva seen between the flowers.

A Greek, however, would have regarded this blossom simply with the eyes of a Devonshire farmer, as bearing on the probable price of cider, and would have called it red, cerulean, purple, white, hyacinthine, or generally "aglaos", agreeable, as happened to suit his verse.

Modern Painters, vol. III, ch. xiv, pars. 43–46.

(*e*) *Grass and Flowers*

There are, it seems to me, several important deductions to be made from these facts. The Greeks, we have seen, delighted in the grass for its usefulness; the mediæval, as also we moderns, for its colour and beauty. But both dwell on it as the *first* element of the lovely landscape; we saw its use in Homer, we see also that Dante thinks the righteous spirits of the heathen enough comforted in Hades by having even the *image* of green grass put beneath their feet;[43] the happy resting-place in Purgatory has no other delight than its grass and flowers; and, finally, in the terrestrial paradise, the feet of Matilda pause where the Lethe stream first bends the blades of grass.[44] Consider a little what a depth there is in this great instinct of the human race. Gather a single blade of grass, and examine for a minute, quietly, its narrow sword-shaped strip of fluted green. Nothing, as it seems there, of notable goodness or beauty. A very little strength, and a very little tallness, and a few delicate long lines meeting in a point,–not a perfect point neither, but blunt and unfinished, by no means a creditable or apparently much cared for example of Nature's workmanship; made, as it seems, only to be trodden on to-day, and to-morrow to be cast into the oven; and a little pale and hollow stalk, feeble and flaccid, leading down to the dull brown fibres of roots. And yet, think of it well, and judge whether of all the

[43] Vide *Inferno*, IV, 118.
[44] *Purg.* XVIII, 27.

gorgeous flowers that beam in summer air, and of all strong and goodly trees, pleasant to the eyes or good for food,—stately palm and pine, strong ash and oak, scented citron, burdened vine,—there be any by man so deeply loved, by God so highly graced, as that narrow point of feeble green.

Modern Painters, vol. III, ch. xiv, par. 51.

(*f*) *Mountains*

To Dante, mountains are inconceivable except as great broken stones or crags; all their broad contours and undulations seem to have escaped his eye. It is, indeed, with his usual undertone of symbolic meaning that he describes the great broken stones, and the fall of the shattered mountain, as the entrance to the circle appointed for the punishment of the violent; meaning that the violent and cruel, notwithstanding all their iron hardness of heart, have no true strength, but, either by earthquake, or want of support, fall at last into desolate ruin, naked, loose, and shaking under the tread. But in no part of the poem do we find allusion to mountains in any other than a stern light; nor the slightest evidence that Dante cared to look at them. From that hill of San Miniato, whose steps he knew so well, the eye commands, at the farther extremity of the Val d'Arno, the whole purple range of the mountains of Carrara, peaked and mighty, seen always against the sunset light in silent outline, the chief forms that rule the scene as twilight fades away. By this vision Dante seems to have been wholly unmoved, and, but for Lucan's mention of Aruns at Luna,[45] would seemingly not have spoken of the Carrara hills in the whole course of his poem: when he does allude to them,[46] he speaks of their white marble, and their command of stars and sea, but has evidently no regard for the hills themselves. There is not a single phrase or syllable throughout the poem which indicates such a regard. Ugolino, in his dream, seemed to him-

[45] *Pharsalia,* I, 575.
[46] *Inferno,* xx, 46.

self to be in the mountains, "by cause of which the Pisan cannot see Lucca";[47] and it is impossible to look up from Pisa to that hoary slope without remembering the awe that there is in the passage; nevertheless, it was as a hunting-ground only that he remembered those hills. Adam of Brescia, tormented with eternal thirst, remembers the hills of Romena, but only for the sake of their sweet waters:

> The rills that glitter down the grassy slopes
> Of Casentino, making fresh and soft
> The banks whereby they glide to Arno's stream,
> Stand ever in my view.[48]

And, whenever hills are spoken of as having any influence on character, the repugnance to them is still manifest; they are always causes of rudeness or cruelty:

> But that ungrateful and malignant race,
> Who in old times came down from Fesole,
> *Ay, and still smack of their rough mountain flint,*
> Will, for thy good deeds, show thee enmity.
> Take heed thou cleanse thee of their ways.[49]

So again—

> As one *mountain-bred,*
> Rugged, and clownish, if some city's walls
> He chance to enter, round him stares agape.[50]

Finally, although the Carrara mountains are named as having command of the stars and sea, the *Alps* are never specially mentioned but in bad weather, or snow. On the sand of the circle of the blasphemers—

> Fell slowly wafting down
> Dilated flakes of fire, as flakes of snow
> On Alpine summit, when the wind is hushed.[51]

47 *Inferno,* XXXIII, 30.
48 *Inferno,* XV, 61.
49 *Inferno,* XXX, 63.
50 *Purg.* XXVI, 60.
51 *Inferno,* XIV, 25.

So the Paduans have to defend their town and castles against inundations,

> Ere the genial warmth be felt,
> On Chiarentana's top.[52]

The clouds of anger, in Purgatory, can only be figured to the reader who has

> On an Alpine height been ta'en by cloud,
> Through which thou sawest no better than the mole
> Doth through opacous membrane.[53]

And in approaching the second branch of Lethe, the seven ladies pause,—

> Arriving at the verge
> Of a dim umbrage hoar, such as is seen
> Beneath green leaves and gloomy branches oft
> To overbrow a bleak and alpine cliff.[54]

Modern Painters, vol. III, ch. XV, pars. 17–18.

(g) *The Sky*

There is only one more point to be noticed in the Dantesque landscape; namely, the feeling entertained by the poet towards the sky. And the love of mountains is so closely connected with the love of clouds, the sublimity of both depending much on their association, that, having found Dante regardless of the Carrara mountains as seen from San Miniato, we may well expect to find him equally regardless of the clouds in which the sun sank behind them. Accordingly, we find that his only pleasure in the sky depends on its "white clearness",—that turning into "bianca aspetto di cilestro" which is so peculiarly characteristic of fine days in Italy. His pieces of pure pale light are always exquisite. In the dawn on the purgatorial moun-

[52] *Inferno,* XV, 9.
[53] *Purg.* XVII, 2.
[54] *Purg.* XXXIII, 107.

tain, first, in its pale white, he sees the "tremola della marina"—trembling of the sea; then it becomes vermilion; and at last, near sunrise, orange.[55] These are precisely the changes of a calm and perfect dawn. The scenery of Paradise begins with "Day added to day", the light of the sun so flooding the heavens, that "never rain nor river made lake so wide";[56] and throughout the Paradise all the beauty depends on spheres of light, or stars, never on clouds. But the pit of the Inferno is at first sight obscure, deep, and so *cloudy* that at its bottom nothing could be seen.[57] When Dante and Virgil reach the marsh in which the souls of those who have been angry and sad in their lives are for ever plunged, they find it covered with thick fog; and the condemned souls say to them,—

We once were sad,
In the *sweet air made gladsome by the sun.*
Now in these murky settlings are we sad.[58]

Even the angel crossing the marsh to help them is annoyed by this bitter marsh smoke, "fummo acerbo", and continually sweeps it with his hand from before his face.[59]

Anger, on the purgatorial mountain, is in like manner imaged, because of its blindness and wildness, by the Alpine clouds. As they emerge from its mist they see the white light radiated through the fading folds of it; and, except this appointed cloud, no other can touch the mountain of purification.

Tempest none, shower, hail, or snow,
Hoar-frost, or dewy moistness, higher falls,
Than that brief scale of threefold steps. Thick clouds,
Nor scudding rack, are ever seen, swift glance
Ne'er lightens, nor Thaumantian iris gleams.[60]

55 *Purg.* I, 117; II, 7–9.
56 *Par.* I, 61.
57 *Inferno,* IV, 10.
58 *Inferno,* VII, 121.
59 *Inferno,* IX, 82.
60 *Purg.* XXI, 46.

Dwell for a little while on this intense love of Dante for light,—taught, as he is at last by Beatrice, to gaze on the sun itself like an eagle,[61]—and endeavour to enter into his equally intense detestation of all mist, rack of cloud, or dimness of rain; and then consider with what kind of temper he would have regarded a landscape of Copley Fielding's or passed a day in the Highlands. He has, in fact, assigned to the souls of the gluttonous no other punishment in the Inferno than perpetuity of Highland weather:

Showers
Ceaseless, accursed, heavy and cold, unchanged
For ever, both in kind and in degree,—
Large hail, discoloured water, sleety flaw,
Through the dim midnight air streamed down amain.[62]

Modern Painters, vol. III, ch. XV, par. 20.

5. MODERN LANDSCAPE— CLOUDINESS AND LIBERTY

We turn our eyes, therefore, as boldly and as quickly as may be, from these serene fields and skies of mediæval art, to the most characteristic examples of modern landscape. And, I believe, the first thing that will strike us, or that ought to strike us, is their *cloudiness.*

Out of perfect light and motionless air, we find ourselves on a sudden brought under sombre skies, and into drifting wind; and, with fickle sunbeams flashing in our face, or utterly drenched with sweep of rain, we are reduced to track the changes of the shadows on the grass, or watch the rents of twilight through angry cloud. And we find that whereas all the pleasure of the mediæval was in *stability, definiteness,* and *luminousness,* we are expected to rejoice in darkness, and triumph in mutability; to lay the foundation of happiness in things which mo-

[61] *Par.* I, 47.
[62] *Inferno,* VI, 7.

mentarily change or fade; and to expect the utmost satisfaction and instruction from what it is impossible to arrest, and difficult to comprehend.

We find, however, together with this general delight in breeze and darkness, much attention to the real form of clouds, and careful drawing of effects of mist; so that the appearance of objects, as seen through it, becomes a subject of science with us; and the faithful representation of that appearance is made of primal importance, under the name of aërial perspective. The aspects of sunset and sunrise, with all their attendant phenomena of cloud and mist, are watchfully delineated; and in ordinary daylight landscape, the sky is considered of so much importance, that a principal mass of foliage, or a whole foreground, is unhesitatingly thrown into shade merely to bring out the form of a white cloud. So that, if a general and characteristic name were needed for modern landscape art, none better could be invented than "the service of clouds".

The next thing that will strike us, after this love of clouds, is the love of liberty. Whereas the mediæval was always shutting himself into castles, and behind fosses, and drawing brickwork neatly, and beds of flowers primly, our painters delight in getting to the open fields and moors; abhor all hedges and moats; never paint anything but free-growing trees, and rivers gliding "at their own sweet will"; eschew formality down to the smallest detail; break and displace the brickwork which the mediæval would have carefully cemented; leave unpruned the thickets he would have delicately trimmed; and, carrying the love of liberty even to license, and the love of wildness even to ruin, take pleasure at last in every aspect of age and desolation which emancipates the objects of nature from the government of men;—on the castle wall displacing its tapestry with ivy, and spreading, through the garden, the bramble for the rose.

Connected with this love of liberty we find a singular manifestation of love of mountains, and see our painters traversing the wildest places of the globe in order to obtain subjects with craggy foregrounds and purple distances. Some few of them remain content with pollards and flat land; but these are always men of third-rate order; and the leading masters, while they do not reject the beauty of the low grounds, reserve their highest powers to paint Alpine peaks or Italian promontories. And it is eminently noticeable, also, that this pleasure in the mountains is never mingled with fear, or tempered by a spirit of meditation, as with the mediæval; but it is always free and fearless, brightly exhilarating, and wholly unreflective; so that the painter feels that his mountain foreground may be more consistently animated by a sportsman than a hermit; and our modern society in general goes to the mountains, not to fast, but to feast, and leaves their glaciers covered with chicken-bones and egg-shells.

Connected with this want of any sense of solemnity in mountain scenery, is a general profanity of temper in regarding all the rest of nature; that is to say, a total absence of faith in the presence of any deity therein. Whereas the mediæval never painted a cloud, but with the purpose of placing an angel in it; and a Greek never entered a wood without expecting to meet a god in it; *we* should think the appearance of an angel in the cloud wholly unnatural, and should be seriously surprised by meeting a god anywhere. Our chief ideas about the wood are connected with poaching. We have no belief that the clouds contain more than so many inches of rain or hail, and from our ponds and ditches expect nothing more divine than ducks and watercresses.

Finally: connected with this profanity of temper is a strong tendency to deny the sacred element of colour, and make our boast in blackness. For though occasionally glaring or violent, modern colour is on the whole eminently sombre, tending continually to grey or brown, and by many of our best painters consistently falsified, with a confessed pride in what they call chaste or subdued tints; so that, whereas a mediæval paints his sky bright blue and his foreground bright green, gilds the towers of his castles, and clothes his figures with purple and white, we paint our sky grey, our foreground black, and our foliage brown, and think that enough is sacrificed to the sun in admitting the dangerous brightness of a scarlet cloak or a blue jacket.

It is evident that the title "Dark Ages", given to the mediæval centuries, is, respecting art, wholly inapplicable. They were, on the contrary, the bright ages; ours are the dark ones. I do not mean metaphysically, but literally. They were the ages of gold; ours are the ages of umber.

This is partly mere mistake in us; we build brown brick walls, and wear brown coats, because we have been blunderingly taught to do so, and go on doing so mechanically. There is, however, also some cause for the change in our own tempers. On the whole, these are much *sadder* ages than the early ones; not sadder in a noble and deep way, but in a dim wearied way,—the way of ennui, and jaded intellect, and uncomfortableness of soul and body. The Middle Ages had their wars and agonies, but also intense delights. Their gold was dashed with blood; but ours is sprinkled with dust. Their life was inwoven with white and purple: ours is one seamless stuff of brown. Not that we are without apparent festivity, but festivity more or less forced, mistaken, embittered, incomplete—not of the heart. How wonderfully, since Shakespeare's time, have we lost the power of laughing at bad jests! The very finish of our wit belies our gaiety.

The profoundest reason of this darkness of heart is, I believe, our want of faith. There never yet was a generation of men (savage or civilized) who, taken as a body, so wofully fulfilled the words "having no hope, and without God in the world", as the present civilized European race. A Red Indian or Otaheitan savage has more sense of a divine existence round him, or government over him, than the plurality of refined Londoners and Parisians: and those among us who may in some sense be said to believe, are divided almost without exception into two broad classes, Romanist and Puritan; who, but for the interference of the unbelieving portions of society, would, either of them, reduce the other sect as speedily as possible to ashes; the Romanist having always done so whenever he could, from the beginning of their separation, and the Puritan at this time holding himself in complacent expectation of the destruction of Rome by volcanic fire. Such division as this between persons nominally of one religion, that is to say, believing in the same God, and the same Revelation, cannot but become a stumbling-block of the gravest kind to all thoughtful and far-sighted men,—a stumbling-block which they can only surmount under the most favourable circumstances of early education. Hence, nearly all our powerful men in this age of the world are unbelievers; the best of them in doubt and misery; the worst in reckless defiance; the plurality, in plodding hesitation, doing, as well as they can, what practical work lies ready to their hands. Most of our scientific men are in this last class: our popular authors either set themselves definitely against all religious form, pleading for simple truth and benevolence, (Thackeray, Dickens,) or give themselves up to bitter and fruitless statement of facts, (De Balzac,) or surface-painting, (Scott,) or careless blasphemy, sad or smiling, (Byron, Beranger). Our earnest poets and deepest thinkers are doubtful and indignant, (Tennyson, Carlyle); one or two, anchored, indeed, but anxious or weeping, (Wordsworth, Mrs Browning); and of these two, the first is not so sure of his anchor, but that now and then it drags with him, even to make him cry out,—

Great God, I had rather be
A Pagan suckled in some creed outworn;
So might I, standing on this pleasant lea,
Have glimpses that would make me less forlorn.[63]

In politics, religion is now a name; in art, a hypocrisy or affectation. Over German religious pictures the inscription, "See how Pious I am", can be read at a glance by any clear-sighted person. Over French and English religious pictures, the inscription, "See how Impious I am",

[63] *Miscellaneous Sonnets,* pt. 1, no. 33.

is equally legible. All sincere and modest art is, among us, profane.

Modern Painters, vol. III, ch. xvi, pars. 1–2; 5–10.

SCOTT AS REPRESENTATIVE OF THE MIND OF THE AGE

I think it probable that many readers may be surprised at my calling Scott the great representative of the mind of the age in literature. Those who can perceive the intense penetrative depth of Wordsworth, and the exquisite finish and melodious power of Tennyson, may be offended at my placing in higher rank that poetry of careless glance, and reckless rhyme, in which Scott poured out the fancies of his youth; and those who are familiar with the subtle analysis of the French novelists, or who have in anywise submitted themselves to the influence of German philosophy, may be equally indignant at my ascribing a principality to Scott among the literary men of Europe, in an age which has produced De Balzac and Goethe. I can only crave the reader's patience, and his due consideration of the following reasons for my doing so, together with those advanced in the farther course of the work.

I believe the first test of a truly great man is his humility. I do not mean, by humility, doubt of his own power, or hesitation in speaking his opinions; but a right understanding of the relation between what *he* can do and say, and the rest of the world's sayings and doings. All great men not only know their business, but usually know that they know it; and are not only right in their main opinions, but they usually know that they are right in them; only, they do not think much of themselves on that account. Arnolfo knows he can build a good dome at Florence; Albert Dürer writes calmly to one who had found fault with his work, "It cannot be better done"; Sir Isaac Newton knows that he has worked out a problem or two that would have puzzled anybody else,—only they do not expect their fellow-men therefore to fall down and worship them; they have a curious under-sense of powerlessness, feeling that the greatness is not *in* them, but *through* them; that they could not do or be anything else than God made them. And they see something divine and God-made in every other man they meet, and are endlessly, foolishly, incredibly merciful.

Now, I find among the men of the present age, as far as I know them, this character in Scott and Turner preeminently; I am not sure if it is not in them alone. I do not find Scott talking about the dignity of literature, nor Turner about the dignity of painting. They do their work, feeling that they cannot well help it; the story must be told, and the effect put down; and if people like it, well and good; and, if not, the world will not be much the worse.

I believe a very different impression of their estimate of themselves and their doings will be received by anyone who reads the conversations of Wordsworth or Goethe. The *slightest* manifestation of jealousy or self-complacency is enough to mark a second-rate character of the intellect; and I fear that, especially in Goethe, such manifestations are neither few nor slight.

Connected with this general humility, is the total absence of affectation in these men,—that is to say, of any assumption of manner or behaviour in their work, in order to attract attention. Not but that they are mannerists both. Scott's verse is strongly mannered, and Turner's oil painting; but the manner of it necessitated by the feelings of the men, entirely natural to both, never exaggerated for the sake of show. I hardly know any other literary or pictorial work of the day which is not in some degree affected. I am afraid Wordsworth was often affected in his simplicity, and De Balzac in his finish. Many fine French writers are affected in their reserve, and full of sage tricks in placing of sentences. It is lucky if in German writers we ever find so much as a sentence without affectation.

Again: another very important, though not infallible, test of greatness is, as we have often said, the appearance of Ease with which the thing is done. It may be that, as with Dante and Leonardo, the finish given to the work effaces the evidence of ease; but where the ease is manifest, as in Scott, Turner, and Tintoret, and the thing done is very noble, it is a strong reason for placing the men above those who confessedly work with great pains. Scott writing his chapter or two before breakfast—not retouching; Turner finishing a whole drawing in a forenoon before he goes out to shoot (providing always the chapter and drawing be good), are instantly to be set above men who confessedly have spent a day over the work, and think the hours well spent if it has been a little mended between sunrise and sunset. Indeed, it is no use for men to think to appear great by working fast, dashing, and scrawling; the thing they do must be good and great, cost what time it may; but if it *be* so, and they have honestly and unaffectedly done it with *no effort,* it is probably a greater and better thing than the result of the hardest efforts of others.

Then, as touching the kind of work done by these two men, the more I think of it I find this conclusion more impressed upon me,—that the greatest thing a human soul ever does in this world is to *see* something, and tell what it *saw* in a plain way. Hundreds of people can talk for one who can think, but thousands can think for one who can see. To see clearly is poetry, prophecy, and religion,—all in one.

Therefore, finding the world of Literature more or less divided into Thinkers and Seers, I believe we shall find also that the Seers are wholly the greater race of the two. A true Thinker, who has practical purpose in his thinking, and is sincere, as Plato, or Carlyle, or Helps, becomes in some sort a seer, and must be always of infinite use in his generation; but an affected Thinker, who supposes his thinking of any other importance than as it tends to work, is about the vainest kind of person that can be found in the occupied classes. Nay, I believe that metaphysicians and philosophers are, on the whole, the greatest troubles the world has got to deal with; and that while a tyrant or bad man is of some use in teaching people submission or indignation, and a thoroughly idle man is only harmful in setting an idle example, and communicating to other lazy people his own lazy misunderstandings, busy metaphysicians are always entangling *good* and *active* people, and weaving cobwebs among the finest wheels of the world's business; and are as much as possible, by all prudent persons, to be brushed out of their way, like spiders, and the meshed weed that has got into the Cambridgeshire canals, and other such impediments to barges and business. And if we thus clear the metaphysical element out of modern literature, we shall find its bulk amazingly diminished, and the claims of the remaining writers, or of those whom we have thinned by this abstraction of their straw stuffing, much more easily adjusted.*

Again: the mass of sentimental literature, concerned with the analysis and description of emotion, headed by the poetry of Byron, is altogether of lower rank than the literature which merely describes what it saw. The true Seer always feels as intensely as any one else; but he does not much describe his feelings. He tells you whom he met, and what they said; leaves you to make out, from that, what they feel, and what he feels, but goes into little detail. And, generally speaking, pathetic writing and careful explanation of passion are quite easy, compared with this plain recording of what people said or did, or with the right invention of what they are likely to say and do; for this reason, that to invent a story, or admirably and thoroughly tell any part of a story, it is necessary to grasp the entire mind of every personage concerned in it, and

* Observe, I do not speak thus of metaphysics because I have no pleasure in them. When I speak contemptuously of philology, it may be answered me, that I am a bad scholar; but I cannot be so answered touching metaphysics, for every one conversant with such subjects may see that I have strong inclination that way, which would, indeed have led me far astray long ago, if I had not learned also some use of my hands, eyes, and feet.

know precisely how they would be affected by what happens; which to do requires a colossal intellect: but to describe a separate emotion delicately, it is only needed that one should feel it oneself; and thousands of people are capable of feeling this or that noble emotion, for one who is able to enter into all the feelings of somebody sitting on the other side of the table. Even, therefore, where this sentimental literature is first rate, as in passages of Byron, Tennyson, and Keats, it ought not to be ranked so high as the Creative; and though perfection, even in narrow fields, is perhaps as rare as in the wider, and it may be as long before we have another *In Memoriam* as another *Guy Mannering*, I unhesitatingly receive as a greater manifestation of power the right invention of a few sentences spoken by Pleydell and Mannering across their supper-table, than the most tender and passionate melodies of the self-examining verse.

Having, therefore, cast metaphysical writers out of our way, and sentimental writers into the second rank, I do not think Scott's supremacy among those who remain will any more be doubtful; nor would it, perhaps, have been doubtful before, had it not been encumbered by innumerable faults and weaknesses. But it is pre-eminently in these faults and weaknesses that Scott is representative of the mind of his age; and because he is the greatest man born amongst us, and intended for the enduring type of us, all our principal faults must be laid on his shoulders, and he must bear down the dark marks to the latest ages; while the smaller men, who have some special work to do, perhaps not so much belonging to this age as leading out of it to the next, are often kept providentially quit of the encumbrances which they had not strength to sustain, and are much smoother and pleasanter to look at, in their way: only that is a smaller way.

Thus, the most startling fault of the age being its faithlessness, it is necessary that its greatest man should be faithless. Nothing is more notable or sorrowful in Scott's mind than its incapacity of steady belief in anything. He cannot even resolve hardily to believe in a ghost, or a water-spirit; always explains them away in an apologetic manner, not believing, all the while, even in his own explanation. He never can clearly ascertain whether there is anything behind the arras but rats; never draws sword, and thrusts at it for life or death; but goes on looking at it timidly, and saying, "it must be the wind". He is educated a Presbyterian, and remains one, because it is the most sensible thing he can do if he is to live in Edinburgh; but he thinks Romanism more picturesque, and profaneness more gentlemanly; does not see that anything affects human life but love, courage, and destiny; which are, indeed, not matters of faith at all, but of sight. Any gods but those are very misty in outline to him; and when the love is laid ghastly in poor Charlotte's coffin,[1] and the courage is no more of use,—the pen having fallen from between the fingers; and destiny is sealing the scroll,—the God-light is dim in the tears that fall on it.

He is in all this the epitome of his epoch.

Again: as another notable weakness of the age is its habit of looking back, in a romantic and passionate idleness, to the past ages, not understanding them all the while, nor really desiring to understand them, so Scott gives up nearly the half of his intellectual power to a fond, yet purposeless, dreaming over the past, and spends half his literary labours in endeavours to revive it, not in reality, but on the stage of fiction; endeavours which were the best of the kind that modernism made, but still successful only so far as Scott put, under the old armour, the everlasting human nature which he knew; and totally unsuccessful, so far as concerned the painting of the armour itself, which he knew *not*. The excellence of Scott's work is precisely in proportion to the degree in which it is sketched from present nature. His familiar life is inimitable; his quiet scenes of introductory conversation, as the beginning of *Rob Roy* and *Redgauntlet*, and all his living Scotch characters, mean or noble, from Andrew Fairservice to Jeanie Deans, are simply right, and can never be

[1] Scott's wife, died 1826.

bettered. But his romance and antiquarianism, his knighthood and monkery, are all false, and he knows them to be false; does not care to make them earnest; enjoys them for their strangeness, but laughs at his own antiquarianism, all through his own third novel,—with exquisite modesty indeed, but with total misunderstanding of the function of an Antiquary. He does not see how anything is to be got out of the past but confusion, old iron on drawing-room chairs, and serious inconvenience to Dr Heavysterne.

Again: more than any age that had preceded it, ours had been ignorant of the meaning of the word "Art". It had not a single fixed principle, and what unfixed principles it worked upon were all wrong. It was necessary that Scott should know nothing of art. He neither cared for painting nor sculpture, and was totally incapable of forming a judgment about them. He had some confused love of Gothic architecture, because it was dark, picturesque, old, and like nature; but could not tell the worst from the best, and built for himself perhaps the most incongruous and ugly pile that gentlemanly modernism ever designed; marking, in the most curious and subtle way, that mingling of reverence with irreverence which is so striking in the age; he reverences Melrose, yet casts one of its piscinas, puts a modern steel grate into it, and makes it his fireplace. Like all pure moderns, he supposes the Gothic barbarous, notwithstanding his love of it; admires, in an equally ignorant way, totally opposite styles; is delighted with the new town of Edinburgh; mistakes its dulness for purity of taste, and actually compares it, in its deathful formality of street, as contrasted with the rudeness of the old town, to Britomart taking off her armour.[2]

Again: as in reverence and irreverence, so in levity and melancholy, we saw that the spirit of the age was strangely interwoven. Therefore, also, it is necessary that Scott should be light, careless, unearnest, and yet eminently sorrowful. Throughout all his work there is no evi-

[2] *Marmion,* Introd. to Canto v.

dence of any purpose but to while away the hour. His life had no other object than the pleasure of the instant, and the establishing of a family name. All his thoughts were, in their outcome and end, less than nothing, and vanity. And yet, of all poetry that I know, none is so sorrowful as Scott's. Other great masters are pathetic in a resolute and predetermined way, when they choose; but, in their own minds, are evidently stern, or hopeful, or serene; never really melancholy. Even Byron is rather sulky and desperate than melancholy; Keats is sad because he is sickly; Shelley because he is impious; but Scott is inherently and consistently sad. Around all his power, and brightness, and enjoyment of eye and heart, the far-away Æolian knell is for ever sounding; there is not one of those loving or laughing glances of his but it is brighter for the film of tears; his mind is like one of his own hill rivers,—it is white, and flashes in the sun fairly, careless, as it seems, and hasty in its going, but

> Far beneath, where slow they creep
> From pool to eddy, dark and deep,
> Where alders moist, and willows weep,
>   You hear her streams repine.[3]

Life begins to pass from him very early; and while Homer sings cheerfully in his blindness, and Dante retains his courage, and rejoices in hope of Paradise, through all his exile, Scott, yet hardly past his youth, lies pensive in the sweet sunshine and among the harvest of his native hills.

> Blackford, on whose uncultured breast,
>   Among the broom, and thorn, and whin,
> A truant boy, I sought the nest,
> Or listed as I lay at rest,
>   While rose on breezes thin
> The murmur of the city crowd,
> And, from his steeple jangling loud,
>   St Giles's mingling din!

[3] *Marmion*, IV, 10.

Now, from the summit to the plain,
Waves all the hill with yellow grain;
  And on the landscape as I look,
Nought do I see unchanged remain,
  Save the rude cliffs and chiming brook;
To me they make a heavy moan
Of early friendships past and gone.[4]

Modern Painters, vol. III, ch. XVI, pars. 23–24.

SCOTT AND NATURE

In consequence of his unselfishness and humility, Scott's enjoyment of nature is incomparably greater than that of any other poet I know. All the rest carry their cares to her, and begin maundering in her ears about their own affairs. Tennyson goes out on a furzy common, and sees it is calm autumn sunshine, but it gives him no pleasure. He only remembers that it is

Dead calm in that noble breast
Which heaves but with the heaving deep.[1]

He sees a thundercloud in the evening, and *would* have "doted and pored" on it, but cannot, for fear it should bring the ship bad weather. Keats drinks the beauty of nature violently; but has no more real sympathy with her than he has with a bottle of claret. His palate is fine; but he "bursts joy's grape against it",[2] gets nothing but misery, and a bitter taste of dregs, out of his desperate draught.

Byron and Shelley are nearly the same, only with less truth of perception, and even more troublesome selfishness. Wordsworth is more like Scott, and understands how to be happy, but yet cannot altogether rid himself of the

[4] *Marmion,* IV, 24.
[1] *In Memoriam,* XI.
[2] *Ode to Melancholy.*

sense that he is a philosopher, and ought always to be saying something wise. He has also a vague notion that Nature would not be able to get on well without Wordsworth; and finds a considerable part of his pleasure in looking at himself as well as at her. But with Scott the love is entirely humble and unselfish. "I, Scott, am nothing, and less than nothing; but these crags, and heaths, and clouds, how great they are, how lovely, how for ever to be beloved, only for their own silent, thoughtless sake!"

Modern Painters, vol. III, ch. XVI, par. 38.

NATURAL INSPIRATION

We seem to have involved the supposition that mountain influence is either unfavourable or inessential to literary power; but for this also the mountain influence is still necessary, only in a subordinate degree. It is true, indeed, that the Avon is no mountain torrent, and that the hills round the vale of Stratford are not sublime; true, moreover, that the cantons Berne and Uri have never yet, so far as I know, produced a great poet; but neither, on the other hand, has Antwerp or Amsterdam. And, I believe, the natural scenery which will be found, on the whole, productive of most literary intellect is that mingled of hill and plain, as all available light is of flame and darkness; the flame being the active element, and the darkness the tempering one.

In noting such evidence as bears upon this subject, the reader must always remember that the mountains are at an unfair disadvantage, in being much *out of the way* of the masses of men employed in intellectual pursuits. The position of a city is dictated by military necessity or commercial convenience: it rises, flourishes, and absorbs into its activity whatever leading intellect is in the surrounding population. The persons who are able and desirous to give their children education naturally resort to it; the best schools, the best society, and the strongest motives assist and excite those born within its walls; and youth after youth rises to distinction out of its streets, while among the blue mountains, twenty miles away, the goatherds live and die in unregarded lowliness. And yet this is no proof that the mountains have little effect upon the mind, or that the streets have a helpful one. The men who are formed by the schools and polished by the society of the capital, may yet in many ways have their powers shortened by the absence of natural scenery; and the mountaineer, neglected, ignorant, and unambitious, may have been taught things by the clouds and streams which he could not have learned in a college, or a coterie.

And in reasoning about the effect of mountains we are therefore under a difficulty like that which would occur to us if we had to determine the good or bad effect of light on the human constitution, in some place where all corporal exercise was necessarily in partial darkness, and only idle people lived in the light. The exercise might give an advantage to the occupants of the gloom, but we should neither be justified in therefore denying the preciousness of light in general, nor the necessity to the workers of the few rays they possessed; and thus I suppose the hills around Stratford, and such glimpses as Shakespeare had of sandstone and pines in Warwickshire, or of chalk cliffs in Kent, to have been essential to the development of his genius. This supposition can only be proved false by the rising of a Shakespeare at Rotterdam or Bergen-op-Zoom, which I think not probable; whereas, on the other hand, it is confirmed by myriads of collateral evidences. The matter could only be *tested* by placing for half a century the British universities at Keswick and Beddgelert, and making Grenoble the capital of France; but if, throughout the history of Britain and France, we contrast the general invention and pathetic power, in ballads or legends, of the inhabitants of the Scottish Border with those manifested in Suffolk or Essex; and similarly the inventive power of Normandy, Provence, and the Bearnois with that of Champagne or Picardy, we shall obtain some convincing evidence respecting the operation of hills on the masses of mankind, and be disposed to admit, with less hesitation, that the apparent inconsistencies in the effect of scenery on greater minds proceed in each case from specialties of education, accident, and original temper, which it would be impossible to follow out in detail. Sometimes only, when the original resemblance in character of intellect is very marked in two individuals, and they are submitted to definitely contrary circumstances of education, an approximation to evidence may be obtained. Thus Bacon and Pascal appear to be men naturally very similar in their temper and powers of minds. One, born in York House, Strand, of courtly parents, educated in court atmosphere, and replying, almost as soon as he could speak, to the queen asking how old he was—"Two years younger than Your Majesty's happy reign!"—has the world's meanness and cunning engrafted into his intellect, and remains smooth, serene, unenthusiastic, and in some degree base, even with all his sincere devotion and universal wisdom; bearing, to the end of life, the likeness of a marble palace in the street of a great city, fairly furnished within, and bright in wall and battlement, yet noisome in places about the foundations. The other, born at Clermont, in Auvergne, under the shadow of the Puy de Dôme, though taken to Paris at eight years old, retains for ever the impress of his birthplace; pursuing natural philosophy with the same zeal as Bacon, he returns to his own mountains to put himself under their tutelage, and by their help first discovers the great relations of the earth and the air: struck at last with mortal disease; gloomy, enthusiastic, and superstitious, with a conscience burning like lava, and inflexible like iron, the clouds gather about the majesty of him, fold after fold; and, with his spirit buried in ashes, and rent by earthquake, yet fruitful of true thought and faithful affection, he stands like that mound of desolate scoria that crowns the hill ranges of his native land, with its sable summit far in heaven, and its foundations green with the ordered garden and the trellised vine.

When, however, our inquiry thus branches into the successive analysis of individual characters, it is time for us to leave it; noting only one or two points respecting Shakespeare. He seems to have been sent essentially to take universal and equal grasp of the *human* nature; and to have been removed, therefore, from all influences which could in the least warp or bias his thoughts. It was necessary that he should lean *no* way; that he should contemplate, with absolute equality of judgment, the life of the court, cloister, and tavern, and be able to sympathize so completely with all creatures as to deprive himself, together with his personal identity, even of his conscience, as he casts himself into their hearts. He must be able to enter into the soul of Falstaff or Shylock with no more sense of contempt or horror than Falstaff or Shylock themselves feel for or in themselves; otherwise his own conscience and indignation would make him unjust to them; he would turn aside from something, miss some good, or overlook some essential palliation. He must be utterly without anger, utterly without purpose; for if a man has any serious purpose in life, that which runs counter to it, or is foreign to it, will be looked at frowningly or carelessly by him. Shakespeare was forbidden of Heaven to have any *plans*. To *do* any good or *get* any good, in the common sense of good, was not to be within his permitted range of work. Not, for him, the founding of institutions, the preaching of doctrines, or the repression of abuses. Neither he, nor the sun, did on any morning that they rose together, receive charge from their Maker concerning such things. They were both of them to shine on the evil and good; both to behold unoffendedly all that was upon the earth, to burn unappalled upon the spears of kings, and undisdaining, upon the reeds of the river.

Therefore, so far as nature had influence over the early training of this man, it was essential to his perfectness that the nature should be quiet. No mountain passions were to be allowed in him. Inflict upon him but one pang of the monastic conscience; cast upon him but one cloud of the mountain gloom; and his serenity had been gone for ever—his equity—his infinity. You would have made another Dante of him; and all that he would have ever uttered about poor, soiled, and frail humanity would have been the quarrel between Simon and Adam of Brescia,—speedily retired from, as not worthy a man's hearing, nay, not to be heard without heavy fault. All your Falstaffs, Slenders, Quicklys, Sir Tobys, Lances, Touchstones, and Quinces, would have been lost in that. Shakespeare could be allowed no mountains; nay, not even any supreme natural beauty. He had to be left with his kingcups and clover;—pansies—the passing clouds—the Avon's flow—and the undulating hills and woods of Warwick; nay, he was not to love even these in any exceeding measure, lest it might make him in the least overrate their power upon the strong, full-fledged minds of men. He makes the quarrelling fairies concerned about them; poor lost Ophelia find some comfort in them; fearful, fair, wise-hearted Perdita trust the speaking of her good will and good hostess-ship to them; and one of the brothers of Imogen confide his sorrow to them,—rebuked instantly by his brother for "wench-like words";* but any thought of them in his mighty men I do not find: it is not usually in the nature of such men; and if he had loved the flowers the *least* better himself, he would assuredly have been offended at this, and given a botanical turn of mind to Cæsar, or Othello.

And it is even among the most curious proofs of the necessity to all high imagination that it should paint straight from the life, that he has *not* given such a turn of mind to some of his great men;—Henry the Fifth, for instance. Doubtless some of my readers, having been accustomed to hear it repeated thoughtlessly from mouth to mouth that Shakespeare conceived the spirit of all ages, were as much offended as surprised at my saying that he

* "With fairest flowers
While summer lasts, and I live here, Fidele,
I'll sweeten thy sad grave. Thou shalt not lack
The flower that's like thy face—pale primrose, nor
The azured harebell—like thy veins; no, nor
The leaf of eglantine, whom not to slander,
Outsweetened not thy breath. The ruddock would
With charitable bill bring thee all this;
Yea, and furr'd moss besides, when flowers are none,
To winter-ground thy corse.
Gui. Prithee, have done,
And do not play in wench-like words with that
Which is so serious."

Imogen herself, afterwards, in deeper passion, will give weeds —not flowers,—and something more:

"And when
With wildwood leaves and weeds, I have strewed his grave,
And on it said a century of prayers,
Such as I can, twice o'er, I'll weep, and sigh,
And, leaving so his service, follow you."
(*Cymbeline,* IV, 2.)

only painted human nature as he saw it in his own time. They will find, if they look into his work closely, as much antiquarianism as they do geography, and no more. The commonly received notions about the things that had been, Shakespeare took as he found them, animating them with pure human nature, of any time and all time; but inquiries into the minor detail of temporary feeling, he despised as utterly as he did maps; and wheresoever the temporary feeling was in anywise contrary to that of his own day, he errs frankly, and paints from his own time. For instance in this matter of love of flowers; we have traced already, far enough for our general purposes, the mediæval interest in them, whether to be enjoyed in the fields, or to be used for types of ornamentation in dress. If Shakespeare had cared to enter into the spirit even of the early fifteenth century, he would assuredly have marked this affection in some of his knights, and indicated even then, in heroic tempers, the peculiar respect for loveliness of *dress* which we find constantly in Dante. But he could not do this; he had not seen it in real life. In his time dress had become an affectation and absurdity. Only fools, or wise men in their weak moments, showed much concern about it; and the facts of human nature which appeared to him general in the matter were the soldier's disdain, and the coxcomb's care of it. Hence Shakespeare's good soldier is almost always in plain or battered armour; even the speech of Vernon in Henry the Fourth,[1] which, as far as I remember, is the only one that bears fully upon the beauty of armour, leans more upon the spirit and hearts of men—"bated, like eagles having lately bathed"; and has an under-current of slight contempt running through the following line, "Glittering in golden coats, *like images*"; while the beauty of the young Harry is essentially the beauty of fiery and perfect youth, answering as much to the Greek, or Roman, or Elizabethan knight as to the mediæval one; whereas the definite interest in armour and dress is opposed by Shakespeare in the French

[1] 1 *Henry IV*, IV, 1.

(meaning to depreciate them), to the English rude soldierliness:

Con. Tut, I have the best armour in the world. Would it were day!
Orl. You have an excellent armour, but let my horse have his due.

And again:

My lord constable, the armour that I saw in your tent to-night, are those stars, or suns, upon it?

while Henry, half proud of his poorness of array, speaks of armorial splendour scornfully; the main idea being still of its being a gilded show and vanity—

Our gayness and our *gilt* are all besmirched.[2]

This is essentially Elizabethan. The quarterings on a knight's shield, or the inlaying of his armour, would never have been thought of by him as mere "gayness or gilt" in earlier days.* In like manner, throughout every scale of rank or feeling, from that of the French knights down to Falstaff's "I looked he should have sent me two-and-twenty yards of satin, as I am true knight, and he sends me security!"[3] care for dress is always considered by Shakespeare as contemptible; and Mrs Quickly distinguishes herself from a true fairy by her solicitude to scour the *chairs of order*—and "each fair instalment, coat, and several crest";[4] and the association in her mind of the flowers in the fairy rings with the

* If the reader thinks that in Henry the Fifth's time the Elizabethan temper might already have been manifesting itself, let him compare the English herald's speech, act 2 scene 2 of King John; and by way of specimen of Shakespeare's historical care, or regard of mediæval character, the large use of *artillery* in the previous scene.

[2] *Henry V*, III, 7; IV, 3.
[3] 2 *Henry IV*, I, 2.
[4] *Merry Wives of Windsor*, V, 5.

Sapphire, pearl, and rich embroidery,
Buckled below fair knighthood's bending knee;

while the true fairies, in field simplicity, are only anxious to "sweep the dust behind the door"; and

With this field dew consecrate,
Every several chamber bless
Through this palace with sweet peace.[5]

Note the expression "Field dew consecrate". Shakespeare loved courts and camps; but he felt that sacredness and peace were in the dew of the Fields only.

There is another respect in which he was wholly incapable of entering into the spirit of the Middle Ages. He had no great art of any kind around him in his own country, and was, consequently, just as powerless to conceive the general influence of former art, as a man of the most inferior calibre. Shakespeare's evidence in matters of art is as narrow as the range of Elizabethan art in England, and resolves itself wholly into admiration of two things,—mockery of life, as in the instance of Hermione as a statue, or absolute splendour, as in the close of *Romeo and Juliet,* where the notion of *gold* as the chief source of dignity of aspect, coming down to Shakespeare from the times of the Field of the Cloth of Gold, and, as I said before, strictly Elizabethan, would interfere seriously with the pathos of the whole passage, but for the sense of sacrifice implied in it:

As *rich* shall Romeo by his lady lie
Poor sacrifices of our enmity.[6]

And observe, I am not giving these examples as proof of any smallness in Shakespeare, but of his greatness; that is to say, of his contentment, like every other great man who ever breathed, to paint nothing but *what he saw;* and therefore giving perpetual evidence that his sight was of the sixteenth, and not of the thirteenth century, be-

[5] *Midsummer Night's Dream,* v, 2.
[6] *Romeo and Juliet,* v, 3.

neath all the broad and eternal humanity of his imagination. How far in these modern days, emptied of splendour, it may be necessary for great men having certain sympathies for those earlier ages, to act in this differently from all their predecessors; and how far they may succeed in the resuscitation of the past by habitually dwelling in all their thoughts among vanished generations, are questions, of all practical and present ones concerning art, the most difficult to decide; for already in poetry several of our truest men have set themselves to this task, and have indeed put more vitality into the shadows of the dead than most others can give the presences of the living. Thus Longfellow, in the *Golden Legend,* has entered more closely into the temper of the Monk, for good and for evil, than ever yet theological writer or historian, though they may have given their life's labour to the analysis: and, again, Robert Browning is unerring in every sentence he writes of the Middle Ages; always vital, right, and profound; so that in the matter of art, with which we have been specially concerned, there is hardly a principle connected with the mediæval temper, that he has not struck upon in those seemingly careless and too rugged rhymes of his. There is a curious instance, by the way, in a short poem referring to this very subject of tomb and image sculpture; and illustrating just one of those phases of local human character which, though belonging to Shakespeare's own age, he never noticed, because it was specially Italian and un-English; connected also closely with the influence of mountains on the heart, and therefore with our immediate inquiries. I mean the kind of admiration with which a southern artist regarded the *stone* he worked in; and the pride which populace or priest took in the possession of precious mountain substance, worked into the pavements of their cathedrals, and the shafts of their tombs.

Observe, Shakespeare, in the midst of architecture and tombs of wood, or freestone, or brass, naturally thinks of *gold* as the best enriching and ennobling substance for them;[7]—in the midst also of the fever of the Renaissance he writes, as every one else did, in praise of precisely the most vicious master of that school—Giulio Romano,[8] but the modern poet, living much in Italy, and quit of the Renaissance influence, is able fully to enter into the Italian feeling, and to see the evil of the Renaissance tendency, not because he is greater than Shakespeare, but because he is in another element, and has *seen* other things. I miss fragments here and there not needed for my purpose in the passage quoted, without putting asterisks, for I weaken the poem enough by the omissions, without spoiling it also by breaks.

"The Bishop orders his tomb in St Praxed's Church

As here I lie
In this state chamber, dying by degrees,
Hours, and long hours, in the dead night, I ask
Do I live—am I dead? Peace, peace seems all:
St Praxed's ever was the church for peace.
And so, about this tomb of mine. I fought
With tooth and nail to save my niche, ye know;
Old Gandolf[9] cozened me, despite my care.
Shrewd was that snatch from out the corner south
He graced his carrion with.
Yet still my niche is not so cramped but thence
One sees the pulpit o' the epistle side,
And somewhat of the choir, those silent seats;
And up into the aery dome where live
The angels, and a sunbeam's sure to lurk.
And I shall fill my slab of basalt there,
And 'neath my tabernacle take my rest,
With those nine columns round me, two and two,
The odd one at my feet, where Anselm[10] stands;
Peach-blossom marble all.
Swift as a weaver's shuttle fleet our years:

[7] Vide *Romeo and Juliet,* v, 3, line 299.
[8] Vide *Winter's Tale,* v, 2.
[9] The last bishop.
[10] His favourite son; nominally his nephew.

Man goeth to the grave, and where is he?
Did I say basalt for my slab, sons? Black—
'Twas ever antique-black I meant! How else
Shall ye contrast my frieze to come beneath?
The bas-relief in bronze ye promised me,
Those Pans and Nymphs ye wot of, and perchance
Some tripod, thyrsus, with a vase or so,
The Saviour at his sermon on the mount,
St Praxed in a glory, and one Pan,
And Moses with the tables . . . but I know
Ye mark me not! What do they whisper thee,
Child of my bowels, Anselm? Ah, ye hope
To revel down my villas while I gasp,
Bricked o'er with beggar's mouldy travertine,
Which Gandolf from his tomb-top chuckles at!
Nay, boys, ye love me—all of jasper, then!
There's plenty jasper somewhere in the world—
And have I not St Praxed's ear to pray
Horses for ye, and brown Greek manuscripts?
That's if ye carve my epitaph aright,
Choice Latin, picked phrase, Tully's every word,
No gaudy ware like Gandolf's second line—
Tully, my masters? Ulpian serves *his* need."

I know no other piece of modern English, prose or poetry, in which there is so much told, as in these lines, of the Renaissance spirit,—its worldliness, inconsistency, pride, hypocrisy, ignorance of itself, love of art, of luxury, and of good Latin. It is nearly all that I said of the central Renaissance in thirty pages of the *Stones of Venice* put into as many lines, Browning's being also the antecedent work. The worst of it is that this kind of concentrated writing needs so much *solution* before the reader can fairly get the good of it, that people's patience fails them, and they give the thing up as insoluble; though, truly, it ought to be to the current of common thought like Saladin's talisman, dipped in clear water, not soluble altogether, but making the element medicinal.[11]

[11] Vide Scott: *Talisman,* I, 8–9.

It is interesting, by the way, with respect to this love of stones in the Italian mind, to consider the difference necessitated in the English temper merely by the general domestic use of wood instead of marble. In that old Shakespearian England, men must have rendered a grateful homage to their oak forests, in the sense of all that they owed to their goodly timbers in the wainscot and furniture of the rooms they loved best, when the blue of the frosty midnight was contrasted, in the dark diamonds of the lattice, with the glowing brown of the warm, fire-lighted, crimson-tapestried walls. Not less would an Italian look with a grateful regard on the hill summits, to which he owed, in the scorching of his summer noonday, escape into the marble corridor or crypt palpitating only with cold and smooth variegation of the unfevered mountain veins. In some sort, as, both in our stubbornness and our comfort, we not unfitly describe ourselves typically as Hearts of Oak, the Italians might in their strange and variegated mingling of passion, like purple colour, with a cruel sternness, like white rock, truly describe themselves as Hearts of Stone.

Into this feeling about marble in domestic use, Shakespeare, having seen it even in northern luxury, could partly enter, and marks it in several passages of his Italian plays. But if the reader still doubts his limitation to his own experience in all subjects of imagination, let him consider how the removal from mountain influence in his youth, so necessary for the perfection of his lower human sympathy, prevented him from ever rendering with any force the feelings of the mountain anchorite, or indicating in any of his monks the deep spirit of monasticism. Worldly cardinals or nuncios he can fathom to the uttermost; but where, in all his thoughts, do we find St Francis, or Abbot Samson? The "Friar" of Shakespeare's plays is almost the only stage conventionalism which he admitted; generally nothing more than a weak old man, who lives in a cell, and has a rope about his waist.

While, finally, in such slight allusions as he makes to mountain scenery itself, it is very curious to observe the accurate limitation of his sympathies to such things as he had known in his youth; and his entire preference of human interest, and of courtly and kingly dignities, to the nobleness of the hills. This is most marked in *Cymbeline*, where the term "mountaineer" is, as with Dante, always one of reproach, and the noble birth of Arviragus and Guiderius is shown by their holding their mountain cave as

> A cell of ignorance; travelling abed;
> A prison for a debtor;

and themselves, educated among hills, as in all things contemptible:

> We are beastly; subtle as the fox, for prey;
> Like warlike as the wolf, for what we eat;
> Our valour is to chase what flies; our cage
> We make our choir, as doth the prisoned bird.[12]

A few phrases occur here and there which might justify the supposition that he had seen high mountains, but never implying awe or admiration. Thus Demetrius:

> These things seem *small* and *indistinguishable,*
> *Like far off mountains, turned into clouds.*[13]

"Taurus snow", and the "frosty Caucasus", are used merely as types of purity or cold; and though the avalanche is once spoken of as an image of power, it is with instantly following depreciation:

> Rush on his host, as doth the melted snow
> Upon the valleys whose low vassal seat
> The Alps doth spit, and void his rheum upon.[14]

There was only one thing belonging to hills that Shakespeare seemed to feel as noble—the pine tree, and that was because he had seen it in Warwickshire, clumps of pine occasionally rising on little sandstone mounds, as at the

[12] *Cymbeline,* III, 3.
[13] *Midsummer Night's Dream,* IV, 1.
[14] *Henry V,* III, 5.

place of execution of Piers Gaveston, above the lowland woods. He touches on this tree fondly again and again:

As rough,
Their royal blood enchafed, as the rud'st wind,
That by his top doth take the mountain pine,
And make him stoop to the vale.[15]

The strong-based promontory
Have I made shake, and by the spurs plucked up
The pine and cedar.[16]

Where note his observance of the peculiar horizontal roots of the pine, spurred as it is by them like the claw of a bird, and partly propped, as the aiguilles by those rock promontories at their bases which I have always called their spurs, this observance of the pine's strength and animal-like grasp being the chief reason for his choosing it, above other trees, for Ariel's prison. Again:

You may as well forbid the mountain pines
To wag their high tops, and to make no noise
When they are fretted with the gusts of heaven.[17]

And yet again:

But when, from under this terrestrial ball,
He fires the proud tops of the eastern pines.[18]

We may judge, by the impression which this single feature of hill scenery seems to have made on Shakespeare's mind, because he had seen it in his youth, how his whole temper would have been changed if he had lived in a more sublime country, and how essential it was to his power of contemplation of mankind that he should be removed from the sterner influences of nature. For the rest, so far as Shakespeare's work has imperfections of any kind,—the trivialness of many of his adopted plots, for

[15] *Cymbeline,* IV, 2.
[16] *Tempest,* V, 1.
[17] *Merchant of Venice,* IV, 1.
[18] *Richard II,* III, 2.

instance, and the comparative rarity with which he admits the ideal of an enthusiastic virtue arising out of principle; virtue being with him, for the most part, founded simply on the affections joined with inherent purity in his women, or on mere manly pride and honour in his men;* —in a word, whatever difference, involving inferiority, there exists between him and Dante, in his conceptions of the relation between this world and the next, we may partly trace, as we did the difference between Bacon and Pascal, to the less noble character of the scenes around

* I mean that Shakespeare almost always implies a total difference in *nature* between one human being and another; one being from the birth pure and affectionate, another base and cruel; and he displays each, in its sphere, as having the nature of dove, wolf, or lion, never much implying the government or change of nature by any external principle. There can be no question that in the main he is right in this view of human nature: still, the other form of virtue does exist occasionally, and was never, as far as I recollect, taken much note of by him. And with this stern view of humanity, Shakespeare joined a sorrowful view of Fate, closely resembling that of the ancients. He is distinguished from Dante eminently by his always dwelling on last causes instead of first causes. Dante invariably points to the moment of the soul's choice which fixed its fate, to the instant of the day when it read no farther, or determined to give bad advice about Penestrino.[19] But Shakespeare always leans on the force of Fate, as it urges the final evil; and dwells with infinite bitterness on the power of the wicked, and the infinitude of result dependent seemingly on little things. A fool brings the last piece of news from Verona, and the dearest lives of its noble houses are lost; they might have been saved if the sacristan had not stumbled as he walked. Othello mislays his handkerchief, and there remains nothing for him but death. Hamlet gets hold of the wrong foil, and the rest is silence. Edmund's runner is a moment too late at the prison, and the feather will not move at Cordelia's lips. Salisbury a moment too late at the tower, and Arthur lies on the stones dead. Goneril and Iago have on the whole, in this world, Shakespeare sees, much their own way, though they come to a bad end. It is a pin that Death pierces the king's fortress wall with; and Carelessness and Folly sit sceptred and dreadful, side by side with the pin-armed skeleton.

---

[19] *Inferno,* IV, 135; XXVII, 102.

him in his youth; and admit that, though it was necessary for his special work that he should be put, as it were, on a level with his race, on those plains of Stratford, we should see in this a proof, instead of a negation, of the mountain power over human intellect. For breadth and perfectness of condescending sight, the Shakespearian mind stands alone; but in *ascending* sight it is limited. The breadth of grasp is innate; the stoop and slightness of it were given by the circumstances of scene: and the difference between those careless masques of heathen gods, or unbelieved, though mightily conceived visions of fairy, witch, or risen spirit, and the earnest faith of Dante's vision of Paradise, is the true measure of the difference in influence between the willowy banks of Avon, and the purple hills of Arno.

Modern Painters, vol. IV, ch. XX, pars. 25–38.

THE INSPIRATION OF THE SEA

The glory of a boat is, first its steadiness of poise—its assured standing on the clear softness of the abyss; and, after that, so much capacity of progress by oar or sail as shall be consistent with this defiance of the treachery of the sea. And, this being understood, it is very notable how commonly the poets, creating for themselves an ideal of motion, fasten upon the charm of a boat. They do not usually express any desire for wings, or, if they do, it is only in some vague and half-unintended phrase, such as "flit or soar", involving wingedness. Seriously, they are evidently content to let the wings belong to Horse, or Muse, or Angel, rather than to themselves; but they all, somehow or other, express an honest wish for a Spiritual Boat. I will not dwell on poor Shelley's paper navies, and seas of quicksilver, lest we should begin to think evil of boats in general because of this traitorous one in Spezzia Bay; but it is a triumph to find the pastorally minded Wordsworth imagine no other way of visiting the stars than in a boat "no bigger than the crescent moon";[1] and to find Tennyson—although his boating, in an ordinary way, has a very marshy and punt-like character—at last, in his highest inspiration, enter in where the wind began "to sweep a music out of sheet and shroud".[2] But the chief triumph of all is in Dante. He had known all manner of travelling; had been borne through vacancy on the shoulders of chimeras, and lifted through upper heaven in the grasp of its spirits; but yet I do not remember that he ever expresses any positive *wish* on such matters, except for a boat.

[1] Prologue to *Peter Bell.*

[2] *In Memoriam,* ci.

Guido, I wish that Lapo, thou, and I,
  Led by some strong enchantment, might ascend
  A magic ship, whose charmëd sails should fly
  With winds at will where'er our thoughts might wend,
So that no change nor any evil chance
  Should mar our joyous voyage; but it might be
  That even satiety should still enhance
  Between our souls their strict community:
And that the bounteous wizard then would place
  Vanna and Bice, and our Lapo's love,
  Companions of our wandering, and would grace
With passionate talk, wherever we might rove,
Our time, and each were as content and free
As I believe that thou and I should be.[3]

And of all the descriptions of motion in the *Divina Commedia,* I do not think there is another quite so fine as that in which Dante has glorified the old fable of Charon by giving a boat also to the bright sea which surrounds the mountain of Purgatory, bearing the redeemed souls to their place of trial; only an angel is now the pilot, and there is no stroke of labouring oar, for his wings are the sails.

  My preceptor silent yet
Stood, while the brightness that we first discerned
Opened the form of wings: then, when he knew
The pilot, cried aloud, "Down, down; bend low
Thy knees; behold God's angel: fold thy hands:
Now shalt thou see true ministers indeed.
Lo! how all human means he sets at nought;
So that nor oar he needs, nor other sail
Except his wings, between such distant shores.
Lo! how straight up to heaven he holds them reared,
Winnowing the air with those eternal plumes,
That not like mortal hairs fall off or change."
  As more and more toward us came, more bright
Appeared the bird of God, nor could the eye
Endure his splendour near: I mine bent down.
He drove ashore in a small bark so swift

[3] Dante: *Sonnet to Guido Cavalcanti.*

And light, that in its course no wave it drank.
The heavenly steersman at the prow was seen,
Visibly written blessed in his looks.
Within, a hundred spirits and more there sat.[4]

I have given this passage at length, because it seems to me that Dante's most inventive adaptation of the fable of Charon to Heaven has not been regarded with the interest that it really deserves; and because, also, it is a description that should be remembered by every traveller when first he sees the white fork of the felucca sail shining on the Southern Sea. Not that Dante had ever seen such sails; his thought was utterly irrespective of the form of canvas in any ship of the period; but it is well to be able to attach this happy image to those felucca sails, as they now float white and soft above the blue glowing of the bays of Adria. Nor are other images wanting in them. Seen far away on the horizon, the Neapolitan felucca has all the aspect of some strange bird stooping out of the air and just striking the water with its claws; while the Venetian, when its painted sails are at full swell in sunshine, is as beautiful as a butterfly with its wings half-closed. There is something also in them that might remind us of the variegated and spotted angel wings of Orcagna, only the Venetian sail never looks majestic; it is too quaint and strange, yet with no peacock's pride or vulgar gaiety,—nothing of Milton's Dalilah:

So bedecked, ornate and gay
Like a stately ship
Of Tarsus, bound for the Isles
Of Javan or Gadire
With all her bravery on and tackle trim,
Sails filled and streamers waving.[5]

That description could only have been written in a time of vulgar women and vulgar vessels. The utmost vanity of dress in a woman of the fourteenth century would have

[4] *Purgatorio,* II, 25–45.
[5] *Samson Agonistes,* 712.

given no image of "sails filled or streamers waving"; nor does the look or action of a really "stately" ship ever suggest any image of the motion of a weak or vain woman. The beauties of the Court of Charles II, and the gilded galleys of the Thames, might fitly be compared; but the pomp of the Venetian fisher-boat is like neither. The sail seems dyed in its fulness by the sunshine, as the rainbow dyes a cloud; the rich stains upon it fade and reappear, as its folds swell or fall; worn with the Adrian storms, its rough woof has a kind of noble dimness upon it, and its colours seem as grave, inherent, and free from vanity as the spots of the leopard, or veins of the seashell.

Yet, in speaking of poets' love of boats, I ought to have limited the love to *modern* poets; Dante, in this respect, as in nearly every other, being far in advance of his age. It is not often that I congratulate myself upon the days in which I happen to live; but I do so in this respect, that, compared with every other period of the world, this nineteenth century (or rather, the period between 1750 and 1850) may not improperly be called the Age of Boats; while the classic and chivalric times, in which boats were partly dreaded, partly despised, may respectively be characterised, with regard to their means of locomotion, as the Age of Chariots, and the Age of Horses.

It is very interesting to note how repugnant every oceanic idea appears to be to the whole nature of our principal English mediæval poet, Chaucer. Read first the *Man of Lawe's Tale,* in which the Lady Constance is continually floated up and down the Mediterranean, and the German Ocean, in a ship by herself; carried from Syria all the way to Northumberland, and there wrecked upon the coast; thence yet again driven up and down among the waves for five years, she and her child; and yet, all this while, Chaucer does not let fall a single word descriptive of the sea, or express any emotion whatever about it, or about the ship. He simply tells us the lady sailed here and was wrecked there; but neither he nor his audience appear to be capable of receiving any sensation, but one of simple aversion, from waves, ships, or sands. Compare with his absolutely apathetic recital, the description by a modern poet of the sailing of a vessel, charged with the fate of another Constance:

> It curled not Tweed alone, that breeze—
> For far upon Northumbrian seas
>   It freshly blew, and strong;
> Where from high Whitby's cloistered pile,
> Bound to St Cuthbert's holy isle,
>   It bore a bark along.
> Upon the gale she stooped her side,
> And bounded o'er the swelling tide
>   As she were dancing home.
> The merry seamen laughed to see
> Their gallant ship so lustily
>   Furrow the green sea foam.[6]

Now just as Scott enjoys this sea breeze, so does Chaucer the soft air of the woods; the moment the older poet lands, he is himself again, his poverty of language in speaking of the ship is not because he despises description, but because he has nothing to describe. Hear him upon the ground in Spring:

> These woodes else recoveren greene,
> That drie in winter ben to sene,
> And the erth waxeth proud withall,
> For sweet dewes that on it fall,
> And the poore estate forget,
> In which that winter had it set:
> And than becomes the ground so proude,
> That it wol have a newe shroude,
> And maketh so queint his robe and faire,
> That it had hewes an hundred paire,
> Of grasse and floures, of Inde and Pers,
> And many hewes full divers:
> That is the robe I mean ywis,
> Through which the ground to praisen is.[7]

[6] *Marmion*, II, 1.
[7] *Romaunt of the Rose*, 57–70.

In like manner, wherever throughout his poems we find Chaucer enthusiastic, it is on a sunny day in the "good greenwood", but the slightest approach to the sea-shore makes him shiver; and his antipathy finds at last positive expression, and becomes the principal foundation of the Frankeleine's Tale, in which a lady, waiting for her husband's return in a castle by the sea, behaves and expresses herself as follows:—

> Another time ther wold she sit and thinke,
> And cast her eyen dounward fro the brinke;
> But whan she saw the grisly rockes blake,
> For veray fere so wold hire herte quake
> That on hire feet she might hire not sustene
> Than wold she sit adoun upon the grene,
> And pitously into the see behold,
> And say right thus, with sorweful sighes cold.
> "Eterne God, that thurgh thy purveance
> Ledest this world by certain governance,
> In idel, as men sain, ye nothing make.
> *But, lord, thise grisly fendly rockes blake,*
> *That semen rather a foule confusion*
> *Of werk, than any faire creation*
> Of swiche a parfit wise God and stable,
> Why han ye wrought this werk unresonable?"[8]

The desire to have the rocks out of her way is indeed severely punished in the sequel of the tale; but it is not the less characteristic of the age, and well worth meditating upon, in comparison with the feelings of an unsophisticated modern French or English girl among the black rocks of Dieppe or Ramsgate.

On the other hand, much might be said about that peculiar love of *green fields and birds* in the Middle Ages; and of all with which it is connected, purity and health in manners and heart, as opposed to the too frequent condition of the modern mind—

[8] *Frankeleines Tale,* 129–144.

As for the birds in the thicket,
Thrush or ousel in leafy niche,
Linnet or finch—she was far too rich
To care for a morning concert to which
She was welcome, without a ticket.[9]

But this would lead us far afield, and the main fact I have to point out to the reader is the transition of human grace and strength from the exercises of the land to those of the sea in the course of the last three centuries.

Harbours of England, Introduction.

[9] Thomas Hood: *Miss Kilmansegg and her Precious Leg.*

INVENTION (1)

Men in their several professed employments, looked at broadly, may be properly arranged under five classes:—

1. Persons who see. These, in modern language, are sometimes called sight-seers, that being an occupation coming more and more into vogue every day. Anciently they used to be called, simply, seers.

2. Persons who talk. These, in modern language, are usually called talkers, or speakers, as in the House of Commons, and elsewhere. They used to be called prophets.

3. Persons who make. These, in modern language, are usually called manufacturers. Anciently they were called poets.

4. Persons who think. There seems to be no very distinct modern title for this kind of person, anciently called philosophers; nevertheless we have a few of them among us.

5. Persons who do: in modern language, called practical persons; anciently, believers.

Modern Painters, vol. v, Pt. VIII, Ch. 1, par. 14.

INVENTION (2)

A poet, or creator, is therefore a person who puts things together, not as a watchmaker steel, or a shoemaker leather, but who puts life into them.

His work is essentially this: it is the gathering and arranging of material by imagination, so as to have in it at least the harmony or helpfulness of life, and the passion or emotion of life. Mere fitting and adjustment of material is nothing; that is watchmaking. But helpful and passionate harmony, essentially choral harmony, so called from the Greek word "rejoicing", is the harmony of Apollo and the Muses; the word Muse and Mother being derived from the same root, meaning "passionate seeking", or love, of which the issue is passionate finding, or sacred INVENTION.

Modern Painters, vol. v, Pt. VIII, Ch. 1, par. 20.

THE TRAGEDIANS AND HOMER

The ruling purpose of Greek poetry is the assertion of victory, by heroism, over fate, sin, and death. The terror of these great enemies is dwelt upon chiefly by the tragedians. The victory over them, by Homer.

The adversary chiefly contemplated by the tragedians is Fate, or predestinate misfortune. And that under three principal forms.

(A) Blindness or ignorance; not in itself guilty, but inducing acts which otherwise would have been guilty; and leading, no less than guilt, to destruction.*

(B) Visitation upon one person of the sin of another.

(C) Repression by brutal, or tyrannous strength, of a benevolent will.

In all these cases sorrow is much more definitely con-

* The speech of Achilles to Priam expresses this idea of fatality and submission clearly, there being two vessels—one full of sorrow, the other of great and noble gifts (a sense of disgrace mixing with that of sorrow, and of honour with that of joy), from which Jupiter pours forth the destinies of men; the idea partly corresponding to the scriptural—"In the hand of the Lord there is a cup, and the wine is red; it is full mixed, and He poureth out of the same."[1] But the title of the gods, nevertheless, both with Homer and Hesiod, is given not from the cup of sorrow, but of good: "givers of good" (δωτῆρες ἐάων). —Hes. *Theog.* 664; *Odyss.* VIII, 325.

[1] *Iliad,* XXIV, 527 *seq.; Psalm* LXXV, 8.

nected with sin by the Greek tragedians than by Shakespeare. The "fate" of Shakespeare is, indeed, a form of blindness, but it issues in little more than haste or indiscretion. It is, in the literal sense, "fatal", but hardly criminal.

The "I am fortune's fool" of Romeo,[2] expresses Shakespeare's primary idea of tragic circumstance. Often his victims are entirely innocent, swept away by mere current of strong encompassing calamity (Ophelia, Cordelia, Arthur, Queen Katherine). This is rarely so with the Greeks. The victim may indeed be innocent, as Antigone, but is in some way resolutely entangled with crime, and destroyed by it, as if it struck by pollution, no less than participation.

The victory over sin and death is therefore also with the Greek tragedians more complete than with Shakespeare. As the enemy has more direct moral personality, —as it is sinfulness more than mischance, it is met by a higher moral resolve, a greater preparation of heart, a more solemn patience and purposed self-sacrifice. At the close of a Shakespeare tragedy, nothing remains but dead march and clothes of burial. At the close of a Greek tragedy there are far-off sounds of a divine triumph, and a glory as of resurrection.*

The Homeric temper is wholly different. Far more tender, more practical, more cheerful; bent chiefly on present things and giving victory now, and here, rather than in hope, and hereafter. The enemies of mankind, in Homer's conception, are more distinctly conquerable; they are ungoverned passions, especially anger, and unreasonable impulse generally (ἀτή). Hence the anger of Achilles, misdirected by pride, but rightly directed by friendship, is the subject of the *Iliad.* The anger of Ulysses ('Οδυσσεὺς, "the angry"), misdirected at first into idle and irregular hostilities, directed at last to execution of sternest justice, is the subject of the *Odyssey.*

* The *Alcestis* is perhaps the central example of the *idea* of all Greek drama.

2 *Romeo and Juliet,* III, 1.

Though this is the central idea of the two poems, it is connected with general display of the evil of all unbridled passions, pride, sensuality, indolence, or curiosity. The pride of Atrides, the passion of Paris, the sluggishness of Elpenor, the curiosity of Ulysses himself about the Cyclops, the impatience of his sailors in untying the winds, and all other faults or follies down to that—(evidently no small one in Homer's mind)—of domestic disorderliness, are throughout shown in contrast with conditions of patient affection and household peace.

Also, the wild powers and mysteries of Nature are in the Homeric mind among the enemies of man; so that all the labours of Ulysses are an expression of the contest of manhood, not only with its own passions or with the folly of others, but with the merciless and mysterious powers of the natural world.[3]

This is perhaps the chief signification of the seven years' stay with Calypso, "the concealer". Not, as vulgarly thought, the concealer of Ulysses, but the great concealer—the hidden power of natural things. She is the daughter of Atlas and the Sea, (Atlas, the sustainer of heaven, and the Sea, the disturber of the Earth). She dwells in the island of Ogygia ("the ancient or venerable"). (Whenever Athens, or any other Greek city, is spoken of with any peculiar reverence, it is called "Ogygian".[4]) Escaping from this goddess of secrets, and from other spirits, some of destructive natural force (Scylla), others signifying the enchantment of mere natural beauty (Circe, daughter of the Sun and Sea), he arrives at last at the Phæacian land, whose king is "strength with intellect", and whose queen, "virtue".[5] These restore him to his country.

Now observe that in their dealing with all these subjects the Greeks never shrink from horror; down to its ut-

[3] Vide *Odyssey*, x, 266; viii, 166; xix, 479.

[4] Vide Aeschylus, *Pers.* 37 and 974; and Sophocles, *Œd. Col.* 1770.

[5] *Odyssey*, vii.

termost depth, to its most appalling physical detail, they strive to sound the secrets of sorrow. For them there is no passing by on the other side, no turning away the eyes to vanity from pain. Literally, they have not "lifted up their souls unto vanity". Whether there be consolation for them or not, neither apathy nor blindness shall be their saviour; if, for them, thus knowing the facts of the grief of earth, any hope, relief, or triumph may hereafter seem possible,—well; but if not, still hopeless, reliefless, eternal, the sorrow shall be met face to face. This Hector, so righteous, so merciful, so brave, has, nevertheless, to look upon his dearest brother in miserablest death. His own soul passes away in hopeless sobs through the throat-wound of the Grecian spear. That is one aspect of things in this world, a fair world truly, but having, among its other aspects, this one, highly ambiguous.

Meeting it boldly as they may, gazing right into the skeleton face of it, the ambiguity remains; nay, in some sort gains upon them. We trusted in the gods;—we thought that wisdom and courage would save us. Our wisdom and courage themselves deceive us to our death. Athena had the aspect of Deiphobus—terror of the enemy. She has not terrified him, but left us, in our mortal need.[6]

And beyond that mortality, what hope have we? Nothing is clear to us on that horizon, nor comforting. Funeral honours; perhaps also rest; perhaps a shadowy life—artless, joyless, loveless. No devices in that darkness of the grave, nor daring, nor delight. Neither marrying nor giving in marriage, nor casting of spears, nor rolling of chariots, nor voice of fame. Lapped in pale Elysian mist, chilling the forgetful heart and feeble frame, shall we waste on for ever? Can the dust of earth claim more of immortality than this? Or shall we have even so much as rest? May we, indeed, lie down again in the dust: or have not our sins hidden from us even the things that belong to that peace? May not chance and the whirl of passion govern us

[6] Vide *Iliad,* XXII, 226 *seq.*

there: when there shall be no thought, nor work, nor wisdom, nor breathing of the soul?*

Be it so. With no better reward, no brighter hope, we will be men while we may: men, just, and strong, and fearless, and up to our power, perfect. Athena herself, our wisdom and our strength, may betray us:—Phœbus, our sun, smite us with plague, or hide his face from us helpless;—Jove and all the powers of fate oppress us, or give us up to destruction. While we live, we will hold fast our integrity; no weak tears shall blind us, no untimely tremors abate our strength of arm nor swiftness of limb. The gods have given us at least this glorious body and this righteous conscience; these will we keep bright and pure to the end. So may we fall to misery, but not to baseness; so may we sink to sleep, but not to shame.

And herein was conquest. So defied, the betraying and accusing shadows shrank back; the mysterious horror subdued itself to majestic sorrow. Death was swallowed up in victory. Their blood, which seemed to be poured out upon the ground, rose into hyacinthine flowers. All the beauty of earth opened to them; they had ploughed into its darkness, and they reaped its gold; the gods, in whom they had trusted through all semblance of oppression, came down to love them and be their helpmates. All nature round them became divine,—one harmony of power and peace. The sun hurt them not by day, nor the moon by night; the earth opened no more her jaws into the pit: the sea whitened no more against them the teeth of his devouring waves. Sun, and moon, and earth, and sea,—all melted into grace and love; the fatal arrows rang not now at the shoulders of Apollo, the healer; lord of life, and of the three great spirits of life—Care, Memory, and Melody. Great Artemis guarded their flocks by night; Selene kissed in love the eyes of those who slept. And from all came the help of heaven to body and soul; a strange spirit lifting the lovely limbs; strange light glowing on the golden

* τῷ καὶ τεθνειῶτι νόον πόρε Περσεφόνεια,
οἴῳ πεπνύσθαι· τοὶ δὲ σκιαὶ ἀίσσουσιν. *Od.* x, 495.

hair; and strangest comfort filling the trustful heart, so that they could put off their armour, and lie down to sleep, —their work well done, whether at the gates of their temples[7] or of their mountains;[8] accepting the death they once thought terrible, as the gift of Him who knew and granted what was best.

Modern Painters, vol. v, Pt. IX, Ch. II, pars. 14–20.

MYTH OF THE HESPERIDES

The fable of the Hesperides had, it seems to me, in the Greek mind two distinct meanings; the first referring to natural phenomena, and the second to moral. The natural meaning of it I believe to have been this:—

The Garden of the Hesperides was supposed to exist in the westernmost part of the Cyrenaica; it was generally the expression for the beauty and luxuriant vegetation of the coast of Africa in that district. The centre of the Cyrenaica "is occupied by a moderately elevated table-land, whose edge runs parallel to the coast, to which it sinks down in a succession of terraces, clothed with verdure, intersected by mountain-streams running through ravines filled with the richest vegetation; well watered by frequent rains, exposed to the cool sea-breeze from the north, and sheltered by the mass of the mountain from the sands and hot winds of the Sahara."*

The Greek colony of Cyrene itself was founded ten miles from the sea-shore, "in a spot backed by the mountains on the south, and thus sheltered from the fiery blasts

* Smith's *Dictionary of Greek and Roman Geography.* Art. "Cyrenaica."

---

[7] οὐκέτι ἀνέστησαν, ἀλλ' ἐν τέλει τούτῳ ἔσχοντο. Herod. I, 31.

[8] ὁ δὲ ἀποπεμπόμενος, αὐτὸς μὲν οὐκ ἀπελίπετο· τὸν δὲ παῖδα συστρατευόμενον ἐόντα οἱ μουνογενέα, ἀπέπεμψε. Herod. VII, 221.

of the desert; while at the height of about 1,800 feet an inexhaustible spring bursts forth amidst luxuriant vegetation, and pours its waters down to the Mediterranean through a most beautiful ravine."

The nymphs of the west, or Hesperides, are, therefore, I believe, as natural types, the representatives of the soft western winds and sunshine, which were in this district most favourable to vegetation. In this sense they are called daughters of Atlas and Hesperis, the western winds being cooled by the snow of Atlas.[1] The dragon, on the contrary, is the representative of the Sahara wind, or Simoom, which blew over the garden from above the hills on the south, and forbade all advance of cultivation beyond their ridge. Whether this was the physical meaning of the tradition in the Greek mind or not, there can be no doubt of its being Turner's first interpretation of it. A glance at the picture may determine this: a clear fountain being made the principal object in the foreground,—a bright and strong torrent in the distance,—while the dragon, wrapped in flame and whirlwind, watches from the top of the cliff.

But, both in the Greek mind and in Turner's, this natural meaning of the legend was a completely subordinate one. The moral significance of it lay far deeper. In the second, but principal sense, the Hesperides were not daughters of Atlas, nor connected with the winds of the west, but with its splendour. They are properly the nymphs of the sunset, and are the daughters of night, having many brothers and sisters, of whom I shall take Hesiod's account.[2]

"And the Night begat Doom, and short-withering Fate, and Death.

"And begat Sleep, and the company of Dreams, and Censure, and Sorrow.

"And the Hesperides, who keep the golden fruit beyond the mighty Sea.

[1] See Diodorus Siculus, iv. 27.

[2] *Theogony,* 211 *seq.*

"And the Destinies, and the Spirits of merciless punishment.

"And Jealousy, and Deceit, and Wanton Love; and Old Age, that fades away; and Strife, whose will endures."

We have not, I think, hitherto quite understood the Greek feeling about those nymphs and their golden apples, coming as a light in the midst of a cloud;—between Censure, and Sorrow,—and the Destinies. We must look to the precise meaning of Hesiod's words, in order to get the force of the passage.

"The night begat Doom"; that is to say, the doom of unforeseen accident—doom essentially of darkness.

"And short-withering Fate." Ill translated. I cannot do it better. It means especially the sudden fate which brings untimely end to all purpose, and cuts off youth and its promise: called, therefore (the epithet hardly ever leaving it), "black Fate."

"And Death." This is the universal, inevitable death, opposed to the interfering, untimely death. These three are named as the elder children. Hesiod pauses, and repeats the word "begat" before going on to number the others.

"And begat Sleep, and the Company of Dreams."

"And *Censure*." "Momus," the Spirit of Blame—the spirit which desires to blame rather than to praise;—false, base, unhelpful, unholy judgment;—ignorant and blind, child of the Night.

"And Sorrow." Accurately, sorrow of mourning; the sorrow of the night when no man can work: of the night that falls when what was the light of the eyes is taken from us; lamenting, sightless sorrow, without hope,—child of Night.

"And the Hesperides." We will come back to these.

"And the Destinies, and the Spirits of Merciless Punishment." These are the great Fates which have rule over conduct; the first fate spoken of (short-withering) is that which has rule over occurrence. These great Fates are Clotho, Lachesis, Atropos. Their three powers are,—

Clotho's over the clue, the thread, or connecting energy, —that is, the conduct of life; Lachesis' over the lot—that is to say, the chance which warps, entangles, or bends the course of life. Atropos, inflexible, cuts the thread for ever.

"And Jealousy," especially the jealousy of Fortune, in balancing all good by evil. The Greeks had a peculiar dread of this form of fate.

"And Deceit, and sensual Love. And Old Age that fades, and Strife that endures"; that is to say, old age, which, growing not in wisdom, is marked only by its failing power—by the gradual gaining of darkness on the faculties, and helplessness on the frame. Such age is the forerunner of true death—the child of Night. "And Strife," the last and the mightiest, the nearest to man of the Night-children—blind leader of the blind.[3]

Understanding thus whose sisters they are, let us consider of the Hesperides themselves—spoken of commonly as the "Singing Nymphs."[4] They are four.[5]

Their names are, Æglé,—Brightness; Erytheia,—Blushing; Hestia,—the (spirit of the) Hearth; Arethusa,—the Ministering.

O English reader! hast thou ever heard of these fair and true daughters of Sunset, beyond the mighty sea?

And was it not well to trust to such keepers the guarding of the golden fruit which the earth gave to Juno at her marriage? Not fruit only: fruit on the tree, given by the earth, the great mother, to Juno (female power), at her marriage with Jupiter, or *ruling* manly power (distinguished from the tried and *agonizing* strength of Hercules). I call Juno, briefly, female power. She is, especially, the goddess presiding over marriage, regarding the woman as the mistress of a household. Vesta (the goddess

[3] Matthew xv. 14.

[4] So in Euripides, *Hercules Furens*, 394.

[5] Their names are given by Apollodorus, ii. 5, 11. The ordinary mythology, however, speaks of only three—Æglé, Erytheia, and Hesperethusa; so in Milton (*Comus*, 981):—

> "All amidst the gardens fair
> Of Hesperus, and his daughters three."

of the hearth*), with Ceres, and Venus, are variously dominant over marriage, as the fulfilment of love; but Juno is pre-eminently the housewives' goddess. She therefore represents, in her character, whatever good or evil may result from female ambition, or desire of power: and, as to a housewife, the earth presents its golden fruit to her, which she gives to two kinds of guardians. The wealth of the earth, as the source of household peace and plenty, is watched by the singing nymphs—the Hesperides. But, as the source of household sorrow and desolation, it is watched by the Dragon.

We must, therefore, see who the Dragon was, and what kind of dragon.

The reader will, perhaps, remember that we traced in an earlier chapter, the birth of the Gorgons, through Phorcys and Ceto, from Nereus. The youngest child of Phorcys and Ceto is the Dragon of the Hesperides;[6] but this latest descent is not, as in Northern traditions,[7] a sign of fortunateness: on the contrary, the children of Nereus receive gradually more and more terror and power, as they are later born, till this last of the Nereids unites horror and power at their utmost. Observe the gradual change. Nereus himself is said to have been perfectly *true,* and *gentle.*

This is Hesiod's account of him:—

"And Pontus begat Nereus, simple and true, the oldest of children; but they call him the aged man, in that he is

* Her name is also that of the Hesperid nymph; but I give the Hesperid her Greek form of name, to distinguish her from the goddess. The Hesperid Arethusa has the same subordinate relation to Ceres; and Erytheia, to Venus. Ægle signifies especially the spirit of brightness or cheerfulness; including even the subordinate idea of household neatness or cleanliness.

---

[6] Hesiod, *Theogony,* 334, 335: "And Ceto mingling in love with Phorcys brought forth, as youngest born, a terrible serpent which in the secret places of dark earth guards the all-golden apples," etc.

[7] See, for example, Grimm's *Fairy Tales,* often based on Scandinavian and North German legends, in which the youngest son succeeds, where his elder brothers have failed.

errorless and kind; neither forgets he what is right; but knows all just and gentle counsel."[8]

Now the children of Nereus, like the Hesperides themselves, bear a twofold typical character; one physical, the other moral. In his physical symbolism, Nereus himself is the calm and gentle sea, from which rise, in gradual increase of terror, the clouds and storms. In his moral character, Nereus is the type of the deep, pure, rightly-tempered human mind, from which, in gradual degeneracy, spring the troubling passions.

Keeping this double meaning in view, observe the whole line of descent to the Hesperides' Dragon. Nereus, by the Earth, begets (1) Thaumas (the wonderful), physically, the father of the Rainbow; morally, the type of the enchantments and dangers of imagination. His grandchildren, besides the Rainbow, are the Harpies. (2) Phorcys (Orcus?), physically, the treachery or devouring spirit of the sea; morally, covetousness or malignity of heart. (3) Ceto, physically, the deep places of the sea; morally, secretness of heart, called "fair-cheeked," because tranquil in outward aspect. (4) Eurybia (wide strength), physically, the flowing, especially the tidal power of the sea (she, by one of the sons of Heaven, becomes the mother of three great Titans,[9] one of whom, Astræus, and the Dawn, are the parents of the four Winds); morally, the healthy passion of the heart. Thus far the children of Nereus.

Next, Phorcys and Ceto, in their physical characters (the grasping or devouring of the sea, reaching out over the land, and its depth), beget the Clouds and Storms —namely, first, the Graiæ, or soft rain-clouds; then the Gorgons, or storm-clouds; and youngest and last, the Hesperides' Dragon,—Volcanic or earth-storm, associated, in conception, with the Simoom and fiery African winds.

But, in its moral significance, the descent is this. Covetousness, or malignity (Phorcys), and Secretness (Ceto), beget, first, the darkening passions, whose hair is always

[8] *Theogony*, 233–236.

[9] Hesiod, *Theogony*, 375, 378.

gray; then the stormy and merciless passions, brazen-winged (the Gorgons), of whom the dominant, Medusa, is ice-cold, turning all who look on her to stone. And, lastly, the consuming (poisonous and volcanic) passions—the "flame-backed dragon,"[10] uniting the powers of poison, and instant destruction. Now the reader may have heard, perhaps, in other books of Genesis than Hesiod's, of a dragon being busy about a tree which bore apples, and of crushing the head of that dragon; but seeing how, in the Greek mind, this serpent was descended from the sea, he may, perhaps, be surprised to remember another verse, bearing also on the matter:—"Thou brakest the heads of the dragons in the waters";[11] and yet more surprised, going on with the Septuagint version, to find where he is being led: "Thou brakest the head of the dragon, and gavest him to be meat to the Ethiopian people. Thou didst tear asunder the strong fountains and the storm-torrents; thou didst dry up the rivers of Etham," πηγὰς καὶ χειμάρρους, the Pegasus fountains—"Etham on the edge of the wilderness."

Returning then to Hesiod, we find he tells us of the Dragon himself:—"He, in the secret places of the desert land, kept the all-golden apples in his great knots" (coils of rope, or extremities of anything).[12] With which compare Euripides' report of him:—"And Hercules came to the Hesperian dome, to the singing maidens, plucking the apple-fruit from the golden petals; slaying the flame-backed dragon, who, twined round and round, kept guard in unapproachable spires"[13] (spirals or whirls, as of a whirlwind-vortex).

Farther, we hear from other scattered syllables of tra-

[10] Euripides, *Hercules Furens*, 398.

[11] Psalm lxxiv. 13, 14, 15. In the second of these verses the Septuagint has, however, "the head*s* of the dragon"; for "Etham *in* the wilderness," see Exodus xiii. 20.

[12] *Theogony*, 334, 335.

[13] *Hercules Furens*, 394–400.

dition, that this dragon was sleepless, and that he was able to take various tones of human voice.[14]

And we find a later tradition than Hesiod's calling him a child of Typhon and Echidna. Now Typhon is volcanic storm, generally the evil spirit of tumult.

Echidna (the adder) is a descendant of Medusa.[15] She is a daughter of Chrysaor (the lightning), by Callirhoë (the fair flowing), a daughter of Ocean;—that is to say, she joins the intense fatality of the lightning with perfect gentleness. In form she is half-maiden, half-serpent; therefore she is the spirit of all the fatallest evil, veiled in gentleness: or, in one word, treachery;—having dominion over many gentle things;—and chiefly over a kiss, given, indeed, in another garden than that of the Hesperides, yet in relation to keeping of treasure also.

Having got this farther clue, let us look who it is whom Dante makes the typical Spirit of Treachery. The eighth or lowest pit of hell is given to its keeping; at the edge of which pit, Virgil casts a *rope* down for a signal; instantly there rises, as from the sea, "as one returns who hath been down to loose some anchor," "the fell monster with the deadly sting, who passes mountains, breaks through fenced walls, and firm embattled spears; and with his filth taints all the world."[16]

Think for an instant of another place:—"Sharp stones are under him, he laugheth at the shaking of a spear."[17] We must yet keep to Dante, however. Echidna, remember, is half-maiden, half-serpent;—hear what Dante's Fraud is like:—

> "Forthwith that image vile of Fraud appear'd,
> His head and upper part exposed on land,
> But laid not on the shore his bestial train.

[14] Apollodorus, ii. 5, 11.

[15] Here we revert to Hesiod, who makes Chrysaor spring from Medusa, and Chrysaor, by union with Callirhoë, bear Echidna (*Theogony,* 281, 287, 295).

[16] *Inferno,* xvi. 133; xvii. 1–3 (Cary's translation, which also is followed in the next passage, *ibid.,* 7–27).

[17] Job xli. 29.

His face the semblance of a just man's wore,
So kind and gracious was its outward cheer;
The rest was serpent all: two shaggy claws
Reach'd to the armpits; and the back and breast,
And either side, were painted o'er with nodes
And orbits. Colours variegated more
Nor Turks nor Tartars e'er on cloth of state
With interchangeable embroidery wove,
Nor spread Arachne o'er her curious loom.
As oft-times a light skiff moor'd to the shore,
Stands part in water, part upon the land;
Or, as where dwells the greedy German boor,
The beaver settles, watching for his prey;
So on the rim, that fenced the sand with rock,
Sat perch'd the fiend of evil. In the void
Glancing, his tail upturn'd, its venomous fork
With sting like scorpion's arm'd."

You observe throughout this description the leaning on the character of the *Sea* Dragon; a little farther on, his way of flying is told us:—

"As a small vessel, backening out from land,
Her station quits; so thence the monster loos'd,
And, when he felt himself at large, turn'd round
There, where the breast had been, his forked tail.
Thus, like an eel, outstretch'd, at length he steer'd,
Gathering the air up with retractile claws."[18]

And, lastly, his name is told us: Geryon.[19] Whereupon, looking back to Hesiod, we find that Geryon is Echidna's brother.[20] Man-serpent, therefore, in Dante, as Echidna is woman-serpent.

We find next that Geryon lived in the island of Erytheia (blushing), only another kind of blushing than that of the Hesperid Erytheia. But it is on, also, a western island, and Geryon kept red oxen in it (said to be near

[18] *Inferno*, xvii. 100–105 (again Cary's translation).
[19] *Ibid.*, 133.
[20] *Theogony*, 287 *seq.*

the red setting sun); and Hercules kills him, as he does the Hesperian dragon: but in order to be able to reach him, a golden boat is given to Hercules by the Sun, to cross the sea in.

We will return to this part of the legend presently, having enough of it now collected to get at the complete idea of the Hesperian dragon, who is, in fine, the "Pluto il gran nemico" of Dante;[21] the demon of all evil passions connected with covetousness; that is to say, essentially of fraud, rage, and gloom. Regarded as the demon of Fraud, he is said to be descended from the viper Echidna, full of deadly cunning, in whirl on whirl; as the demon of consuming Rage from Phorcys; as the demon of Gloom, from Ceto;—in his watching and melancholy, he is sleepless (compare the Micyllus dialogue of Lucian[22]); breathing whirlwind and fire, he is the destroyer, descended from Typhon as well as Phorcys; having, moreover, with all these, the irresistible strength of his ancestral sea.

Now, look at him, as Turner has drawn him. I cannot reduce the creature to this scale without losing half his power; his length, especially, seems to diminish more than it should in proportion to his bulk. In the picture he is far in the distance, cresting the mountain; and may be, perhaps, three-quarters of a mile long. The actual length on the canvas is a foot and eight inches; so that it may be judged how much he loses by the reduction, not to speak of my imperfect etching, and of the loss which, however well he might have been engraved, he would still have sustained, in the impossibility of expressing the lurid colour of his armour, alternate bronze and blue.

Still, the main points of him are discernible enough: and among all the wonderful things that Turner did in his day, I think this nearly the most wonderful. How far he had really found out for himself the collateral bearings of the Hesperid tradition I know not; but that he had got the

21 *Inferno,* vi., last line: "Quivi trovammo Pluto il gran nemico."

22 Where the eternal disquietude of Wealth and High Estate are contrasted with the easy sleep of poverty.

main clue of it, and knew who the Dragon was, there can be no doubt; the strange thing is, that his conception of it throughout, down to the minutest detail, fits every one of the circumstances of the Greek traditions. There is, first, the Dragon's descent from Medusa and Typhon, indicated in the serpent-clouds floating from his head; then note the grovelling and ponderous body, ending in a serpent, of which we do not see the end. He drags the weight of it forward by his claws, not being able to lift himself from the ground ("Mammon, the least erected spirit that fell"[23]); then the grip of the claws themselves as if they would clutch (rather than tear) the rock itself into pieces; but chiefly, the designing of the body. Remember, one of the essential characters of the creature, as descended from Medusa, is its coldness and petrifying power; this, in the demon of covetousness, must exist to the utmost; breathing fire, he is yet himself of ice. Now, if I were merely to draw this dragon as white, instead of dark, and take his claws away, his body would become a representation of a great glacier, so nearly perfect, that I know no published engraving of glacier breaking over a rocky brow so like the truth as this dragon's shoulders[24] would be, if they were thrown out in light; there being only this difference, that they have the form, but not the fragility of the ice; they are at once ice and iron. "His bones are like solid pieces of brass; his bones are like bars of iron; by his neesings a light doth shine."[25]

The strange unity of vertebrated action, and of a true bony contour, infinitely varied in every vertebra, with this glacial outline;—together with the adoption of the head of the Ganges crocodile, the fish-eater, to show his sea

[23] *Paradise Lost*, i. 679.

[24] The resemblance of the glacier to a serpent was seized also by Shelley in his lines on "Mont Blanc," written in the Vale of Chamouni:—

"The glaciers creep
Like snakes that watch their prey, from their far fountains,
Slow rolling on."

[25] Job xli. 18.

descent (and this in the year 1806, when hardly a single fossil saurian skeleton existed within Turner's reach), renders the whole conception one of the most curious exertions of the imaginative intellect with which I am acquainted in the arts.

Thus far then, of the dragon; next, we have to examine the conception of the Goddess of Discord. We must return, for a moment, to the tradition about Geryon. I cannot yet decipher the meaning of his oxen, said to be fed together with those of Hades; nor of the journey of Hercules, in which, after slaying Geryon, he returns through Europe like a border forager, driving these herds, and led into farther battle in protection or recovery of them.[26] But it seems to me the main drift of the legend cannot be mistaken; viz., that Geryon is the evil spirit of wealth, as arising from commerce; hence, placed as a guardian of isles in the most distant sea, and reached in a golden boat; while the Hesperian dragon is the evil spirit of wealth, as possessed in households; and associated, therefore, with the true household guardians, or singing nymphs. Hercules (manly labour), slaying both Geryon and Ladon, presents oxen and apples to Juno who is their proper mistress; but the Goddess of Discord, contriving that one portion of this household wealth shall be ill bestowed by Paris, he, according to Coleridge's interpretation,[27] choosing pleasure instead of wisdom or power;—there issue from this evil choice the catastrophe of the Trojan war, and the wanderings of Ulysses, which are essentially, both in the *Iliad* and *Odyssey*, the troubling of household peace; terminating with the restoration of this peace by repentance and patience; Helen and Penelope seen at last sitting upon their household thrones, in the Hesperian light of age.

[26] See Apollodorus, ii. 106 *seq.*, for these legends.

[27] The editors do not find this reference in Coleridge, though he discusses the choice of Hercules (in *The Friend*, introduction to the Second Section). Probably Ruskin, recollecting that, wrote "Coleridge" by a slip for "Bacon"; the interpretation is given in *The Advancement of Learning* (i. 8, 7).

We have, therefore, to regard Discord, in the Hesperides garden, eminently as the disturber of households, assuming a different aspect from Homer's wild and fierce discord of war. They are, nevertheless, one and the same power; for she changes her aspect at will. I cannot get at the root of her name, Eris.[28] It seems to me as if it ought to have one in common with Erinnys (Fury); but it means always contention, emulation, or competition, either in mind or in words;—the final work of Eris is essentially "division," and she is herself always double-minded; shouts two ways at once (in *Iliad,* xi. 6), and wears a mantle rent in half (*Æneid,* viii. 702). Homer makes her loud-voiced,[29] and insatiably covetous. This last attribute is, with him, the source of her usual title. She is little when she first is seen, then rises till her head touches heaven.[30] By Virgil she is called mad; and her hair is of serpents, bound with bloody garlands.[31]

This is the conception first adopted by Turner, but combined with another which he found in Spenser; only note that there is some confusion in the minds of English poets between Eris (Discord) and Até (Error), who is a daughter of Discord, according to Hesiod.[32] She is properly—mischievous error, tender-footed;[33] for she does not walk on the earth, but on heads of men (*Iliad,* xix. 92); *i.e.,* not on the solid ground, but on human vain thoughts; therefore, her hair is glittering (*Iliad,* xix. 126). I think she is mainly the confusion of mind coming of pride, as Eris comes of covetousness; therefore, Homer makes her a daughter of Jove.[34] Spenser, under the name of Até, describes Eris. I referred to his account of her in my notice of the Discord on the Ducal Palace of Venice (remember the inscription there, *Discordia sum, discordans*).

[28] According to some, akin to *irasci:* the angry one.
[29] See *Iliad,* xi. 10.
[30] See *Iliad,* iv. 442, 443.
[31] *Æneid,* vi. 280.
[32] *Theogony,* 230.
[33] *Iliad,* xix. 92.
[34] *Iliad,* xix. 91.

(*Stones of Venice,* II. viii. 71.) But the stanzas from which Turner derived his conception of her are these—[35]

"Als, as she double spake, so heard she double,
With matchless eares deformed and distort,
Fild with false rumors and seditious trouble,
Bred in assemblies of the vulgar sort,
That still are led with every light report:
And as her eares, so eke her feet were odde,
And much unlike; th' one long, the other short,
And both misplast; that, when th' one forward yode,
The other backe retired and contrárie trode.

"Likewise unequall were her handës twaine;
That one did reach, the other pusht away;
That one did make, the other mard againe,
And sought to bring all things unto decay;
Whereby great riches, gathered manie a day,
She in short space did often bring to nought,
And their possessours often did dismay:
For all her studie was, and all her thought,
How she might overthrow the things that Concord wrought.

"So much her malice did her might surpas,
That even th' Almightie selfe she did maligne,
Because to man so merciful He was,
And unto all His creatures so benigne,
Sith she herself was of His grace indigne:
For all this worlds faire workmanship she tride
Unto his last confusion to bring,
And that great golden chaine quite to divide,
With which it blessed Concord hath together tide."

All these circumstances of decrepitude and distortion Turner has followed, through hand and limb, with patient care: he has added one final touch of his own. The nymph who brings the apples to the goddess, offers her one in

[35] The following stanzas are from the *Faerie Queene,* book iv. canto i. 27–29.

each hand; and Eris, of the divided mind, cannot choose.

One farther circumstance must be noted, in order to complete our understanding of the picture,—the gloom extending, not to the dragon only, but also to the fountain and the tree of golden fruit. The reason of this gloom may be found in two other passages of the authors from which Turner had taken his conception of Eris—Virgil and Spenser. For though the Hesperides in their own character, as the nymphs of domestic joy, are entirely bright (and the garden always bright around them), yet seen or remembered in sorrow, or in the presence of discord, they deepen distress. Their entirely happy character is given by Euripides:—"The fruit-planted shore of the Hesperides,—songstresses,—where the ruler of the purple lake allows not any more to the sailor his way, assigning the boundary of Heaven which Atlas holds; where the ambrosial fountains flow, and the fruitful and divine land increases the happiness of the gods."[36]

But to the thoughts of Dido, in her despair, they recur under another aspect; she remembers their priestess as a great enchantress; who *feeds the dragon* and preserves the boughs of the trees; sprinkling moist honey and drowsy poppy; who also has power over ghosts; "and the earth shakes and the forests stoop from the hills at her bidding."[37]

This passage Turner must have known well, from his continual interest in Carthage: but his diminution of the splendour of the old Greek garden was certainly caused chiefly by Spenser's describing the Hesperides fruit as growing first in the garden of Mammon:—

"There mournfull cypresse grew in greatest store
And trees of bitter gall; and heben sad;
Dead sleeping poppy; and black hellebore;
Cold coloquintida; and tetra mad;
Mortal samnitis; and cicuta bad,
With which th' unjust Atheniens made to dy

36 *Hippolytus,* 741 *seq.*
37 *Æneid,* iv. 484–486.

Wise Socrates, who, thereof quaffing glad,
Pourd out his life and last philosophy.

* * * * *

"The gardin of Prosérpina this hight:
And in the midst thereof a silver seat,
With a thick arber goodly over-dight,
In which she often usd from open heat
Herselfe to shroud, and pleasures to entreat:
Next thereunto did grow a goodly tree,
With braunches broad dispredd and body great,
Clothed with leaves, that none the wood mote see,
And loaden all with fruit as thick as it might bee.

"Their fruit were golden apples glistring bright,
That goodly was their glory to behold;
On earth like never grew, ne living wight
Like ever saw, but they from hence were sold;
For those, which Hercules with conquest bold
Got from great Atlas daughters, hence began.

* * * * *

"Here eke that famous golden apple grew,
The which emongst the gods false Até threw."[38]

There are two collateral evidences in the pictures of Turner's mind having been partly influenced by this passage. The excessive darkness of the stream,—though one of the Cyrene fountains—to remind us of Cocytus; and the breaking of the bough of the tree by the weight of its apples—not healthily, but as a diseased tree would break.

Such then is our English painter's first great religious picture; and exponent of our English faith. A sad-coloured work, not executed in Angelico's white and gold; nor in Perugino's crimson and azure; but in a sulphurous hue, as relating to a paradise of smoke. That power, it appears, on the hill-top, is our British Madonna: whom, reverently, the English devotional painter must paint, thus enthroned,

[38] *Faerie Queene,* book ii. canto vii. 52, 53, 54, 55.

with nimbus about the gracious head. Our Madonna,—or our Jupiter on Olympus,—or, perhaps, more accurately still, our unknown god, sea-born, with the cliffs, not of Cyrene, but of England, for his altar; and no chance of any Mars' Hill proclamation concerning him, "whom therefore ye ignorantly worship."[39]

This is no irony. The fact is verily so. The greatest man of our England, in the first half of the nineteenth century, in the strength and hope of his youth, perceives this to be the thing he has to tell us of utmost moment, connected with the spiritual world. In each city and country of past time, the master-minds had to declare the chief worship which lay at the nation's heart; to define it; adorn it; show the range and authority of it. Thus in Athens, we have the triumph of Pallas; and in Venice the Assumption of the Virgin; here, in England, is our great spiritual fact for ever interpreted to us—the Assumption of the Dragon. No St. George any more to be heard of; no more dragon-slaying possible: this child, born on St. George's Day, can only make manifest the dragon, not slay him, sea-serpent as he is; whom the English Andromeda, not fearing, takes for her lord. The fairy English Queen once thought to command the waves, but it is the sea-dragon now who commands her valleys; of old the Angel of the Sea ministered to them, but now the Serpent of the Sea; where once flowed their clear springs now spreads the black Cocytus pool; and the fair blooming of the Hesperid meadows fades into ashes beneath the Nereid's Guard.

Yes, Albert of Nuremberg; the time has at last come. Another nation has arisen in the strength of its Black anger; and another hand has pourtrayed the spirit of its toil. Crowned with fire, and with the wings of the bat.

Modern Painters, vol. v, ch. x, pars. 4–25.

[39] Acts xvii. 23.

THE ALLEGORY OF AVARICE

It is a strange habit of wise humanity to speak in enigmas only, so that the highest truths and usefullest laws must be hunted for through whole picture-galleries of dreams, which to the vulgar seem dreams only. Thus Homer, the Greek tragedians, Plato, Dante, Chaucer, Shakspeare, and Goethe, have hidden all that is chiefly serviceable in their work, and in all the various literature they absorbed and re-embodied, under types which have rendered it quite useless to the multitude. What is worse, the two primal declarers of moral discovery, Homer and Plato, are partly at issue; for Plato's logical power quenched his imagination, and he became incapable of understanding the purely imaginative element either in poetry or painting: he therefore somewhat overrates the pure discipline of passionate art in song and music, and misses that of meditative art. There is, however, a deeper reason for his distrust of Homer. His love of justice, and reverently religious nature, made him dread, as death, every form of fallacy; but chiefly, fallacy respecting the world to come (his own myths being only symbolic exponents of a rational hope). We shall perhaps now every day discover more clearly how right Plato was in this, and feel ourselves more and more wonderstruck that men such as Homer and Dante (and, in an inferior sphere, Milton), not to speak of the great sculptors and painters of every age, have permitted themselves, though full of all nobleness and wisdom, to coin idle imaginations of the mysteries of eternity, and guide the faiths of the families of the earth by the courses of their own vague and visionary arts: while the indisputable truths of human life and duty, respecting which they all have but one voice, lie hidden behind these veils of phantasy, unsought, and often unsuspected. I will gather carefully, out of Dante and Homer, what, in this kind, bears on our subject, in its due place; the first broad intention of their symbols may be sketched at once.

The rewards of a worthy use of riches, subordinate to other ends, are shown by Dante in the fifth and sixth orbs of Paradise; for the punishment of their unworthy use, three places are assigned; one for the avaricious and prodigal whose souls are lost (*Hell,* canto 7); one for the avaricious and prodigal whose souls are capable of purification (*Purgatory,* canto 19); and one for the usurers, of whom *none* can be redeemed (*Hell,* canto 17). The first group, the largest in all hell ("gente più che altrove troppa," compare Virgil's "quæ maxima turba"[1]), meet in contrary currents, *as the waves of Charybdis,* casting weights at each other from opposite sides. This weariness of contention is the chief element of their torture; so marked by the beautiful lines beginning "Or puoi, figliuol," etc.: (but the usurers, who made their money inactively, *sit* on the sand, equally without rest, however. "Di qua, di là, soccorrien," etc.) For it is not avarice, but *contention* for riches, leading to this double misuse of them, which, in Dante's sight, is the unredeemable sin. The place of its punishment is guarded by Plutus, "the great enemy," and "la fièra crudele,"[2] a spirit quite different from the Greek Plutus, who, though old and blind, is not cruel, and is curable, so as to become far-sighted. (οὐ τυφλὸς ἀλλ' ὀξὺ βλέπων—Plato's epithets in first book of the *Laws.*[3]) Still more does this Dantesque type differ from the resplendent Plutus of Goethe in the second part of *Faust,* who is the personified power of wealth for good or evil—not the passion for wealth; and again from the Plutus of Spenser, who is the passion of mere aggregation.[4] Dante's Plutus is specially and definitely the Spirit of Contention and Compe-

1 *Æneid,* vi. 611.

2 *Inferno,* vi., last line: "Quivi trovammo Pluto il gran nemico."

3 "Of the lesser gods the first is health, the second beauty, the third strength . . . and the fourth is wealth, not the blind god, but one who is keen of sight, and has wisdom for a companion."

4 See *The Faerie Queene,* book ii. canto vii. 24 *seq.*

tition, or Evil Commerce; because, as I showed before, this kind of commerce "makes all men strangers"; his speech is therefore unintelligible, and no single soul of all those ruined by him *has recognizable features.*[5]

On the other hand, the redeemable sins of avarice and prodigality are, in Dante's sight, those which are without deliberate or calculated operation. The lust, or lavishness, of riches can be purged, so long as there has been no servile consistency of dispute and competition for them. The sin is spoken of as that of degradation by the love of earth; it is purified by deeper humiliation—the souls crawl on their bellies; their chant is, "my soul cleaveth unto the dust."[6] But the spirits thus condemned are all recognizable, and even the worst examples of the thirst for gold, which they are compelled to tell the histories of during the night, are of men swept by the passion of avarice into violent crime, but not sold to its steady work.

The precept given to each of these spirits for its deliverance is—Turn thine eyes to the lucre (lure)[7] which the Eternal King rolls with the mighty wheels. Otherwise, the wheels of the "Greater Fortune," of which the constellation is ascending when Dante's dream begins.[8] Compare George Herbert—

> "Lift up thy head;
> Take stars for money; stars, not to be told
> By any art, yet to be purchased."[9]

And Plato's notable sentence in the third book of the *Polity:*—"Tell them they have divine gold and silver in their souls for ever; that they need no money stamped of men—neither may they otherwise than impiously mingle

[5] The reference is to the *Inferno,* vii. 53–54 ("La sconoscente vita, che i fe' sozzi, Ad ogni . . .": "the ignoble life which made them sordid now makes them unto all discernment dim").

[6] Psalms cxix. 25, quoted by Dante from the Vulgate: see *Purgatorio,* xix. 73.

[7] *Logoro* (lure) in Dante.

[8] *Purgatorio,* xix. 4–7.

[9] *The Church Porch,* xxix. Ruskin quotes from memory; the first words are "Raise thy head."

the gathering of the divine with the mortal treasure, *for through that which the law of the multitude has coined, endless crimes have been done and suffered; but in theirs is neither pollution nor sorrow.*"[10]

At the entrance of this place of punishment an evil spirit is seen by Dante, quite other than the "Gran Nemico." The great enemy is obeyed knowingly and willingly; but the spirit—feminine—and called a Siren[11]—is the "*Deceitfulness* of riches," ἀπάτη πλούτου of the Gospels,[12] winning obedience by guile. This is the Idol of riches, made doubly phantasmal by Dante's seeing her in a dream. She is lovely to look upon, and enchants by her sweet singing, but her womb is loathsome. Now, Dante does not call her one of the Sirens carelessly, any more than he speaks of Charybdis carelessly; and though he had got at the meaning of Homeric fable only through Virgil's obscure tradition of it,[13] the clue he has given us is quite enough. Bacon's interpretation, "the Sirens, *or pleasures*,"[14] which has become universal since his time, is opposed alike to Plato's meaning and Homer's. The Sirens are not pleasures, but *Desires:* in the *Odyssey* they are the phantoms of vain desire;[15] but in Plato's Vision of Destiny, phantoms of divine desire; singing each a different note on the circles of the distaff of Necessity, but forming one harmony, to which the three great Fates put words.[16] Dante, how-

[10] *Republic*, iii. 416 E.

[11] *Purgatorio*, xix. 19.

[12] Matthew xiii. 22.

[13] In *Æneid*, v. 864 *seq*.

[14] The title of ch. xxxi. in his *De Sapientia Veterum*.

[15] *Odyssey*, xii. 40–54, 153–200.

[16] *Republic*, x. 617 B.: "The spindle turns on the knees of Necessity; and on the upper surface of each circle is a Siren, who goes round with them, hymning a single sound and note. The eight together form one harmony; and round about, at equal intervals, there is another band, three in number, each sitting upon her throne: these are the Fates, daughters of Necessity, who are clothed in white raiment and have garlands upon their heads, Lachesis and Clotho and Atropos, who accompany with their voices the harmony of the Sirens—Lachesis singing of the past, Clotho of the present, Atropos of the future" (Jowett's version).

ever, adopted the Homeric conception of them,[17] which was that they were demons of the Imagination, not carnal; (desire of the eyes; not lust of the flesh;[18]) therefore said to be daughters of the Muses.[19] Yet not of the Muses, heavenly or historical, but of the Muse of pleasure; and they are at first winged, because even vain hope excites and helps when first formed; but afterwards, contending for the possession of the imagination with the Muses themselves, they are deprived of their wings.

And thus we are to distinguish the Siren power from the power of Circe, who is no daughter of the Muses, but of the strong elements, Sun and Sea;[20] her power is that of frank, and full vital pleasure, which, if governed and watched, nourishes men; but, unwatched, and having no "moly," bitterness or delay, mixed with it, turns men into beasts, but does not slay them,—leaves them, on the contrary, power of revival. She is herself indeed an Enchantress;—pure Animal life; transforming—or degrading—but always wonderful (she puts the stores on board the ship invisibly, and is gone again, like a ghost[21]); even the wild beasts rejoice and are softened around her cave; the transforming poisons she gives to men are mixed with no rich feast, but with pure and right nourishment,—Pramnian wine, cheese, and flour;[22] that is, wine, milk, and corn, the three great sustainers of life—it is their own fault if

[17] Probably, however, not consciously so; for Dante, as Ruskin has just said, seems to have been ignorant of Homer's account: see Paget Toynbee's *Dante Dictionary,* under "Sirena."

[18] Ezekiel xxiv. 16; 1 John ii. 16.

[19] Here Ruskin passes to versions of the legend later than Homer. Apollonius Rhodius (iv. 894) makes the Sirens daughters of the Muse Terpsichore; and other writers tell of a contest, on lyre and flute, between the Sirens and the Muses, in which the victors fell upon the Sirens, plucked their feathers, and wore them in token of victory (Julian, *Epist.* 41; Pausanias, ix. 34, 3).

[20] *Odyssey,* x. 138, 139. For the herb "moly" as a countercharm, see *ibid.,* 305.

[21] *Odyssey,* x. 571–574.

[22] *Odyssey,* x. 235.

these make swine of them; and swine are chosen merely as the type of consumption; as Plato's ὑῶν πόλις, in the second book of the *Polity*,[23] and perhaps chosen by Homer with a deeper knowledge of the likeness in variety of nourishment, and internal form of body.

"Et quel est, s'il vous plait, cet audacieux animal qui se permet d'être bâti au dedans comme une jolie petite fille?

"Hélas! chère enfant, j'ai honte de le nommer, et il ne faudra pas m'en vouloir. C'est . . . c'est le cochon. Ce n'est pas précisément flatteur pour vous; mais nous en sommes tout là, et si cela vous contrarie par trop, il faut aller vous plaindre au bon Dieu qui a voulu que les choses fussent arrangées ainsi: seulement le cochon, qui ne pense qu'à manger, a l'estomac bien plus vaste que nous et c'est toujours une consolation."—(*Histoire d'une Bouchée de Pain*, Lettre ix.[24])

But the deadly Sirens are in all things opposed to the Circean power. They promise pleasure, but never give it. They nourish in no wise; but slay by slow death. And whereas they corrupt the heart and the head, instead of merely betraying the senses, there is no recovery from their power; they do not tear nor scratch, like Scylla, but the men who have listened to them are poisoned, and waste away. Note that the Sirens' field is covered, not merely with the bones, but with the *skins*,[25] of those who have been consumed there. They address themselves, in the part of the song which Homer gives, not to the passions of Ulysses, but to his vanity, and the only man who ever came within hearing of them, and escaped untempted, was Orpheus, who silenced the vain imaginations by singing the praises of the gods.[26]

[23] *Republic*, 372.

[24] Jean Macé, *Histoire d'une Bouchée de Pain: lettres à une petite fille sur la vie de l'homme et des animaux*, 1861 (an English translation, by Mrs A. Gatty, was published in 1864).

[25] See *Odyssey*, xii. 46; and for the Sirens' song, *ibid.*, 184–191.

[26] See Apollodorus, i. 9, 25; and compare Apollonius Rhodius, iv. 905.

It is, then, one of these Sirens whom Dante takes as the phantasm or deceitfulness of riches; but note further, that she says it was her song that deceived Ulysses.[27] Look back to Dante's account of Ulysses' death, and we find it was not the love of money, but pride of knowledge,[28] that betrayed him; whence we get the clue to Dante's complete meaning: that the souls whose love of wealth is pardonable have been first deceived into pursuit of it by a dream of its higher uses, or by ambition. His Siren is therefore the Philotimé of Spenser, daughter of Mammon—

> "Whom all that folk with such contention
> Do flock about, my deare, my daughter is—
> Honour and dignitie from her alone
> Derived are."[29]

By comparing Spenser's entire account of this Philotimé with Dante's of the Wealth-Siren, we shall get at the full meaning of both poets; but that of Homer lies hidden much more deeply. For his Sirens are indefinite; and they are desires of any evil thing; power of wealth is not specially indicated by him, until, escaping the harmonious danger of imagination, Ulysses has to choose between two practical ways of life, indicated by the two *rocks* of Scylla and Charybdis. The monsters that haunt them are quite distinct from the rocks themselves, which, having many other subordinate significations, are in the main Labour and Idleness, or getting and spending; each with its attendant monster, or betraying demon. The rock of gaining

[27] *Purgatorio,* xix. 22: "I, from his course, Ulysses by my lay enchanted drew."

[28] *Inferno,* xxvi. 94–99:—
> "Nor fondness for my son, nor reverence
> Of my old father, nor return of love,
> That should have crown'd Penelope with joy,
> Could overcome in me the zeal I had
> To explore the world, and search the ways of life,
> Man's evil and his virtue."

[29] *The Faerie Queene,* ii. 7, 48.

has its summit in the clouds, invisible, and not to be climbed; that of spending is low, but marked by the cursed fig-tree, which has leaves, but no fruit. We know the type elsewhere;[30] and there is a curious lateral allusion to it by Dante when Jacopo di Sant' Andrea, who had ruined himself by profusion and committed suicide, scatters the leaves of the bush of Lotto degli Agli, endeavouring to hide himself among them.[31] We shall hereafter examine the type completely; here I will only give an approximate rendering of Homer's words, which have been obscured more by translation than even by tradition.[32]

"They are overhanging rocks. The great waves of blue water break round them; and the blessed Gods call them the Wanderers.

"By one of them no winged thing can pass—not even the wild doves that bring ambrosia to their father Jove—but the smooth rock seizes its sacrifice of them." (Not even ambrosia to be had without Labour. The word is peculiar—as a part of anything is offered for sacrifice; especially used of heave-offering.[33]) "It reaches the wide heaven with its top, and a dark-blue cloud rests on it, and never passes; neither does the clear sky hold it, in summer nor in harvest. Nor can any man climb it—not if he had twenty feet and hands, for it is as smooth as though it were hewn.

"And in the midst of it is a cave which is turned the way of hell. And therein dwells Scylla, whining for prey; her cry, indeed, is no louder than that of a newly-born whelp: but she herself is an awful thing—nor can any creature see her face and be glad; no, though it were a

[30] See Matthew xxi. 19; Mark xi. 13; and for the parable, Luke xiii. 6.

[31] *Inferno*, xiii. 115 *seq*.

[32] *Odyssey*, xii. 59–64. Then Ruskin omits several lines, and continues with 73–81, 85–92, 101–107.

[33] Homer's word is ἀφαιρεῖται. The word ἀφαίρεμα is used in the Septuagint (Numbers xv. 20, 21; xviii. 27; xxxi. 41) of heave-offerings (*i.e.*, in the Levitical law offerings which were heaved or elevated by the priest).

god that rose against her. For she had twelve feet, all fore-feet, and six necks, and terrible heads on them; and each has three rows of teeth, full of black death.

"But the opposite rock is lower than this, though but a bow-shot distant; and upon it there is a great fig-tree, full of leaves; and under it the terrible Charybdis sucks down the black water. Thrice in the day she sucks it down, and thrice casts it up again; be not thou there when she sucks down, for Neptune himself could not save thee."

Munera Pulveris, pars. 87–94.

SHAKESPEARE'S NAMES

Of Shakespeare's names I will afterwards speak at more length: they are curiously—often barbarously—much by Providence,—but assuredly not without Shakespeare's cunning purpose—mixed out of the various traditions he confusedly adopted, and languages which he imperfectly knew. Three of the clearest in meaning have been already noticed. Desdemona, "δυσδαιμονία", "miserable fortune", is also plain enough. Othello is, I believe, "the careful;" all the calamity of the tragedy arising from the single flaw and error in his magnificently collected strength. Ophelia, "serviceableness", the true lost wife of Hamlet, is marked as having a Greek name by that of her brother, Laertes; and its signification is once exquisitely alluded to in that brother's last word of her, where her gentle preciousness is opposed to the uselessness of the churlish clergy—"A *ministering* angel shall my sister be, when thou liest howling." Hamlet is, I believe, connected in some way with "homely", the entire event of the tragedy turning on betrayal of home duty. Hermione (ἕρμα), "pillar-like" (ἣ εἶδος ἔχε χρυσέης 'Αφροδίτης). Titania (τιτήνη), "the queen"; Benedict and Beatrice, "blessed and blessing"; Valentine and Proteus, enduring (or strong), (valens), and changeful. Iago and Iachimo have evidently the same root—probably the Spanish Iago, Jacob, "the supplanter". Leonatus, and other such names, are interpreted, or played with, in the plays themselves.

Munera Pulveris, par. 134.

MILTON'S *LYCIDAS*

Last came, and last did go,
The pilot of the Galilean lake.
Two massy keys he bore of metals twain,
(The golden opes, the iron shuts amain,)
He shook his mitred locks, and stern bespake,
"How well could I have spared for thee, young swain,
Enow of such as for their bellies' sake
Creep, and intrude, and climb into the fold!
Of other care they little reckoning make,
Than how to scramble at the shearers' feast,
And shove away the worthy bidden guest;
Blind mouths! that scarce themselves know how to hold
A sheep-hook, or have learn'd aught else, the least
That to the faithful herdman's art belongs!
What recks it them? What need they? They are sped;
And when they list, their lean and flashy songs
Grate on their scrannel pipes of wretched straw;
The hungry sheep look up, and are not fed,
But, swoln with wind, and the rank mist they draw,
Rot inwardly, and foul contagion spread;
Besides what the grim wolf with privy paw
Daily devours apace, and nothing said."[1]

Let us think over this passage, and examine its words.

First, is it not singular to find Milton assigning to St Peter, not only his full episcopal function, but the very types of it which Protestants usually refuse most passionately? His "mitred" locks! Milton was no Bishop-lover; how comes St Peter to be "mitred"? "Two massy keys he bore." Is this, then, the power of the keys claimed by the Bishops of Rome? and is it acknowledged here by Milton only in a poetical licence, for the sake of its picturesque-

[1] *Lycidas,* 108.

ness, that he may get the gleam of the golden keys to help his effect? Do not think it. Great men do not play stage tricks with the doctrines of life and death: only little men do that. Milton means what he says; and means it with his might too—is going to put the whole strength of his spirit presently into the saying of it. For though not a lover of false bishops, he *was* a lover of true ones; and the Lake-pilot is here, in his thoughts, the type and head of true episcopal power. For Milton reads that text, "I will give unto thee the keys of the kingdom of Heaven", quite honestly. Puritan though he be, he would not blot it out of the book because there have been bad bishops; nay, in order to understand *him,* we must understand that verse first; it will not do to eye it askance, or whisper it under our breath, as if it were a weapon of an adverse sect. It is a solemn, universal assertion, deeply to be kept in mind by all sects. But perhaps we shall be better able to reason on it if we go on a little farther, and come back to it. For clearly this marked insistence on the power of the true episcopate is to make us feel more weightily what is to be charged against the false claimants of episcopate; or generally, against false claimants of power and rank in the body of the clergy; they who, "for their bellies' sake, creep, and intrude, and climb into the fold".

Never think Milton uses those three words to fill up his verse, as a loose writer would. He needs all the three;—specially those three, and no more than those—"creep", and "intrude", and "climb"; no other words would or could serve the turn, and no more could be added. For they exhaustively comprehend the three classes, correspondent to the three characters, of men who dishonestly seek ecclesiastical power. First, those who "*creep*" into the fold; who do not care for office, nor name, but for secret influence, and do all things occultly and cunningly, consenting to any servility of office or conduct, so only that they may intimately discern, and unawares direct, the minds of men. Then those who "intrude" (thrust, that is) themselves into the fold, who by natural insolence of heart, and stout eloquence of tongue, and fearlessly perseverant self-assertion, obtain hearing and authority with the common crowd. Lastly, those who "climb", who, by labour and learning, both stout and sound, but selfishly exerted in the cause of their own ambition, gain high dignities and authorities, and become "lords over the heritage", though not "ensamples to the flock".

Now go on:–

> Of other care they little reckoning make,
> Than how to scramble at the shearers' feast.
> *Blind mouths*—

I pause again, for this is a strange expression; a broken metaphor, one might think, careless and unscholarly.

Not so: its very audacity and pithiness are intended to make us look close at the phrase and remember it. Those two monosyllables express the precisely accurate contraries of right character, in the two great offices of the Church–those of bishop and pastor.

A "Bishop" means "a person who sees".

A "Pastor" means "a person who feeds".

The most unbishoply character a man can have is therefore to be Blind.

The most unpastoral is, instead of feeding, to want to be fed,–to be a Mouth.

Take the two reverses together, and you have "blind mouths". We may advisably follow out this idea a little. Nearly all the evils in the Church have arisen from bishops desiring *power* more than *light*. They want authority, not outlook. Whereas their real office is not to rule; though it may be vigorously to exhort and rebuke: it is the king's office to rule; the bishop's office is to *oversee* the flock; to number it, sheep by sheep; to be ready always to give full account of it. Now it is clear he cannot give account of the souls, if he has not so much as numbered the bodies, of his flock. The first thing, therefore, that a bishop has to do is at least to put himself in a position in which, at any moment, he can obtain the history, from childhood, of every living soul in his diocese, and of its present state. Down in that back street, Bill, and Nancy, knocking each other's teeth out!—Does the bishop know all about it? Has he his eye upon them? Has he *had* his eye upon them? Can he circumstantially explain to us how Bill got into the habit of beating Nancy about the head? If he cannot, he is no bishop, though he had a mitre as high as Salisbury steeple; he is no bishop,—he has sought to be at the helm instead of the mast-head; he has no sight of things. "Nay", you say, "it is not his duty to look after Bill in the back street." What! the fat sheep that have full fleeces—you think it is only those he should look after while (go back to your Milton) "the hungry sheep look up, and are not fed, besides what the grim wolf, with privy paw" (bishops knowing nothing about it) "daily devours apace, and nothing said"?

"But that's not our idea of a bishop." Perhaps not; but it was St Paul's; and it was Milton's. They may be right, or we may be; but we must not think we are reading either one or the other by putting our meaning into their words.

I go on.

> But swoln with wind, and the rank mist they draw.

This is to meet the vulgar answer that "if the poor are not looked after in their bodies, they are in their souls; they have spiritual food".

And Milton says, "They have no such thing as spiritual food; they are only swollen with wind." At first you may think that is a coarse type, and an obscure one. But again, it is a quite literally accurate one. Take up your Latin and Greek dictionaries, and find out the meaning of "Spirit". It is only a contraction of the Latin word "breath", and an indistinct translation of the Greek word for "wind". The same word is used in writing, "The wind bloweth where it listeth"; and in writing, "So is every one that is born of the Spirit"; born of the *breath*, that is; for it means the breath of God, in soul and body. We have the true sense of it in our words "inspiration" and "expire". Now, there are two kinds of breath with which the flock may be filled,—God's breath, and man's. The breath of God is health, and life, and peace to them, as the air of heaven is to the flocks on the hills; but man's breath—the word which *he* calls spiritual—is disease and contagion to them, as the fog of the fen. They rot inwardly with it; they are puffed up by it, as a dead body by the vapours of its own decomposition. This is literally true of all false religious teaching; the first and last, and fatalest sign of it is that "puffing up". Your converted children, who teach their parents; your converted convicts, who teach honest men; your converted dunces, who, having lived in cretinous stupefaction half their lives, suddenly awaking to the fact of there being a God, fancy themselves therefore His peculiar people and messengers; your sectarians of every species, small and great, Catholic or Protestant, of high church or low, in so far as they think themselves exclusively in the right and others wrong; and pre-eminently, in every sect, those who hold that men can be saved by thinking rightly instead of doing rightly, by word instead of act, and wish instead of work;—these are the true fog children—clouds, these, without water; bodies, these, of putrescent vapour and skin, without blood or flesh: blown bag-pipes for the fiends to pipe with—corrupt, and corrupting,—"Swoln with wind, and the rank mist they draw."

Lastly, let us return to the lines respecting the power of the keys, for now we can understand them. Note the difference between Milton and Dante in their interpretation of this power: for once, the latter is weaker in thought; he supposes *both* the keys to be of the gate of heaven; one is of gold, the other of silver: they are given by St Peter to the sentinel angel; and it is not easy to determine the meaning either of the substances of the three steps of the gate, or of the two keys. But Milton makes one, of gold, the key of heaven; the other, of iron, the key of the prison in which the wicked teachers are to be bound who "have taken away the key of knowledge, yet entered not in themselves".

We have seen that the duties of bishop and pastor are to see, and feed; and of all who do so it is said, "He that watereth, shall be watered also himself." But the reverse is truth also. He that watereth not, shall be *withered* himself; and he that seeth not, shall himself be shut out of sight—shut into the perpetual prison-house. And that prison opens here, as well as hereafter: he who is to be bound in heaven must first be bound on earth. That command to the strong angels, of which the rock-apostle is the image, "Take him, and bind him hand and foot, and cast him out", issues, in its measure, against the teacher, for every help withheld, and for every truth refused, and for every falsehood enforced; so that he is more strictly fettered the more he fetters, and farther outcast as he more and more misleads, till at last the bars of the iron cage close upon him, and as "the golden opes, the iron shuts amain".

We have got something out of the lines, I think, and much more is yet to be found in them; but we have done enough by way of example of the kind of word-by-word examination of your author which is rightly called "reading"; watching every accent and expression, and putting ourselves always in the author's place, annihilating our own personality, and seeking to enter into his, so as to be able assuredly to say, "Thus Milton thought", not "Thus *I* thought, in mis-reading Milton". And by this process you will gradually come to attach less weight to your own "Thus I thought" at other times. You will begin to perceive that what *you* thought was a matter of no serious importance;—that your thoughts on any subject are not perhaps the clearest and wisest that could be arrived at thereupon:—in fact, that unless you are a very singular person, you cannot be said to have any "thoughts" at all; that you have no materials for them, in any serious matters;—no right to "think", but only to try to learn more of the facts.

Sesame and Lilies, lect. I, pars. 20–25.

LILIES OF QUEENS' GARDENS

"Be thou glad, oh thirsting Desert; let the desert be made cheerful, and bloom as the lily; and the barren places of Jordan shall run wild with wood." — ISAIAH XXXV. 1. (Septuagint).

It will, perhaps, be well, as this Lecture is the sequel of one previously given, that I should shortly state to you my general intention in both. The questions specially proposed to you in the first, namely, How and What to Read, rose out of a far deeper one, which it was my endeavour to make you propose earnestly to yourselves, namely, *Why* to Read. I want you to feel, with me, that whatever advantages we possess in the present day in the diffusion of education and of literature, can only be rightly used by any of us when we have apprehended clearly what education is to lead to, and literature to teach. I wish you to see that both well-directed moral training and well-chosen reading lead to the possession of a power over the ill-guided and illiterate, which is, according to the measure of it, in the truest sense, *kingly;* conferring indeed the purest kingship that can exist among men: too many other kingships (however distinguished by visible insignia or material power) being either spectral, or tyrannous;—spectral—that is to say, aspects and shadows only of royalty, hollow as death, and which only the "likeness of a kingly crown have on:"[1] or else—tyrannous—that is to say, substituting their own will for the law of justice and love by which all true kings rule.

There is, then, I repeat—and as I want to leave this idea with you, I begin with it, and shall end with it—only one pure kind of kingship; an inevitable and eternal kind, crowned or not; the kingship, namely, which consists in

[1] *Paradise Lost,* ii. 673.

a stronger moral state, and a truer thoughtful state, than that of others; enabling you, therefore, to guide, or to raise them. Observe that word "State"; we have got into a loose way of using it. It means literally the standing and stability of a thing; and you have the full force of it in the derived word "statue"—"the immovable thing." A king's majesty or "state," then, and the right of his kingdom to be called a state, depends on the movelessness of both: —without tremor, without quiver of balance; established and enthroned upon a foundation of eternal law which nothing can alter, nor overthrow.

Believing that all literature and all education are only useful so far as they tend to confirm this calm, beneficent, and *therefore* kingly, power—first, over ourselves, and, through ourselves, over all around us,—I am now going to ask you to consider with me farther, what special portion or kind of this royal authority, arising out of noble education, may rightly be possessed by women; and how far they also are called to a true queenly power,—not in their households merely, but over all within their sphere. And in what sense, if they rightly understood and exercised this royal or gracious influence, the order and beauty induced by such benignant power would justify us in speaking of the territories over which each of them reigned, as "Queens' Gardens."

And here, in the very outset, we are met by a far deeper question, which—strange though this may seem—remains among many of us yet quite undecided in spite of its infinite importance.

We cannot determine what the queenly power of women should be, until we are agreed what their ordinary power should be. We cannot consider how education may fit them for any widely extending duty, until we are agreed what is their true constant duty. And there never was a time when wilder words were spoken, or more vain imagination permitted, respecting this question—quite vital to all social happiness. The relations of the womanly to the manly nature, their different capacities of intellect or of virtue, seem never to have been yet estimated with entire consent. We hear of the "mission" and of the "rights" of Woman, as if these could ever be separate from the mission and the rights of Man—as if she and her lord were creatures of independent kind, and of irreconcilable claim. This, at least, is wrong. And not less wrong—perhaps even more foolishly wrong (for I will anticipate thus far what I hope to prove)—is the idea that woman is only the shadow and attendant image of her lord, owing him a thoughtless and servile obedience, and supported altogether in her weakness by the pre-eminence of his fortitude.

This, I say, is the most foolish of all errors respecting her who was made to be the helpmate of man. As if he could be helped effectively by a shadow, or worthily by a slave!

Let us try, then, whether we cannot get at some clear and harmonious idea (it must be harmonious if it is true) of what womanly mind and virtue are in power and office, with respect to man's; and how their relations, rightly accepted, aid and increase the vigour and honour and authority of both.

And now I must repeat one thing I said in the last lecture: namely, that the first use of education was to enable us to consult with the wisest and the greatest men on all points of earnest difficulty. That to use books rightly, was to go to them for help: to appeal to them, when our own knowledge and power of thought failed: to be led by them into wider sight,—purer conception,—than our own, and receive from them the united sentence of the judges and councils of all time, against our solitary and unstable opinion.

Let us do this now. Let us see whether the greatest, the wisest, the purest-hearted of all ages are agreed in any wise on this point: let us hear the testimony they have left respecting what they held to be the true dignity of woman and her mode of help to man.

And first let us take Shakespeare.

Note broadly in the outset, Shakespeare has no heroes; —he has only heroines. There is not one entirely heroic figure in all his plays, except the slight sketch of Henry the Fifth, exaggerated for the purposes of the stage; and the still slighter Valentine in *The Two Gentlemen of Verona.* In his laboured and perfect plays you have no hero. Othello would have been one, if his simplicity had not been so great as to leave him the prey of every base practice round him; but he is the only example even approximating to the heroic type. Coriolanus—Cæsar—Antony stand in flawed strength, and fall by their vanities;—Hamlet is indolent, and drowsily speculative; Romeo an impatient boy; the Merchant of Venice languidly submissive to adverse fortune; Kent, in *King Lear,* is entirely noble at heart, but too rough and unpolished to be of true use at the critical time, and he sinks into the office of a servant only. Orlando, no less noble, is yet the despairing toy of chance, followed, comforted, saved by Rosalind. Whereas there is hardly a play that has not a perfect woman in it, steadfast in grave hope, and errorless purpose: Cordelia, Desdemona, Isabella, Hermione, Imogen, Queen Catherine, Perdita, Sylvia, Viola, Rosalind, Helena, and last, and perhaps loveliest, Virgilia, are all faultless; conceived in the highest heroic type of humanity.

Then observe, secondly,

The catastrophe of every play is caused always by the folly or fault of a man; the redemption, if there be any, is by the wisdom and virtue of a woman, and, failing that, there is none. The catastrophe of King Lear is owing to his own want of judgment, his impatient vanity, his misunderstanding of his children; the virtue of his one true daughter would have saved him from all the injuries of the others, unless he had cast her away from him; as it is, she all but saves him.

Of Othello I need not trace the tale;—nor the one weakness of his so mighty love; nor the inferiority of his perceptive intellect to that even of the second woman character in the play, the Emilia who dies in wild testimony against his error:—

"Oh, murderous coxcomb! what should such a fool
Do with so good a wife?"[2]

In *Romeo and Juliet*, the wise and brave stratagem of the wife is brought to ruinous issue by the reckless impatience of her husband. In *Winter's Tale*, and in *Cymbeline*, the happiness and existence of two princely households, lost through long years, and imperilled to the death by the folly and obstinacy of the husbands, are redeemed at last by the queenly patience and wisdom of the wives. In *Measure for Measure*, the foul injustice of the judge, and the foul cowardice of the brother, are opposed to the victorious truth and adamantine purity of a woman. In *Coriolanus*, the mother's counsel, acted upon in time, would have saved her son from all evil; his momentary forgetfulness of it is his ruin; her prayer, at last granted, saves him—not, indeed, from death, but from the curse of living as the destroyer of his country.

And what shall I say of Julia, constant against the fickleness of a lover who is a mere wicked child?—of Helena, against the petulance and insult of a careless youth?—of the patience of Hero, the passion of Beatrice, and the calmly devoted wisdom of the "unlessoned girl,"[3] who appears among the helplessness, the blindness, and the vindictive passions of men, as a gentle angel, bringing courage and safety by her presence, and defeating the worst malignities of crime by what women are fancied most to fail in,—precision and accuracy of thought?

Observe, further, among all the principal figures in Shakespeare's plays, there is only one weak woman—Ophelia; and it is because she fails Hamlet at the critical moment, and is not, and cannot in her nature be, a guide to him when he needs her most, that all the bitter catastrophe follows. Finally, though there are three wicked women among the principal figures—Lady Macbeth, Regan, and Goneril—they are felt at once to be frightful ex-

[2] Act v. sc. 2, 236.

[3] Portia's description of herself: *Merchant of Venice*, iii. 2, 159.

ceptions to the ordinary laws of life; fatal in their influence also, in proportion to the power for good which they have abandoned.

Such, in broad light, is Shakespeare's testimony to the position and character of women in human life. He represents them as infallibly faithful and wise counsellors,—incorruptibly just and pure examples—strong always to sanctify, even when they cannot save.

Not as in any wise comparable in knowledge of the nature of man,—still less in his understanding of the causes and courses of fate,—but only as the writer who has given us the broadest view of the conditions and modes of ordinary thought in modern society, I ask you next to receive the witness of Walter Scott.

I put aside his merely romantic prose writings as of no value, and though the early romantic poetry is very beautiful, its testimony is of no weight, other than that of a boy's ideal. But his true works, studied from Scottish life, bear a true witness; and in the whole range of these, there are but three men who reach the heroic type*—Dandie Dinmont, Rob Roy, and Claverhouse; of these, one is a border farmer; another a freebooter; the third a soldier in a bad cause. And these touch the ideal of heroism only in their courage and faith, together with a strong, but uncultivated, or mistakenly applied, intellectual power; while his younger men are the gentlemanly playthings of fantastic fortune, and only by aid (or accident) of that fortune, survive, not vanquish, the trials they involuntarily sustain. Of any disciplined, or consistent character, earnest in a purpose wisely conceived, or dealing with forms

* I ought, in order to make this assertion fully understood, to have noted the various weaknesses which lower the ideal of other great characters of men in the Waverley novels—the selfishness and narrowness of thought in Redgauntlet, the weak religious enthusiasm in Edward Glendinning, and the like; and I ought to have noticed that there are several quite perfect characters sketched sometimes in the backgrounds; three—let us accept joyously this courtesy to England and her soldiers—are English officers: Colonel Gardiner, Colonel Talbot, and Colonel Mannering.

of hostile evil, definitely challenged and resolutely subdued, there is no trace in his conceptions of young men. Whereas in his imaginations of women,—in the characters of Ellen Douglas, of Flora MacIvor, Rose Bradwardine, Catherine Seyton, Diana Vernon, Lilias Redgauntlet, Alice Bridgenorth, Alice Lee, and Jeanie Deans,—with endless varieties of grace, tenderness, and intellectual power, we find in all a quite infallible sense of dignity and justice; a fearless, instant, and untiring self-sacrifice, to even the appearance of duty, much more to its real claims; and, finally, a patient wisdom of deeply-restrained affection, which does infinitely more than protect its objects from a momentary error; it gradually forms, animates, and exalts the characters of the unworthy lovers, until, at the close of the tale, we are just able, and no more, to take patience in hearing of their unmerited success.

So that, in all cases, with Scott as with Shakespeare, it is the woman who watches over, teaches, and guides the youth; it is never, by any chance, the youth who watches over, or educates, his mistress.

Next take, though more briefly, graver testimony—that of the great Italians and Greeks. You know well the plan of Dante's great poem—that it is a love-poem to his dead lady; a song of praise for her watch over his soul. Stooping only to pity, never to love, she yet saves him from destruction—saves him from hell. He is going eternally astray in despair; she comes down from heaven to his help, and throughout the ascents of Paradise is his teacher, interpreting for him the most difficult truths, divine and human; and leading him, with rebuke upon rebuke, from star to star.

I do not insist upon Dante's conception; if I began I could not cease: besides, you might think this a wild imagination of one poet's heart. So I will rather read to you a few verses of the deliberate writing of a knight of Pisa to his living lady, wholly characteristic of the feeling of all the noblest men of the thirteenth, or early fourteenth, century, preserved among many other such records of knightly honour and love, which Dante Rossetti has gathered for us from among the early Italian poets.[4]

"For lo! thy law is passed
That this my love should manifestly be
To serve and honour thee:
And so I do; and my delight is full,
Accepted for the servant of thy rule.

"Without almost, I am all rapturous,
Since thus my will was set
To serve, thou flower of joy, thine excellence:
Nor ever seems it anything could rouse
A pain or a regret.
But on thee dwells my every thought and sense;
Considering that from thee all virtues spread
As from a fountain head,—
That in thy gift is wisdom's best avail,
And honour without fail,
With whom each sovereign good dwells separate,
Fulfilling the perfection of thy state.

"Lady, since I conceived
Thy pleasurable aspect in my heart,
My life has been apart
In shining brightness and the place of truth;
Which till that time, good sooth,
Groped among shadows in a darken'd place,
Where many hours and days
It hardly ever had remember'd good.
But now my servitude
Is thine, and I am full of joy and rest.
A man from a wild beast
Thou madest me, since for thy love I lived."

You may think perhaps a Greek knight would have had a lower estimate of women than this Christian lover. His spiritual subjection to them was indeed not so absolute;

[4] The poem is by Pannuccio dal Bagno, Pisano: see Rossetti's *Dante and his Circle*, pp. 331–332 (ed. 1874).

but as regards their own personal character, it was only because you could not have followed me so easily, that I did not take the Greek women instead of Shakespeare's; and instance, for chief ideal types of human beauty and faith, the simple mother's and wife's heart of Andromache; the divine, yet rejected wisdom of Cassandra; the playful kindness and simple princess-life of happy Nausicaa; the housewifely calm of that of Penelope, with its watch upon the sea; the ever patient, fearless, hopelessly devoted piety of the sister, and daughter, in Antigone; the bowing down of Iphigenia, lamb-like and silent; and finally, the expectation of the resurrection, made clear to the soul of the Greeks in the return from her grave of that Alcestis, who, to save her husband, had passed calmly through the bitterness of death.

Now I could multiply witness upon witness of this kind upon you if I had time. I would take Chaucer, and show you why he wrote a Legend of Good Women; but no Legend of Good Men. I would take Spenser, and show you how all his fairy knights are sometimes deceived and sometimes vanquished; but the soul of Una is never darkened, and the spear of Britomart is never broken. Nay, I could go back into the mythical teaching of the most ancient times, and show you how the great people,—by one of whose princesses it was appointed that the Lawgiver of all the earth should be educated rather than by his own kindred;—how that great Egyptian people, wisest then of nations, gave to their Spirit of Wisdom the form of a Woman; and into her hand, for a symbol, the weaver's shuttle; and how the name and the form of that spirit, adopted, believed, and obeyed by the Greeks, became that Athena of the olive-helm, and cloudy shield, to faith in whom you owe, down to this date, whatever you hold most precious in art, in literature, or in types of national virtue.

But I will not wander into this distant and mythical element; I will only ask you to give its legitimate value to the testimony of these great poets and men of the world,—consistent, as you see it is, on this head. I will ask you whether it can be supposed that these men, in the main work of their lives, are amusing themselves with a fictitious and idle view of the relations between man and woman; —nay, worse than fictitious or idle; for a thing may be imaginary, yet desirable, if it were possible: but this, their ideal of woman, is, according to our common idea of the marriage relation, wholly undesirable. The woman, we say, is not to guide, nor even to think for herself. The man is always to be the wiser; he is to be the thinker, the ruler, the superior in knowledge and discretion, as in power.

Is it not somewhat important to make up our minds on this matter? Are all these great men mistaken, or are we? Are Shakespeare and Æschylus, Dante and Homer, merely dressing dolls for us; or, worse than dolls, unnatural visions, the realization of which, were it possible, would bring anarchy into all households and ruin into all affections? Nay, if you can suppose this, take lastly the evidence of facts, given by the human heart itself. In all Christian ages which have been remarkable for their purity or progress, there has been absolute yielding of obedient devotion, by the lover, to his mistress. I say *obedient;*—not merely enthusiastic and worshipping in imagination, but entirely subject, receiving from the beloved woman, however young, not only the encouragement, the praise, and the reward of all toil, but, so far as any choice is open, or any question difficult of decision, the *direction* of all toil. That chivalry, to the abuse and dishonour of which are attributable primarily whatever is cruel in war, unjust in peace, or corrupt and ignoble in domestic relations; and to the original purity and power of which we owe the defence alike of faith, of law, and of love; that chivalry, I say, in its very first conception of honourable life, assumes the subjection of the young knight to the command—should it even be the command in caprice—of his lady. It assumes this, because its masters knew that the first and necessary impulse of every truly taught and knightly heart is this of blind service to its lady: that where that true faith and captivity are not, all wayward and wicked passion must be; and that in this rapturous obedience to the single love of his youth, is the sanctification of all man's strength, and the continuance of all his purposes. And this, not because such obedience would be safe, or honourable, were it ever rendered to the unworthy; but because it ought to be impossible for every noble youth—it *is* impossible for every one rightly trained—to love any one whose gentle counsel he cannot trust, or whose prayerful command he can hesitate to obey.

I do not insist by any farther argument on this, for I think it should commend itself at once to your knowledge of what has been and to your feeling of what should be. You cannot think that the buckling on of the knight's armour by his lady's hand was a mere caprice of romantic fashion. It is the type of an eternal truth—that the soul's armour is never well set to the heart unless a woman's hand has braced it; and it is only when she braces it loosely that the honour of manhood fails. Know you not those lovely lines—I would they were learned by all youthful ladies of England:—

> Ah, wasteful woman, she who may
> On her sweet self set her own price,
> Knowing he cannot choose but pay,
> How has she cheapen'd Paradise;
> How given for nought her priceless gift,
> How spoiled the bread and spill'd the wine,
> Which, spent with due, respective thrift,
> Had made brutes men, and men divine!*

Thus much, then, respecting the relations of lovers I believe you will accept. But what we too often doubt is the fitness of the continuance of such a relation throughout the whole of human life. We think it right in the lover and mistress, not in the husband and wife. That is to say,

* Coventry Patmore. You cannot read him too often or too carefully; as far as I know he is the only living poet who always strengthens and purifies; the others sometimes darken, and nearly always depress and discourage, the imagination they deeply seize.

we think that a reverent and tender duty is due to one whose affection we still doubt, and whose character we as yet do but partially and distantly discern; and that this reverence and duty are to be withdrawn when the affection has become wholly and limitlessly our own, and the character has been so sifted and tried that we fear not to entrust it with the happiness of our lives. Do you not see how ignoble this is, as well as how unreasonable? Do you not feel that marriage,—when it is marriage at all,—is only the seal which marks the vowed transition of temporary into untiring service, and of fitful into eternal love?

But how, you will ask, is the idea of this guiding function of the woman reconcilable with a true wifely subjection? Simply in that it is a *guiding*, not a determining, function. Let me try to show you briefly how these powers seem to be rightly distinguishable.

We are foolish, and without excuse foolish, in speaking of the "superiority" of one sex to the other, as if they could be compared in similar things. Each has what the other has not: each completes the other, and is completed by the other: they are in nothing alike, and the happiness and perfection of both depends on each asking and receiving from the other what the other only can give.

Now their separate characters are briefly these. The man's power is active, progressive, defensive. He is eminently the doer, the creator, the discoverer, the defender. His intellect is for speculation and invention; his energy for adventure, for war, and for conquest, wherever war is just, wherever conquest necessary. But the woman's power is for rule, not for battle,—and her intellect is not for invention or creation, but for sweet ordering, arrangement, and decision. She sees the qualities of things, their claims, and their places. Her great function is Praise; she enters into no contest, but infallibly adjudges the crown of contest. By her office, and place, she is protected from all danger and temptation. The man, in his rough work in open world, must encounter all peril and trial;—to him, therefore, must be the failure, the offence, the inevitable error: often he must be wounded, or subdued; often misled; and *always* hardened. But he guards the woman from all this; within his house, as ruled by her, unless she herself has sought it, need enter no danger, no temptation, no cause of error or offence. This is the true nature of home —it is the place of Peace; the shelter, not only from all injury, but from all terror, doubt, and division. In so far as it is not this, it is not home; so far as the anxieties of the outer life penetrate into it, and the inconsistently-minded, unknown, unloved, or hostile society of the outer world is allowed by either husband or wife to cross the threshold, it ceases to be home; it is then only a part of that outer world which you have roofed over, and lighted fire in. But so far as it is a sacred place, a vestal temple, a temple of the hearth watched over by Household Gods, before whose faces none may come but those whom they can receive with love,—so far as it is this, and roof and fire are types only of a nobler shade and light,—shade as of the rock in a weary land,[5] and light as of the Pharos in the stormy sea;—so far it vindicates the name, and fulfils the praise, of Home.

And wherever a true wife comes, this home is always round her. The stars only may be over her head; the glowworm in the night-cold grass may be the only fire at her foot; but home is yet wherever she is; and for a noble woman it stretches far round her, better than ceiled with cedar, or painted with vermilion,[6] shedding its quiet light far, for those who else were homeless.

This, then, I believe to be,—will you not admit it to be? —the woman's true place and power. But do not you see that, to fulfil this, she must—as far as one can use such terms of a human creature—be incapable of error? So far as she rules, all must be right, or nothing is. She must be enduringly, incorruptibly good; instinctively, infallibly wise—wise, not for self-development, but for self-renunciation: wise, not that she may set herself above her husband, but that she may never fail from his side: wise, not

[5] Isaiah xxxii. 2.
[6] Jeremiah xxii. 14.

with the narrowness of insolent and loveless pride, but with the passionate gentleness of an infinitely variable, because infinitely applicable, modesty of service—the true changefulness of woman. In that great sense—"La donna è mobile," not "Qual piúm' al vento";[7] no, nor yet "Variable as the shade, by the light quivering aspen made";[8] but variable as the *light*, manifold in fair and serene division, that it may take the colour of all that it falls upon, and exalt it.

I have been trying, thus far, to show you what should be the place, and what the power of woman. Now, secondly, we ask, What kind of education is to fit her for these?

And if you indeed think this a true conception of her office and dignity, it will not be difficult to trace the course of education which would fit her for the one, and raise her to the other.

The first of our duties to her—no thoughtful persons now doubt this,—is to secure for her such physical training and exercise as may confirm her health, and perfect her beauty; the highest refinement of that beauty being unattainable without splendour of activity and of delicate strength. To perfect her beauty, I say, and increase its power; it cannot be too powerful, nor shed its sacred light too far: only remember that all physical freedom is vain to produce beauty without a corresponding freedom of heart. There are two passages of that poet who is distinguished, it seems to me, from all others—not by power, but by exquisite *rightness*—which point you to the source, and describe to you, in a few syllables, the completion of womanly beauty. I will read the introductory stanzas, but the last is the one I wish you specially to notice:—

"Three years she grew in sun and shower,
Then Nature said, 'A lovelier flower
On earth was never sown;
This child I to myself will take;

[7] The song in Verdi's *Rigoletto*.
[8] *Marmion*, canto vi. 30.

She shall be mine, and I will make
A lady of my own.

'Myself will to my darling be
Both law and impulse; and with me
The girl, in rock and plain,
In earth and heaven, in glade and bower,
Shall feel an overseeing power
To kindle, or restrain.

'The floating clouds their state shall lend
To her, for her the willow bend;
Nor shall she fail to see,
Even in the motions of the storm,
Grace that shall mould the maiden's form
By silent sympathy.

'And *vital feelings of delight*
Shall rear her form to stately height,—
Her virgin bosom swell.
Such thoughts to Lucy I will give,
While she and I together live,
Here in this happy dell.' "*

"*Vital* feelings of delight," observe. There are deadly feelings of delight; but the natural ones are vital, necessary to very life.

And they must be feelings of delight, if they are to be vital. Do not think you can make a girl lovely, if you do not make her happy. There is not one restraint you put on a good girl's nature—there is not one check you give to her instincts of affection or of effort—which will not be indelibly written on her features, with a hardness which is all the more painful because it takes away the brightness from the eyes of innocence, and the charm from the brow of virtue.

This for the means: now note the end. Take from the same poet, in two lines, a perfect description of womanly beauty—

* Observe, it is "Nature" who is speaking throughout, and who says, "while she and I together live."

"A countenance in which did meet
Sweet records, promises as sweet."[9]

The perfect loveliness of a woman's countenance can only consist in that majestic peace, which is founded in the memory of happy and useful years,—full of sweet records; and from the joining of this with that yet more majestic childishness, which is still full of change and promise;—opening always—modest at once, and bright, with hope of better things to be won, and to be bestowed. There is no old age where there is still that promise.

Thus, then, you have first to mould her physical frame, and then, as the strength she gains will permit you, to fill and temper her mind with all knowledge and thoughts which tend to confirm its natural instincts of justice, and refine its natural tact of love.

All such knowledge should be given her as may enable her to understand, and even to aid, the work of men: and yet it should be given, not as knowledge,—not as if it were, or could be, for her an object to know; but only to feel, and to judge. It is of no moment, as a matter of pride or perfectness in herself, whether she knows many languages or one; but it is of the utmost, that she should be able to show kindness to a stranger, and to understand the sweetness of a stranger's tongue. It is of no moment to her own worth or dignity that she should be acquainted with this science or that; but it is of the highest that she should be trained in habits of accurate thought; that she should understand the meaning, the inevitableness, and the loveliness of natural laws; and follow at least some one path of scientific attainment, as far as to the threshold of that bitter Valley of Humiliation,[10] into which only the wisest and bravest of men can descend, owning themselves for ever children, gathering pebbles on a boundless shore.[11]

[9] From the poem beginning "She was a phantom of delight."

[10] Through which Christian had to pass in Bunyan's *Pilgrim's Progress.*

[11] "As children gathering pebbles on the shore": *Paradise Regained,* iv. 330.

It is of little consequence how many positions of cities she knows, or how many dates of events, or names of celebrated persons—it is not the object of education to turn the woman into a dictionary; but it is deeply necessary that she should be taught to enter with her whole personality into the history she reads; to picture the passages of it vitally in her own bright imagination; to apprehend, with her fine instincts, the pathetic circumstances and dramatic relations, which the historian too often only eclipses by his reasoning, and disconnects by his arrangement: it is for her to trace the hidden equities of divine reward, and catch sight, through the darkness, of the fateful threads of woven fire that connect error with retribution. But, chiefly of all, she is to be taught to extend the limits of her sympathy with respect to that history which is being for ever determined as the moments pass in which she draws her peaceful breath; and to the contemporary calamity, which, were it but rightly mourned by her, would recur no more hereafter. She is to exercise herself in imagining what would be the effects upon her mind and conduct, if she were daily brought into the presence of the suffering which is not the less real because shut from her sight. She is to be taught somewhat to understand the nothingness of the proportion which that little world in which she lives and loves, bears to the world in which God lives and loves;[12]—and solemnly she is to be taught to strive that her thoughts of piety may not be feeble in proportion to the number they embrace, nor her prayer more languid than it is for the momentary relief from pain of her husband or her child, when it is uttered for the multitudes of those who have none to love them,—and is "for all who are desolate and oppressed."

Thus far, I think, I have had your concurrence; perhaps you will not be with me in what I believe is most needful

[12] See the last stanza of *In Memoriam:*—

"That God, which ever lives and loves,
One God, one law, one element,
And one far-off divine event,
To which the whole creation moves."

for me to say. There *is* one dangerous science for women —one which they must indeed beware how they profanely touch—that of theology. Strange, and miserably strange, that while they are modest enough to doubt their powers, and pause at the threshold of sciences where every step is demonstrable and sure, they will plunge headlong, and without one thought of incompetency, into that science in which the greatest men have trembled, and the wisest erred. Strange, that they will complacently and pridefully bind up whatever vice or folly there is in them, whatever arrogance, petulance, or blind incomprehensiveness, into one bitter bundle of consecrated myrrh. Strange, in creatures born to be Love visible, that where they can know least, they will condemn first, and think to recommend themselves to their Master, by crawling up the steps of His judgment-throne to divide it with Him. Strangest of all that they should think they were led by the Spirit of the Comforter into habits of mind which have become in them the unmixed elements of home discomfort; and that they dare to turn the Household Gods of Christianity into ugly idols of their own;—spiritual dolls, for them to dress according to their caprice; and from which their husbands must turn away in grieved contempt, lest they should be shrieked at for breaking them.

I believe, then, with this exception, that a girl's education should be nearly, in its course and material of study, the same as a boy's; but quite differently directed. A woman, in any rank of life, ought to know whatever her husband is likely to know, but to know it in a different way. His command of it should be foundational and progressive; hers, general and accomplished for daily and helpful use. Not but that it would often be wiser in men to learn things in a womanly sort of way, for present use, and to seek for the discipline and training of their mental powers in such branches of study as will be afterwards fittest for social service; but, speaking broadly, a man ought to know any language or science he learns, thoroughly—while a woman ought to know the same language, or science, only so far as may enable her to sympathise in her husband's pleasures, and in those of his best friends.

Yet, observe, with exquisite accuracy as far as she reaches. There is a wide difference between elementary knowledge and superficial knowledge—between a firm beginning, and an infirm attempt at compassing. A woman may always help her husband by what she knows, however little; by what she half-knows, or mis-knows, she will only tease him.

And indeed, if there were to be any difference between a girl's education and a boy's, I should say that of the two the girl should be earlier led, as her intellect ripens faster, into deep and serious subjects: and that her range of literature should be, not more, but less frivolous; calculated to add the qualities of patience and seriousness to her natural poignancy of thought and quickness of wit; and also to keep her in a lofty and pure element of thought. I enter not now into any question of choice of books; only let us be sure that her books are not heaped up in her lap as they fall out of the package of the circulating library, wet with the last and lightest spray of the fountain of folly.

Or even of the fountain of wit; for with respect to the sore temptation of novel reading, it is not the badness of a novel that we should dread, so much as its over-wrought interest. The weakest romance is not so stupefying as the lower forms of religious exciting literature, and the worst romance is not so corrupting as false history, false philosophy, or false political essays. But the best romance becomes dangerous, if, by its excitement, it renders the ordinary course of life uninteresting, and increases the morbid thirst for useless acquaintance with scenes in which we shall never be called upon to act.

I speak therefore of good novels only; and our modern literature is particularly rich in types of such. Well read, indeed, these books have serious use, being nothing less than treatises on moral anatomy and chemistry; studies of human nature in the elements of it. But I attach little weight to this function: they are hardly ever read with earnestness enough to permit them to fulfil it. The utmost they usually do is to enlarge somewhat the charity of a kind reader, or the bitterness of a malicious one; for each will gather, from the novel, food for her own disposition. Those who are naturally proud and envious will learn from Thackeray to despise humanity; those who are naturally gentle, to pity it; those who are naturally shallow, to laugh at it. So, also, there might be a serviceable power in novels to bring before us, in vividness, a human truth which we had before dimly conceived; but the temptation to picturesqueness of statement is so great, that often the best writers of fiction cannot resist it; and our views are rendered so violent and one-sided, that their vitality is rather a harm than good.

Without, however, venturing here on any attempt at decision how much novel reading should be allowed, let me at least clearly assert this,—that whether novels, or poetry, or history be read, they should be chosen, not for their freedom from evil, but for their possession of good. The chance and scattered evil that may here and there haunt, or hide itself in, a powerful book, never does any harm to a noble girl; but the emptiness of an author oppresses her, and his amiable folly degrades her. And if she can have access to a good library of old and classical books, there need be no choosing at all. Keep the modern magazine and novel out of your girl's way: turn her loose into the old library every wet day, and let her alone. She will find what is good for her; you cannot: for there is just this difference between the making of a girl's character and a boy's—you may chisel a boy into shape, as you would a rock, or hammer him into it, if he be of a better kind, as you would a piece of bronze. But you cannot hammer a girl into anything. She grows as a flower does,—she will wither without sun; she will decay in her sheath, as a narcissus will, if you do not give her air enough; she may fall, and defile her head in dust, if you leave her without help at some moments of her life; but you cannot fetter her; she must take her own fair form and way, if she take any, and in mind as in body, must have always

"Her household motions light and free
And steps of virgin liberty."[13]

Let her loose in the library, I say, as you do a fawn in a field. It knows the bad weeds twenty times better than you; and the good ones too, and will eat some bitter and prickly ones, good for it, which you had not the slightest thought would have been so.

Then, in art, keep the finest models before her, and let her practice in all accomplishments be accurate and thorough, so as to enable her to understand more than she accomplishes. I say the finest models—that is to say, the truest, simplest, usefullest. Note those epithets: they will range through all the arts. Try them in music, where you might think them the least applicable. I say the truest, that in which the notes most closely and faithfully express the meaning of the words, or the character of intended emotion; again, the simplest, that in which the meaning and melody are attained with the fewest and most significant notes possible; and, finally, the usefullest, that music which makes the best words most beautiful, which enchants them in our memories each with its own glory of sound, and which applies them closest to the heart at the moment we need them.

And not only in the material and in the course, but yet more earnestly in the spirit of it, let a girl's education be as serious as a boy's. You bring up your girls as if they were meant for sideboard ornaments, and then complain of their frivolity. Give them the same advantages that you give their brothers—appeal to the same grand instincts of virtue in them; teach *them,* also, that courage and truth are the pillars of their being:—do you think that they would not answer that appeal, brave and true as they are even now, when you know that there is hardly a girls' school in this Christian kingdom where the children's courage or sincerity would be thought of half so much impor-

[13] Again a quotation from the poem beginning "She was a phantom of delight."

tance as their way of coming in at a door; and when the whole system of society, as respects the mode of establishing them in life, is one rotten plague of cowardice and imposture—cowardice, in not daring to let them live, or love, except as their neighbours choose; and imposture, in bringing, for the purposes of our own pride, the full glow of the world's worst vanity upon a girl's eyes, at the very period when the whole happiness of her future existence depends upon her remaining undazzled?

And give them, lastly, not only noble teachings, but noble teachers. You consider somewhat before you send your boy to school, what kind of a man the master is;—whatsoever kind of a man he is, you at least give him full authority over your son, and show some respect to him yourself;—if he comes to dine with you, you do not put him at a side table: you know also that, at college, your child's immediate tutor will be under the direction of some still higher tutor, for whom you have absolute reverence. You do not treat the Dean of Christ Church or the Master of Trinity as your inferiors.

But what teachers do you give your girls, and what reverence do you show to the teachers you have chosen? Is a girl likely to think her own conduct, or her own intellect, of much importance, when you trust the entire formation of her character, moral and intellectual, to a person whom you let your servants treat with less respect than they do your housekeeper (as if the soul of your child were a less charge than jams and groceries), and whom you yourself think you confer an honour upon by letting her sometimes sit in the drawing-room in the evening?

Thus, then, of literature as her help, and thus of art. There is one more help which she cannot do without—one which, alone, has sometimes done more than all other influences besides,—the help of wild and fair nature. Hear this of the education of Joan of Arc:—

> "The education of this poor girl was mean, according to the present standard; was ineffably grand, according to a purer philosophic standard; and only not

good for our age, because for us it would be unattainable. * * *

"Next after her spiritual advantages, she owed most to the advantages of her situation. The fountain of Domrémy was on the brink of a boundless forest; and it was haunted to that degree by fairies, that the parish priest (*curé*) was obliged to read mass there once a year, in order to keep them in decent bounds. * * *

"But the forests of Domrémy—those were the glories of the land; for in them abode mysterious powers and ancient secrets that towered into tragic strength. 'Abbeys there were, and abbey windows,'—'like Moorish temples of the Hindoos,' that exercised even princely power both in Lorraine and in the German Diets. These had their sweet bells that pierced the forests for many a league at matins or vespers, and each its own dreamy legend. Few enough, and scattered enough, were these abbeys, so as in no degree to disturb the deep solitude of the region; yet many enough to spread a network or awning of Christian sanctity over what else might have seemed a heathen wilderness."*

Now, you cannot, indeed, have here in England, woods eighteen miles deep to the centre; but you can, perhaps, keep a fairy or two for your children yet, if you wish to keep them. But *do* you wish it? Suppose you had each, at the back of your houses, a garden, large enough for your children to play in, with just as much lawn as would give them room to run,—no more—and that you could not change your abode; but that, if you chose, you could double your income, or quadruple it, by digging a coal shaft in the middle of the lawn, and turning the flowerbeds into heaps of coke. Would you do it? I hope not. I can tell you, you would be wrong if you did, though it gave you income sixty-fold instead of four-fold.

Yet this is what you are doing with all England. The

* "Joan of Arc: in reference to M. Michelet's *History of France*." De Quincey's Works. Vol. iii. p. 217 [edition of 1862].

whole country is but a little garden, not more than enough for your children to run on the lawns of, if you would let them *all* run there. And this little garden you will turn into furnace ground, and fill with heaps of cinders, if you can; and those children of yours, not you, will suffer for it. For the fairies will not be all banished; there are fairies of the furnace as of the wood, and their first gifts seem to be "sharp arrows of the mighty"; but their last gifts are "coals of juniper."[14]

And yet I cannot—though there is no part of my subject that I feel more—press this upon you; for we made so little use of the power of nature while we had it that we shall hardly feel what we have lost. Just on the other side of the Mersey you have your Snowdon, and your Menai Straits, and that mighty granite rock beyond the moors of Anglesea, splendid in its heathery crest, and foot planted in the deep sea, once thought of as sacred—a divine promontory, looking westward; the Holy Head or Headland, still not without awe when its red light glares first through storm. These are the hills, and these the bays and blue inlets, which, among the Greeks, would have been always loved, always fateful in influence on the national mind. That Snowdon is your Parnassus; but where are its Muses? That Holyhead mountain is your Island of Ægina; but where is its temple to Minerva?

Shall I read you what the Christian Minerva had achieved under the shadow of our Parnassus up to the year 1848?—Here is a little account of a Welsh school, from page 261 of the Report on Wales, published by the Committee of Council on Education. This is a school close to a town containing 5000 persons:—

> "I then called up a larger class, most of whom had recently come to the school. Three girls repeatedly declared they had never heard of Christ, and two that they had never heard of God. Two out of six thought Christ was on earth now" (they might have had a worse thought perhaps), "three knew nothing about

[14] Psalms cxx. 4.

> the Crucifixion. Four out of seven did not know the names of the months nor the number of days in a year. They had no notion of addition beyond two and two, or three and three; their minds were perfect blanks."

Oh, ye women of England! from the Princess of that Wales to the simplest of you, do not think your own children can be brought into their true fold of rest, while these are scattered on the hills, as sheep having no shepherd.[15] And do not think your daughters can be trained to the truth of their own human beauty, while the pleasant places, which God made at once for their schoolroom and their playground, lie desolate and defiled. You cannot baptize them rightly in those inch-deep fonts of yours, unless you baptize them also in the sweet waters which the great Lawgiver strikes forth for ever from the rocks of your native land—waters which a Pagan would have worshipped in their purity, and you worship only with pollution. You cannot lead your children faithfully to those narrow axe-hewn church altars of yours, while the dark azure altars in heaven—the mountains that sustain your island throne,—mountains on which a Pagan would have seen the powers of heaven rest in every wreathed cloud—remain for you without inscription; altars built, not to, but by an Unknown God.

Thus far, then, of the nature, thus far of the teaching, of woman, and thus of her household office, and queenliness. We now come to our last, our widest question.—What is her queenly office with respect to the state?

Generally, we are under an impression that a man's duties are public, and a woman's private. But this is not altogether so. A man has a personal work or duty, relating to his own home, and a public work or duty, which is the expansion of the other, relating to the state. So a woman has a personal work or duty, relating to her own home, and a public work or duty, which is also the expansion of that.

Now the man's work for his own home is, as has been

[15] Matthew ix. 36.

said, to secure its maintenance, progress, and defence; the woman's to secure its order, comfort, and loveliness.

Expand both these functions. The man's duty as a member of a commonwealth, is to assist in the maintenance, in the advance, in the defence of the state. The woman's duty, as a member of the commonwealth, is to assist in the ordering, in the comforting, and in the beautiful adornment of the state.

What the man is at his own gate, defending it, if need be, against insult and spoil, that also, not in a less, but in a more devoted measure, he is to be at the gate of his country, leaving his home, if need be, even to the spoiler, to do his more incumbent work there.

And, in like manner, what the woman is to be within her gates, as the centre of order, the balm of distress, and the mirror of beauty: that she is also to be without her gates, where order is more difficult, distress more imminent, loveliness more rare.

And as within the human heart there is always set an instinct for all its real duties,—an instinct which you cannot quench, but only warp and corrupt if you withdraw it from its true purpose:—as there is the intense instinct of love, which, rightly disciplined, maintains all the sanctities of life, and, misdirected, undermines them; and *must* do either the one or the other;—so there is in the human heart an inextinguishable instinct, the love of power, which, rightly directed, maintains all the majesty of law and life, and, misdirected, wrecks them.

Deep rooted in the innermost life of the heart of man, and of the heart of woman, God set it there, and God keeps it there.—Vainly, as falsely, you blame or rebuke the desire of power!—For Heaven's sake, and for Man's sake, desire it all you can. But *what* power? That is all the question. Power to destroy? the lion's limb, and the dragon's breath? Not so. Power to heal, to redeem, to guide, and to guard. Power of the sceptre and shield; the power of the royal hand that heals in touching,—that binds the fiend, and looses the captive; the throne that is founded on the rock of Justice, and descended from only by steps of

Mercy. Will you not covet such power as this, and seek such throne as this, and be no more housewives, but queens?

It is now long since the women of England arrogated, universally, a title which once belonged to nobility only; and, having once been in the habit of accepting the simple title of gentlewoman as correspondent to that of gentleman, insisted on the privilege of assuming the title of "Lady," which properly corresponds only to the title of "Lord."

I do not blame them for this; but only for their narrow motive in this. I would have them desire and claim the title of Lady, provided they claim, not merely the title, but the office and duty signified by it. Lady means "bread-giver" or "loaf-giver," and Lord means "maintainer of laws,"[16] and both titles have reference, not to the law which is maintained in the house, nor to the bread which is given to the household; but to law maintained for the multitude, and to bread broken among the multitude. So that a Lord has legal claim only to his title in so far as he is the maintainer of the justice of the Lord of lords; and a Lady has legal claim to her title only so far as she communicates that help to the poor representatives of her Master, which women once, ministering to Him of their substance, where permitted to extend to that Master Himself; and when she is known, as He Himself once was, in breaking of bread.[17]

And this beneficent and legal dominion, this power of the Dominus, or House-Lord, and of the Domina, or House-Lady, is great and venerable, not in the number of those through whom it has lineally descended, but in the number of those whom it grasps within its sway; it is always regarded with reverent worship wherever its dynasty

[16] According to Skeat (*Etymological Dictionary*) *lord* means "loaf-keeper (Anglo-Saxon *hláford* (loaf-ward)," and lady, "loaf-kneader (Anglo-Saxon *hláf* and *dáege* (kneader)." Ruskin, it will be seen, assumes a different derivation for "lord," deriving it from the Anglo-Saxon *lágu* (law).

[17] Luke xxiv. 30, 31, 35.

is founded on its duty, and its ambition co-relative with its beneficence. Your fancy is pleased with the thought of being noble ladies, with a train of vassals. Be it so; you cannot be too noble, and your train cannot be too great; but see to it that your train is of vassals whom you serve and feed, not merely of slaves who serve and feed *you;* and that the multitude which obeys you is of those whom you have comforted, not oppressed,—whom you have redeemed, not led into captivity.

And this, which is true of the lower or household dominion, is equally true of the queenly dominion; that highest dignity is open to you, if you will also accept that highest duty. Rex et Regina—Roi et Reine—"*Right*-doers"; they differ but from the Lady and Lord, in that their power is supreme over the mind as over the person—that they not only feed and clothe, but direct and teach. And whether consciously or not, you must be, in many a heart, enthroned: there is no putting by that crown; queens you must always be: queens to your lovers; queens to your husbands and your sons; queens of higher mystery to the world beyond, which bows itself, and will for ever bow, before the myrtle crown[18] and the stainless sceptre of womanhood. But, alas! you are too often idle and careless queens, grasping at majesty in the least things, while you abdicate it in the greatest; and leaving misrule and violence to work their will among men, in defiance of the power which, holding straight in gift from the Prince of all Peace, the wicked among you betray, and the good forget.

"Prince of Peace."[19] Note that name. When kings rule in that name, and nobles, and the judges of the earth, they also, in their narrow place, and mortal measure, receive the power of it. There are no other rulers than they; other rule than theirs is but *mis*rule; they who govern verily "Dei Gratiâ" are all princes, yes, or princesses of Peace.

[18] For the myrtle as sacred to Venus, see Virgil, *Eclogues,* vii. 61.

[19] Isaiah ix. 6.

There is not a war in the world, no, nor an injustice, but you women are answerable for it; not in that you have provoked, but in that you have not hindered. Men, by their nature, are prone to fight; they will fight for any cause, or for none. It is for you to choose their cause for them, and to forbid them when there is no cause. There is no suffering, no injustice, no misery, in the earth, but the guilt of it lies with you. Men can bear the sight of it, but you should not be able to bear it. Men may tread it down without sympathy in their own struggle; but men are feeble in sympathy, and contracted in hope; it is you only who can feel the depths of pain, and conceive the way of its healing. Instead of trying to do this, you turn away from it; you shut yourselves within your park walls and garden gates; and you are content to know that there is beyond them a whole world in wilderness—a world of secrets which you dare not penetrate; and of suffering which you dare not conceive.

I tell you that this is to me quite the most amazing among the phenomena of humanity. I am surprised at no depths to which, when once warped from its honour, that humanity can be degraded. I do not wonder at the miser's death, with his hands, as they relax, dropping gold. I do not wonder at the sensualist's life, with the shroud wrapped about his feet. I do not wonder at the single-handed murder of a single victim, done by the assassin in the darkness of the railway, or reed shadow of the marsh. I do not even wonder at the myriad-handed murder of multitudes, done boastfully in the daylight, by the frenzy of nations, and the immeasurable, unimaginable guilt heaped up from hell to heaven, of their priests, and kings. But this is wonderful to me—oh, how wonderful!—to see the tender and delicate woman among you, with her child at her breast, and a power, if she would wield it, over it, and over its father, purer than the air of heaven, and stronger than the seas of earth—nay, a magnitude of blessing which her husband would not part with for all that earth itself, though it were made of one entire and perfect chrysolite:[20]—to see her abdicate this majesty to play at precedence with her next-door neighbour! This is wonderful—oh, wonderful!—to see her, with every innocent feeling fresh within her, go out in the morning into her garden to play with the fringes of its guarded flowers, and lift their heads when they are drooping, with her happy smile upon her face, and no cloud upon her brow, because there is a little wall around her place of peace: and yet she knows, in her heart, if she would only look for its knowledge, that, outside of that little rose-covered wall, the wild grass, to the horizon, is torn up by the agony of men, and beat level by the drift of their life-blood.

Have you ever considered what a deep under meaning there lies, or at least may be read, if we choose, in our custom of strewing flowers before those whom we think most happy? Do you suppose it is merely to deceive them into the hope that happiness is always to fall thus in showers at their feet?—that wherever they pass they will tread on herbs of sweet scent, and that the rough ground will be made smooth for them by depths of roses? So surely as they believe that, they will have, instead, to walk on bitter herbs and thorns; and the only softness to their feet will be of snow. But it is not thus intended they should believe; there is a better meaning in that old custom. The path of a good woman is indeed strewn with flowers; but they rise behind her steps, not before them. "Her feet have touched the meadows, and left the daisies rosy."[21]

[20] *Othello*, v. 2, 146:—

"Had she been true,
If Heaven would make me such another world,
Of one entire and perfect chrysolite,
I'd not have sold her for it."

[21] Tennyson: *Maud*, i. xii. 6. Ruskin, it will be seen, treats the passage as "a lover's fancy, false and vain"; as an instance, that is, of the "Pathetic Fallacy". The poet resented this interpretation. "Why," he said to Thomas Wilson, "the very day I wrote it, I saw the daisies rosy in Maiden's Croft, and thought of enclosing one to Ruskin labelled 'A pathetic fallacy'" (*Memoir*, by his son, vol. i. p. 511).

You think that only a lover's fancy;—false and vain! How if it could be true? You think this also, perhaps, only a poet's fancy—

"Even the light harebell raised its head
Elastic from her airy tread."[22]

But it is little to say of a woman, that she only does not destroy where she passes. She should revive; the harebells should bloom, not stoop, as she passes. You think I am rushing into wild hyperbole! Pardon me, not a whit—I mean what I say in calm English, spoken in resolute truth. You have heard it said—(and I believe there is more than fancy even in that saying, but let it pass for a fanciful one)—that flowers only flourish rightly in the garden of some one who loves them. I know you would like that to be true; you would think it a pleasant magic if you could flush your flowers into brighter bloom by a kind look upon them: nay, more, if your look had the power, not only to cheer, but to guard;—if you could bid the black blight turn away, and the knotted caterpillar spare—if you could bid the dew fall upon them in the drought, and say to the south wind, in frost—"Come, thou south, and breathe upon my garden, that the spices of it may flow out."[23] This you would think a great thing? And do you think it not a greater thing, that all this, (and how much more than this!) you *can* do, for fairer flowers than these—flowers that could bless you for having blessed them, and will love you for having loved them; flowers that have thoughts like yours, and lives like yours; and which, once saved, you save for ever? Is this only a little power? Far among the moorlands and the rocks,—far in the darkness of the terrible streets,—these feeble florets are lying, with all their fresh leaves torn, and their stems broken: will you never go down to them, nor set them in order in their little fragrant beds, nor fence them in their trembling, from the fierce wind? Shall morning follow morning, for you, but

[22] From Scott's description of Ellen Douglas: *Lady of the Lake*, i. 18. "Light" is "slight" in the original.

[23] Song of Solomon iv. 16.

not for them; and the dawn rise to watch, far away, those frantic Dances of Death; but no dawn rise to breathe upon these living banks of wild violet, and woodbine, and rose; nor call to you, through your casement—call (not giving you the name of the English poet's lady, but the name of Dante's great Matilda, who, on the edge of happy Lethe, stood, wreathing flowers with flowers), saying:—

> "Come into the garden, Maud,
> For the black bat, night, has flown,
> And the woodbine spices are wafted abroad,
> And the musk of the roses blown"?[24]

Will you not go down among them?—among those sweet living things, whose new courage, sprung from the earth with the deep colour of heaven upon it, is starting up in strength of goodly spire; and whose purity, washed from the dust, is opening, bud by bud, into the flower of promise;—and still they turn to you, and for you, "The Larkspur listens—I hear, I hear! And the Lily whispers—I wait."[25]

Did you notice that I missed two lines when I read you that first stanza; and think that I had forgotten them? Hear them now:—

> "Come into the garden, Maud,
> For the black bat, night, has flown,
> Come into the garden, Maud,
> I am here at the gate, alone."

Who is it, think you, who stands at the gate of this sweeter garden alone, waiting for you? Did you ever hear, not of a Maud, but a Madeleine, who went down to her garden in the dawn, and found One waiting at the gate, whom she supposed to be the gardener?[26] Have you not sought Him often;—sought Him in vain, all through

[24] *Maud,* part i. canto xxii. verse 1 (the first two and the last two lines).

[25] From verse 10 of the same canto.

[26] John xx. 15. The other Biblical references are to Genesis iii. 24; Song of Solomon vii. 12, and ii. 15; Matthew viii. 20.

the night;—sought Him in vain at the gate of that old garden where the fiery sword is set? He is never there; but at the gate of *this* garden He is waiting always—waiting to take your hand—ready to go down to see the fruits of the valley, to see whether the vine has flourished, and the pomegranate budded. There you shall see with Him the little tendrils of the vines that His hand is guiding—there you shall see the pomegranate springing where His hand cast the sanguine seed;—more: you shall see the troops of the angel keepers that, with their wings, wave away the hungry birds from the path-sides where He has sown, and call to each other between the vineyard rows, "Take us the foxes, the little foxes, that spoil the vines, for our vines have tender grapes." Oh—you queens—you queens! among the hills and happy greenwood of this land of yours, shall the foxes have holes, and the birds of the air have nests; and in your cities, shall the stones cry out against you, that they are the only pillows where the Son of Man can lay His head?

Sesame and Lilies, lect. 2.

A MYSTERY OF LIFE

But farther, you may, perhaps, think it a beneficent ordinance for the generality of men that they do not, with earnestness or anxiety, dwell on such questions of the future because the business of the day could not be done if this kind of thought were taken by all of us for the morrow. Be it so: but at least we might anticipate that the greatest and wisest of us, who were evidently the appointed teachers of the rest, would set themselves apart to seek out whatever could be surely known of the future destinies of their race; and to teach this in no rhetorical or ambiguous manner, but in the plainest and most severely earnest words.

Now, the highest representatives of men who have thus endeavoured, during the Christian era, to search out these deep things, and relate them, are Dante and Milton. There are none who for earnestness of thought, for mastery of word, can be classed with these. I am not at present, mind you, speaking of persons set apart in any priestly or pastoral office, to deliver creeds to us, or doctrines; but of men who try to discover and set forth, as far as by human intellect is possible, the facts of the other world. Divines may perhaps teach us how to arrive there, but only these two poets have in any powerful manner striven to discover, or in any definite words professed to tell, what we shall see and become there; or how those upper and nether worlds are, and have been, inhabited.

And what have they told us? Milton's account of the most important event in his whole system of the universe, the fall of the angels, is evidently unbelievable to himself; and the more so, that it is wholly founded on, and in a great part spoiled and degraded from, Hesiod's account of the decisive war of the younger gods with the Titans. The rest of his poem is a picturesque drama, in which every artifice of invention is visibly and consciously employed; not a single fact being, for an instant, conceived as tenable by any living faith. Dante's conception is far more intense, and, by himself, for the time, not to be escaped from; it is indeed a vision, but a vision only, and that one of the wildest that ever entranced a soul—a dream in which every grotesque type or phantasy of heathen tradition is renewed, and adorned; and the destinies of the Christian Church, under their most sacred symbols, become literally subordinate to the praise, and are only to be understood by the aid, of one dear Florentine maiden.

I tell you truly that, as I strive more with this strange lethargy and trance in myself, and awake to the meaning and power of life, it seems daily more amazing to me that men such as these should dare to play with the most precious truths, (or the most deadly untruths,) by which the whole human race listening to them could be informed, or deceived;—all the world their audiences for ever, with pleased ear, and passionate heart;—and yet, to this submissive infinitude of souls, and ever more succeeding and succeeding multitude, hungry for bread of life, they do but play upon sweetly modulated pipes; with pompous nomenclature adorn the councils of hell;[1] touch a troubadour's guitar to the courses of the suns;[2] and fill the openings of eternity, before which prophets have veiled their faces, and which angels desire to look into,[3] with idle puppets of their scholastic imagination, and melancholy lights of frantic faith in their lost mortal love.

Is not this a mystery of life?

But more. We have to remember that these two great teachers were both of them warped in their temper, and thwarted in their search for truth. They were men of intellectual war, unable, through darkness of controversy, or stress of personal grief, to discern where their own ambition modified their utterances of the moral law; or their own agony mingled with their anger at its violation. But greater men than these have been—innocent-hearted—too great for contest. Men, like Homer and Shakespeare, of so unrecognized personality, that it disappears in future ages, and becomes ghostly, like the tradition of a lost heathen god. Men, therefore, to whose unoffended, uncondemning sight, the whole of human nature reveals itself in a pathetic weakness, with which they will not strive; or in mournful and transitory strength, which they dare not praise. And all Pagan and Christian Civilization thus becomes subject to them. It does not matter how little, or how much, any of us have read, either of Homer or Shakespeare; everything round us, in substance, or in thought, has been moulded by them. All Greek gentlemen were educated under Homer. All Roman gentlemen, by Greek literature. All Italian, and French, and English gentlemen, by Roman literature, and by its principles. Of the scope of

[1] See *Paradise Lost,* books ii. and x.

[2] The reference is, of course, to the *Divina Commedia,* in which the story of the poet's love threads the general scheme.

[3] Isaiah vi. 2; 1 Peter i. 12.

Shakespeare, I will say only, that the intellectual measure of every man since born, in the domains of creative thought, may be assigned to him, according to the degree in which he has been taught by Shakespeare. Well, what do these two men, centres of mortal intelligence, deliver to us of conviction respecting what it most behoves that intelligence to grasp? What is their hope—their crown of rejoicing?[4] what manner of exhortation have they for us, or of rebuke? what lies next their own hearts, and dictates their undying words? Have they any peace to promise to our unrest—any redemption to our misery?

Take Homer first, and think if there is any sadder image of human fate than the great Homeric story. The main features in the character of Achilles are its intense desire of justice, and its tenderness of affection. And in that bitter song of the *Iliad*, this man, though aided continually by the wisest of the gods, and burning with the desire of justice in his heart, becomes yet, through ill-governed passion, the most unjust of men: and, full of the deepest tenderness in his heart, becomes yet, through ill-governed passion, the most cruel of men. Intense alike in love and in friendship, he loses, first his mistress, and then his friend; for the sake of the one, he surrenders to death the armies of his own land; for the sake of the other, he surrenders all. Will a man lay down his life for his friend?[5] Yea—even for his *dead* friend, this Achilles, though goddess-born, and goddess-taught, gives up his kingdom, his country, and his life—casts alike the innocent and guilty, with himself, into one gulf of slaughter, and dies at last by the hand of the basest of his adversaries.[6]

Is not this a mystery of life?

But what, then, is the message to us of our own poet,

[4] 1 Thessalonians ii. 19.

[5] John xiii. 15.

[6] The references are to Achilles, born of Thetis and advised by Athena; to his abstention from battle because Agamemnon had robbed him of Briseis; to his return on account of the death of Patroclus; to his dragging of the body of Hector round the walls of Troy; to his death at the hands of Paris.

and searcher of hearts, after fifteen hundred years of Christian faith have been numbered over the graves of men? Are his words more cheerful than the Heathen's—is his hope more near—his trust more sure—his reading of fate more happy? Ah, no! He differs from the Heathen poet chiefly in this—that he recognizes, for deliverance, no gods nigh at hand; and that, by petty chance—by momentary folly—by broken message—by fool's tyranny—or traitor's snare, the strongest and most righteous are brought to their ruin, and perish without word of hope.[7] He indeed, as part of his rendering of character, ascribes the power and modesty of habitual devotion to the gentle and the just. The death-bed of Katharine is bright with visions of angels;[8] and the great soldier-king, standing by his few dead,[9] acknowledges the presence of the Hand that can save alike by many or by few.[10] But observe that from those who with deepest spirit, meditate, and with deepest passion, mourn, there are no such words as these; nor in their hearts are any such consolations. Instead of the perpetual sense of the helpful presence of the Deity, which, through all heathen tradition, is the source of heroic strength, in battle, in exile, and in the valley of the shadow of death,[11] we find only in the great Christian poet, the consciousness of a moral law, through which "the gods are just, and of our pleasant vices make instruments to scourge us";[12] and of the resolved arbitration of the destinies, that conclude into precision of doom what we feebly and blindly began; and force us, when our indiscretion serves us, and our deepest plots do pall, to the

[7] "By petty chance," as by the changing of the foils in *Hamlet;* "by momentary folly," as by Cordelia in *King Lear* (i. 1); "by broken message," as in *Romeo and Juliet* (iv. 2); "by fool's tyranny," as of Leontes in *Winter's Tale;* "or traitor's snare," as Iago's in *Othello.*

[8] *Henry VIII.*, Act iv. sc. 2.

[9] *Henry V.*, Act iv. sc. 8.

[10] 1 Samuel xiv. 6.

[11] Psalms xxiii. 4.

[12] *King Lear*, v. 3, lines 170–171.

confession, that "there's a divinity that shapes our ends, rough hew them how we will."[13]

Is not this a mystery of life?

Be it so, then. About this human life that is to be, or that is, the wise religious men tell us nothing that we can trust; and the wise contemplative men, nothing that can give us peace. But there is yet a third class, to whom we may turn—the wise practical men. We have sat at the feet of the poets who sang of heaven, and they have told us their dreams. We have listened to the poets who sang of earth, and they have chanted to us dirges and words of despair. But there is one class of men more:—men, not capable of vision, nor sensitive to sorrow, but firm of purpose—practised in business; learned in all that can be, (by handling,) known. Men, whose hearts and hopes are wholly in this present world, from whom, therefore, we may surely learn, at least, how, at present, conveniently to live in it. What will *they* say to us, or show us by example? These kings—these councillors—these statesmen and builders of kingdoms—these capitalists and men of business, who weigh the earth, and the dust of it, in a balance. They know the world, surely; and what is the mystery of life to us, is none to them. They can surely show us how to live, while we live, and to gather out of the present world what is best.

Sesame and Lilies, lect. 3, pars. 110–116.

[13] *Hamlet,* v. 2, lines 7–10:—

"Our indiscretion sometimes serves us well,
When our deep plots shall pall: and that should teach us
There's a divinity that shapes our ends,
Rough-hew them how we will."

FAIRY STORIES

And the effect of the endeavour to make stories moral upon the literary merit of the work itself, is as harmful as the motive of the effort is false. For every fairy tale worth recording at all is the remnant of a tradition possessing true historical value;—historical, at least, in so far as it has naturally arisen out of the mind of a people under special circumstances, and risen not without meaning, nor removed altogether from their sphere of religious faith. It sustains afterwards natural changes from the sincere action of the fear or fancy of successive generations; it takes new colour from their manner of life, and new form from their changing moral tempers. As long as these changes are natural and effortless, accidental and inevitable, the story remains essentially true, altering its form, indeed, like a flying cloud, but remaining a sign of the sky; a shadowy image, as truly a part of the great firmament of the human mind as the light of reason which it seems to interrupt. But the fair deceit and innocent error of it cannot be interpreted nor restrained by a wilful purpose, and all additions to it by art do but defile, as the shepherd disturbs the flakes of morning mist with smoke from his fire of dead leaves.

There is also a deeper collateral mischief in this indulgence of licentious change and retouching of stories to suit particular tastes, or inculcate favourite doctrines. It directly destroys the child's power of rendering any such belief as it would otherwise have been in his nature to give to an imaginative vision. How far it is expedient to occupy his mind with ideal forms at all may be questionable to many, though not to me; but it is quite beyond question that if we do allow of the fictitious representation, that representation should be calm and complete, possessed to the full, and read down its utmost depth. The little reader's attention should never be confused or disturbed, whether he is possessing himself of fairy tale or history. Let him know his fairy tale accurately, and have perfect joy or awe in the conception of it as if it were real; thus he will always be exercising his power of grasping realities: but a confused, careless, and discrediting tenure of the fiction will lead to as confused and careless reading of fact. Let the circumstances of both be strictly perceived, and long dwelt upon, and let the child's own mind develop fruit of thought from both. It is of the greatest importance early to secure this habit of contemplation, and therefore it is a grave error, either to multiply unnecessarily, or to illustrate with extravagant richness, the incidents presented to the imagination. It should multiply and illustrate them for itself; and, if the intellect is of any real value, there will be a mystery and wonderfulness in its own dreams which would only be thwarted by external illustration. Yet I do not bring forward the text or the etchings in this volume as examples of what either ought to be in works of the kind: they are in many respects common, imperfect, vulgar; but their vulgarity is of a wholesome and harmless kind. It is not, for instance, graceful English, to say that a thought "popped into Catherine's head"; but it nevertheless is far better, as an initiation into literary style, that a child should be told this than that "a subject attracted Catherine's attention." And in genuine forms of minor tradition, a rude and more or less illiterate tone will always be discernible; for all the best fairy tales have owed their birth, and the greater part of their power, to narrowness of social circumstances; they belong properly to districts in which walled cities are surrounded by bright and unblemished country, and in which a healthy and bustling town life, not highly refined, is relieved by, and contrasted with, the calm enchantment of pastoral and woodland scenery, either under humble cultivation by peasant masters, or left in its natural solitude. Under conditions of this kind the imagination is enough excited to invent instinctively, (and rejoice in the invention of) spiritual forms of wildness and beauty, while yet it is restrained and made cheerful by the familiar accidents and relations of town life, mingling always in its fancy humorous and vulgar circumstances with pathetic ones, and never so much impressed with its supernatural phantasies as to be in danger of retaining them as any part of its religious faith. The good spirit descends gradually from an angel into a fairy, and the demon shrinks into a playful grotesque of diminutive malevolence, while yet both keep an accredited and vital influence upon the character and mind. But the language in which such ideas will be usually clothed must necessarily partake of their narrowness; and art is systematically incognizant of them, having only strength under the conditions which awake them to express itself in an irregular and gross grotesque, fit only for external architectural decoration.

"Fairy Stories," pars. 5–6.

THE QUEEN OF THE AIR

PREFACE

My days and strength have lately been much broken; and I never more felt the insufficiency of both than in preparing for the press the following desultory memoranda on a most noble subject. But I leave them now as they stand, for no time nor labour would be enough to complete them to my contentment; and I believe that they contain suggestions which may be followed with safety, by persons who are beginning to take interest in the aspects of mythology, which only recent investigation has removed from the region of conjecture into that of rational inquiry.[1] I have some advantage, also, from my field work, in the interpretation of myths relating to natural phenomena: and I have had always near me, since we were at college together, a sure, and unweariedly kind, guide, in my friend Charles Newton, to whom we owe the finding of more treasure in mines of marble, than, were it rightly estimated, all California could buy. I must not, however, permit the chance of his name being in any wise associated with my errors. Much of my work has been done obstinately in my own way; and he is never responsible for me, though he has often kept me right, or at least enabled me to advance in a right direction. Absolutely right no one can be in such matters; nor does a day pass without convincing every honest student of antiquity of some partial error, and showing him better how to think, and where to look. But I knew that there was no hope of my being able to enter with advantage on the fields of history opened by the splendid investigation of

[1] The date, 1869, should be remembered. Ruskin was thinking of the school of comparative mythology founded on philology (see a few lines lower down), not of the later method of anthropology.

recent philologists; though I could qualify myself, by attention and sympathy, to understand, here and there, a verse of Homer's or Hesiod's, as the simple people did for whom they sang.

Even while I correct these sheets for press, a lecture by Professor Tyndall has been put into my hands, which I ought to have heard last 16th of January, but was hindered by mischance; and which, I now find, completes, in two important particulars, the evidence of an instinctive truth in ancient symbolism; showing, first, that the Greek conception of an ethereal element pervading space is justified by the closest reasoning of modern physicists; and, secondly, that the blue of the sky, hitherto thought to be caused by watery vapour, is, indeed, reflected from the divided air itself; so that the bright blue of the eyes of Athena, and the deep blue of her ægis, prove to be accurate mythic expressions of natural phenomena which it is an uttermost triumph of recent science to have revealed.

Indeed, it would be difficult to imagine triumph more complete. To form, "within an experimental tube, a bit of more perfect sky than the sky itself!" here is magic of the finest sort! singularly reversed from that of old time, which only asserted its competency to enclose in bottles elementary forces that were—not of the sky.

Let me, in thanking Professor Tyndall for the true wonder of this piece of work, ask his pardon, and that of all masters in physical science, for any words of mine, either in the following pages or elsewhere, that may ever seem to fail in the respect due to their great powers of thought, or in the admiration due to the far scope of their discovery. But I will be judged by themselves, if I have not bitter reason to ask them to teach us more than yet they have taught.

This first day of May, 1869, I am writing where my work was begun thirty-five years ago, within sight of the snows of the higher Alps. In that half of the permitted life of man, I have seen strange evil brought upon every scene that I best loved, or tried to make beloved by others. The light which once flushed those pale summits with its rose at dawn, and purple at sunset, is now umbered and faint; the air which once inlaid the clefts of all their golden crags with azure is now defiled with languid coils of smoke, belched from worse than volcanic fires; their very glacier waves are ebbing, and their snows fading, as if Hell had breathed on them; the waters that once sank at their feet into crystalline rest are now dimmed and foul, from deep to deep, and shore to shore. These are no careless words —they are accurately—horribly—true. I know what the Swiss lakes were; no pool of Alpine fountain at its source was clearer. This morning, on the Lake of Geneva, at half a mile from the beach, I could scarcely see my oar-blade a fathom deep.

The light, the air, the waters, all defiled! How of the earth itself? Take this one fact for type of honour done by the modern Swiss to the earth of his native land. There used to be a little rock at the end of the avenue by the port of Neuchâtel; there, the last marble of the foot of Jura, sloping to the blue water, and (at this time of year) covered with bright pink tufts of Saponaria. I went, three days since, to gather a blossom at the place. The goodly native rock and its flowers were covered with the dust and refuse of the town; but, in the middle of the avenue, was a newly-constructed artificial rockery, with a fountain twisted through a spinning spout, and an inscription on one of its loose-tumbled stones,—

"Aux Botanistes,
Le club Jurassique."

Ah, masters of modern science, give me back my Athena out of your vials, and seal, if it may be, once more, Asmodeus therein.[2] You have divided the elements, and united them; enslaved them upon the earth, and discerned them in the stars. Teach us, now, but this of them, which is all that man need know,—that the Air is given to him for his

[2] For Asmodeus, the evil spirit of destruction, see the Book of Tobit, *Paradise Lost* (iv. 168), and Le Sage's *Asmodeus; or, The Devil on Two Sticks* (*Le Diable Boiteux*); to which latter work reference is here made.

life; and the Rain to his thirst, and for his baptism; and the Fire for warmth; and the Sun for sight; and the Earth for his meat—and his Rest.

VEVAY, *May 1, 1869.*

I

*ATHENA CHALINITIS**

(*Athena in the Heavens*)

Lecture on the Greek Myths of Storm, given (partly) in University College, London, March 9th, 1869

1. I will not ask your pardon for endeavouring to interest you in the subject of Greek Mythology; but I must ask your permission to approach it in a temper differing from that in which it is frequently treated. We cannot justly interpret the religion of any people, unless we are prepared to admit that we ourselves, as well as they, are liable to error in matters of faith; and that the convictions of others, however singular, may in some points have been well founded, while our own, however reasonable, may in some particulars be mistaken. You must forgive me, therefore, for not always distinctively calling the creeds of the past, "superstition," and the creeds of the present day, "religion"; as well as for assuming that a faith now confessed may sometimes be superficial, and that a faith long forgotten may once have been sincere. It is the task of the Divine to condemn the errors of antiquity, and of the Philologist to account for them: I will only pray you to read, with patience and human sympathy, the thoughts of men who lived without blame in a darkness they could

* "Athena the Restrainer." The name is given to her as having helped Bellerophon to bridle Pegasus, the flying cloud. *Cp.* Pausanias, *Corinthiaca* 4, and Bellerophon's dream, Pind. *Ol.* 13, 97.

not dispel; and to remember that, whatever charge of folly may justly attach to the saying,—"There is no God,"[1] the folly is prouder, deeper, and less pardonable, in saying, "There is no God but for me."

2. A myth, in its simplest definition, is a story with a meaning attached to it, other than it seems to have at first; and the fact that it has such a meaning is generally marked by some of its circumstances being extraordinary, or, in the common use of the word, unnatural. Thus, if I tell you that Hercules killed a water-serpent in the lake of Lerna, and if I mean, and you understand, nothing more than that fact, the story, whether true or false, is not a myth. But if by telling you this, I mean that Hercules purified the stagnation of many streams from deadly miasmata, my story, however simple, is a true myth; only, as, if I left it in that simplicity, you would probably look for nothing beyond, it will be wise in me to surprise your attention by adding some singular circumstance; for instance, that the water-snake had several heads, which revived as fast as they were killed, and which poisoned even the foot that trode upon them as they slept. And in proportion to the fulness of intended meaning I shall probably multiply and refine upon these improbabilities; as, suppose, if, instead of desiring only to tell you that Hercules purified a marsh, I wished you to understand that he contended with the venom and vapour of envy and evil ambition, whether in other men's souls or in his own, and choked *that* malaria only by supreme toil—I might tell you that this serpent was formed by the Goddess whose pride was in the trial of Hercules; and that its place of abode was by a palm tree; and that for every head of it that was cut off, two rose up with renewed life; and that the hero found at last he could not kill the creature at all by cutting its heads off or crushing them; but only by burning them down; and that the midmost of them could not be killed even that way, but had to be buried alive. Only, in proportion as I mean more I shall certainly appear more

[1] Psalms liii. 1.

absurd in my statement, and at last, when I get unendurably significant, all practical persons will agree that I was talking mere nonsense from the beginning, and never meant anything at all.

3. It is just possible, however, also, that the story-teller may all along have meant nothing but what he said; and that, incredible as the events may appear, he himself literally believed—and expected you also to believe—all this about Hercules, without any latent moral or history whatever. And it is very necessary, in reading traditions of this kind, to determine, first of all, whether you are listening to a simple person, who is relating what, at all events, he believes to be true (and may, therefore, possibly have been so to some extent), or to a reserved philosopher, who is veiling a theory of the universe under the grotesque of a fairy tale. It is, in general, more likely that the first supposition should be the right one:—simple and credulous persons are, perhaps fortunately, more common than philosophers: and it is of the highest importance that you should take their innocent testimony as it was meant, and not efface, under the graceful explanation which your cultivated ingenuity may suggest, either the evidence their story may contain (such as it is worth) of an extraordinary event having really taken place, or the unquestionable light which it will cast upon the character of the person by whom it was frankly believed. And to deal with Greek religion honestly, you must at once understand that this literal belief was, in the mind of the general people, as deeply rooted as ours in the legends of our own sacred book; and that a basis of unmiraculous event was as little suspected, and an explanatory symbolism as rarely traced, by them, as by us.

You must, therefore, observe that I deeply degrade the position which such a myth as that just referred to occupied in the Greek mind, by comparing it (for fear of offending you) to our story of St. George and the Dragon. Still, the analogy is perfect in minor respects; and though it fails to give you any notion of the vitally religious earnestness of the Greek faith, it will exactly illustrate the manner in which faith laid hold of its objects.

4. This story of Hercules and the Hydra, then, was to the general Greek mind, in its best days, a tale about a real hero and a real monster. Not one in a thousand knew anything of the way in which the story had arisen, any more than the English peasant generally is aware of the plebeian origin of St. George; or supposes that there were once alive in the world, with sharp teeth and claws, real, and very ugly, flying dragons. On the other hand, few persons traced any moral or symbolical meaning in the story, and the average Greek was as far from imagining any interpretation like that I have just given you, as an average Englishman is from seeing in St. George the Red Cross Knight of Spenser, or in the dragon the Spirit of Infidelity. But, for all that, there was a certain undercurrent of consciousness in all minds, that the figures meant more than they at first showed; and according to each man's own faculties of sentiment, he judged and read them; just as a Knight of the Garter reads more in the jewel on his collar than the George and Dragon of a public-house expresses to the host or to his customers. Thus, to the mean person the myth always meant little; to the noble person, much: and the greater their familiarity with it, the more contemptible it became to the one, and the more sacred to the other: until vulgar commentators explained it entirely away, while Virgil made it the crowning glory of his choral hymn to Hercules:

"Around thee, powerless to infect thy soul,
Rose, in his crested crown, the Lerna worm."

"Non te rationis egentem
Lernæus turbâ capitum circumstetit anguis."[2]

And although, in any special toil of the hero's life, the moral interpretation was rarely with definiteness attached to its event, yet in the whole course of the life, not only a symbolical meaning, but the warrant for the existence of

[2] *Æneid,* viii. 300.

a real spiritual power, was apprehended of all men. Hercules was no dead hero, to be remembered only as a victor over monsters of the past—harmless now, as slain. He was the perpetual type and mirror of heroism, and its present and living aid against every ravenous form of human trial and pain.

5. But, if we seek to know more than this, and to ascertain the manner in which the story first crystallized into its shape, we shall find ourselves led back generally to one or other of two sources—either to actual historical events, represented by the fancy under figures personifying them; or else to natural phenomena similarly endowed with life by the imaginative power, usually more or less under the influence of terror. The historical myths we must leave the masters of history to follow; they, and the events they record, being yet involved in great, though attractive and penetrable, mystery. But the stars, and hills, and storms are with us now, as they were with others of old; and it only needs that we look at them with the earnestness of those childish eyes to understand the first words spoken of them by the children of men. And then, in all the most beautiful and enduring myths, we shall find, not only a literal story of a real person,—not only a parallel imagery of moral principle,—but an underlying worship of natural phenomena, out of which both have sprung, and in which both for ever remain rooted. Thus, from the real sun, rising and setting;—from the real atmosphere, calm in its dominion of unfading blue, and fierce in its descent of tempest,—the Greek forms, first, the idea of two entirely personal and corporeal gods, whose limbs are clothed in divine flesh, and whose brows are crowned with divine beauty; yet so real that the quiver rattles at their shoulder, and the chariot bends beneath their weight. And on the other hand, collaterally with these corporeal images, and never for one instant separated from them, he conceives also two omnipresent spiritual influences, of which one illuminates, as the sun, with a constant fire, whatever in humanity is skilful and wise; and the other, like the living air, breathes the calm of heavenly fortitude, and strength

of righteous anger, into every human breast that is pure and brave.

6. Now, therefore, in nearly every myth of importance, and certainly in every one of those of which I shall speak to-night, you have to discern these three structural parts —the root and the two branches:—the root, in physical existence, sun, or sky, or cloud, or sea; then the personal incarnation of that; becoming a trusted and companionable deity, with whom you may walk hand in hand, as a child with its brother or its sister; and, lastly, the moral significance of the image, which is in all the great myths eternally and beneficently true.

7. The great myths; that is to say, myths made by great people. For the first plain fact about myth-making is one which has been most strangely lost sight of,—that you cannot make a myth unless you have something to make it of. You cannot tell a secret which you don't know. If the myth is about the sky, it must have been made by somebody who had looked at the sky. If the myth is about justice and fortitude, it must have been made by some one who knew what it was to be just or patient. According to the quantity of understanding in the person will be the quantity of significance in his fable; and the myth of a simple and ignorant race must necessarily mean little, because a simple and ignorant race have little to mean. So the great question in reading a story is always, not what wild hunter dreamed, or what childish race first dreaded it; but what wise man first perfectly told, and what strong people first perfectly lived by it. And the real meaning of any myth is that which it has at the noblest age of the nation among whom it is current.[3] The farther back you pierce, the less significance you will find, until you come to the first narrow thought, which, indeed, contains the germ of the accomplished tradition; but only as the seed contains the flower. As the intelligence and passion of the race develop, they cling to and nourish their beloved and sacred legend; leaf by leaf, it expands, under the touch

[3] Compare *Fors Clavigera,* Letter 71: "a great myth can only be written in the central time of a nation's power."

of more pure affections, and more delicate imagination, until at last the perfect fable burgeons out into symmetry of milky stem, and honeyed bell.

8. But through whatever changes it may pass, remember that our right reading of it is wholly dependent on the materials we have in our own minds for an intelligent answering sympathy. If it first arose among a people who dwelt under stainless skies, and measured their journeys by ascending and declining stars, we certainly cannot read their story, if we have never seen anything above us in the day but smoke; nor anything round us in the night but candles. If the tale goes on to change clouds or planets into living creatures,—to invest them with fair forms—and inflame them with mighty passions, we can only understand the story of the human-hearted things, in so far as we ourselves take pleasure in the perfectness of visible form, or can sympathise, by an effort of imagination, with the strange people who had other loves than that of wealth, and other interests than those of commerce. And, lastly, if the myth complete itself to the fulfilled thoughts of the nation, by attributing to the gods, whom they have carved out of their fantasy, continual presence with their own souls; and their every effort for good is finally guided by the sense of the companionship, the praise, and the pure will of Immortals, we shall be able to follow them into this last circle of their faith only in the degree in which the better parts of our own beings have been also stirred by the aspects of nature, or strengthened by her laws. It may be easy to prove that the ascent of Apollo in his chariot signifies nothing but the rising of the sun. But what does the sunrise itself signify to us? If only languid return to frivolous amusement, or fruitless labour, it will, indeed, not be easy for us to conceive the power, over a Greek, of the name of Apollo. But if, for us also, as for the Greek, the sunrise means daily restoration to the sense of passionate gladness, and of perfect life—if it means the thrilling of new strength through every nerve,—the shedding over us of a better peace than the peace of night, in the power of the dawn,—and the purging of evil

vision and fear by the baptism of its dew; if the sun itself is an influence, to us also, of spiritual good—and becomes thus in reality, not in imagination, to us also, a spiritual power,—we may then soon over-pass the narrow limit of conception which kept that power impersonal, and rise with the Greek to the thought of an angel who rejoiced as a strong man to run his course, whose voice, calling to life and to labour, rang round the earth, and whose going forth was to the ends of heaven.[4]

9. The time, then, at which I shall take up for you, as well as I can decipher it, the tradition of the Gods of Greece, shall be near the beginning of its central and formed faith,—about 500 B.C.,—a faith of which the character is perfectly represented by Pindar and Æschylus, who are both of them out-spokenly religious, and entirely sincere men; while we may always look back to find the less developed thought of the preceding epoch given by Homer, in a more occult, subtle, half-instinctive and involuntary way.

10. Now, at that culminating period of the Greek religion we find, under one governing Lord of all things, four subordinate elemental forces, and four spiritual powers living in them, and commanding them. The elements are of course the well-known four of the ancient world—the earth, the waters, the fire, and the air; and the living powers of them are Demeter, the Latin Ceres; Poseidon, the Latin Neptune; Apollo, who has retained always his Greek name; and Athena, the Latin Minerva. Each of these is descended from, or changed from, more ancient, and therefore more mystic deities of the earth and heaven, and of a finer element of æther supposed to be beyond the heavens; but at this time we find the four quite definite, both in their kingdoms and in their personalities. They are the rulers of the earth that we tread upon, and the air that we breathe; and are with us as closely, in their vivid humanity, as the dust that they animate, and the winds that they bridle. I shall briefly define for you the range

[4] Psalms xix. 5, 6 (Prayer-book version).

of their separate dominions, and then follow, as far as we have time, the most interesting of the legends which relate to the queen of the air.

11. The rule of the first spirit, Demeter, the earth mother, is over the earth, first, as the origin of all life—the dust from whence we were taken: secondly, as the receiver of all things back at last into silence—"Dust thou art, and unto dust shalt thou return." And, therefore, as the most tender image of this appearing and fading life, in the birth and fall of flowers, her daughter Proserpine plays in the fields of Sicily, and thence is torn away into darkness, and becomes the Queen of Fate—not merely of death, but of the gloom which closes over and ends, not beauty only, but sin; and chiefly of sins, the sin against the life she gave: so that she is, in her highest power, Persephone, the avenger and purifier of blood,—"The voice of thy brother's blood cries to me *out of the ground.*" Then, side by side with this queen of the earth, we find a demigod of agriculture by the plough—the lord of grain, or of the thing ground by the mill. And it is a singular proof of the simplicity of Greek character at this noble time, that of all representations left to us of their deities by their art, few are so frequent, and none perhaps so beautiful, as the symbol of this spirit of agriculture.

12. Then the dominant spirit of the element of water is Neptune, but subordinate to him are myriads of other water spirits, of whom Nereus is the chief, with Palæmon, and Leucothea, the "white lady" of the sea; and Thetis, and nymphs innumerable, who, like her, could "suffer a sea change," while the river deities had each independent power, according to the preciousness of their streams to the cities fed by them,—the "fountain Arethuse, and thou, honoured flood, smooth sliding Mincius, crowned with vocal reeds."[5] And, spiritually, this king of the waters is lord of the strength and daily flow of human life—he gives it material force and victory; which is the meaning of the

[5] *Lycidas,* 85, 86.

dedication of the hair, as the sign of the strength of life, to the river of the native land.

13. Demeter, then, over the earth, and its giving and receiving of life. Neptune over the waters, and the flow and force of life,—always among the Greeks typified by the horse, which was to them as a crested sea-wave, animated and bridled. Then the third element, fire, has set over it two powers: over earthly fire, the assistant of human labour, is set Hephæstus, lord of all labour in which is the flush and the sweat of the brow; and over heavenly fire, the source of day, is set Apollo, the spirit of all kindling, purifying, and illuminating intellectual wisdom; each of these gods having also their subordinate or associated powers—servant, or sister, or companion muse.

14. Then, lastly, we come to the myth which is to be our subject of closer inquiry—the story of Athena and of the deities subordinate to her. This great goddess, the Neith of the Egyptians, the Athena or Athenaia of the Greeks, and, with broken power, half usurped by Mars, the Minerva of the Latins, is, physically, the queen of the air; having supreme power both over its blessings of calm, and wrath of storm; and spiritually, she is the queen of the breath of man, first of the bodily breathing which is life to his blood, and strength to his arm in battle; and then of the mental breathing, or inspiration, which is his moral health and habitual wisdom; wisdom of conduct and of the heart, as opposed to the wisdom of imagination and the brain; moral, as distinct from intellectual; inspired, as distinct from illuminated.

15. By a singular, and fortunate, though I believe wholly accidental coincidence, the heart-virtue, of which she is the spirit, was separated by the ancients into four divisions, which have since obtained acceptance from all men as rightly discerned, and have received, as if from the quarters of the four winds of which Athena is the natural queen, the name of "Cardinal" virtues: namely, Prudence, (the right seeing, and foreseeing, of events through darkness); Justice, (the righteous bestowal of favour and of indignation); Fortitude, (patience under trial

by pain); and Temperance, (patience under trial by pleasure). With respect to these four virtues, the attributes of Athena are all distinct. In her prudence, or sight in darkness, she is "Glaukopis," owl-eyed. In her justice, which is the dominant virtue, she wears two robes, one of light and one of darkness; the robe of light, saffron colour, or the colour of the daybreak, falls to her feet, covering her wholly with favour and love,—the calm of the sky in blessing; it is embroidered along its edge with her victory over the giants, (the troublous powers of the earth,) and the likeness of it was woven yearly by the Athenian maidens and carried to the temple of their own Athena,—not to the Parthenon, that was the temple of all the world's Athena,—but this they carried to the temple of their own only one, who loved them, and stayed with them always. Then her robe of indignation is worn on her breast and left arm only, fringed with fatal serpents, and fastened with Gorgonian cold, turning men to stone; physically, the lightning and the hail of chastisement by storm. Then in her fortitude she wears the crested and unstooping helmet;* and lastly, in her temperance, she is the queen of maidenhood—stainless as the air of heaven.

16. But all these virtues mass themselves in the Greek mind into the two main ones—of Justice, or noble passion, and Fortitude, or noble patience; and of these, the chief powers of Athena, the Greeks had divinely written for them, and for all men after them, two mighty songs,—one, of the Menis,† mens, passion, or zeal, of Athena, breathed into a mortal whose name is "Ache of heart," and whose short life is only the incarnate brooding and burst of storm; and the other is of the foresight and fortitude of Athena, maintained by her in the heart of a mortal whose name is given to him from a longer grief, Odysseus the

* I am compelled, for clearness' sake, to mark only one meaning at a time. Athena's helmet is sometimes a mask—sometimes a sign of anger—sometimes of the highest light of æther: but I cannot speak of all this at once.

† This first word of the *Iliad,* Menis, afterwards passes into the Latin Mens; is the root of the Latin name for Athena, "Minerva," and so of the English "mind."

full of sorrow, the much-enduring, and the long-suffering.

17. The minor expressions by the Greeks in word, in symbol, and in religious service, of this faith, are so many and so beautiful, that I hope some day to gather at least a few of them into a separate body of evidence respecting the power of Athena, and its relations to the ethical conception of the Homeric poems, or rather, to their ethical nature; for they are not conceived didactically, but are didactic in their essence, as all good art is. There is an increasing insensibility to this character, and even an open denial of it, among us, now, which is one of the most curious errors of modernism,—the peculiar and judicial blindness of an age which, having long practised art and poetry for the sake of pleasure only, has become incapable of reading their language when they were both didactic: and also having been itself accustomed to a professedly didactic teaching, which yet, for private interests, studiously avoids collision with every prevalent vice of its day (and especially with avarice), has become equally dead to the intensely ethical conceptions of a race which habitually divided all men into two broad classes of worthy or worthless;—good and good for nothing. And even the celebrated passage of Horace about the *Iliad*[6] is now misread or disbelieved, as if it was impossible that the *Iliad* could be instructive because it is not like a sermon. Horace does not say that it is like a sermon, and would have been still less likely to say so, if he ever had had the advantage of hearing a sermon. "I having been reading that story of Troy again" (thus he writes to a noble youth of Rome whom he cared for), "quietly at Præneste, while you have been busy at Rome; and truly I think that what is base and what is noble, and what useful and useless, may be better learned from that than from all Chrysippus' and Crantor's talk put together."* Which is profoundly true, not of the *Iliad* only, but of all other great art whatso-

* Note, once for all, that unless when there is question about some particular expression, I never translate literally, but give the real force of what is said, as I best can, freely.

[6] *Epistles*, i. 2.

ever; for all pieces of such art are didactic in the purest way, indirectly and occultly, so that, first, you shall only be bettered by them if you are already hard at work in bettering yourself; and when you *are* bettered by them it shall be partly with a general acceptance of their influence, so constant and subtle that you shall be no more conscious of it than of the healthy digestion of food; and partly by a gift of unexpected truth, which you shall only find by slow mining for it;—which is withheld on purpose, and close-locked, that you may not get it till you have forged the key of it in a furnace of your own heating. And this withholding of their meaning is continual, and confessed, in the great poets. Thus Pindar says of himself: "There is many an arrow in my quiver, full of speech to the wise, but, for the many, they need interpreters."[7] And neither Pindar, nor Æschylus, nor Hesiod, nor Homer, nor any of the greater poets or teachers of any nation or time, ever spoke but with intentional reservation: nay, beyond this, there is often a meaning which they themselves cannot interpret,—which it may be for ages long after them to interpret,—in what they said, so far as it recorded true imaginative vision. For all the greatest myths have been seen, by the men who tell them, involuntarily and passively—seen by them with as great distinctness (and in some respects, though not in all, under conditions as far beyond the control of their will) as a dream sent to any of us by night when we dream clearest; and it is this veracity of vision that could not be refused, and of moral that could not be foreseen, which in modern historical inquiry has been left wholly out of account: being indeed the thing which no merely historical investigator can understand, or even believe; for it belongs exclusively to the creative or artistic group of men, and can only be interpreted by those of their race, who themselves in some measure also see visions and dream dreams.[8]

So that you may obtain a more truthful idea of the nature of Greek religion and legend from the poems of Keats,

[7] *Olympia,* ii. 83–86.
[8] Joel ii. 28; Acts ii. 17.

and the nearly as beautiful, and, in general grasp of subject, far more powerful, recent work of Morris,[9] than from frigid scholarship, however extensive. Not that the poet's impressions or renderings of things are wholly true, but their truth is vital, not formal. They are like sketches from life by Reynolds or Gainsborough, which may be demonstrably inaccurate or imaginary in many traits, and indistinct in others, yet will be in the deepest sense like, and true; while the work of historical analysis is too often weak with loss, through the very labour of its miniature touches, or useless in clumsy and vapid veracity of externals, and complacent security of having done all that is required for the portrait, when it has measured the breadth of the forehead, and the length of the nose.

18. The first of requirements, then, for the right reading of myths, is the understanding of the nature of all true vision by noble persons; namely, that it is founded on constant laws common to all human nature; that it perceives, however darkly, things which are for all ages true; —that we can only understand it so far as we have some perception of the same truth;—and that its fulness is developed and manifested more and more by the reverberation of it from minds of the same mirror-temper, in succeeding ages. You will understand Homer better by seeing his reflection in Dante, as you may trace new forms and softer colours in a hillside, redoubled by a lake.

I shall be able partly to show you, even to-night, how much, in the Homeric vision of Athena, has been made clearer by the advance of time, being thus essentially and eternally true; but I must in the outset indicate the relation to that central thought of the imagery of the inferior deities of storm.

19. And first I will take the myth of Æolus (the "sage Hippotades" of Milton's *Lycidas*[10]), as it is delivered pure by Homer from the early times.

[9] William Morris had published *The Life and Death of Jason* in 1867, and the first portion of *The Earthly Paradise* in 1868.

[10] Æolus, son of Hippotes. Line 96:—

"And questioned every gust of rugged wings

Why do you suppose Milton calls him "sage"? One does not usually think of the winds as very thoughtful or deliberate powers. But hear Homer:[11] "Then we came to the Æolian island, and there dwelt Æolus Hippotades, dear to the deathless gods: there he dwelt in a floating island, and round it was a wall of brass that could not be broken; and the smooth rock of it ran up sheer. To whom twelve children were born in the sacred chamber—six daughters and six strong sons; and they dwell for ever with their beloved father, and their mother strict in duty; and with them are laid up a thousand benefits; and the misty house around them rings with fluting all the day long." Now, you are to note first, in this description, the wall of brass and the sheer rock. You will find, throughout the fables of the tempest-group, that the brazen wall and precipice (occurring in another myth as the brazen tower of Danaë) are always connected with the idea of the towering cloud lighted by the sun, here truly described as a floating island. Secondly, you hear that all treasures were laid up in them; therefore, you know this Æolus is lord of the beneficent winds ("he bringeth the wind out of his treasuries"[12]); and presently afterwards Homer calls him the "steward" of the winds,[13] the master of the storehouse of them. And this idea of gifts and preciousness in the winds of heaven is carried out in the well-known sequel of the fable:—Æolus gives them to Ulysses, all but one, bound in a leathern bag,[14] with a glittering cord of silver; and so like a bag of treasures that the sailors think it is one, and open it to see. And when Ulysses is thus driven back to Æolus, and prays him again to help him, note the deliberate words of the King's refusal,—"Did I not,"

That blows from off each beakèd promontory.
They knew not of his story;
And sage Hippotades their answer brings."

[11] *Odyssey*, x. 1–10.

[12] Psalms cxxxv. 7.

[13] ταμίην ἀνέμων—*Odyssey*, x. 21.

[14] But it was only "the blustering winds," (*Odyssey*, x. 20), that Æolus had tied up. "That is indeed an important mistake about the bag," wrote Ruskin to Professor Norton. "Of course

he says, "send thee on thy way heartily, that thou mightest reach thy country, thy home, and whatever is dear to thee? It is not lawful for me again to send forth favourably on his journey a man hated by the happy gods."[15] This idea of the beneficence of Æolus remains to the latest times, though Virgil, by adopting the vulgar change of the cloud island into Lipari, has lost it a little; but even when it is finally explained away by Diodorus, Æolus is still a kind-hearted monarch, who lived on the coast of Sorrento, invented the use of sails, and established a system of storm signals.[16]

20. Another beneficent storm-power, Boreas, occupies an important place in early legend, and a singularly principal one in art; and I wish I could read to you a passage of Plato[17] about the legend of Boreas and Oreithyia,* and the breeze and shade of the Ilissus—notwithstanding its severe reflection upon persons who waste their time on mythological studies; but I must go on at once to the fable with which you are all generally familiar,—that of the Harpies.

This is always connected with that of Boreas or the north wind, because the two sons of Boreas are enemies of the Harpies, and drive them away into frantic flight.†

* Translated by Max Müller in the opening of his essay on "Comparative Mythology." (*Chips from a German Workshop;* vol. ii.)

† Zetes and Calaïs, Pind. *Pyth.*, 4, 324, have *rough purple* (*i.e.*, fiery) wings.[18]

---

these stories are all first fixed in my mind by my boy's reading of Pope—then I read in the Greek rapidly to hunt out the points I want to work on, and am always liable to miss an immaterial point. But it is strange that I hardly ever get anything stated without some grave mistake, however true in my main discoveries" (*Letters to Charles Eliot Norton,* vol. ii. p. 20).

15 *Odyssey,* x. 65, 66, 72, 73.

16 See Diodorus Siculus, v. 7 *ad fin.*

17 See *Phædrus,* 229 B. and C.

18 "Willingly and with glad heart their father Boreas, king of winds, harnessed Zetes and Calaïs, men both with purple wings shooting from their backs."

The myth in its first literal form means only the battle between the fair north wind and the foul south one: the two Harpies, "Storm-swift," and "Swiftfoot," are the sisters of the rainbow[19]—that is to say, they are the broken drifts of the showery south wind, and the clear north wind drives them back; but they quickly take a deeper and more malignant significance. You know the short, violent, spiral gusts that lift the dust before coming rain: the Harpies get identified first with these, and then with more violent whirlwinds, and so they are called "Harpies," "the Snatchers," and are thought of as entirely destructive; their manner of destroying being twofold—by snatching away, and by defiling and polluting. This is a month in which you may really see a small Harpy at her work almost whenever you choose. The first time that there is threatening of rain after two or three days of fine weather, leave your window well open to the street, and some books or papers on the table; and if you do not, in a little while, know what the Harpies mean; and how they snatch, and how they defile, I'll give up my Greek myths.

21. That is the physical meaning. It is now easy to find the mental one. You must all have felt the expression of ignoble anger in those fitful gusts of sudden storm. There is a sense of provocation and apparent bitterness of purpose in their thin and senseless fury, wholly different from the noble anger of the greater tempests. Also, they seem useless and unnatural, and the Greek thinks of them always as vile in malice, and opposed, therefore, to the sons of Boreas, who are kindly winds, that fill sails, and wave

[19] See Hesiod: *Theogony,* 265–269: "And Thaumas wedded Electra, daughter of deep-flowing Ocean; she bare rapid Iris, and the fair-tressed Harpies, Aello and Ocypete, who accompany the wind-blasts and birds, with swift wings, for they fly high above the earth." *Aello,* "storm-swift"; *Ocypete,* "swift-flying." But already in Homer the "more malignant significance" is present: see *Odyssey,* i. 241—"but now the harpies (spirits of the storm) have swept him away inglorious"—and compare *ibid.,* xx. 66, 77.

harvests,—full of bracing health and happy impulses.* From this lower and merely malicious temper, the Harpies rise into a greater terror, always associated with their whirling motion, which is indeed indicative of the most destructive winds: and they are thus related to the nobler tempests, as Charybdis to the sea; they are devouring and desolating, merciless, making all things disappear that come in their grasp: and so, spiritually, they are the gusts of vexatious, fretful, lawless passion, vain and over-shadowing, discontented and lamenting, meagre and insane,—spirits of wasted energy, and wandering disease, and unappeased famine, and unsatisfied hope. So you have, on the one side, the winds of prosperity and health, on the other, of ruin and sickness. Understand that, once, deeply—any who have ever known the weariness of vain desires; the pitiful, unconquerable, coiling and recoiling, and self-involved returns of some sickening famine and thirst of heart:—and you will know what was in the sound of the Harpy Celæno's shriek from her rock;[21] and why, in the seventh circle of the *Inferno*, the Harpies make their nests in the warped branches of the trees that are the souls of suicides.[22]

22. Now you must always be prepared to read Greek legends as you trace threads through figures on a silken damask: the same thread runs through the web, but it makes part of different figures. Joined with other colours you hardly recognize it, and in different lights it is dark or light. Thus the Greek fables blend and cross curiously in different directions, till they knit themselves into an arabesque where sometimes you cannot tell black from purple, nor blue from emerald—they being all the truer

* Conf. Refreshment of Sarpedon, *Il.* v. 697.[20]

[20] In Pope's version:—

"The fainting soul stood ready winged for flight,
And o'er his eyeballs swam the shades of night;
But Boreas rising fresh, with gentle breath,
Recalled his spirit from the gates of death."

[21] *Æneid,* iii. 245 *seq.*

[22] *Inferno,* xiii. 10, 94–108.

for this, because the truths of emotion they represent are interwoven in the same way, but all the more difficult to read, and to explain in any order. Thus the Harpies, as they represent vain desire, are connected with the Sirens, who are the spirits of constant desire: so that it is difficult sometimes in early art to know which are meant, both being represented alike as birds with women's heads: only the Sirens are the great constant desires—the infinite sicknesses of heart—which, rightly placed, give life, and, wrongly placed, waste it away; so that there are two groups of Sirens, one noble and saving, as the other is fatal. But there are no animating or saving Harpies; their nature is always vexing and full of weariness, and thus they are curiously connected with the whole group of legends about Tantalus.

23. We all know what it is to be tantalized; but we do not often think of asking what Tantalus was tantalized for—what he had done, to be for ever kept hungry in sight of food? Well; he had not been condemned to this merely for being a glutton. By Dante the same punishment is assigned to simple gluttony, to purge it away;[23]—but the sins of Tantalus were of a much wider and more mysterious kind. There are four great sins attributed to him—one, stealing the food of the Gods to give it to men: another, sacrificing his son to feed the Gods themselves (it may remind you for a moment of what I was telling you of the earthly character of Demeter, that, while the other Gods all refuse, she, dreaming about her lost daughter, eats part of the shoulder of Pelops before she knows what she is doing); another sin is, telling the secrets of the Gods; and only the fourth—stealing the golden dog of Pandareos —is connected with gluttony. The special sense of this myth is marked by Pandareos receiving the happy privilege of never being troubled with indigestion; the dog, in general, however, mythically represents all utterly senseless and carnal desires, mainly that of gluttony; and in the mythic sense of Hades—that is to say, so far as it represents spiri-

[23] *Purgatorio,* xxii.–xxiv.

tual ruin in this life, and not a literal hell—the dog Cerberus is its gate-keeper—with this special marking of his character of sensual passion, that he fawns on all those who descend, but rages against all who would return (the Virgilian "facilis descensus"[24] being a later recognition of this mythic character of Hades): the last labour of Hercules is the dragging him up to the light; and in some sort, he represents the voracity or devouring of Hades itself; and the mediæval representation of the mouth of hell perpetuates the same thought. Then, also, the power of evil passion is partly associated with the red and scorching light of Sirius, as opposed to the pure light of the sun:—he is the dog-star of ruin; and hence the continual Homeric dwelling upon him, and comparison of the flame of anger to his swarthy light;[25] only, in his scorching, it is thirst, not hunger, over which he rules physically; so that the fable of Icarius, his first master, corresponds, among the Greeks, to the legend of the drunkenness of Noah.[26]

The story of Actæon, the raging death of Hecuba, and the tradition of the white dog which ate part of Hercules' first sacrifice, and so gave name to the Cynosarges, are all various phases of the same thought—the Greek notion of the dog being throughout confused between its serviceable fidelity, its watchfulness, its foul voracity, shamelessness, and deadly madness, while with the curious reversal or recoil of the meaning which attaches itself to nearly every great myth—and which we shall presently see notably exemplified in the relations of the serpent to Athena, —the dog becomes in philosophy a type of severity and abstinence.

24. It would carry us too far aside were I to tell you the story of Pandareos' dog—or rather, of Jupiter's dog, for Pandareos was its guardian only; all that bears on our present purpose is that the guardian of this golden dog had three daughters, one of whom was subject to the

[24] *Æneid,* vi. 126.

[25] See, for instance, *Iliad,* xxii. 25 *seq.*

[26] For the legend of Icarius, who introduced Dionysus into Attica, see Apollodorus, iii. 14.

power of the Sirens, and is turned into the nightingale; and the other two were subject to the power of the Harpies, and this was what happened to them.[27] They were very beautiful, and they were beloved by the gods in their youth, and all the great goddesses were anxious to bring them up rightly. Of all types of young ladies' education, there is nothing so splendid as that of the younger daughters of Pandareos. They have literally the four greatest goddesses for their governesses. Athena teaches them domestic accomplishments; how to weave, and sew, and the like; Artemis teaches them to hold themselves up straight; Hera, how to behave proudly and oppressively to company; and Aphrodite—delightful governess—feeds them with cakes and honey all day long. All goes well, until just the time when they are going to be brought out; then there is a great dispute whom they are to marry, and in the midst of it they are carried off by the Harpies, given by them to be slaves to the Furies, and never seen more. But of course there is nothing in Greek myths; and one never heard of such things as vain desires, and empty hopes, and clouded passions, defiling and snatching away the souls of maidens, in a London season.

I have no time to trace for you any more harpy legends, though they are full of the most curious interest; but I may confirm for you my interpretation of this one, and prove its importance in the Greek mind, by noting that Polygnotus painted these maidens, in his great religious series of paintings at Delphi, crowned with flowers, and playing at dice;[28] and that Penelope remembers them in her last fit of despair, just before the return of Ulysses; and prays bitterly that she may be snatched away at once into nothingness by the Harpies, like Pandareos' daughters, rather than be tormented longer by her deferred hope, and anguish of disappointed love.[29]

25. I have hitherto spoken only of deities of the winds. We pass now to a far more important group, the Deities

[27] The story is told by Homer (*Odyssey*, xx. 66–78).
[28] See, again, Pausanias, x. 30, 2.
[29] See, again, *Odyssey*, xx. 66 *seq*.

of Cloud. Both of these are subordinate to the ruling power of the air, as the demigods of the fountains and minor seas are to the great deep: but as the cloud-firmament detaches itself more from the air, and has a wider range of ministry than the minor streams and sea, the highest cloud deity, Hermes, has a rank more equal with Athena than Nereus or Proteus with Neptune; and there is greater difficulty in tracing his character, because his physical dominion over the clouds can, of course, be asserted only where clouds are; and, therefore, scarcely at all in Egypt:* so that the changes which Hermes undergoes in becoming a Greek from an Egyptian and Phœnician god, are greater than in any other case of adopted tradition. In Egypt Hermes is a deity of historical record, and a conductor of the dead to judgment; the Greeks take away much of this historical function, assigning it to the Muses; but, in investing him with the physical power over clouds, they give him that which the Muses disdain—the power of concealment, and of theft. The snatching away by the Harpies is with brute force; but the snatching away by the clouds is connected with the thought of hiding, and of making things seem to be what they are not; so that Hermes is the god of lying, as he is of mist; and yet, with this ignoble function of making things vanish and disappear, is connected the remnant of his grand Egyptian authority of leading away souls in the cloud of death (the actual dimness of sight caused by mortal wounds physically suggesting the darkness and descent of clouds, and continually being so described in the *Iliad*); while the sense of the need of guidance on the untrodden road follows necessarily. You cannot but remember how this thought of

* I believe that the conclusions of recent scholarship are generally opposed to the Herodotean ideas of any direct acceptance by the Greeks of Egyptian Myths: and very certainly, Greek art is developed by giving the veracity and simplicity of real life to Eastern savage grotesque; and not by softening the severity of pure Egyptian designs. But it is of no consequence whether one conception was, or was not, in this case, derived from the other; my object is only to mark the essential differences between them.

cloud guidance, and cloud receiving of souls at death, has been elsewhere ratified.[30]

26. Without following that higher clue, I will pass to the lovely group of myths connected with the birth of Hermes on the Greek mountains. You know that the valley of Sparta is one of the noblest mountain ravines in the world, and that the western flank of it is formed by an unbroken chain of crags, forty miles long, rising, opposite Sparta, to a height of 8,000 feet, and known as the chain of Taygetus. Now the nymph from whom that mountain ridge is named, was the mother of Lacedæmon; therefore, the mythic ancestress of the Spartan race. She is the nymph Taygeta, and one of the seven stars of spring; one of those Pleiades of whom is the question to Job,—"Canst thou bind the sweet influences of Pleiades, or loose the bands of Orion?"[31] "The sweet influences of Pleiades," of the stars of spring,—nowhere sweeter than among the pineclad slopes of the hills of Sparta and Arcadia, when the snows of their higher summits, beneath the sunshine of April, fell into fountains, and rose into clouds; and in every ravine was a newly-awakened voice of waters,—soft increase of whisper among its sacred stones: and on every crag its forming and fading veil of radiant cloud; temple above temple, of the divine marble that no tool can pollute, nor ruin undermine. And, therefore, beyond this central valley, this great Greek vase of Arcadia, on the "*hollow*" mountain, Cyllene, or "pregnant" mountain, called also "cold," because there the vapours rest,* and born of the eldest of those stars of spring, that Maia, from whom your own month of May has its name, bringing to you, in the green of her garlands and the white of her hawthorn, the unrecognized symbols of the pastures and the wreathed snows of Arcadia, where long ago she was queen

* On the altar of Hermes on its summit, as on that of the Lacinian Hera, no wind ever stirred the ashes. Beside those altars, the Gods of Heaven were appeased: and all their storms at rest.

---

30 Acts i. 9: "and a cloud received Him out of their sight."
31 Job xxxviii. 31.

of stars: there—first cradled and wrapt in swaddling-clothes; then raised, in a moment of surprise, into his wandering power—is born the shepherd of the clouds,[32] winged-footed and deceiving,—blinding the eyes of Argus, —escaping from the grasp of Apollo—restless messenger between the highest sky and topmost earth—

> "the herald Mercury,
> New-lighted on a heaven-kissing hill."[33]

27. Now, it will be wholly impossible, at present, to trace for you any of the minor Greek expressions of this thought, except only that Mercury, as the cloud shepherd, is especially called Eriophoros, the wool-bearer.[34] You will recollect the name from the common woolly rush "eriophorum," which has a cloud of silky seed; and note also that he wears distinctively the flat cap, *petasos,* named from a word meaning to expand; which shaded from the sun, and is worn on journeys. You have the epithet of mountains "cloud-capped" as an established form with every poet, and the Mont Pilate of Lucerne is named from a Latin word signifying specially a *woollen* cap; but Mercury has, besides, a general Homeric epithet, curiously and intensely concentrated in meaning, "the profitable or serviceable by wool," that is to say, by shepherd wealth; hence, "pecuniarily," rich, or serviceable, and so he passes at last into a general mercantile deity; while yet the cloud sense of the wool is retained by Homer always, so that he gives him this epithet when it would otherwise have been quite meaningless, (in *Iliad,* xxiv. 440,) when he drives Priam's chariot, and breathes force into his horses, precisely as we shall find Athena drive Diomed: and yet the serviceable and profitable sense, and something also of gentle and soothing character in the mere wool-softness,

[32] See the opening lines of the Homeric Hymn: "Of Hermes sing, O Muse, the son of Zeus and Maia, Lord of Cyllene, and Arcadia rich in sheep," etc.

[33] *Hamlet,* iii. 4, 58.

[34] This is a puzzling statement, for no instance can be found of the application of this rare epithet to Hermes.

as used for dress, and religious rites, is retained also in the epithet, and thus the gentle and serviceable Hermes is opposed to the deceitful one.

28. In connection with this driving of Priam's chariot, remember that as Autolycus is the son of Hermes the Deceiver, Myrtilus (the Auriga of the Stars) is the son of Hermes the Guide. The name Hermes itself means Impulse; and he is especially the shepherd of the flocks of the sky, in driving, or guiding, or stealing them; and yet his great name, Argeiphontes, not only—as in different passages of the olden poets—means "Shining White," which is said of him as being himself the silver cloud lighted by the sun; but "Argus-Killer," the killer of brightness, which is said of him as he veils the sky, and especially the stars, which are the eyes of Argus; or, literally, eyes of brightness, which Juno, who is, with Jupiter, part of the type of highest heaven, keeps in her peacock's train. We know that this interpretation is right, from a passage in which Euripides describes the shield of Hippomedon,[35] which bore for its sign, "Argus the all-seeing, covered with eyes; open towards the rising of the stars, and closed towards their setting."

And thus Hermes becomes the spirit of the movement of the sky or firmament; not merely the fast flying of the transitory cloud, but the great motion of the heavens and stars themselves. Thus, in his highest power, he corresponds to the "primo mobile" of the later Italian philosophy,[36] and, in his simplest, is the guide of all mysterious and cloudy movement, and of all successful subtleties. Perhaps the prettiest minor recognition of his character is when, on the night foray of Ulysses and Diomed, Ulysses

[35] *Phœnissæ,* 116.

[36] The *primum mobile* was in the Ptolemaic system of astronomy the tenth sphere, supposed to revolve from east to west in twenty-four hours, carrying with it all the other spheres. Thus in Milton (*Paradise Lost,* iii. 481–483):—

> "They pass the planets seven, and pass the fixed,
> And that crystalline sphere whose balance weighs
> The trepidation talked, and that *first moved.*"

wears the helmet stolen by Autolycus the son of Hermes.[37]

29. The position in the Greek mind of Hermes as the Lord of cloud is, however, more mystic and ideal than that of any other deity, just on account of the constant and real presence of the cloud itself under different forms, giving rise to all kinds of minor fables. The play of the Greek imagination in this direction is so wide and complex, that I cannot even give you an outline of its range in my present limits. There is first a great series of storm-legends connected with the family of the historic Æolus, centralized by the story of Athamas, with his two wives "the Cloud" and the "White Goddess,"[38] ending in that of Phrixus and Helle, and of the golden fleece (which is only the cloud-burden of Hermes Eriophoros). With this, there is the fate of Salmoneus, and the destruction of Glaucus by his own horses;[39] all these minor myths of storm concentrating themselves darkly into the legend of Bellerophon and the Chimæra, in which there is an under story about the vain subduing of passion and treachery, and the end of life in fading melancholy,[40]—which, I hope,

[37] *Iliad,* x. 261 *seq.*

[38] Athamas, son of Æolus, married first Nephele; and then Ino, daughter of Cadmus, worshipped as a sea-goddess under the name Leucothea (*Odyssey,* v. 333). She was jealous of Phrixus and Helle, the children of Athamas by Nephele, and resolved to destroy them; but they escaped from her fury to Colchis, on a golden ram.

[39] The story of Glaucus, son of Sisyphus, destroyed by his own mares, is told by Hyginus (250), and referred to by Virgil (*Georgics,* ii. 267).

[40] Here Ruskin rationalises the story of Bellerophon as told by the fabulists and poets. Bellerophon, after the murder of his brother, had fled to the court of Prœtus, King of Argos; and there he resisted the advances of Stenobœa, the king's wife. But she accused him to her husband, who sent him to his father-in-law, Jobates, King of Lycia, to be murdered treacherously. Jobates, not wishing to put him straight to death, imposed on Bellerophon many dangerous labours; amongst others, the slaying of the Chimæra. In vain did Bellerophon surmount them; for when he tried to escape to heaven on Pegasus, Zeus stung the horse and Bellerophon fell to earth, wandering about henceforth in deep dejection.

not many of you could understand even were I to show it you: (the merely physical meaning of the Chimæra is the cloud of volcanic lightning, connected wholly with earth-fire, but resembling the heavenly cloud in its height and its thunder). Finally, in the Æolic group, there is the legend of Sisyphus, which I mean to work out thoroughly by itself: its root is in the position of Corinth as ruling the isthmus and the two seas—the Corinthian Acropolis, two thousand feet high, being the centre of the crossing currents of the winds, and of the commerce of Greece. Therefore, Athena, and the fountain cloud Pegasus, are more closely connected with Corinth than even with Athens in their material, though not in their moral power; and Sisyphus founds the Isthmian games in connection with a melancholy story about the sea gods;[41] but he himself is the most "gaining" and subtle of men:[42] who, having the key of the Isthmus, becomes the type of transit, transfer, or trade, as such; and of the apparent gain from it, which is not gain; and this is the real meaning of his punishment in hell—eternal toil and recoil (the modern idol of capital being, indeed, the stone of Sisyphus with a vengeance, *crushing* in its recoil). But, throughout, the old ideas of the cloud power and cloud feebleness,—the deceit of its hiding,—and the emptiness of its vanishing, —the Autolycus enchantment of making black seem white, —and the disappointed fury of Ixion (taking shadow for power), mingle in the moral meaning of this and its collateral legends; and give an aspect, at last, not only of foolish cunning, but of impiety or literal "idolatry," "imagination worship," to the dreams of avarice and injustice, until this notion of atheism and insolent blindness becomes

[41] Pausanias ii. 1, 3: "they say that the child Melicertes was landed on this spot by a dolphin, and that Sisyphus found him lying, buried him on the isthmus, and instituted the Isthmian games in his honour." Melicertes, son of Athamas and Ino, had been saved by his mother from the fury of his father. She in despair had thrown herself with her son in her arms into the sea; but Poseidon, pitying her, changed her into a sea-goddess, Leucothea.

[42] *Iliad,* vi. 153.

principal; and the *Clouds* of Aristophanes, with the personified "just" and "unjust" sayings in the latter part of the play, foreshadow, almost feature by feature, in all that they were written to mock and to chastise, the worst elements of the impious "δῖνος"[43] and tumult in men's thoughts, which have followed on their avarice in the present day, making them alike forsake the laws of their ancient gods, and misapprehend or reject the true words of their existing teachers.

30. All this we have from the legends of the historic Æolus only; but, besides these, there is the beautiful story of Semele, the mother of Bacchus.[44] She is the cloud with the strength of the vine in its bosom, consumed by the light which matures the fruit; the melting away of the cloud into the clear air at the fringe of its edges being exquisitely rendered by Pindar's epithet for her, Semele, "with the stretched-out hair."[45] Then there is the entire tradition of the Danaïdes, and of the tower of Danaë and golden shower; the birth of Perseus connecting this legend with that of the Gorgons and Graiæ, who are the true clouds of thunderous and ruinous tempest. I must, in passing, mark for you that the form of the sword or sickle of Perseus, with which he kills Medusa, is another image of the whirling harpy vortex, and belongs especially to the sword of destruction or annihilation; whence it is given to the two angels who gather for destruction the evil harvest and evil vintage of the earth (Rev. xiv. 15). I will collect afterwards and complete what I have already written respecting the Pegasean and Gorgonian legends, noting here only what is necessary to explain the central myth of Athena herself, who represents the ambient air, which included all cloud, and rain, and dew, and darkness, and

[43] See *Clouds*, 380, where Socrates is represented as putting Δῖνος (whirling, rotation) in place of Δῖος (Zeus).

[44] Here Ruskin explains as a nature-myth the story of Semele, who was visited by Zeus attended with clouds, lightning, and thunderbolt, and, unable to endure so much majesty, was consumed by fire.

[45] *Olymp.*, ii. 46.

peace, and wrath of heaven. Let me now try to give you, however briefly, some distinct idea of the several agencies of this great goddess.

31. I. She is the air giving life and health to all animals.

II. She is the air giving vegetative power to the earth.

III. She is the air giving motion to the sea, and rendering navigation possible.

IV. She is the air nourishing artificial light, torch or lamplight; as opposed to that of the sun, on one hand, and of *consuming** fire on the other.

V. She is the air conveying vibration of sound.

I will give you instances of her agency in all these functions.

32. First, and chiefly, she is air as the spirit of life, giving vitality to the blood. Her psychic relation to the vital force in matter lies deeper, and we will examine it afterwards; but a great number of the most interesting passages in Homer regard her as flying over the earth in local and transitory strength, simply and merely the goddess of fresh air.

It is curious that the British city which has somewhat saucily styled itself the Modern Athens, is indeed more under her especial tutelage and favour in this respect than perhaps any other town in the island. Athena is first simply what in the Modern Athens you so practically find her, the breeze of the mountain and the sea; and wherever she comes, there is purification, and health, and power. The sea-beach round this isle of ours is the frieze of our Parthenon, every wave that breaks on it thunders with Athena's voice; nay, whenever you throw your window wide open in the morning, you let in Athena, as wisdom and fresh air at the same instant; and whenever you draw a pure, long, full breath of right heaven, you take Athena into your heart, through your blood; and with the blood, into the thoughts of your brain.

* Not a scientific, but a very practical and expressive distinction.

Now this giving of strength by the air, observe, is mechanical as well as chemical. You cannot strike a good blow but with your chest full; and in hand to hand fighting, it is not the muscle that fails first, it is the breath; the longest-breathed will, on the average, be the victor,—not the strongest. Note how Shakspeare always leans on this. Of Mortimer, in "changing hardiment with great Glendower":[46]

"Three times they breathed, and three times did they drink,
Upon agreement, of swift Severn's flood."

And again, Hotspur sending challenge to Prince Harry:—

"That none might draw short breath to-day
But I and Harry Monmouth."

Again, of Hamlet, before he receives his wound:—

"He's fat, and scant of breath."

Again, Orlando in the wrestling:—

"Yes, I beseech your grace: I am not yet well breathed."

Now of all people that ever lived, the Greeks knew best what breath meant, both in exercise and in battle; and therefore the queen of the air becomes to them at once the queen of bodily strength in war; not mere brutal muscular strength,—that belongs to Ares,—but the strength of young lives passed in pure air and swift exercise,—Camilla's virginal force, that "flies o'er the unbending corn, and skims along the main."[47]

33. Now I will rapidly give you two or three instances of her direct agency in this function. First, when she wants to make Penelope bright and beautiful; and to do away with the signs of her waiting and her grief. "Then Athena thought of another thing; she laid her into deep

[46] The passages referred to are in *1 Henry IV.*, i. 3, and v. 2 ("And that no man," etc.: Ruskin quotes from memory); *Hamlet*, v. 2; *As You Like It*, i. 2.

[47] *Æneid*, vii. 808.

sleep, and loosed all her limbs, and made her taller, and made her smoother, and fatter, and whiter than sawn ivory; and breathed ambrosial brightness over her face; and so she left her and went up to heaven."[48] Fresh air and sound sleep at night, young ladies! You see you may have Athena for lady's maid whenever you choose. Next, hark how she gives strength to Achilles when he is broken with fasting and grief. Jupiter pities him and says to her, —"'Daughter mine, are you forsaking your own soldier, and don't you care for Achilles any more? see how hungry and weak he is,—go and feed him with ambrosia.' So he urged the eager Athena; and she leapt down out of heaven like a harpy falcon, shrill voiced; and she poured nectar and ambrosia, full of delight, into the breast of Achilles, that his limbs might not fail with famine: then she returned to the solid dome of her strong father."[49] And then comes the great passage about Achilles arming—for which we have no time. But here is again Athena giving strength to the whole Greek army. She came as a falcon to Achilles, straight at him;—a sudden drift of breeze; but to the army she must come widely,—she sweeps round them all. "As when Jupiter spreads the purple rainbow over heaven, portending battle or cold storm, so Athena, wrapping herself round with a purple cloud, stooped to the Greek soldiers, and raised up each of them."[50] Note that purple, in Homer's use of it, nearly always means "fiery," "full of light." It is the light of the rainbow, not the colour of it, which Homer means you to think of.

34. But the most curious passage of all, and fullest of meaning, is when she gives strength to Menelaus, that he may stand unwearied against Hector. He prays to her: "And blue-eyed Athena was glad that he prayed to her, first; and she gave him strength in his shoulders, and in his limbs, and she gave him the courage"—of what animal, do you suppose? Had it been Neptune or Mars, they would have given him the courage of a bull, or lion; but

[48] *Odyssey*, xviii. 187–197.
[49] *Iliad*, xix. 342–351.
[50] *Ibid.*, xvii. 547–552.

Athena gives him the courage of the most fearless in attack of all creatures—small or great—and very small it is, but wholly incapable of terror,—she gives him the courage of a fly.[51]

35. Now this simile of Homer's is one of the best instances I can give you of the way in which great writers seize truths unconsciously which are for all time. It is only recent science which has completely shown the perfectness of this minute symbol of the power of Athena; proving that the insect's flight and breath are co-ordinated; that its wings are actually forcing pumps, of which the stroke compels the thoracic respiration; and that it thus breathes and flies simultaneously by the action of the same muscles, so that respiration is carried on most vigorously during flight, "while the air-vessels, supplied by many pairs of lungs instead of one, traverse the organs of flight in far greater numbers than the capillary blood-vessels of our own system, and give enormous and untiring muscular power, a rapidity of action measured by thousands of strokes in the minute, and an endurance, by miles and hours of flight."*

Homer could not have known this; neither that the buzzing of the fly was produced as in a wind instrument, by a constant current of air through the trachea. But he had seen, and, doubtless, meant us to remember, the marvellous strength and swiftness of the insect's flight (the glance of the swallow itself is clumsy and slow compared to the darting of common house-flies at play); he probably attributed its murmur to the wings, but in this also there was a type of what we shall presently find recognized in the name of Pallas,—the vibratory power of the air to convey sound,—while, as a purifying creature, the fly holds its place beside the old symbol of Athena in Egypt, the vulture; and as a venomous and tormenting creature, has more than the strength of the serpent in proportion to its size, being thus entirely representative

* Ormerod. *Natural History of Wasps.*

---

51 *Iliad,* xvii. 566–570.

of the influence of the air both in purification and pestilence; and its courage is so notable that, strangely enough, forgetting Homer's simile, I happened to take the fly for an expression of the audacity of freedom in speaking of quite another subject. Whether it should be called courage, or mere mechanical instinct, may be questioned, but assuredly no other animal, exposed to continual danger, is so absolutely without sign of fear.

36. You will, perhaps, have still patience to hear two instances, not of the communication of strength, but of the personal agency of Athena as the air. When she comes down to help Diomed against Ares, she does not come to fight instead of him, but she takes his charioteer's place.

"She snatched the reins, she lashed with all her force,
And full on Mars impelled the foaming horse."[52]

Ares is the first to cast his spear; then, note this:—Pope says—

"Pallas opposed her hand, and caused to glance,
Far from the car, the strong immortal lance."[53]

She does not *oppose* her hand in the Greek, for the wind could not meet the lance straight. She catches it in her hand, and throws it off. There is no instance in which a lance is so parried by a mortal hand in all the *Iliad;* and it is exactly the way the wind would parry it, catching it and turning it aside. If there be any good rifleshots here, they know something about Athena's parrying—and in old times the English masters of feathered artillery knew more yet. Compare also the turning of Hector's lance from Achilles: *Iliad,* xx. 439.

37. The last instance I will give you is as lovely as it is subtle. Throughout the *Iliad* Athena is herself the will or Menis of Achilles. If he is to be calmed, it is she who calms him; if angered, it is she who inflames him. In the first quarrel with Atrides, when he stands at pause, with the great sword half drawn, "Athena came from heaven,

52 *Iliad,* v. 840, 841; 1034, 1035 in Pope's version.
53 *Ibid.,* 1046, 1047 in Pope's version.

and stood behind him, and caught him by the yellow hair."[54] Another god would have stayed his hand upon the hilt, but Athena only lifts his hair. "And he turned and knew her, and her dreadful eyes shone upon him."[55] There is an exquisite tenderness in this laying her hand upon his hair, for it is the talisman of his life, vowed to his own Thessalian river if he ever returned to its shore, and cast upon Patroclus' pile, so ordaining that there should be no return.[56]

38. Secondly—Athena is the air giving vegetative impulse to the earth. She is the wind and the rain—and yet more the pure air itself, getting at the earth fresh turned by spade or plough—and, above all, feeding the fresh leaves; for though the Greeks knew nothing about carbonic acid, they did know that trees fed on the air.

Now, note first in this, the myth of the air getting at ploughed ground. You know I told you the Lord of all labour by which man lived was Hephæstus; therefore Athena adopts a child of his, and of the earth,—Erichthonius,—literally, "the tearer up of the ground"—who is the head (though not in direct line) of the kings of Attica; and having adopted him, she gives him to be brought up by the three nymphs of the dew. Of these, Aglauros, the dweller in the fields, is the envy or malice of the earth; she answers nearly to the envy of Cain, the tiller of the ground, against his shepherd brother, in her own envy against her two sisters, Herse, the cloud dew, who is the beloved of the shepherd Mercury; and Pandrosos, the diffused dew, or dew of heaven. Literally, you have in this myth the words of the blessing of Esau—"Thy dwelling shall be of the fatness of the earth, and of the dew of

54 *Iliad,* i. 194–197.

55 *Ibid.,* 199, 200.

56 *Ibid.,* xxiii. 140 *seq.* (thus rendered by Pope):—

"But great Achilles stands apart in prayer,
And from his head divides the yellow hair;
Those curling locks which from his youth he vowed,
And sacred grew, to Sperchius' honoured flood:
Then sighing, to the deep his looks he cast,
And rolled his eyes around the watery waste."

heaven from above."[57] Aglauros is for her envy turned into a black stone; and hers is one of the voices,—the other being that of Cain,—which haunts the circle of envy in the Purgatory:—

"Io sono Aglauro, chi divenne sasso."[58]

But to her two sisters, with Erichthonius, (or the hero Erectheus,) is built the most sacred temple of Athena in Athens; the temple to their own dearest Athena—to her, and to the dew together: so that it was divided into two parts: one, the temple of Athena of the city, and the other that of the dew.[59] And this expression of her power, as the air bringing the dew to the hill pastures, in the central temple of the central city of the heathen, dominant over the future intellectual world, is, of all the facts connected with her worship as the spirit of life, perhaps the most important. I have no time now to trace for you the hundredth part of the different ways in which it bears both upon natural beauty, and on the best order and happiness of men's lives. I hope to follow out some of these trains of thought in gathering together what I have to say about field herbage; but I must say briefly here that the great sign, to the Greeks, of the coming of spring in the pastures, was not, as with us, in the primrose, but in the various flowers of the asphodel tribe (of which I will give you some separate account presently); therefore it is that the earth answers with crocus flame to the cloud on Ida;[60] and the power of Athena in eternal life is written by the light of the asphodel on the Elysian fields.

57 Genesis xxvii. 39.

58 *Purgatorio,* xiv. 139.

59 The Erechtheum seems to have included three distinct shrines—the Temple of Athena Polias, the most revered sanctuary of Athens; the shrines of Erechtheus and Poseidon; and, thirdly, the Pandroseion.

60 See *Iliad,* xiv. 347 *seq.*, where in the recesses of Mount Ida "beneath them the divine earth caused fresh grass to spring up, and dewy lotus and crocus . . . and they were clothed with a cloud, beauteous, golden." The passage is imitated by Tennyson in his description of "a vale in Ida" (*Œnone,* 97):—

But farther, Athena is the air, not only to the lilies of the field, but to the leaves of the forest. We saw before the reason why Hermes is said to be the son of Maia, the eldest of the sister stars of spring. Those stars are called not only Pleiades, but Vergiliæ, from a word mingling the ideas of the turning or returning of spring-time with the out-pouring of rain. The mother of Virgil bearing the name of Maia, Virgil himself received his name from the seven stars; and he, in forming, first, the mind of Dante, and through him that of Chaucer (besides whatever special minor influence came from the *Pastorals* and *Georgics*), became the fountain-head of all the best literary power connected with the love of vegetative nature among civilized races of men. Take the fact for what it is worth; still it is a strange seal of coincidence, in word and in reality, upon the Greek dream of the power over human life, and its purest thoughts, in the stars of spring. But the first syllable of the name of Virgil has relation also to another group of words, of which the English ones, virtue, and virgin, bring down the force to modern days. It is a group containing mainly the idea of "spring," or increase of life in vegetation—the rising of the new branch of the tree out of the bud, and of the new leaf out of the ground. It involves, secondarily, the idea of greenness and of strength, but primarily, that of living increase of a new rod from a stock, stem, or root; ("There shall come forth a rod out of the stem of Jesse;"[61]) and chiefly the stem of certain plants—either of the rose tribe, as in the budding of the almond rod of Aaron; or of the olive tribe, which has triple significance in this symbolism, from the use of its oil for sacred anointing, for strength in the gymnasium, and for light. Hence, in numberless divided and reflected ways, it is connected with the power of Hercules and Athena: Hercules plants the wild olive, for its shade, on

---

"It was the deep mid-noon: one silvery cloud
Had lost his way between the piney sides
Of this long glen. Then to the bower they came,
Naked they came to that smooth-swarded bower,
And at their feet the crocus brake like flame."

[61] Isaiah xi. 1.

the course of Olympia, and it thenceforward gives the Olympic crown, of consummate honour and rest;[62] while the prize at the Panathenaic games is a vase of its oil, (meaning encouragement to continuance of effort); and from the paintings on these Panathenaic vases we get the most precious clue to the entire character of Athena. Then to express its propagation by slips, the trees from which the oil was to be taken were called "Moriai," trees of division (being all descendants of the sacred one in the Erechtheum). And thus, in one direction, we get to the "children like olive plants round about thy table" and the olive grafting of St. Paul;[63] while the use of the oil for anointing gives chief name to the rod itself of the stem of Jesse, and to all those who were by that name signed for his disciples first in Antioch. Remember, farther, since that name was first given, the influence of the symbol, both in extreme unction, and in consecration of priests and kings to their "divine right"; and think, if you can reach with any grasp of thought, what the influence on the earth has been, of those twisted branches whose leaves give grey bloom to the hillsides under every breeze that blows from the midland sea. But, above and beyond all, think how strange it is that the chief Agonia of humanity, and the chief giving of strength from heaven for its fulfilment, should have been under its night shadow in Palestine.[64]

39. Thirdly—Athena is the air in its power over the sea.

On the earliest Panathenaic vase known—the "Burgon" vase in the British Museum—Athena has a dolphin on her shield. The dolphin has two principal meanings in Greek symbolism. It means, first, the sea; secondarily, the ascending and descending course of any of the heavenly bodies from one sea horizon to another—the dolphin's arching rise and re-plunge (in a summer evening, out of

62 See Pausanias, v. 7, 4.

63 Psalms cxxviii. 3; Romans xi. 17. Christ, the anointed; and "the disciples were called Christians first in Antioch" (Acts xi. 26).

64 See Matthew xxvi. 30, 36. The traditional site of the Garden of Gethsemane is at the foot of Mount Olivet.

calm sea, their black backs roll round with exactly the slow motion of a water-wheel; but I do not know how far Aristotle's exaggerated account of their leaping or their swiftness has any foundation,[65]) being taken as a type of the emergence of the sun or stars from the sea in the east and plunging beneath in the west. Hence, Apollo, when in his personal power he crosses the sea, leading his Cretan colonists to Pytho, takes the form of a dolphin, becomes Apollo Delphinius, and names the founded colony "Delphi." The lovely drawing of the Delphic Apollo on the hydria of the Vatican, gives the entire conception of this myth. Again, the beautiful coins of Tarentum represent Taras coming to found the city, riding on a dolphin, whose leaps and plunges have partly the rage of the sea in them, and partly the spring of the horse, because the splendid riding of the Tarentines had made their name proverbial in Magna Græcia. The story of Arion is a collateral fragment of the same thought; and again, the plunge before their transformation, of the ships of Æneas.[66] Then, this idea of career upon, or conquest of the sea, either by the creatures themselves, or by dolphin-like ships, (compare the Merlin prophecy,—

"They shall ride
Over ocean wide
With hempen bridle, and horse of tree,"[67])

connects itself with the thought of undulation, and of the wave-power in the sea itself, which is always expressed by the serpentine bodies either of the sea-gods or of the sea-horse; and when Athena carries, as she does often in later work, a serpent for her shield-sign, it is not so much the repetition of her own ægis-snakes as the farther expression of her power over the sea-wave; which, finally, Virgil gives in its perfect unity with her own anger, in the approach

[65] *Hist. An.*, ix. 48, 4, where it is said that the dolphin leaps over the masts of ships, and darts as quick as an arrow.

[66] *Æneid*, ix. 119.

[67] Thomas of Ercildoune.

of the serpents against Laocoon from the sea:[68] and then, finally, when her own storm-power is fully put forth on the ocean also, and the madness of the ægis-snake is given to the wave-snake, the sea-wave becomes the devouring hound at the waist of Scylla, and Athena takes Scylla for her helmet-crest; while yet her beneficent and essential power on the ocean, in making navigation possible, is commemorated in the Panathenaic festival by her peplus being carried to the Erechtheum suspended from the mast of a ship.

In Plate cxv. of vol. ii., Lenormant,[69] are given two sides of a vase, which, in rude and childish way, assembles most of the principal thoughts regarding Athena in this relation. In the first the sunrise is represented by the ascending chariot of Apollo, foreshortened; the light is supposed to blind the eyes, and no face of the god is seen. (Turner, in the Ulysses and Polyphemus sunrise, loses the form of the god in light, giving the chariot-horses only;[70] rendering in his own manner, after 2,200 years of various fall and revival of the arts, precisely the same thought as the old Greek potter.) He ascends out of the sea; but the sea itself has not yet caught the light. In the second design, Athena as the morning breeze, and Hermes as the morning cloud, fly over the sea before the sun. Hermes turns back his head; his face is unseen in the cloud, as Apollo's in the light; the grotesque appearance of an animal's face is only the cloud-phantasm modifying a frequent form of the hair of Hermes beneath the back of his cap. Under the morning breeze, the dolphins leap from the rippled sea, and their sides catch the light.

The coins of the Lucanian Heracleia give a fair representation of the helmed Athena, as imagined in later Greek art, with the embossed Scylla.

40. Fourthly—Athena is the air nourishing artificial light —unconsuming fire. Therefore, a lamp was always kept

[68] *Æneid,* ii. 205.

[69] From a small Bacchic amphora, black-figured, in the Cabinet de Médailles at the Louvre.

[70] No. 508 in the National Gallery

burning in the Erechtheum; and the torch-race belongs chiefly to her festival,[71] of which the meaning is to show the danger of the perishing of the light even by excess of the air that nourishes it: and so that the race is not to the swift,[72] but to the wise. The household use of her constant light is symbolized in the lovely passage in the *Odyssey*, where Ulysses and his son move the armour while the servants are shut in their chambers, and there is no one to hold torches for them; but Athena herself, "having a golden lamp,"[73] fills all the rooms with light. Her presence in war-strength with her favourite heroes is always shown by the "unwearied"[74] fire hovering on their helmets and shields; and the image gradually becomes constant and accepted, both for the maintenance of household watchfulness, as in the parable of the ten virgins, or as the symbol of direct inspiration, in the rushing wind and divided flames of Pentecost:[75] but, together with this thought of unconsuming and constant fire, there is always mingled in the Greek mind the sense of the consuming by excess, as of the flame by the air, so also of the inspired creature by its own fire (thus, again, "the zeal of thine house hath eaten me up"—"my zeal hath consumed me, because of thine enemies,"[76] and the like); and especially Athena has this aspect towards the truly sensual and bodily strength; so that to Ares, who is himself insane and consuming, the opposite wisdom seems to be insane and consuming: "All we the other gods have thee against us, O Jove! when we would give grace to men; for thou hast begotten the maid without a mind—the mischievous creature, the doer of unseemly evil. All we obey thee, and are ruled by thee. Her only thou wilt not resist in anything she says or does,

[71] "Callimachus made a golden lamp for the goddess. They fill the lamp with oil, and wait till the same day next year, and the oil suffices for the lamp during all the intervening time, though it is burning night and day" (Pausanias, i. 26, 7).

[72] Ecclesiastes ix. 11.

[73] *Odyssey*, xix. 34.

[74] *Iliad*, v. 4, where Athena gives strength to Diomede.

[75] Matthew xxv.; Acts ii. 2, 3.

[76] Psalms lxix. 9; cxix. 139.

because thou didst bear her—consuming child as she is."[77]

41. Lastly—Athena is the air conveying vibration of sound.

In all the loveliest representations in central Greek art of the birth of Athena, Apollo stands close to the sitting Jupiter, singing, with a deep, quiet joyfulness, to his lyre. The sun is always thought of as the master of time and rhythm, and as the origin of the composing and inventive discovery of melody; but the air, as the actual element and substance of the voice, the prolonging and sustaining power of it, and the symbol of its moral passion. Whatever in music is measured and designed, belongs therefore to Apollo and the Muses; whatever is impulsive and passionate, to Athena: hence her constant strength of voice or cry (as when she aids the shout of Achilles[78]) curiously opposed to the dumbness of Demeter.[79] The Apolline lyre, therefore, is not so much the instrument producing sound, as its measurer and divider by length or tension of string into given notes; and I believe it is, in a double connection with its office as a measurer of time or motion, and its relation to the transit of the sun in the sky, that Hermes forms it from the tortoise-shell, which is the image of the dappled concave of the cloudy sky. Thenceforward all the limiting or restraining modes of music belong to the Muses; but the passionate music is wind music, as in the Doric flute. Then, when this inspired music becomes degraded in its passion, it sinks into the pipe of Pan, and the double pipe of Marsyas, and is then rejected by Athena.[80] The myth which rep-

[77] *Iliad,* v. 872–880.

[78] *Iliad,* xviii. 217–218.

[79] Who, however, had reason for her silence in absorbing grief for her daughter. "In silence she waited, casting down her lovely eyes. . . . Then sat she down and held the veil before her face; long in sorrow and silence sat she so, and spake to no man nor made any sign, but smileless she sat, nor tasted meat nor drink, wasting with long desire for her deep-bosomed daughter" (*Homeric Hymn to Demeter:* Lang's translation).

[80] In a letter to Charles Eliot Norton, Ruskin says: "I found out the Piping and Fluting from the Pindaric ode which de-

resents her doing so is that she invented the double pipe from hearing the hiss of the Gorgonian serpents; but when she played upon it, chancing to see her face reflected in water, she saw that it was distorted, whereupon she threw down the flute, which Marsyas found. Then, the strife of Apollo and Marsyas represents the enduring contest between music in which the words and thought lead, and the lyre measures or melodizes them, (which Pindar means when he calls his hymns "kings over the lyre,"[81]) and music in which the words are lost, and the wind or impulse leads,—generally, therefore, between intellectual, and brutal, or meaningless, music. Therefore, when Apollo prevails, he flays Marsyas, taking the limit and external bond of his shape from him, which is death, without touching the mere muscular strength; yet shameful and dreadful in dissolution.

42. And the opposition of these two kinds of sound is continually dwelt upon by the Greek philosophers, the real fact at the root of all their teaching being this,—that true music is the natural expression of a lofty passion for a right cause; that in proportion to the kingliness and force of any personality, the expression either of its joy or suffering becomes measured, chastened, calm, and capable of interpretation only by the majesty of ordered, beautiful, and worded sound. Exactly in proportion to the degree in which we become narrow in the cause and conception of our passions, incontinent in the utterance of them, feeble of perseverance in them, sullied or shameful in the indulgence of them, their expression by musical sound becomes broken, mean, fatuitous, and at last impossible; the measured waves of the air of heaven will not

---

scribes Athena making the Pan's pipe out of Medusa's hair." The reference is to the Twelfth Pythian Ode, but the suggestion that Athena made the pipe out of Medusa's hair is Ruskin's own. Pindar says: "But the Maiden, when that she had delivered her well-beloved from these toils, contrived the manifold music of the flute, that with such instrument she might repeat the shrill lament that reached her from Euryale's ravening jaws" (Myers).

[81] *Olymp.*, ii. 1.

lend themselves to expression of ultimate vice, it must be for ever sunk into discordance or silence. And since, as before stated, every work of right art has a tendency to reproduce the ethical state which first developed it, this, which of all the arts is most directly ethical in origin, is also the most direct in power of discipline; the first, the simplest, the most effective of all instruments of moral instruction; while in the failure and betrayal of its functions, it becomes the subtlest aid of moral degradation. Music is thus, in her health, the teacher of perfect order, and is the voice of the obedience of angels, and the companion of the course of the spheres of heaven; and in her depravity she is also the teacher of perfect disorder and disobedience, and the Gloria in Excelsis becomes the Marseillaise. In the third section of this volume, I reprint two chapters from another essay of mine, (*The Cestus of Aglaia*) on modesty or measure, and on liberty, containing farther reference to music in her two powers; and I do this now, because, among the many monstrous and misbegotten fantasies which are the spawn of modern licence, perhaps the most impishly opposite to the truth is the conception of music which has rendered possible the writing, by educated persons, and, more strangely yet, the tolerant criticism, of such words as these:—"*This so persuasive art is the only one that has no didactic efficacy, that engenders no emotions save such as are without issue on the side of moral truth, that expresses nothing of God, nothing of reason, nothing of human liberty.*" I will not give the author's name; the passage is quoted in the *Westminster Review* for last January (1869), p. 153.

43. I must also anticipate something of what I have to say respecting the relation of the power of Athena to organic life, so far as to note that her name, Pallas, probably refers to the quivering or vibration of the air; and to its power, whether as vital force, or communicated wave, over every kind of matter, in giving it vibratory movement; first, and most intense, in the voice and throat of the bird, which is the air incarnate; and so descending through the various orders of animal life to the vibrating

and semi-voluntary murmur of the insect; and, lower still, to the hiss, or quiver of the tail, of the half-lunged snake and deaf adder; all these, nevertheless, being wholly under the rule of Athena as representing either breath, or vital nervous power; and, therefore, also, in their simplicity, the "oaten pipe and pastoral song," which belong to her dominion over the asphodel meadows, and breathe on their banks of violets.

Finally, is it not strange to think of the influence of this one power of Pallas in vibration; (we shall see a singular mechanical energy of it presently in the serpent's motion), in the voices of war and peace? How much of the repose—how much of the wrath, folly, and misery of men, has literally depended on this one power of the air; —on the sound of the trumpet and of the bell—on the lark's song, and the bee's murmur!

44. Such is the general conception in the Greek mind of the physical power of Athena. The spiritual power associated with it is of two kinds:—first, she is the Spirit of Life in material organism; not strength in the blood only, but formative energy in the clay: and, secondly, she is inspired and impulsive wisdom in human conduct and human art, giving the instinct of infallible decision, and of faultless invention.

It is quite beyond the scope of my present purpose—and, indeed, will only be possible for me at all after marking the relative intention of the Apolline myths—to trace for you the Greek conception of Athena as the guide of moral passion. But I will at least endeavour, on some near occasion, to define some of the actual truths respecting the vital force in created organism, and inventive fancy in the works of man, which are more or less expressed by the Greeks, under the personality of Athena. You would, perhaps, hardly bear with me if I endeavoured farther to show you—what is nevertheless perfectly true—the analogy between the spiritual power of Athena in her gentle ministry, yet irresistible anger, with the ministry of another Spirit whom we also, believing in as the universal power of life, are forbidden, at our worst peril, to quench or to grieve.[82]

45. But, I think, to-night, you should not let me close, without requiring of me an answer on one vital point, namely, how far these imaginations of Gods—which are vain to us—were vain to those who had no better trust? and what real belief the Greek had in these creations of his own spirit, practical and helpful to him in the sorrow of earth? I am able to answer you explicitly in this. The origin of his thoughts is often obscure, and we may err in endeavouring to account for their form of realization; but the effect of that realization on his life is not obscure at all. The Greek creed was, of course, different in its character, as our own creed is, according to the class of persons who held it. The common people's was quite literal, simple, and happy: their idea of Athena was as clear as a good Roman Catholic peasant's idea of the Madonna. In Athens itself, the centre of thought and refinement, Pisistratus obtained the reins of government through the ready belief of the populace that a beautiful woman, armed like Athena, was the goddess herself. Even at the close of the last century some of this simplicity remained among the inhabitants of the Greek islands; and when a pretty English lady first made her way into the grotto of Antiparos, she was surrounded, on her return, by all the women of the neighbouring village, believing her to be divine, and praying her to heal them of their sicknesses.

46. Then, secondly, the creed of the upper classes was more refined and spiritual, but quite as honest, and even more forcible in its effect on the life. You might imagine that the employment of the artifice just referred to implied utter unbelief in the persons contriving it; but it really meant only that the more worldly of them would play with a popular faith for their own purposes, as doubly-minded persons have often done since, all the while sincerely holding the same ideas themselves in a more

[82] 1 Thessalonians v. 19: "Quench not the Spirit." Ephesians iv. 30: "And grieve not the Holy Spirit of God, whereby ye are sealed unto the day of redemption."

abstract form; while the good and unworldly men, the true Greek heroes, lived by their faith as firmly as S. Louis, or the Cid, or the Chevalier Bayard.

47. Then, thirdly, the faith of the poets and artists was, necessarily, less definite, being continually modified by the involuntary action of their own fancies; and by the necessity of presenting, in clear verbal or material form, things of which they had no authoritative knowledge. Their faith was, in some respects, like Dante's or Milton's: firm in general conception, but not able to vouch for every detail in the forms they gave it: but they went considerably farther, even in that minor sincerity, than subsequent poets; and strove with all their might to be as near the truth as they could. Pindar says, quite simply, "I cannot think so-and-so of the Gods. It must have been this way—it cannot have been that way—that the thing was done." And as late among the Latins as the days of Horace, this sincerity remains. Horace is just as true and simple in his religion as Wordsworth; but all power of understanding any of the honest classic poets has been taken away from most English gentlemen by the mechanical drill in verse-writing at school. Throughout the whole of their lives afterwards, they never can get themselves quit of the notion that all verses were written as an exercise, and that Minerva was only a convenient word for the last of an hexameter, and Jupiter for the last but one.

48. It is impossible that any notion can be more fallacious or more misleading in its consequences. All great song, from the first day when human lips contrived syllables, has been sincere song. With deliberate didactic purpose the tragedians—with pure and native passion the lyrists—fitted their perfect words to their dearest faiths. "Operosa parvus carmina fingo."[83] "I, little thing that I am, weave my laborious songs" as earnestly as the bee among the bells of thyme on the Matin mountains. Yes, and he dedicates his favourite pine to Diana, and he chants his autumnal hymn to Faunus guarding his fields, and he

[83] Horace: *Odes,* iv. 2, 27–32.

guides the noble youths and maids of Rome in their choir to Apollo, and he tells the farmer's little girl that the Gods will love her, though she has only a handful of salt and meal to give them[84]—just as earnestly as ever English gentleman taught Christian faith to English youth, in England's truest days.

49. Then, lastly, the creed of the philosophers or sages varied according to the character and knowledge of each; —their relative acquaintance with the secrets of natural science—their intellectual and sectarian egotism—and their mystic or monastic tendencies, for there is a classic as well as a mediæval monasticism. They ended in losing the life of Greece in play upon words; but we owe to their early thought some of the soundest ethics, and the foundation of the best practical laws, yet known to mankind.

50. Such was the general vitality of the heathen creed in its strength. Of its direct influence on conduct, it is, as I said, impossible for me to speak now; only, remember always, in endeavouring to form a judgment of it, that what of good or right the heathens did, they did looking for no reward. The purest forms of our own religion have always consisted in sacrificing less things to win greater;—time, to win eternity,—the world, to win the skies. The order, "sell that thou hast," is not given without the promise,—"thou shalt have treasure in heaven;"[85] and well for the modern Christian if he accepts the alternative as his Master left it—and does not practically read the command and promise thus: "Sell that thou hast in the best market, and thou shalt have treasure in eternity also." But the poor Greeks of the great ages expected no reward from heaven but honour, and no reward from earth but rest; —though, when, on those conditions, they patiently, and proudly, fulfilled their task of the granted day, an unrea-

[84] The references here are to *Odes,* iii. 22—which in a list of titles for all the *Odes* Ruskin calls "Diana's Pine"; iii. 18 ("Faune, Nympharum"); i. 21 ("Dianam teneræ. . . . Vos Tempe totidem. . . . Natalemque, mares, Delon Apollinis"); and iii. 23, 17–20.

[85] Matthew xix. 21.

soning instinct of an immortal benediction broke from their lips in song: and they, even they, had sometimes a prophet to tell them of a land "where there is sun alike by day, and alike by night—where they shall need no more to trouble the earth by strength of hands for daily bread—but the ocean breezes blow around the blessed islands, and golden flowers burn on their bright trees for evermore."[86]

II

*ATHENA KERAMITIS**

(*Athena in the Earth*)

Study, supplementary to the preceding lecture, of the supposed, and actual, relations of Athena to the vital force in material organism.

51. It has been easy to decipher approximately the Greek conception of the physical power of Athena in cloud and sky, because we know ourselves what clouds and skies are, and what the force of the wind is in forming them. But it is not at all easy to trace the Greek thoughts about the power of Athena in giving life, because we do not ourselves know clearly what life is, or in what way the air is necessary to it, or what there is, besides the air, shaping the forms that it is put into. And it is comparatively of small consequence to find out what the Greeks thought or meant, until we have determined what we ourselves think, or mean, when we translate the Greek word for "breathing" into the Latin-English word "spirit."

52. But it is of great consequence that you should fix in your minds—and hold, against the baseness of mere

* "Athena, fit for being made into pottery." I coin the expression as a counterpart of "Clay intact."

[86] Rendered freely from Pindar, *Olymp.*, ii. 109–130.

materialism on the one hand, and against the fallacies of controversial speculation on the other—the certain and practical sense of this word "spirit";—the sense in which you may all know that its reality exists, as the power which shaped you into your shape, and by which you love, and hate, when you have received that shape. You need not fear, on the one hand, that either the sculpturing or the loving power can ever be beaten down by the philosophers into a metal or evolved by them into a gas: but, on the other hand, take care that you yourselves, in trying to elevate your conception of it, do not lose its truth in a dream, or even in a word. Beware always of contending for words: you will find them not easy to grasp, if you know them in several languages. This very word, which is so solemn in your mouths, is one of the most doubtful. In Latin it means little more than breathing, and may mean merely accent; in French it is not breath, but wit, and our neighbours are therefore obliged, even in their most solemn expressions, to say "wit" when we say "ghost." In Greek, "pneuma," the word we translate "ghost," means either wind or breath, and the relative word "psyche" has, perhaps, a more subtle power; yet St. Paul's words "pneumatic body" and "psychic body"[1] involve a difference in his mind which no words will explain. But in Greek and in English, and in Saxon and in Hebrew, and in every articulate tongue of humanity, the "spirit of man" truly means his passion and virtue, and is stately according to the height of his conception, and stable according to the measure of his endurance.

53. Endurance, or patience, that is the central sign of spirit; a constancy against the cold and agony of death; and as, physically, it is by the burning power of the air that the heat of the flesh is sustained, so this Athena, spiritually, is the queen of all glowing virtue, the unconsuming fire and inner lamp of life. And thus, as Hephæstus is lord of the fire of the hand, and Apollo of the fire of the brain, so Athena of the fire of the heart; and as

[1] 1 Corinthians xv. 44.

Hercules wears for his chief armour the skin of the Nemean lion, his chief enemy, whom he slew; and Apollo has for his highest name "the Pythian," from his chief enemy, the Python, slain; so Athena bears always on her breast the deadly face of her chief enemy slain, the Gorgonian cold, and venomous agony, that turns living men to stone.

54. And so long as you have that fire of the heart within you, and know the reality of it, you need be under no alarm as to the possibility of its chemical or mechanical analysis. The philosophers are very humorous in their ecstasy of hope about it; but the real interest of their discoveries in this direction is very small to human kind. It is quite true that the tympanum of the ear vibrates under sound, and that the surface of the water in a ditch vibrates too: but the ditch hears nothing for all that; and my hearing is still to me as blessed a mystery as ever, and the interval between the ditch and me, quite as great. If the trembling sound in my ears was once of the marriage bell which began my happiness, and is now of the passing bell which ends it, the difference between those two sounds to me cannot be counted by the number of concussions. There have been some curious speculations lately as to the conveyance of mental consciousness by "brain-waves." What does it matter how it is conveyed? The consciousness itself is not a wave. It may be accompanied here or there by any quantity of quivers and shakes, up or down, of anything you can find in the universe that is shakeable—what is that to me? My friend is dead, and my —according to modern views—vibratory sorrow is not one whit less, or less mysterious to me, than my old quiet one.

55. Beyond, and entirely unaffected by, any questionings of this kind, there are, therefore, two plain facts which we should all know: first, that there is a power which gives their several shapes to things, or capacities of shape; and, secondly, a power which gives them their several feelings, or capacities of feeling; and that we can increase or destroy both of these at our will. By care and tenderness, we can extend the range of lovely life in plants and animals; by our neglect and cruelty, we can arrest it,

and bring pestilence in its stead. Again, by right discipline we can increase our strength of noble will and passion, or destroy both. And whether these two forces are local conditions of the elements in which they appear, or are part of a great force in the universe, out of which they are taken, and to which they must be restored, is not of the slightest importance to us in dealing with them; neither is the manner of their connection with light and air. What precise meaning we ought to attach to expressions such as that of the prophecy to the four winds that the dry bones might be breathed upon,[2] and might live, or why the presence of the vital power should be dependent on the chemical action of the air, and its awful passing away materially signified by the rendering up of that breath or ghost, we cannot at present know, and need not at any time dispute. What we assuredly know is that the states of life and death are different, and the first more desirable than the other, and by effort attainable, whether we understand being "born of the spirit"[3] to signify having the breath of heaven in our flesh, or its power in our hearts.

56. As to its power on the body, I will endeavour to tell you, having been myself much led into studies involving necessary reference both to natural science and mental phenomena, what, at least, remains to us after science has done its worst;—what the Myth of Athena, as a Formative and Decisive power—a Spirit of Creation and Volition, —must eternally mean for all of us.

57. It is now (I believe I may use the strong word) "ascertained" that heat and motion are fixed in quantity, and measurable in the portions that we deal with. We can measure out portions of power, as we can measure portions of space; while yet, as far as we know, space may be infinite, and force infinite. There may be heat as much greater than the sun's, as the sun's heat is greater than a candle's; and force as much greater than the force by which the world swings, as that is greater than the force by which a cobweb trembles. Now, on heat and force, life

[2] Ezekiel i. 1–9.
[3] John iii. 5.

is inseparably dependent; and I believe, also, on a form of substance, which the philosophers call "protoplasm." I wish they would use English instead of Greek words. When I want to know why a leaf is green, they tell me it is coloured by "chlorophyll," which at first sounds very instructive; but if they would only say plainly that a leaf is coloured green by a thing which is called "green leaf," we should see more precisely how far we had got. However, it is a curious fact that life is connected with a cellular structure called protoplasm, or, in English, "first stuck together": whence conceivably through deutoroplasms or second stickings, and tritoplasms, or third stickings, we reach the highest plastic phase in the human pottery, which differs from common china-ware, primarily, by a measurable degree of heat, developed in breathing, which it borrows from the rest of the universe while it lives, and which it as certainly returns to the rest of the universe, when it dies.

58. Again, with this heat certain assimilative powers are connected, which the tendency of recent discovery is to simplify more and more into modes of one force; or finally into mere motion, communicable in various states, but not destructible. We will assume that science has done its utmost; and that every chemical or animal force is demonstrably resolvable into heat or motion, reciprocally changing into each other. I would myself like better, in order of thought, to consider motion as a mode of heat than heat as a mode of motion; still, granting that we have got thus far, we have yet to ask, What is heat? or what, motion? What is this "primo mobile," this transitional power, in which all things live, and move, and have their being? It is by definition something different from matter, and we may call it as we choose—"first cause," or "first light," or "first heat"; but we can show no scientific proof of its not being personal, and coinciding with the ordinary conception of a supporting spirit in all things.

59. Still, it is not advisable to apply the word "spirit" or "breathing" to it, while it is only enforcing chemical affinities; but, when the chemical affinities are brought

under the influence of the air, and of the sun's heat, the formative force enters an entirely different phase. It does not now merely crystallize indefinite masses, but it gives to limited portions of matter the power of gathering, selectively, other elements proper to them, and binding these elements into their own peculiar and adopted form.

This force, now properly called life, or breathing, or spirit, is continually creating its own shells of definite shape out of the wreck around it: and this is what I meant by saying, in the *Ethics of the Dust:*—"you may always stand by form against force." For the mere force of junction is not spirit; but the power that catches out of chaos charcoal, water, lime, or what not, and fastens them down into a given form, is properly called "spirit"; and we shall not diminish, but strengthen our conception of this creative energy by recognizing its presence in lower states of matter than our own;—such recognition being enforced upon us by a delight we instinctively receive from all the forms of matter which manifest it: and yet more, by the glorifying of those forms, in the parts of them that are most animated, with the colours that are pleasantest to our senses. The most familiar instance of this is the best, and also the most wonderful:—the blossoming of plants.

60. The Spirit in the plant—that is to say, its power of gathering dead matter out of the wreck round it, and shaping it into its own chosen shape,—is of course strongest at the moment of its flowering, for it then not only gathers, but forms, with the greatest energy.

And where this Life is in it at full power, its form becomes invested with aspects that are chiefly delightful to our own human passions; namely, first, with the loveliest outlines of shape: and, secondly, with the most brilliant phases of the primary colours, blue, yellow, and red or white, the unison of all; and, to make it all more strange, this time of peculiar and perfect glory is associated with relations of the plants or blossoms to each other, correspondent to the joy of love in human creatures, and having the same object in the continuance of the race. Only, with respect to plants, as animals, we are wrong in speaking as if the object of this strong life were only the bequeathing of itself. The flower is the end or proper object of the seed, not the seed of the flower. The reason for seeds is that flowers may be; not the reason of flowers that seeds may be. The flower itself is the creature which the spirit makes; only, in connection with its perfectness, is placed the giving birth to its successor.

61. The main fact, then, about a flower is that it is the part of the plant's form developed at the moment of its intensest life: and this inner rapture is usually marked externally for us by the flush of one or more of the primary colours. What the character of the flower shall be, depends entirely upon the portion of the plant into which this rapture of spirit has been put. Sometimes the life is put into its outer sheath, and then the outer sheath becomes white and pure, and full of strength and grace; sometimes the life is put into the common leaves, just under the blossom, and they become scarlet or purple; sometimes the life is put into the stalks of the flower, and they flush blue; sometimes in its outer enclosure or calyx; mostly into its inner cup; but in all cases, the presence of the strongest life is asserted by characters in which the human sight takes pleasure, and which seem prepared with distinct reference to us, or rather, bear, in being delightful, evidence of having been produced by the power of the same spirit as our own.

62. And we are led to feel this still more strongly, because all the distinctions of species,* both in plants and animals, appear to have similar connection with human character. Whatever the origin of species may be, or however those species, once formed, may be influenced by external accident, the groups into which birth or acci-

* The facts on which I am about to dwell are in nowise antagonistic to the theories which Mr. Darwin's unwearied and unerring investigations are every day rendering more probable. The æsthetic relations of species are independent of their origin. Nevertheless, it has always seemed to me, in what little work I have done upon organic forms, as if the species mocked us by their deliberate imitation of each other when they met: yet did not pass one into another.

dent reduce them have distinct relation to the spirit of man. It is perfectly possible, and ultimately conceivable, that the crocodile and the lamb may have descended from the same ancestral atom of protoplasm; and that the physical laws of the operation of calcareous slime and of meadow grass, on that protoplasm, may in time have developed the opposite natures and aspects of the living frames; but the practically important fact for us is the existence of a power which creates that calcareous earth itself;—which creates that, separately, and quartz, separately, and gold, separately, and charcoal, separately; and then so directs the relations of these elements that the gold may destroy the souls of men by being yellow; and the charcoal destroy their souls by being hard and bright; and the quartz represent to them an ideal purity; and the calcareous earth, soft, may beget crocodiles, and dry and hard, sheep; and that the aspects and qualities of these two products, crocodiles and lambs, may be, the one repellent to the spirit of man, the other attractive to it, in a quite inevitable way, representing to him states of moral evil and good, and becoming myths to him of destruction or redemption, and, in the most literal sense, "Words" of God.

63. And the force of these facts cannot be escaped from by the thought that there are species innumerable, passing into each other by regular gradations, out of which we choose what we most love or dread, and say they were indeed prepared for us. Species are not innumerable; neither are they now connected by consistent gradation. They touch at certain points only; and even then are connected, when we examine them deeply, in a kind of reticulated way, not in chains, but in chequers; also, however connected, it is but by a touch of the extremities, as it were, and the characteristic form of the species is entirely individual. The rose nearly sinks into a grass in the sanguisorba; but the formative spirit does not the less clearly separate the ear of wheat from the dog-rose, and oscillate with tremulous constancy round the central forms of both, having each their due relation to the mind of man. The

great animal kingdoms are connected in the same way. The bird through the penguin drops towards the fish, and the fish in the cetacean reascends to the mammal, yet there is no confusion of thought possible between the perfect forms of an eagle, a trout, and a war-horse, in their relations to the elements, and to man.

64. Now we have two orders of animals to take some note of in connection with Athena, and one vast order of plants, which will illustrate this matter very sufficiently for us.

The two orders of animals are the serpent and the bird; the serpent, in which the breath, or spirit, is less than in any other creature, and the earth-power greatest:—the bird, in which the breath, or spirit, is more full than in any other creature, and the earth-power least.

65. We will take the bird first. It is little more than a drift of the air brought into form by plumes; the air is in all its quills, it breathes through its whole frame and flesh, and glows with air in its flying, like a blown flame: it rests upon the air, subdues it, surpasses it, outraces it;—*is* the air, conscious of itself, conquering itself, ruling itself.

Also, into the throat of the bird is given the voice of the air. All that in the wind itself is weak, wild, useless in sweetness, is knit together in its song. As we may imagine the wild form of the cloud closed into the perfect form of the bird's wings, so the wild voice of the cloud into its ordered and commanded voice; unwearied, rippling through the clear heaven in its gladness, interpreting all intense passion through the soft spring nights, bursting into acclaim and rapture of choir at daybreak, or lisping and twittering among the boughs and hedges through heat of day, like little winds that only make the cowslip bells shake, and ruffle the petals of the wild rose.

66. Also, upon the plumes of the bird are put the colours of the air: on these the gold of the cloud, that cannot be gathered by any covetousness; the rubies of the clouds, that are not the price of Athena, but *are* Athena; the vermilion of the cloud-bar, and the flame of the cloud-crest, and the snow of the cloud, and its shadow, and the melted

blue of the deep wells of the sky—all these, seized by the creating spirit, and woven by Athena herself into films and threads of plume; with wave on wave following and fading along breast, and throat, and opened wings, infinite as the dividing of the foam and the sifting of the sea-sand; —even the white down of the cloud seeming to flutter up between the stronger plumes, seen, but too soft for touch.

And so the Spirit of the Air is put into, and upon, this created form; and it becomes, through twenty centuries, the symbol of Divine help, descending, as the Fire, to speak, but as the Dove, to bless.

67. Next, in the serpent we approach the source of a group of myths, world-wide, founded on great and common human instincts, respecting which I must note one or two points which bear intimately on all our subject. For it seems to me that the scholars who are at present occupied in interpretation of human myths have most of them forgotten that there are any such things as natural myths; and that the dark sayings of men may be both difficult to read, and not always worth reading; but the dark sayings of nature will probably become clearer for the looking into, and will very certainly be worth reading. And, indeed, all guidance to the right sense of the human and variable myths will probably depend on our first getting at the sense of the natural and invariable ones. The dead hieroglyph may have meant this or that—the living hieroglyph means always the same; but remember, it is just as much a hieroglyph as the other; nay, more,—a "sacred or reserved sculpture," a thing with an inner language. The serpent crest of the king's crown, or of the god's, on the pillars of Egypt, is a mystery; but the serpent itself, gliding past the pillar's foot, is it less a mystery? Is there, indeed, no tongue, except the mute forked flash from its lips, in that running brook of horror on the ground?

68. Why that horror? We all feel it, yet how imaginative it is, how disproportioned to the real strength of the creature! There is more poison in an ill-kept drain,—in a pool of dish-washings at a cottage door,—than in the deadliest asp of Nile. Every back-yard which you look down

into from the railway, as it carries you out by Vauxhall or Deptford, holds its coiled serpent: all the walls of those ghastly suburbs are enclosures of tank temples for serpent worship; yet you feel no horror in looking down into them, as you would if you saw the livid scales and lifted head. There is more venom, mortal, inevitable, in a single word sometimes, or in the gliding entrance of a wordless thought, than ever "vanti Libia con sua rena."[4] But that horror is of the myth, not of the creature. There are myriads lower than this, and more loathsome, in the scale of being; the links between dead matter and animation drift everywhere unseen. But it is the strength of the base element that is so dreadful in the serpent; it is the very omnipotence of the earth. That rivulet of smooth silver—how does it flow, think you? It literally rows on the earth, with every scale for an oar; it bites the dust with the ridges of its body. Watch it, when it moves slowly:—A wave, but without wind! a current, but with no fall! all the body moving at the same instant, yet some of it to one side, some to another, or some forward, and the rest of the coil backwards; but all with the same calm will and equal way —no contraction, no extension; one soundless, causeless march of sequent rings, and spectral procession of spotted dust, with dissolution in its fangs, dislocation in its coils. Startle it;—the winding stream will become a twisted arrow;—the wave of poisoned life will lash through the grass like a cast lance. It scarcely breathes with its one lung (the other shrivelled and abortive); it is passive to the sun and shade, and is cold or hot like a stone; yet, "it can outclimb the monkey, outswim the fish, outleap the jerboa, outwrestle the athlete, and crush the tiger." It is a divine hieroglyph of the demoniac power of the earth,—of the entire earthly nature. As the bird is the clothed power of the air, so this is the clothed power of the dust; as the bird the symbol of the spirit of life, so this of the grasp and sting of death.

[4] *Inferno,* xxiv. 85, where Dante describes a crowd of terrible serpents, so strange and hideous that "let Libya vaunt no more of her sands."

69. Hence the continual change in the interpretation put upon it in various religions. As the worm of corruption, it is the mightiest of all adversaries of the gods—the special adversary of their light and creative power—Python against Apollo. As the power of the earth against the air, the giants are serpent-bodied in the Gigantomachia; but as the power of the earth upon the seed—consuming it into new life ("that which thou sowest is not quickened except it die"[5])—serpents sustain the chariot of the spirit of agriculture.

70. Yet, on the other hand, there is a power in the earth to take away corruption, and to purify, (hence the very fact of burial, and many uses of earth, only lately known); and in this sense, the serpent is a healing spirit,—the representative of Æsculapius, and of Hygieia; and is a sacred earth-type in the temple of the Dew;—being there especially a symbol of the native earth of Athens; so that its departure from the temple was a sign to the Athenians that they were to leave their homes.[6] And then, lastly, as there is a strength and healing in the earth, no less than the strength of air, so there is conceived to be a wisdom of earth no less than a wisdom of the spirit; and when its deadly power is killed, its guiding power becomes true; so that the Python serpent is killed at Delphi, where yet the oracle is from the breath of the earth.

71. You must remember, however, that in this, as in every other instance, I take the myth at its central time. This is only the meaning of the serpent to the Greek mind which could conceive an Athena. Its first meaning to the nascent eyes of men, and its continued influence over degraded races, are subjects of the most fearful mystery. Mr. Fergusson has just collected the principal evidence bearing on the matter in a work of very great value, and if you read his opening chapters, they will put you in possession of the circumstances needing chiefly to be considered. I cannot touch upon any of them here, except

[5] 1 Corinthians xv. 36.

[6] Before the battle of Salamis: see Herodotus, viii. 41.

only to point out that, though the doctrine of the so-called "corruption of human nature," asserting that there is nothing but evil in humanity, is just as blasphemous and false as a doctrine of the corruption of physical nature would be, asserting there was nothing but evil in the earth,—there is yet the clearest evidence of a disease, plague, or cretinous imperfection of development, hitherto allowed to prevail against the greater part of the races of men; and this in monstrous ways, more full of mystery than the serpent-being itself. I have gathered for you to-night only instances of what is beautiful in Greek religion; but even in its best time there were deep corruptions in other phases of it, and degraded forms of many of its deities, all originating in a misunderstood worship of the principle of life; while in the religions of lower races, little else than these corrupted forms of devotion can be found;—all having a strange and dreadful consistency with each other, and infecting Christianity, even at its strongest periods, with fatal terror of doctrine, and ghastliness of symbolic conception, passing through fear into frenzied grotesque, and thence into sensuality.

In the Psalter of S. Louis itself, half of its letters are twisted snakes; there is scarcely a wreathed ornament, employed in Christian dress, or architecture, which cannot be traced back to the serpent's coil; and there is rarely a piece of monkish decorated writing in the world, that is not tainted with some ill-meant vileness of grotesque—nay, the very leaves of the twisted ivy-pattern of the fourteenth century can be followed back to wreaths for the foreheads of bacchanalian gods. And truly, it seems to me, as I gather in my mind the evidences of insane religion, degraded art, merciless war, sullen toil, detestable pleasure, and vain or vile hope, in which the nations of the world have lived since first they could bear record of themselves—it seems to me, I say, as if the race itself were still half-serpent, not extricated yet from its clay; a lacertine breed of bitterness—the glory of it emaciate with cruel hunger, and blotted with venomous stain: and the track of it, on the leaf a glittering slime, and in the sand a useless furrow.

72. There are no myths, therefore, by which the moral state and fineness of intelligence of different races can be so deeply tried or measured, as by those of the serpent and the bird; both of them having an especial relation to the kind of remorse for sin, or grief in fate, of which the national minds that spoke by them had been capable. The serpent and vulture are alike emblems of immortality and purification among races which desired to be immortal and pure: and as they recognize their own misery, the serpent becomes to them the scourge of the Furies, and the vulture finds its eternal prey in their breast. The bird long contests, among the Egyptians, with the still received serpent, the symbol of power. But the Draconian image of evil is established in the serpent Apap;[7] while the bird's wings, with the globe, become part of a better symbol of deity, and the entire form of the vulture, as an emblem of purification, is associated with the earliest conception of Athena.[8] In the type of the dove with the olive branch, the conception of the spirit of Athena in renewed life prevailing over ruin, is embodied for the whole of futurity; while the Greeks, to whom, in a happier climate and higher life than that of Egypt, the vulture symbol of cleansing became unintelligible, took the eagle, instead, for their hieroglyph of supreme spiritual energy, and it thenceforward retains its hold on the human imagination, till it is established among Christian myths as the expression of the most exalted form of evangelistic teaching. The special relation of Athena to her favourite bird we will trace presently; the peacock of Hera, and dove of Aphrodite, are comparatively unimportant myths: but the bird power is soon made entirely human by the Greeks in their flying angel of victory (partially human, with modified

[7] "The battle in heaven with the gigantic Apap, or great serpent; his (Ra's) final triumph, and strangling of the dragon, and his diurnal renewal of the fray, formed the subject of the walls of the tombs and sarcophagi at the time of the 18th and subsequent dynasties" (Wilkinson's *Manners and Customs of the Ancient Egyptians*, ed. 1878, vol. iii. p. 59).

[8] That is, of Neith, the Egyptian form of Athena, who is often represented as vulture-headed.

meaning of evil, in the Harpy and Siren); and thenceforward it associates itself with the Hebrew cherubim, and has had the most singular influence on the Christian religion by giving its wings to render the conception of angels mysterious and untenable, and check rational endeavour to determine the nature of subordinate spiritual agency; while yet it has given to that agency a vague poetical influence of the highest value in its own imaginative way.

73. But with the early serpent-worship there was associated another—that of the groves—of which you will also find the evidence exhaustively collected in Mr. Fergusson's work. This tree-worship may have taken a dark form when associated with the Draconian one; or opposed, as in Judea, to a purer faith;[9] but in itself, I believe, it was always healthy, and though it retains little definite hierogyphic power in subsequent religion, it becomes instead of symbolic, real; the flowers and trees are themselves beheld and beloved with a half-worshipping delight, which is always noble and healthful.

And it is among the most notable indications of the volition of the animating power, that we find the ethical signs of good and evil set on these also, as well as upon animals; the venom of the serpent, and in some respects its image also, being associated even with the passionless growth of the leaf out of the ground; while the distinctions of species seem appointed with more definite ethical address to the intelligence of man as their material products become more useful to him.

74. I can easily show this, and, at the same time, make clear the relation to other plants of the flowers which especially belong to Athena, by examining the natural myths in the groups of the plants which would be used at any country dinner, over which Athena would, in her simplest household authority, cheerfully rule, here, in England. Suppose Horace's favourite dish of beans,[10] with the bacon; potatoes; some savoury stuffing of onions and

[9] See Exodus xxiv. 13; Deuteronomy xvi. 21, etc.
[10] *Satires*, ii. 6, 63.

herbs with the meat; celery, and a radish or two, with the cheese; nuts and apples for dessert, and brown bread.

75. The beans are, from earliest time, the most important and interesting of the seeds of the great tribe of plants from which came the Latin and French name for all kitchen vegetables,—things that are gathered with the hand—podded seeds that cannot be reaped, or beaten, or shaken down, but must be gathered green. "Leguminous" plants, all of them having flowers like butterflies, seeds in (frequently pendent) pods,—"lætum siliqua quassante legumen"[11]—smooth and tender leaves, divided into many minor ones,—strange adjuncts of tendril, for climbing (and sometimes of thorn);—exquisitely sweet, yet pure, scents of blossom, and almost always harmless, if not serviceable, seeds. It is, of all tribes of plants, the most definite; its blossoms being entirely limited in their parts, and not passing into other forms. It is also the most usefully extended in range and scale; familiar in the height of the forest—acacia, laburnum, Judas-tree; familiar in the sown field—bean and vetch and pea; familiar in the pasture—in every form of clustered clover and sweet trefoil tracery; the most entirely serviceable and human of all orders of plants.

76. Next, in the potato, we have the scarcely innocent underground stem of one of a tribe set aside for evil;* having the deadly nightshade for its queen, and including the henbane, the witch's mandrake, and the worst natural curse of modern civilization—tobacco.† And the strange thing about this tribe is, that though thus set aside for evil, they are not a group distinctly separate from those that are happier in function. There is nothing in other tribes of plants like the form of the bean blossom; but there is another family with forms and structure closely

* Some two out of a hundred and fifty species of Solanum are useful to man.

† It is not easy to estimate the demoralizing effect on the youth of Europe of the cigar, enabling them to pass their time happily in idleness.

[11] Virgil, *Georgics,* i. 74: "the pulse which is luxuriant with quivering pod"—a description of the bean.

connected with this venomous one. Examine the purple and yellow bloom of the common hedge nightshade; you will find it constructed exactly like some of the forms of the cyclamen; and, getting this clue, you will find at last the whole poisonous and terrible group to be—sisters of the primulas!

The nightshades are, in fact, primroses with a curse upon them; and a sign set in their petals, by which the deadly and condemned flowers may always be known from the innocent ones,—that the stamens of the nightshades are between the lobes, and of the primulas, opposite the lobes, of the corolla.

77. Next, side by side, in the celery and radish, you have the two great groups of umbelled and cruciferous plants; alike in conditions of rank among herbs: both flowering in clusters; but the umbelled group, flat, the crucifers, in spires:—both of them mean and poor in the blossom, and losing what beauty they have by too close crowding:—both of them having the most curious influence on human character in the temperate zones of the earth, from the days of the parsley crown, and hemlock drink, and mocked Euripidean chervil,[12] until now: but chiefly among the northern nations, being especially plants that are of some humble beauty, and (the crucifers) of endless use, when they are chosen and cultivated; but that run to wild waste, and are the signs of neglected ground, in their rank or ragged leaves, and meagre stalks, and pursed or podded seed clusters. Capable, even under cultivation, of no perfect beauty, though reaching some subdued delightfulness in the lady's smock and the wallflower; for the most part, they have every floral quality meanly, and in vain,—they are white, without purity; golden, without preciousness; redundant, without richness; divided, without fineness; massive, without strength; and slender, without grace. Yet think over that useful vulgarity of theirs; and of the relations of German and En-

[12] The reference is to Aristophanes, *Acharnians,* 478, where, taunting the poet with the lowly station of his mother as a herb-seller, he says "give me chervil, and get it from your mother."

glish peasant character to its food of kraut and cabbage, (as of Arab character to its food of palm-fruit,) and you will begin to feel what purposes of the forming spirit are in these distinctions of species.

78. Next we take the nuts and apples,—the nuts representing one of the groups of catkined trees, whose blossoms are only tufts and dust; and the other, the rose tribe, in which fruit and flower alike have been the types, to the highest races of men, of all passionate temptation, or pure delight, from the coveting of Eve to the crowning of the Madonna, above the

"Rosa sempiterna,
Che si dilata, rigrada, e ridole
Odor di lode al Sol."[13]

We have no time now for these; we must go on to the humblest group of all, yet the most wonderful, that of the grass, which has given us our bread; and from that we will go back to the herbs.

79. The vast family of plants which, under rain, make the earth green for man; and, under sunshine, give him bread; and, in their springing in the early year, mixed with their native flowers, have given us (far more than the new leaves of trees) the thought and word of "spring," divide themselves broadly into three great groups—the grasses, sedges, and rushes. The grasses are essentially a clothing for healthy and pure ground, watered by occasional rain, but in itself dry, and fit for all cultivated pasture and corn. They are distinctively plants with round and jointed stems, which have long green flexible leaves, and heads of seed, independently emerging from them. The sedges are essentially the clothing of waste and more or less poor or uncultivatable soils, coarse in their structure, frequently triangular in stem—hence called "acute" by Virgil[14]—and with their heads of seed not extricated from their leaves. Now, in both the sedges and grasses, the blossom has a

[13] *Paradiso*, xxx. 124.
[14] *Georgics*, iii. 231.

common structure, though undeveloped in the sedges, but composed always of groups of double husks, which have mostly a spinous process in the centre, sometimes projecting into a long awn or beard; this central process being characteristic also of the ordinary leaves of mosses, as if a moss were a kind of ear of corn made permanently green on the ground, and with a new and distinct fructification. But the rushes differ wholly from the sedge and grass in their blossom structure. It is not a dual cluster, but a twice threefold one, so far separate from the grasses, and so closely connected with a higher order of plants, that I think you will find it convenient to group the rushes at once with that higher order, to which, if you will for the present let me give the general name of Drosidæ, or dew-plants, it will enable me to say what I have to say of them much more shortly and clearly.

80. These Drosidæ, then, are plants delighting in interrupted moisture—moisture which comes either partially or at certain seasons—into dry ground. They are not water-plants; but the signs of water resting among dry places. Many of the true water-plants have triple blossoms, with a small triple calyx holding them; in the Drosidæ, the floral spirit passes into the calyx also, and the entire flower becomes a six-rayed star, bursting out of the stem laterally, as if it were the first of flowers, and had made its way to the light by force through the unwilling green. They are often required to retain moisture or nourishment for the future blossom through long times of drought; and this they do in bulbs under ground, of which some become a rude and simple, but most wholesome food for man.

81. So now, observe, you are to divide the whole family of the herbs of the field into three great groups—Drosidæ, Carices, Gramineæ—dew-plants, sedges, and grasses. Then the Drosidæ are divided into five great orders—lilies, asphodels, amaryllids, irids, and rushes. No tribes of flowers have had so great, so varied, or so healthy an influence on man as this great group of Drosidæ, depending not so much on the whiteness of some of their blossoms, or the radiance of others, as on the strength and delicacy of the

substance of their petals; enabling them to take forms of faultless elastic curvature, either in cups, as the crocus, or expanding bells, as the true lily, or heath-like bells, as the hyacinth, or bright and perfect stars, like the star of Bethlehem, or, when they are affected by the strange reflex of the serpent nature which forms the labiate group of all flowers, closing into forms of exquisitely fantastic symmetry in the gladiolus. Put by their side their Nereid sisters, the water-lilies, and you have in them the origin of the loveliest forms of ornamental design, and the most powerful floral myths yet recognized among human spirits, born by the streams of Ganges, Nile, Arno, and Avon.

82. For consider a little what each of those five tribes* has been to the spirit of man. First, in their nobleness; the Lilies gave the lily of the Annunciation; the Asphodels, the flower of the Elysian fields; the Irids, the fleur-de-lys of chivalry; and the Amaryllids, Christ's lily of the field: while the rush, trodden always under foot, became the emblem of humility. Then take each of the tribes, and consider the extent of their lower influence. Perdita's "The crown imperial, lilies of all kinds,"[15] are the first tribe; which, giving the type of perfect purity in the Madonna's lily, have, by their lovely form, influenced the entire decorative design of Italian sacred art; while ornament of war was continually enriched by the curves of the triple petals of the Florentine "giglio," and French fleur-de-lys; so that it is impossible to count their influence for good in the Middle Ages, partly as a symbol of womanly character, and partly of the utmost brightness and refinement of chivalry in the city which was the flower of cities.

Afterwards, the group of the turban-lilies, or tulips, did some mischief, (their splendid stains having made them

* Take this rough distinction of the four tribes:—Lilies, superior ovary, white seeds; Asphodels, superior ovary, black seeds; Irids, inferior ovary, style (typically) rising into central crest; Amaryllids, inferior ovary, stamens (typically) joined in central cup. Then the rushes are a dark group, through which they stoop to the grasses.

---

15 *Winter's Tale,* iv. 3, 126.

the favourite caprice of florists;) but they may be pardoned all such guilt for the pleasure they have given in cottage gardens, and are yet to give, when lowly life may again be possible among us; and the crimson bars of the tulips in their trim beds, with their likeness in crimson bars of morning above them, and its dew glittering heavy, globed in their glossy cups, may be loved better than the grey nettles of the ash heap, under grey sky, unveined by vermilion or by gold.

83. The next great group, of the Asphodels, divides itself also into two principal families; one, in which the flowers are like stars, and clustered characteristically in balls, though opening sometimes into looser heads; and the other, in which the flowers are in long bells, opening suddenly at the lips, and clustered in spires on a long stem, or drooping from it, when bent by their weight.

The star-group, of the squills, garlics, and onions, has always caused me great wonder. I cannot understand why its beauty, and serviceableness, should have been associated with the rank scent which has been really among the most powerful means of degrading peasant life, and separating it from that of the higher classes.

The belled group, of the hyacinth and convallaria, is as delicate as the other is coarse: the unspeakable azure light along the ground of the wood hyacinth in English spring; the grape hyacinth, which is in South France, as if a cluster of grapes and a hive of honey had been distilled and compressed together into one small boss of celled and beaded blue; the lilies of the valley everywhere, in each sweet and wild recess of rocky land;—count the influences of these on childish and innocent life; then measure the mythic power of the hyacinth and asphodel as connected with Greek thoughts of immortality; finally take their useful and nourishing power in ancient and modern peasant life, and it will be strange if you do not feel what fixed relation exists between the agency of the creating spirit in these, and in us who live by them.

84. It is impossible to bring into any tenable compass for our present purpose, even hints of the human influence

of the two remaining orders of Amaryllids and Irids;—only note this generally, that while these in northern countries share with the Primulas the fields of spring, it seems that in Greece, the primulaceæ are not an extended tribe, while the crocus, narcissus, and Amaryllis lutea, the "lily of the field" (I suspect also that the flower whose name we translate "violet" was in truth an Iris) represented to the Greek the first coming of the breath of life on the renewed herbage; and became in his thoughts the true embroidery of the saffron robe of Athena. Later in the year, the dianthus (which, though belonging to an entirely different race of plants, has yet a strange look of having been made out of the grasses by turning the sheath-membrane at the root of their leaves into a flower,) seems to scatter, in multitudinous families, its crimson stars far and wide. But the golden lily and crocus, together with the asphodel, retain always the old Greek's fondest thoughts—they are only "golden" flowers that are to burn on the trees, and float on the streams of paradise.[16]

85. I have but one tribe of plants more to note at our country feast—the savoury herbs; but must go a little out of my way to come at them rightly. All flowers whose petals are fastened together, and most of those whose petals are loose, are best thought of first as a kind of cup or tube opening at the mouth. Sometimes the opening is gradual, as in the convolvulus or campanula; oftener there is a distinct change of direction between the tube and expanding lip, as in the primrose; or even a contraction under the lip, making the tube into a narrow-necked phial or vase, as in the heaths, but the general idea of a tube expanding into a quatrefoil, cinquefoil, or sixfoil, will embrace most of the forms.

86. Now it is easy to conceive that flowers of this kind, growing in close clusters, may, in process of time, have extended their outside petals rather than the interior ones

[16] A reference to the passage in Pindar translated above (§ 50, p. 272), which continues, "golden flowers are glowing, some from the land on trees of splendour, and some the water feedeth, with wreaths whereof they entwine their hands."

(as the outer flowers of the clusters of many umbellifers actually do), and thus, elongated and variously distorted forms have established themselves; then if the stalk is attached to the side instead of the base of the tube, its base becomes a spur, and thus all the grotesque forms of the mints, violets, and larkspurs, gradually might be composed. But, however this may be, there is one great tribe of plants separate from the rest, and of which the influence seems shed upon the rest in different degrees: and these would give the impression, not so much of having been developed by change, as of being stamped with a character of their own, more or less serpentine or dragon-like. And I think you will find it convenient to call these generally, *Draconidæ;* disregarding their present ugly botanical name,[17] which I do not care even to write once —you may take for their principal types the Foxglove, Snapdragon, and Calceolaria; and you will find they all agree in a tendency to decorate themselves by spots, and with bosses or swollen places in their leaves, as if they had been touched by poison. The spot of the Foxglove is especially strange, because it draws the colour out of the tissue all round it, as if it had been stung, and as if the central colour was really an inflamed spot, with paleness round. Then also they carry to its extreme the decoration by bulging or pouting the petal;—often beautifully used by other flowers in a minor degree, like the beating out of bosses in hollow silver, as in the kalmia, beating out apparently in each petal by the stamens instead of a hammer; or the borage, pouting inwards; but the snapdragons and calceolarias carry it to its extreme.

87. Then the spirit of these Draconidæ seems to pass more or less into other flowers, whose forms are properly pure vases; but it affects some of them slightly,—others not at all. It never strongly affects the heaths; never once the roses; but it enters like an evil spirit into the buttercup, and turns it into a larkspur, with a black, spotted, grotesque centre, and a strange, broken blue, gorgeous and

[17] *Scrofulariaceæ.*

intense, yet impure, glittering on the surface as if it were strewn with broken glass, and stained or darkening irregularly into red. And then at last the serpent charm changes the ranunculus into monkshood; and makes it poisonous. It enters into the forget-me-not, and the star of heavenly turquoise is corrupted into the viper's bugloss, darkened with the same strange red as the larkspur, and fretted into a fringe of thorn; it enters, together with a strange insect-spirit, into the asphodels, and (though with a greater interval between the groups,) they change into spotted orchideæ: it touches the poppy, it becomes a fumaria; the iris, and it pouts into a gladiolus; the lily, and it chequers itself into a snake's-head, and secretes in the deep of its bell drops, not of venom indeed, but honey-dew, as if it were a healing serpent. For there is an Æsculapian as well as an evil serpentry among the Draconidæ, and the fairest of them, the "erba della Madonna" of Venice, (Linaria Cymbalaria,) descends from the ruins it delights in to the herbage at their feet, and touches it; and behold, instantly, a vast group of herbs for healing,—all draconid in form,—spotted, and crested, and from their lip-like corollas named "labiatæ"; full of various balm, and warm strength for healing, yet all of them without splendid honour or perfect beauty, "ground ivies," richest when crushed under the foot; the best sweetness and gentle brightness of the robes of the field,—thyme, and marjoram, and Euphrasy.

88. And observe, again and again, with respect to all these divisions and powers of plants; it does not matter in the least by what concurrences of circumstance or necessity they may gradually have been developed: the concurrence of circumstance is itself the supreme and inexplicable fact. We always come at last to a formative cause, which directs the circumstance, and mode of meeting it. If you ask an ordinary botanist the reason of the form of a leaf, he will tell you it is a "developed tubercle," and that its ultimate form "is owing to the direction of its vascular threads." But what directs its vascular threads? "They are seeking for something they want," he will probably answer. What

made them want that? What made them seek for it thus? Seek for it, in five fibres or in three? Seek for it, in serration, or in sweeping curves? Seek for it, in servile tendrils, or impetuous spray? Seek for it, in woollen wrinkles rough with stings, or in glossy surfaces, green with pure strength, and winterless delight?

89. There is no answer. But the sum of all is, that over the entire surface of the earth and its waters, as influenced by the power of the air under solar light, there is developed a series of changing forms, in clouds, plants, and animals, all of which have reference in their action, or nature, to the human intelligence that perceives them; and on which, in their aspects of horror and beauty, and their qualities of good and evil, there is engraved a series of myths, or words of the forming power, which, according to the true passion and energy of the human race, they have been enabled to read into religion. And this forming power has been by all nations partly confused with the breath or air through which it acts, and partly understood as a creative wisdom, proceeding from the Supreme Deity; but entering into and inspiring all intelligences that work in harmony with Him. And whatever intellectual results may be in modern days obtained by regarding this effluence only as a motion or vibration, every formative human art hitherto, and the best states of human happiness and order, have depended on the apprehension of its mystery (which is certain), and of its personality (which is probable).

90. Of its influence on the formative arts, I have a few words to say separately: my present business is only to interpret, as we are now sufficiently enabled to do, the external symbols of the myth under which it was represented by the Greeks as a goddess of counsel, taken first into the breast of their Supreme Deity, then created out of his thoughts, and abiding closely beside him; always sharing and consummating his power.

91. And in doing this we have first to note the meaning of the principal epithet applied to Athena, "Glaukopis," "with eyes full of light," the first syllable being

connected, by its root, with words signifying sight, not with words signifying colour. As far as I can trace the colour perception of the Greeks, I find it all founded primarily on the degree of connection between colour and light; the most important fact to them in the colour of red being its connection with fire and sunshine; so that "purple" is, in its original sense, "fire-colour," and the scarlet, or orange, of dawn, more than any other, fire-colour. I was long puzzled by Homer's calling the sea purple; and misled into thinking he meant the colour of cloud shadows on green sea; whereas he really means the gleaming blaze of the waves under wide light. Aristotle's idea (partly true) is that light, subdued by blackness, becomes red;[18] and blackness heated or lighted, also becomes red. Thus, a colour may be called purple because it is light subdued (and so death is called "purple" or "shadowy" death); or else it may be called purple as being shade kindled with fire, and thus said of the lighted sea; or even of the sun itself, when it is thought of as a red luminary opposed to the whiteness of the moon: "purpureos inter soles, et candida lunæ sidera";[19] or of golden hair: "pro purpureo pœnam solvens scelerata capillo";[20] while both ideas are modified by the influence of an earlier form of the word, which has nothing to do with fire at all, but only with mixing or staining; and then, to make the whole group of thoughts inextricably complex, yet rich and subtle in proportion to their intricacy, the various rose and crimson colours of the murex-dye,—the crimson and purple of the poppy, and fruit of the palm—and the association of all these with the hue of blood;—partly direct, partly through a confusion between the word signifying "slaughter" and "palm-fruit colour," mingle themselves in, and renew the whole nature of the old word; so that, in later literature, it means a different colour, or emotion of colour, in almost every place where it

[18] *De Coloribus,* ch. iii.; compare Vol. VII. p. 159.

[19] Virgil: *Ciris,* 37.

[20] Ruskin quotes from memory, and combines *Georgics,* i. 405 with *Æneid,* ii. 576.

occurs: and casts around for ever the reflection of all that has been dipped in its dyes.

92. So that the word is really a liquid prism, and stream of opal. And then, last of all, to keep the whole history of it in the fantastic course of a dream, warped here and there into wild grotesque, we moderns, who have preferred to rule over coal-mines instead of the sea (and so have turned the everlasting lamp of Athena into a Davy's safety-lamp in the hand of Britannia, and Athenian heavenly lightning into British subterranean "damp"), have actually got our purple out of coal instead of the sea! And thus, grotesquely, we have had enforced on us the doubt that held the old word between blackness and fire, and have completed the shadow, and the fear of it, by giving it a name from battle, "Magenta."

93. There is precisely a similar confusion between light and colour in the word used for the blue of the eyes of Athena—a noble confusion, however, brought about by the intensity of the Greek sense that the heaven is light, more than that it is blue. I was not thinking of this when I wrote, in speaking of pictorial chiaroscuro, "The sky is not blue colour merely: it is blue fire, and cannot be painted"; but it was this that the Greeks chiefly felt of it, and so "Glaukopis" chiefly means grey-eyed: grey standing for a pale or luminous blue; but it only means "owl-eyed" in thought of the roundness and expansion, not from the colour; this breadth and brightness being, again, in their moral sense, typical of the breadth, intensity, and singleness of the sight in prudence ("if thine eye be single, thy whole body shall be full of light"[21]). Then the actual power of the bird to see in twilight enters into the type, and perhaps its general fineness of sense. "Before the human form was adopted, her (Athena's) proper symbol was the owl, a bird which seems to surpass all other creatures in acuteness of organic perception, its eye being calculated to observe objects which to all others are enveloped in darkness, its ear to hear sounds distinctly, and

[21] Matthew vi. 22.

its nostrils to discriminate effluvia with such nicety that it has been deemed prophetic, from discovering the putridity of death even in the first stages of disease."*

I cannot find anywhere an account of the first known occurrence of the type; but, in the early ones on Attic coins, the wide round eyes are clearly the principal things to be made manifest.

94. There is yet, however, another colour of great importance in the conception of Athena—the dark blue of her ægis. Just as the blue or grey of her eyes was conceived as more light than colour, so her ægis was dark blue, because the Greeks thought of this tint more as shade than colour, and, while they used various materials in ornamentation, lapis-lazuli, carbonate of copper, or perhaps, smalt, with real enjoyment of the blue tint, it was yet in their minds as distinctly representative of darkness as scarlet was of light, and, therefore, anything dark,† but espe-

* Payne Knight, in his *Inquiry into the Symbolical Language of Ancient Art* [1818], not trustworthy, being little more than a mass of conjectural memoranda, but the heap is suggestive, if well sifted.

† In the breastplate and shield of Atrides the serpents and bosses are all of this dark colour, yet the serpents are said to be like rainbows;[22] but through all this splendour and opposition of hue, I feel distinctly that the literal "splendour," with its relative shade, are prevalent in the conception; and that there is always a tendency to look through the hue to its cause. And in this feeling about colour the Greeks are separated from the Eastern nations, and from the best designers of Christian times. I cannot find that they take pleasure in colour for its own sake; it may be in something more than colour, or better; but it is not in the hue itself. When Homer describes cloud breaking from a mountain summit the crags became visible in light, not in colour; he feels only their flashing out in bright edges and trenchant shadows: above, the "infinite," "unspeakable" aether is torn open—but not the *blue* of it.[23] He has scarcely any

[22] *Iliad*, xi. 24 *seq.*

[23] *Ibid.*, xvi. 297–300: "As when from the high crest of a great hill, Zeus, the gatherer of the lightning, has stirred a dense cloud, and all the peaks, and sharp promontories, and glades shine forth, and from heaven the infinite air breaks open."

cially the colour of heavy thundercloud, was described by the same term. The physical power of this darkness of the ægis, fringed with lightning, is given quite simply when Jupiter himself uses it to overshadow Ida and the Plain of Troy, and withdraws it at the prayer of Ajax for light;[24] and again when he grants it to be worn for a time by Apollo, who is hidden by its cloud when he strikes down Patroclus:[25] but its spiritual power is chiefly expressed by a word signifying deeper shadow;—the gloom of Erebus, or of our evening, which, when spoken of the ægis, signifies not merely the indignation of Athena, but the entire hiding or withdrawal of her help, and beyond even this, her deadliest of all hostility—the darkness by which she herself deceives and beguiles to final ruin those to whom she is wholly adverse; this contradiction of her

---

abstract pleasure in blue, or green, or gold; but only in their shade or flame.

I have yet to trace the causes of this (which will be a long task, belonging to art questions, not to mythological ones); but it is, I believe, much connected with the brooding of the shadow of death over the Greeks, without any clear hope of immortality. The restriction of the colour on their vases to dim red (or yellow) with black and white, is greatly connected with their sepulchral use, and with all the melancholy of Greek tragic thought; and in this gloom the failure of colour-perception is partly noble, partly base: noble, in its earnestness, which raises the design of Greek vases as far above the designing of mere colourist nations like the Chinese, as men's thoughts are above children's; and yet it is partly base and earthly; and inherently defective in one human faculty: and I believe it was one cause of the perishing of their art so swiftly, for indeed there is no decline so sudden, or down to such utter loss and ludicrous depravity, as the fall of Greek design on its vases from the fifth to the third century, B.C. On the other hand, the pure colour-gift, when employed for pleasure only, degrades in another direction; so that among the Indians, Chinese, and Japanese, all intellectual progress in art has been for ages rendered impossible by the prevalence of that faculty: and yet it is, as I have said again and again, the spiritual power of art; and its true brightness is the essential characteristic of all healthy schools.

---

[24] *Ibid.*, xvii. 593, 594, 626 *seq.*

[25] *Ibid.*, xvi. 777 *seq.*

own glory being the uttermost judgment upon human falsehood. Thus it is she who provokes Pandarus to the treachery which purposed to fulfil the rape of Helen by the murder of her husband in time of truce; and *then* the Greek King, holding his wounded brother's hand, prophesies against Troy the darkness of the ægis which shall be over all, and for ever.*

95. This, then, finally, was the perfect colour-conception of Athena;—the flesh, snow-white, (the hands, feet, and face of marble, even when the statue was hewn roughly in wood); the eyes of keen pale blue, often in statues represented by jewels; the long robe to the feet, crocus-coloured; and the ægis thrown over it of thunderous purple; the helmet golden, (*Il.*, v. 144,) and I suppose its crest also, as that of Achilles.[26]

If you think carefully of the meaning and character which is now enough illustrated for you in each of these colours; and remember that the crocus-colour and the purple were both of them developments, in opposite directions, of the great central idea of fire-colour, or scarlet, you will see that this form of the creative spirit of the earth is conceived as robed in the blue, and purple, and scarlet, the white, and the gold, which have been recognized for the sacred chord of colours, from the day when the cloud descended on a Rock more mighty than Ida.[27]

96. I have spoken throughout, hitherto, of the conception of Athena, as it is traceable in the Greek mind; not as it was rendered by Greek art. It is matter of extreme difficulty, requiring a sympathy at once affectionate and cautious, and a knowledge reaching the earliest springs of the religion of many lands, to discern through the imperfection, and alas! more dimly yet, through the tri-

* *Il.*, iv. 166.

[26] *Iliad*, xviii. 611.

[27] See Exodus xxiv. 18, xxv. 1–4: "And Moses went into the midst of the cloud, and gat him up into the mount. . . . And the Lord spake unto Moses, saying, Speak unto the children of Israel, that they bring me an offering. . . . And blue, and purple, and scarlet."

umphs, of formative art, what kind of thoughts they were that appointed for it the tasks of its childhood, and watched by the awakening of its strength.

The religious passion is nearly always vividest when the art is weakest; and the technical skill reaches its deliberate splendour only when the ecstasy which gave it birth has passed away for ever. It is as vain an attempt to reason out the visionary power or guiding influence of Athena in the Greek heart, from anything we now read, or possess, of the work of Phidias, as it would be for the disciples of some new religion to infer the spirit of Christianity from Titian's "Assumption." The effective vitality of the religious conception can be traced only through the efforts of trembling hands, and strange pleasures of untaught eyes; and the beauty of the dream can no more be found in the first symbols by which it is expressed, than a child's idea of fairyland can be gathered from its pencil scrawl, or a girl's love for her broken doll explained by the defaced features. On the other hand, the Athena of Phidias was, in very fact, not so much the deity, as the darling of the Athenian people. Her magnificence represented their pride and fondness, more than their piety; and the great artist, in lavishing upon her dignities which might be ended abruptly by the pillage they provoked, resigned, apparently without regret, the awe of her ancient memory; and, (with only the careless remonstrance of a workman too strong to be proud,) even the perfectness of his own art. Rejoicing in the protection of their goddess, and in their own hour of glory, the people of Athena robed her, at their will, with the preciousness of ivory and gems; forgot or denied the darkness of the breastplate of judgment, and vainly bade its unappeasable serpents relax their coils in gold.

97. It will take me many a day yet—if days, many or few, be given me—to disentangle in anywise the proud and practised disguises of religious creeds from the instinctive arts which, grotesquely and indecorously, yet with sincerity, strove to embody them, or to relate. But I think the reader, by help even of the imperfect indications al-

ready given to him, will be able to follow, with a continually increasing security, the vestiges of the Myth of Athena; and to reanimate its almost evanescent shade, by connecting it with the now recognized facts of existent nature, which it, more or less dimly, reflected and foretold. I gather these facts together in brief sum.

98. The deep of air that surrounds the earth enters into union with the earth at its surface, and with its waters; so as to be the apparent cause of their ascending into life. First, it warms them, and shades, at once, staying the heat of the sun's rays in its own body, but warding their force with its clouds. It warms and cools at once, with traffic of balm and frost; so that the white wreaths are withdrawn from the field of the Swiss peasant by the glow of Libyan rock. It gives its own strength to the sea; forms and fills every cell of its foam; sustains the precipices, and designs the valleys of its waves; gives the gleam to their moving under the night, and the white fire to their plains under sunrise; lifts their voices along the rocks, bears above them the spray of birds, pencils through them the dimpling of unfooted sands. It gathers out of them a portion in the hollow of its hand: dyes, with that, the hills into dark blue, and their glaciers with dying rose; inlays with that, for sapphire, the dome in which it has to set the cloud; shapes out of that the heavenly flocks: divides them, numbers, cherishes, bears them on its bosom, calls them to their journeys, waits by their rest; feeds from them the brooks that cease not, and strews with them the dews that cease. It spins and weaves their fleece into wild tapestry, rends it, and renews; and flits and flames, and whispers, among the golden threads, thrilling them with a plectrum of strange fire that traverses them to and fro, and is enclosed in them like life.

It enters into the surface of the earth, subdues it, and falls together with it into fruitful dust, from which can be moulded flesh; it joins itself, in dew, to the substance of adamant; and becomes the green leaf out of the dry ground; it enters into the separated shapes of the earth it has tempered, commands the ebb and flow of the current of their life, fills their limbs with its own lightness, measures their existence by its indwelling pulse, moulds upon their lips the words by which one soul can be known to another; is to them the hearing of the ear, and the beating of the heart; and, passing away, leaves them to the peace that hears and moves no more.

99. This was the Athena of the greatest people of the days of old. And opposite to the temple of this Spirit of the breath, and life-blood, of man and of beast, stood, on the Mount of Justice, and near the chasm which was haunted by the goddess-Avengers, an altar to a God unknown;—proclaimed at last to them, as one who, indeed, gave to all men, life, and breath, and all things; and rain from heaven, filling their hearts with food and gladness; —a God who had made of one blood all nations of men who dwell on the face of all the earth, and had determined the times of their fate, and the bounds of their habitation.[28]

100. We ourselves, fretted here in our narrrow days, know less, perhaps, in very deed, than they, what manner of spirit we are of, or what manner of spirit we ignorantly worship.[29] Have we, indeed, desired the Desire of all nations? and will the Master whom we meant to seek, and the Messenger in whom we thought we delighted, confirm, when He comes to His temple,—or not find in its midst,—the tables heavy with gold for bread, and the seats that are bought with the price of the dove? Or is our own land also to be left by its angered Spirit;—left among those, where sunshine vainly sweet, and passionate folly of storm, waste themselves in the silent places of knowledge that has passed away, and of tongues that have ceased?

This only we may discern assuredly: this, every true

[28] The reference is to the preaching of St. Paul on the Areopagus at Athens, opposite to the Acropolis, and close to the cave of the Eumenides; where stood "an altar with this inscription, To the Unknown God" (Acts xvii. 19, 23, 25, 26, xiv. 17).

[29] For the Bible references here, see Acts xvii. 23; Haggai ii. 7; Malachi iii. 1; Matthew xxi. 12.

light of science, every mercifully-granted power, every wisely-restricted thought, teach us more clearly day by day, that in the heavens above, and the earth beneath, there is one continual and omnipotent presence of help, and of peace, for all men who know that they Live, and remember that they Die.

III

*ATHENA ERGANE**

(*Athena in the Heart*)

Various Notes relating to the Conception of Athena as the Directress of the Imagination and Will

101. I have now only a few words to say, bearing on what seems to me present need, respecting the third function of Athena, conceived as the directress of human passion, resolution, and labour.

Few words, for I am not yet prepared to give accurate distinction between the intellectual rule of Athena and that of the Muses: but, broadly, the Muses, with their king, preside over meditative, historical, and poetic arts, whose end is the discovery of light or truth, and the creation of beauty: but Athena rules over moral passion, and practically useful art. She does not make men learned, but prudent and subtle: she does not teach them to make their work beautiful, but to make it right.

In different places of my writings, and through many years of endeavour to define the laws of art, I have insisted on this rightness in work, and on its connection with virtue of character, in so many partial ways, that the impres-

* "Athena the worker, or having rule over work." The name was first given to her by the Athenians.

sion left on the reader's mind—if, indeed, it was ever impressed at all—has been confused and uncertain. In beginning the series of my corrected works, I wish this principle (in my own mind the foundation of every other) to be made plain, if nothing else is: and will try, therefore, to make it so, as far as, by any effort, I can put it into unmistakable words. And, first, here is a very simple statement of it, given lately in a lecture on the Architecture of the Valley of the Somme, which will be better read in this place than in its incidental connection with my account of the porches of Abbeville.

102. I had used, in a preceding part of the lecture, the expression, "by what faults" this Gothic architecture fell. We continually speak thus of works of art. We talk of their faults and merits, as of virtues and vices. What do we mean by talking of the faults of a picture, or the merits of a piece of stone?

The faults of a work of art are the faults of its workman, and its virtues his virtues.

Great art is the expression of the mind of a great man, and mean art, that of the want of mind of a weak man. A foolish person builds foolishly, and a wise one, sensibly; a virtuous one, beautifully; and a vicious one, basely. If stone work is well put together, it means that a thoughtful man planned it, and a careful man cut it, and an honest man cemented it. If it has too much ornament, it means that its carver was too greedy of pleasure; if too little, that he was rude, or insensitive, or stupid, and the like. So that when once you have learned how to spell these most precious of all legends,—pictures and buildings,—you may read the characters of men, and of nations, in their art, as in a mirror;—nay, as in a microscope, and magnified a hundredfold; for the character becomes passionate in the art, and intensifies itself in all its noblest or meanest delights. Nay, not only as in a microscope, but as under a scalpel, and in dissection; for a man may hide himself from you, or misrepresent himself to you, every other way; but he cannot in his work: there, be sure, you have him to the inmost. All that he likes, all that he sees,—all that he can do,—his imagination, his affections, his perseverance, his impatience, his clumsiness, cleverness, everything is there. If the work is a cobweb, you know it was made by a spider; if a honeycomb, by a bee; a worm-cast is thrown up by a worm, and a nest wreathed by a bird; and a house built by a man, worthily, if he is worthy, and ignobly, if he is ignoble.

And always, from the least to the greatest, as the made thing is good or bad, so is the maker of it.

103. You all use this faculty of judgment more or less, whether you theoretically admit the principle or not. Take that floral gable;* you don't suppose the man who built Stonehenge could have built that, or that the man who built that, *would* have built Stonehenge? Do you think an old Roman would have liked such a piece of filigree work? or that Michael Angelo would have spent his time in twisting these stems of roses in and out? Or, of modern handicraftsmen, do you think a burglar, or a brute, or a pickpocket could have carved it? Could Bill Sykes have done it? or the Dodger, dexterous with finger and tool? You will find in the end, that *no man could have done it but exactly the man who did it;* and by looking close at it, you may, if you know your letters, read precisely the manner of man he was.

104. Now I must insist on this matter, for a grave reason. Of all facts concerning art, this is the one most necessary to be known, that, while manufacture is the work of hands only, art is the work of the whole spirit of man; and as that spirit is, so is the deed of it: and by whatever power of vice or virtue any art is produced, the same vice or virtue it reproduces and teaches. That which is born of evil begets evil; and that which is born of valour and honour, teaches valour and honour. All art is either infection or education. It *must* be one or other of these.

* The elaborate pediment above the central porch at the west end of Rouen Cathedral, pierced into a transparent web of tracery, and enriched with a border of "twisted eglantine."[1]

[1] *L'Allegro,* 48.

105. This, I repeat, of all truths respecting art, is the one of which understanding is the most precious, and denial the most deadly. And I assert it the more, because it has of late been repeatedly, expressly, and with contumely denied; and that by high authority: and I hold it one of the most sorrowful facts connected with the decline of the arts among us, that English gentlemen, of high standing as scholars and artists, should have been blinded into the acceptance, and betrayed into the assertion of a fallacy which only authority such as theirs could have rendered for an instant credible. For the contrary of it is written in the history of all great nations; it is the one sentence always inscribed on the steps of their thrones; the one concordant voice in which they speak to us out of their dust.

All such nations first manifest themselves as a pure and beautiful animal race, with intense energy and imagination. They live lives of hardship by choice, and by grand instinct of manly discipline: they become fierce and irresistible soldiers; the nation is always its own army, and their king, or chief head of government, is always their first soldier. Pharaoh, or David, or Leonidas, or Valerius, or Barbarossa, or Cœur de Lion, or S. Louis, or Dandolo, or Frederick the Great:—Egyptian, Jew, Greek, Roman, German, English, French, Venetian,—that is inviolable law for them all; their king must be their first soldier, or they cannot be in progressive power. Then, after their great military period, comes the domestic period; in which, without betraying the discipline of war, they add to their great soldiership the delights and possessions of a delicate and tender home-life: and then, for all nations, is the time of their perfect art, which is the fruit, the evidence, the reward of their national ideal of character, developed by the finished care of the occupations of peace. That is the history of all true art that ever was, or can be: palpably the history of it,—unmistakably,—written on the forehead of it in letters of light,—in tongues of fire, by which the seal of virtue is branded as deep as ever iron burnt into a convict's flesh the seal of crime. But always, hitherto, after the great period, has followed the day of luxury, and pursuit of the arts for pleasure only. And all has so ended.

106. Thus far of Abbeville building. Now I have here asserted two things,—first, the foundation of art in moral character; next, the foundation of moral character in war. I must make both these assertions clearer, and prove them.

First, of the foundation of art in moral character. Of course art-gift and amiability of disposition are two different things; a good man is not necessarily a painter, nor does an eye for colour necessarily imply an honest mind. But great art implies the union of both powers: it is the expression, by an art-gift, of a pure soul. If the gift is not there, we can have no art at all; and if the soul—and a right soul too—is not there, the art is bad, however dexterous.

107. But also, remember, that the art-gift itself is only the result of the moral character of generations. A bad woman may have a sweet voice; but that sweetness of voice comes of the past morality of her race. That she can sing with it at all, she owes to the determination of laws of music by the morality of the past. Every act, every impulse, of virtue and vice, affects in any creature, face, voice, nervous power, and vigour and harmony of invention, at once. Perseverance in rightness of human conduct, renders, after a certain number of generations, human art possible; every sin clouds it, be it ever so little a one; and persistent vicious living and following of pleasure render, after a certain number of generations, all art impossible. Men are deceived by the long-suffering of the laws of nature; and mistake, in a nation, the reward of the virtue of its sires for the issue of its own sins. The time of their visitation will come, and that inevitably; for, it is always true, that if the fathers have eaten sour grapes, the children's teeth are set on edge. And for the individual, as soon as you have learned to read, you may, as I have said, know him to the heart's core, through his art. Let his art-gift be never so great, and cultivated to the height by the schools of a great race of men; and it is still but a tapestry

thrown over his own being and inner soul; and the bearing of it will show, infallibly, whether it hangs on a man, or on a skeleton. If you are dim-eyed, you may not see the difference in the fall of the folds at first, but learn how to look, and the folds themselves will become transparent, and you shall see through them the death's shape, or the divine one, making the tissue above it as a cloud of light, or as a winding-sheet.

108. Then farther, observe, I have said (and you will find it true, and that to the uttermost) that, as all lovely art is rooted in virtue, so it bears fruit of virtue, and is didactic in its own nature. It is often didactic also in actually expressed thought, as Giotto's, Michael Angelo's, Dürer's, and hundreds more; but that is not its special function,—it is didactic chiefly by being beautiful; but beautiful with haunting thought, no less than with form, and full of myths that can be read only with the heart.

For instance, at this moment there is open beside me as I write, a page of Persian manuscript, wrought with wreathed azure and gold, and soft green, and violet, and ruby and scarlet, into one field of pure resplendence. It is wrought to delight the eyes only; and it does delight them; and the man who did it assuredly had eyes in his head; but not much more. It is not didactic art, but its author was happy: and it will do the good, and the harm, that mere pleasure can do. But, opposite me, is an early Turner drawing of the lake of Geneva, taken about two miles from Geneva, on the Lausanne road, with Mont Blanc in the distance. The old city is seen lying beyond the waveless waters, veiled with a sweet misty veil of Athena's weaving: a faint light of morning, peaceful exceedingly, and almost colourless, shed from behind the Voirons, increases into soft amber along the slope of the Salève, and is just seen, and no more, on the fair warm fields of its summit, between the folds of a white cloud that rests upon the grass, but rises, high and towerlike, into the zenith of dawn above.

109. There is not as much colour in that low amber light upon the hill-side as there is in the palest dead leaf.

The lake is not blue, but grey in mist, passing into deep shadow beneath the Voirons' pines; a few dark clusters of leaves, a single white flower—scarcely seen—are all the gladness given to the rocks of the shore. One of the ruby spots of the eastern manuscript would give colour enough for all the red that is in Turner's entire drawing. For the mere pleasure of the eye, there is not so much in all those lines of his, throughout the entire landscape, as in half an inch square of the Persian's page. What made him take pleasure in the low colour that is only like the brown of a dead leaf? in the cold grey of dawn—in the one white flower among the rocks—in these—and no more than these?

110. He took pleasure in them because he had been bred among English fields and hills; because the gentleness of a great race was in his heart, and its power of thought in his brain; because he knew the stories of the Alps, and of the cities at their feet; because he had read the Homeric legends of the clouds, and beheld the gods of dawn, and the givers of dew to the fields; because he knew the faces of the crags, and the imagery of the passionate mountains, as a man knows the face of his friend; because he had in him the wonder and sorrow concerning life and death, which are the inheritance of the Gothic soul from the days of its first sea kings; and also the compassion and the joy that are woven into the innermost fabric of every great imaginative spirit, born now in countries that have lived by the Christian faith with any courage or truth. And the picture contains also, for us, just this which its maker had in him to give; and can convey it to us, just so far as we are of the temper in which it must be received. It is didactic, if we are worthy to be taught, no otherwise. The pure heart, it will make more pure; the thoughtful, more thoughtful. It has in it no words for the reckless or the base.

111. As I myself look at it, there is no fault nor folly of my life,—and both have been many and great,—that does not rise up against me, and take away my joy, and shorten my power of possession, of sight, of understanding.

And every past effort of my life, every gleam of rightness or good in it, is with me now, to help me in my grasp of this art, and its vision. So far as I can rejoice in, or interpret either, my power is owing to what of right there is in me. I dare to say it, that, because through all my life I have desired good, and not evil; because I have been kind to many; have wished to be kind to all; have wilfully injured none; and because I have loved much, and not selfishly;—therefore, the morning light is yet visible to me on those hills, and you, who read, may trust my thought and word in such work as I have to do for you; and you will be glad afterwards that you have trusted them.

112. Yet remember,—I repeat it again and yet again,—that I may for once, if possible, make this thing assuredly clear:—the inherited art-gift must be there, as well as the life in some poor measure, or rescued fragment, right. This art-gift of mine could not have been won by any work, or by any conduct; it belongs to me by birthright, and came by Athena's will, from the air of English country villages, and Scottish hills. I will risk whatever charge of folly may come on me, for printing one of my many childish rhymes, written on a frosty day in Glen Farg, just north of Loch Leven. It bears date 1st January, 1828. I was born on the 8th of February, 1819; and all that I ever could be, and all that I cannot be, the weak little rhyme already shows.

"Papa, how pretty those icicles are,
That are seen so near,—that are seen so far;
—Those dropping waters that come from the rocks
And many a hole, like the haunt of a fox.
That silvery stream that runs babbling along,
Making a murmuring, dancing song.
Those trees that stand waving upon the rock's side,
And men, that, like spectres, among them glide.
And waterfalls that are heard from far,
And come in sight when very near.
And the water-wheel that turns slowly round,
Grinding the corn that—requires to be ground,—

(Political Economy of the future!)

—And mountains at a distance seen,
And rivers winding through the plain.
And quarries with their craggy stones,
And the wind among them moans."

So foretelling Stones of Venice, and this essay on Athena.

Enough now concerning myself.

113. Of Turner's life, and of its good and evil, both great, but the good immeasurably the greater, his work is in all things a perfect and transparent evidence. His biography is simply,—"He did this, nor will ever another do its like again." Yet read what I have said of him, as compared with the great Italians, in the passages taken from the *Cestus of Aglaia*, farther on, § 158.

114. This, then, is the nature of the connection of morals with art. Now, secondly, I have asserted the foundation of both these, at least, hitherto, in war. The reason of this too manifest fact is, that, until now, it has been impossible for any nation, except a warrior one, to fix its mind wholly on its men, instead of on their possessions. Every great soldier nation thinks, necessarily, first of multiplying its bodies and souls of men, in good temper and strict discipline. As long as this is its political aim, it does not matter what it temporarily suffers, or loses, either in numbers or in wealth; its morality and its arts, (if it have national art-gift,) advance together; but so soon as it ceases to be a warrior nation, it thinks of its possessions instead of its men; and then the moral and poetic powers vanish together.

115. It is thus, however, absolutely necessary to the virtue of war that it should be waged by personal strength, not by money or machinery. A nation that fights with a mercenary force, or with torpedoes instead of its own arms, is dying. Not but that there is more true courage in modern than even in ancient war; but this is, first, because all the remaining life of European nations is with a morbid intensity thrown into their soldiers; and, secondly, be-

cause their present heroism is the culmination of centuries of inbred and traditional valour, which Athena taught them by forcing them to govern the foam of the sea-wave and of the horse,—not the steam of kettles.

116. And farther, note this, which is vital to us in the present crisis: If war is to be made by money and machinery, the nation which is the largest and most covetous multitude will win. You may be as scientific as you choose; the mob that can pay more for sulphuric acid and gunpowder will at last poison its bullets, throw acid in your faces, and make an end of you;—of itself, also, in good time, but of you first. And to the English people the choice of its fate is very near now. It may spasmodically defend its property with iron walls a fathom thick, a few years longer—a very few. No walls will defend either it, or its havings, against the multitude that is breeding and spreading, faster than the clouds, over the habitable earth. We shall be allowed to live by small pedlar's business, and ironmongery—since we have chosen those for our line of life—as long as we are found useful black servants to the Americans; and are content to dig coals and sit in the cinders; and have still coals to dig,—they once exhausted, or got cheaper elsewhere, we shall be abolished. But if we think more wisely, while there is yet time, and set our minds again on multiplying Englishmen, and not on cheapening English wares; if we resolve to submit to wholesome laws of labour and economy, and, setting our political squabbles aside, try how many strong creatures, friendly and faithful to each other, we can crowd into every spot of English dominion, neither poison nor iron will prevail against us; nor traffic—nor hatred: the noble nation will yet, by the grace of Heaven, rule over the ignoble, and force of heart hold its own against fire-balls.

117. But there is yet a farther reason for the dependence of the arts on war. The vice and injustice of the world are constantly springing anew, and are only to be subdued by battle; the keepers of order and law must always be soldiers. And now, going back to the myth of Athena, we see that though she is first a warrior maid, she

detests war for its own sake; she arms Achilles and Ulysses in just quarrels, but she *dis*arms Ares. She contends, herself, continually against disorder and convulsion in the Earth giants; she stands by Hercules' side in victory over all monstrous evil: in justice only she judges and makes war.[2] But in this war of hers she is wholly implacable. She has little notion of converting criminals. There is no faculty of mercy in her when she has been resisted. Her word is only, "I will mock when your fear cometh."[3] Note the words that follow: "when your fear cometh as desolation, and your destruction as a whirlwind;" for her wrath is of irresistible tempest: once roused, it is blind and deaf,—rabies—madness of anger—darkness of the Dies Iræ.

And that is, indeed, the sorrowfullest fact we have to know about our own several lives. Wisdom never forgives. Whatever resistance we have offered to her law, she avenges for ever;—the lost hour can never be redeemed, and the accomplished wrong never atoned for. The best that can be done afterwards, but for that, had been better; —the falsest of all the cries of peace, where there is no peace, is that of the pardon of sin, as the mob expect it. Wisdom can "put away" sin,[4] but she cannot pardon it; and she is apt, in her haste, to put away the sinner as well, when the black ægis is on her breast.

118. And this is also a fact we have to know about our national life, that it is ended as soon as it has lost the power of noble Anger. When it paints over, and apologizes for its pitiful criminalities; and endures its false weights, and its adulterated food; dares not decide practically between good and evil, and can neither honour the one, nor smite the other, but sneers at the good, as if it were hidden evil, and consoles the evil with pious sympathy, and conserves it in the sugar of its leaden heart,—the end is come.

119. The first sign, then, of Athena's presence with any people, is that they become warriors, and that the chief

[2] Revelation xix. 11.
[3] Proverbs i. 26, 27.
[4] Hebrews ix. 26.

thought of every man of them is to stand rightly in his rank, and not fail from his brother's side in battle. Wealth, and pleasure, and even love, are all, under Athena's orders, sacrificed to this duty of standing fast in the rank of war.

But farther: Athena presided over industry, as well as battle; typically, over women's industry; that brings comfort with pleasantness. Her word to us all is:—"Be well exercised, and rightly clothed. Clothed, and in your right minds; not insane and in rags, nor in soiled fine clothes clutched from each other's shoulders. Fight and weave. Then I myself will answer for the course of the lance, and the colours of the loom."

And now I will ask the reader to look with some care through these following passages respecting modern multitudes and their occupations, written long ago, but left in fragmentary form, in which they must now stay, and be of what use they can.

120. It is not political economy to put a number of strong men down on an acre of ground, with no lodging, and nothing to eat. Nor is it political economy to build a city on good ground, and fill it with store of corn and treasure, and put a score of lepers to live in it. Political economy creates together the means of life, and the living persons who are to use them; and of both, the best and the most that it can, but imperatively the best, not the most. A few good and healthy men, rather than a multitude of diseased rogues; and a little real milk and wine rather than much chalk and petroleum; but the gist of the whole business is, that the men, and their property, must both be produced together—not one to the loss of the other. Property must not be created in lands desolate by exile of their people,—nor multiplied and depraved humanity, in lands barren of bread.

121. Nevertheless, though the men and their possessions are to be increased at the same time, the first object of thought is always to be the multiplication of a worthy people. The strength of the nation is in its multitude, not in its territory; but only in its sound multitude. It is one

thing, both in a man and a nation, to gain flesh, and another to be swollen with putrid humours. Not that multitude ever ought to be inconsistent with virtue. Two men should be wiser than one, and two thousand than two; nor do I know another so gross fallacy in the records of human stupidity as that excuse for neglect of crime by greatness of cities. As if the first purpose of congregation were not to devise laws and repress crimes! as if bees and wasps could live honestly in flocks,—men, only in separate dens!—as if it were easy to help one another on the opposite sides of a mountain, and impossible on the opposite sides of a street! But when the men are true and good, and stand shoulder to shoulder, the strength of any nation is in its quantity of life, not in its land nor gold. The more good men a state has, in proportion to its territory, the stronger the state. And as it has been the madness of economists to seek for gold instead of life, so it has been the madness of kings to seek for land instead of life. They want the town on the other side of the river, and seek it at the spear point: it never enters their stupid heads that to double the honest souls in the town on *this* side of the river, would make them stronger kings; and that this doubling might be done by the ploughshare instead of the spear, and through happiness instead of misery.

Therefore, in brief, this is the object of all true policy and true economy: "utmost multitude of good men on every given space of ground"—imperatively always, good, sound, honest men, not a mob of white-faced thieves. So that, on the one hand, all aristocracy is wrong which is inconsistent with numbers; and, on the other, all numbers are wrong which are inconsistent with breeding.

122. Then, touching the accumulation of wealth for the maintenance of such men, observe, that you must never use the terms "money" and "wealth" as synonymous. Wealth consists of the good, and therefore useful, things in the possession of the nation: money is only the written or coined sign of the relative quantities of wealth in each person's possession. All money is a divisible title-deed, of immense importance as an expression of right to property;

but absolutely valueless, as property itself. Thus, supposing a nation isolated from all others, the money in its possession is, at its maximum value, worth all the property of the nation, and no more, because no more can be got for it. And the money of all nations is worth, at its maximum, the property of all nations, and no more, for no more can be got for it. Thus, every article of property produced increases, by its value, the value of all the money in the world, and every article of property destroyed diminishes the value of all the money in the world. If ten men are cast away on a rock, with a thousand pounds in their pockets, and there is on the rock neither food nor shelter, their money is worth simply nothing; for nothing is to be had for it: if they build ten huts, and recover a cask of biscuit from the wreck, then their thousand pounds, at its maximum value, is worth ten huts and a cask of biscuit. If they make their thousand pounds into two thousand by writing new notes, their two thousand pounds are still only worth ten huts and a cask of biscuit. And the law of relative value is the same for all the world, and all the people in it, and all their property, as for ten men on a rock. Therefore, money is truly and finally lost in the degree in which its value is taken from it, (ceasing in that degree to be money at all); and it is truly gained in the degree in which value is added to it. Thus, suppose the money coined by the nation to be a fixed sum, divided very minutely, (say into francs and cents), and neither to be added to, nor diminished. Then every grain of food and inch of lodging added to its possessions makes every cent in its pockets worth proportionally more, and every grain of food it consumes, and inch of roof it allows to fall to ruin, makes every cent in its pockets worth less; and this with mathematical precision. The immediate value of the money at particular times and places depends, indeed, on the humours of the possessors of property; but the nation is in the one case gradually getting richer; and will feel the pressure of poverty steadily everywhere relaxing, whatever the humours of individuals may be; and, in the other case, is gradually growing poorer, and the pressure of its poverty will every day tell more and more, in ways that it cannot explain, but will most bitterly feel.

123. The actual quantity of money which it coins, in relation to its real property, is therefore only of consequence for convenience of exchange; but the proportion in which this quantity of money is divided among individuals expresses their various rights to greater or less proportions of the national property, and must not, therefore, be tampered with. The Government may at any time, with perfect justice, double its issue of coinage, if it gives every man who had ten pounds in his pocket, another ten pounds, and every man who had ten pence, another ten pence; for it thus does not make any of them richer; it merely divides their counters for them into twice the number. But if it gives the newly-issued coins to other people, or keeps them itself, it simply robs the former holders to precisely that extent. This most important function of money, as a title-deed, on the non-violation of which all national soundness of commerce and peace of life depend, has been never rightly distinguished by economists from the quite unimportant function of money as a means of exchange. You can exchange goods,—at some inconvenience indeed, but still you can contrive to do it,—without money at all; but you cannot maintain your claim to the savings of your past life without a document declaring the amount of them, which the nation and its Government will respect.

124. And as economists have lost sight of this great function of money in relation to individual rights, so they have equally lost sight of its function as a representative of good things. That, for every good thing produced, so much money is put into everybody's pocket—is the one simple and primal truth for the public to know, and for economists to teach. How many of them have taught it? Some have; but only incidentally; and others will say it is a truism. If it be, do the public know it? Does your ordinary English householder know that every costly dinner he gives has destroyed as much money as it is worth? Does every well-educated girl—do even the women in high political position—know that every fine dress they wear them-

selves, or cause to be worn, destroys precisely so much of the national money as the labour and material of it are worth? If this be a truism, it is one that needs proclaiming somewhat louder.

125. That, then, is the relation of money and goods. So much goods, so much money; so little goods, so little money. But, as there is this true relation between money and "goods," or good things, so there is a false relation between money and "bads," or bad things. Many bad things will fetch a price in exchange; but they do not increase the wealth of the country. Good wine is wealth—drugged wine is not; good meat is wealth—putrid meat is not; good pictures are wealth—bad pictures are not. A thing is worth precisely what it can do for you; not what you choose to pay for it. You may pay a thousand pounds for a cracked pipkin, if you please; but you do not by that transaction make the cracked pipkin worth one that will hold water, nor that, nor any pipkin whatsoever, worth more than it was before you paid such sum for it. You may, perhaps, induce many potters to manufacture fissured pots, and many amateurs of clay to buy them; but the nation is, through the whole business so encouraged, rich by the addition to its wealth of so many potsherds—and there an end. The thing is worth what it CAN do for you, not what you think it can; and most national luxuries, now-a-days, are a form of potsherd provided for the solace of a self-complacent Job, voluntarily sedent on his ash-heap.

126. And, also, so far as good things already exist, and have become media of exchange, the variations in their prices are absolutely indifferent to the nation. Whether Mr. A. buys a Titian from Mr. B. for twenty, or for two thousand, pounds, matters not sixpence to the national revenue: that is to say, it matters in nowise to the revenue whether Mr. A. has the picture, and Mr. B. the money, or Mr. B. the picture, and Mr. A. the money. Which of them will spend the money most wisely, and which of them will keep the picture most carefully, is, indeed, a matter of some importance; but this cannot be known by the mere fact of exchange.

127. The wealth of a nation then, first, and its peace and well-being besides, depend on the number of persons it can employ in making good and useful things. I say its well-being also, for the character of men depends more on their occupations than on any teaching we can give them, or principles with which we can imbue them. The employment forms the habits.

. . . .[5]

132. . . . I find by me a violent little fragment of undelivered lecture, which puts this, perhaps, still more clearly. Your idle people, (it says,) as they are now, are not merely waste coal-beds. They are explosive coal-beds, which you pay a high annual rent for. You are keeping all these idle persons, remember, at far greater cost than if they were busy. Do you think a vicious person eats less than an honest one? or that it is cheaper to keep a bad man drunk, than a good man sober? There is, I suppose, a dim idea in the mind of the public, that they don't pay for the maintenance of people they don't employ. Those staggering rascals at the street corner, grouped around its splendid angle of public-house, we fancy they are no servants of ours! that we pay them no wages! that no cash out of our pocket is spent over that beer-stained counter!

Whose cash is it then they are spending? It is not got honestly by work. You know that much. Where do they get it from? Who has paid for their dinner and their pot? Those fellows can live only in one of two ways—by pillage or beggary. Their annual income by thieving comes out of the public pocket, you will admit. They are not cheaply fed, so far as they are fed by theft. But the rest of their living—all that they don't steal—they must beg. Not with success from you, you think. Wise as benevolent, you never gave a penny in "indiscriminate charity." Well, I congratulate you on the freedom of your conscience from that sin, mine being bitterly burdened with the memory of many a sixpence given to beggars of whom I knew

[5] The rest of § 127 and §§ 128–132 were reprinted from the *Notes on the General Principles of Employment for the Destitute and Criminal Classes.*

nothing, but that they had pale faces and thin waists. But it is not that kind of street beggary that the vagabonds of our people chiefly practise. It is home beggary that is the worst beggars' trade. Home alms which it is their worst degradation to receive. Those scamps know well enough that you and your wisdom are worth nothing to them. They won't beg of you. They will beg of their sisters, and mothers, and wives, and children, and of any one else who is enough ashamed of being of the same blood with them to pay to keep them out of sight. Every one of those blackguards is the bane of a family. *That* is the deadly "indiscriminate charity"—the charity which each household pays to maintain its own private curse.

133. And you think that is no affair of yours? and that every family ought to watch over and subdue its own living plague? Put it to yourselves this way, then: suppose you knew every one of those families kept an idol in an inner room—a big-bellied bronze figure, to which daily sacrifice and oblation was made; at whose feet so much beer and brandy were poured out every morning on the ground; and before which, every night, good meat, enough for two men's keep, was set, and left, till it was putrid, and then carried out and thrown on the dunghill;—you would put an end to that form of idolatry with your best diligence, I suppose. You would understand then that the beer, and brandy, and meat, were wasted; and that the burden imposed by each household on itself lay heavily through them on the whole community? But, suppose farther, that this idol were not of silent and quiet bronze only;—but an ingenious mechanism, wound up every morning, to run itself down in automatic blasphemies; that it struck and tore with its hands the people who set food before it; that it was anointed with poisonous unguents, and infected the air for miles round. You would interfere with the idolatry then, straightway? Will you not interfere with it now, when the infection that the venomous idol spreads is not merely death—but sin?

134. So far the old lecture. Returning to cool English, the end of the matter is, that sooner or later, we shall

have to register our people; and to know how they live; and to make sure, if they are capable of work, that right work is given them to do.

. . . .[6]

I give now, for such farther illustration as they contain of the points I desire most to insist upon with respect both to education and employment, a portion of the series of notes published some time ago in the *Art Journal,* on the opposition of Modesty and Liberty, and the unescapable law of wise restraint. I am sorry that they are written obscurely;—and it may be thought affectedly:—but the fact is, I have always had three different ways of writing: one, with the single view of making myself understood, in which I necessarily omit a great deal of what comes into my head; another, in which I say what I think ought to be said, in what I suppose to be the best words I can find for it; (which is in reality an affected style—be it good or bad;) and my third way of writing is to say all that comes into my head for my own pleasure, in the first words that come, retouching them afterwards into (approximate) grammar. These notes for the *Art Journal* were so written; and I like them myself, of course; but ask the reader's pardon for their confusedness.

135[7]–142. . . . . . .

143. Next to Modesty, and her delight in measures, let us reflect a little on the character of her adversary, the Goddess of Liberty, and her delight in the absence of measures, or in false ones. It is true that there are liberties and liberties. Yonder torrent, crystal-clear, and arrow-swift, with its spray leaping into the air like white troops of fawns, is free enough. Lost, presently, amidst bankless, boundless marsh—soaking in slow shallowness, as it will, hither and thither, listless, among the poisonous reeds and unresisting slime—it is free also. We may choose which

[6] Here the reprint from the pamphlet—*Notes on the General Principles of Employment for the Destitute and Criminal Classes*—was resumed.

[7] Here followed in *The Queen of the Air,* §§ 22–29 of *The Cestus of Aglaia.*

liberty we like,—the restraint of voiceful rock, or the dumb and edgeless shore of darkened sand. Of that evil liberty, which men are now glorifying, and proclaiming as essence of gospel to all the earth, and will presently, I suppose, proclaim also to the stars, with invitation to them *out* of their courses,—and of its opposite continence, which is the clasp and χρυσέη περόνη of Aglaia's cestus, we must try to find out something true. For no quality of art has been more powerful in its influence on public mind. . . .[8]

160. Thus far the notes on Freedom. Now, lastly, here is some talk which I tried at the time to make intelligible; and with which I close this volume, because it will serve sufficiently to express the practical relation in which I think the art and imagination of the Greeks stand to our own; and will show the reader that my view of that relation is unchanged, from the first day on which I began to write, until now.

THE HERCULES OF CAMARINA

Address to the Students of the Art School of South Lambeth, March 15th, 1869

161. Among the photographs of Greek coins which present so many admirable subjects for your study, I must speak for the present of one only: the Hercules of Camarina. You have, represented by a Greek workman, in that coin, the face of a man, and the skin of a lion's head. And the man's face is like a man's face, but the lion's skin is not like a lion's skin.

162. Now there are some people who will tell you that Greek art is fine, because it is true; and because it carves men's faces as like men's faces as it can.

And there are other people who will tell you that Greek art is fine because it is not true; and carves a lion's skin so as to look not at all like a lion's skin.

[8] Here in *The Queen of the Air* (§§ 143–159) are reprinted §§ 69–85 of *The Cestus of Aglaia.*

And you fancy that one or other of these sets of people must be wrong, and are perhaps much puzzled to find out which you should believe.

But neither of them are wrong, and you will have eventually to believe, or rather to understand and know, in reconciliation, the truths taught by each;—but for the present, the teachers of the first group are those you must follow.

It is they who tell you the deepest and usefullest truth, which involves all others in time. *Greek art, and all other art, is fine when it makes a man's face as like a man's face as it can.* Hold to that. All kinds of nonsense are talked to you, now-a-days, ingeniously and irrelevantly about art. Therefore, for the most part of the day, shut your ears, and keep your eyes open: and understand primarily, what you may, I fancy, understand easily, that the greatest masters of all greatest schools—Phidias, Donatello, Titian, Velasquez, or Sir Joshua Reynolds—all tried to make human creatures as like human creatures as they could; and that anything less like humanity than their work, is not so good as theirs.

Get that well driven into your heads; and don't let it out again, at your peril.

163. Having got it well in, you may then farther understand, safely, that there is a great deal of secondary work in pots, and pans, and floors, and carpets, and shawls, and architectural ornament, which ought, essentially, to be *unlike* reality, and to depend for its charm on quite other qualities than imitative ones. But all such art is inferior and secondary—much of it more or less instinctive and animal; and a civilized human creature can only learn its principles rightly, by knowing those of great civilized art first—which is always the representation, to the utmost of its power, of whatever it has got to show—made to look as like the thing as possible. Go into the National Gallery, and look at the foot of Correggio's Venus there. Correggio made it as like a foot as he could, and you won't easily find anything liker. Now, you will find on any Greek vase something meant for a foot, or a hand, which is not at all like

one. The Greek vase is a good thing in its way, but Correggio's picture is the best work.

164. So, again, go into the Turner room of the National Gallery, and look at Turner's drawing of "Ivy Bridge." You will find the water in it is like real water, and the ducks in it are like real ducks. Then go into the British Museum, and look for an Egyptian landscape, and you will find the water in that constituted of blue zigzags, not at all like water; and ducks in the middle of it made of red lines, looking not in the least as if they could stand stuffing with sage and onions. They are very good in their way, but Turner's are better.

165. I will not pause to fence my general principle against what you perfectly well know of the due contradiction,—that a thing may be painted very like, yet painted ill. Rest content with knowing that it *must* be like, if it is painted well; and take this further general law:—Imitation is like charity. When it is done for love, it is lovely; when it is done for show, hateful.

166. Well, then, this Greek coin is fine, first because the face is like a face. Perhaps you think there is something particularly handsome in the face, which you can't see in the photograph, or can't at present appreciate. But there is nothing of the kind. It is a very regular, quiet, commonplace sort of face; and any average English gentleman's, of good descent, would be far handsomer.

167. Fix that in your heads also, therefore, that Greek faces are not particularly beautiful. Of the much nonsense against which you are to keep your ears shut, that which is talked to you of the Greek ideal of beauty, is among the absolutest. There is not a single instance of a very beautiful head left by the highest school of Greek art. On coins, there is even no approximately beautiful one. The Juno of Argos is a virago; the Athena of Athens grotesque; the Athena of Corinth is insipid; and of Thurium, sensual. The Siren Ligeia, and fountain of Arethusa, on the coins of Terina and Syracuse, are prettier, but totally without expression, and chiefly set off by their well-curled hair. You might have expected something subtle in Mercuries; but

the Mercury of Ænus is a very stupid-looking fellow, in a cap like a bowl, with a knob on the top of it. The Bacchus of Thasos is a drayman with his hair pomatum'd. The Jupiter of Syracuse is, however, calm and refined; and the Apollo of Clazomenæ would have been impressive, if he had not come down to us much flattened by friction. But on the whole, the merit of Greek coins does not primarily depend on beauty of features, nor even, in the period of highest art, that of the statues. You may take the Venus of Melos as a standard of beauty of the central Greek type. She has tranquil, regular, and lofty features; but could not hold her own for a moment against the beauty of a simple English girl, of pure race and kind heart.

168. And the reason that Greek art, on the whole, bores you, (and you know it does,) is that you are always forced to look in it for something that is not there; but which may be seen every day, in real life, all round you; and which you are naturally disposed to delight in, and ought to delight in. For the Greek race was not at all one of exalted beauty, but only of general and healthy completeness of form. They were only, and could be only, beautiful in body to the degree that they were beautiful in soul; (for you will find, when you read deeply into the matter, that the body is only the soul made visible). And the Greeks were indeed very good people, much better people than most of us think, or than many of us are; but there are better people alive now than the best of them, and lovelier people to be seen now, than the loveliest of them.

169. Then, what *are* the merits of this Greek art, which make it so exemplary for you? Well, not that it is beautiful, but that it is Right. All that it desires to do, it does, and all that it does, does well. You will find, as you advance in the knowledge of art, that its laws of self-restraint are very marvellous; that its peace of heart, and contentment in doing a simple thing, with only one or two qualities, restrictedly desired, and sufficiently attained, are a most wholesome element of education for you, as opposed to the wild writhing, and wrestling, and longing for the moon, and tilting at windmills, and agony of eyes, and

torturing of fingers, and general spinning out of one's soul into fiddlestrings, which constitute the ideal life of a modern artist.

Also observe, there is entire masterhood of its business up to the required point. A Greek does not reach after other people's strength, nor out-reach his own. He never tries to paint before he can draw; he never tries to lay on flesh where there are no bones; and he never expects to find the bones of anything in his inner consciousness. Those are his first merits—sincere and innocent purpose, strong common sense and principle, and all the strength that comes of these, and all the grace that follows on that strength.

170. But, secondly, Greek art is always exemplary in disposition of masses, which is a thing that in modern days students rarely look for, artists not enough, and the public never. But, whatever else Greek work may fail of, you may be always sure its masses are well placed, and their placing has been the object of the most subtle care. Look, for instance, at the inscription in front of this Hercules of the name of the town—Camarina. You can't read it, even though you may know Greek, without some pains; for the sculptor knew well enough that it mattered very little whether you read it or not, for the Camarina Hercules could tell his own story; but what did above all things matter was, that no K or A or M should come in a wrong place with respect to the outline of the head, and divert the eye from it, or spoil any of its lines. So the whole inscription is thrown into a sweeping curve of gradually diminishing size, continuing from the lion's paws, round the neck, up to the forehead, and answering a decorative purpose as completely as the curls of the mane opposite. Of these, again, you cannot change or displace one without mischief: they are almost as even in reticulation as a piece of basket-work; but each has a different form and a due relation to the rest, and if you set to work to draw that mane rightly, you will find that, whatever time you give to it, you can't get the tresses quite into their places, and that every tress out of its place does an

injury. If you want to test your powers of accurate drawing you may make that lion's mane your *pons asinorum.* I have never yet met with a student who didn't make an ass in a lion's skin of himself, when he tried it.

171. Granted, however, that these tresses may be finely placed, still they are not like a lion's mane. So we come back to the question,—if the face is to be like a man's face, why is not the lion's mane to be like a lion's mane? Well, because it can't be like a lion's mane without too much trouble;—and inconvenience after that, and poor success, after all. Too much trouble, in cutting the die into fine fringes and jags; inconvenience after that,—because fringes and jags would spoil the surface of a coin; poor success after all,—because, though you can easily stamp cheeks and foreheads smooth at a blow, you can't stamp projecting tresses fine at a blow, whatever pains you take with your die.

So your Greek uses his common sense, wastes no time, loses no skill, and says to you, "Here are beautifully set tresses, which I have carefully designed and easily stamped. Enjoy them; and if you cannot understand that they mean lion's mane, heaven mend your wits."

172. See then, you have in this work, well-founded knowledge, simple and right aims, thorough mastery of handicraft, splendid invention in arrangement, unerring common sense in treatment,—merits, these, I think, exemplary enough to justify our tormenting you a little with Greek Art. But it has one merit more than these, the greatest of all. *It always means something worth saying. Not merely worth saying for that time only, but for all time.* What do you think this helmet of lion's hide is always given to Hercules for? You can't suppose it means only that he once killed a lion, and always carried its skin afterwards to show that he had, as Indian sportsmen send home stuffed rugs, with claws at the corners, and a lump in the middle, which one tumbles over every time one stirs the fire. What *was* this Nemean Lion, whose spoils were evermore to cover Hercules from the cold? Not merely a large specimen of Felis Leo, ranging the fields of Nemea,

be sure of that. This Nemean cub was one of a bad litter. Born of Typhon and Echidna,—of the whirlwind and the snake,—Cerberus his brother, the Hydra of Lerna his sister, —it must have been difficult to get his hide off him. He had to be found in darkness too, and dealt upon without weapons, by grip at the throat—arrows and club of no avail against him. What does all that mean?

173. It means that the Nemean Lion is the first great adversary of life, whatever that may be—to Hercules, or to any of us, then or now. The first monster we have to strangle, or to be destroyed by, fighting in the dark, and with none to help us, only Athena standing by, to encourage with her smile. Every man's Nemean Lion lies in wait for him somewhere. The slothful man says, there is a lion in the path. He says well. The quite *un*slothful man says the same, and knows it too. But they differ in their further reading of the text. The slothful man says, *I* shall be slain, and the unslothful, IT shall be. It is the first ugly and strong enemy that rises against us, all future victory depending on victory over that. Kill it; and through all the rest of life, what was once dreadful is your armour, and you are clothed with that conquest for every other, and helmed with its crest of fortitude for evermore.

Alas, we have most of us to walk bareheaded; but that is the meaning of the story of Nemea,—worth laying to heart and thinking of, sometimes, when you see a dish garnished with parsley, which was the crown at the Nemean games.

174. How far, then, have we got, in our list of the merits of Greek art now?

Sound knowledge.

Simple aims.

Mastered craft.

Vivid invention.

Strong common sense.

And eternally true and wise meaning.

Are these not enough? Here is one more then, which will find favour, I should think, with the British Lion. *Greek art is never frightened at anything, it is always cool.*

175. It differs essentially from all other art, past or present, in this *incapability of being frightened.* Half the power and imagination of every other school depend on a certain feverish terror mingling with their sense of beauty; —the feeling that a child has in a dark room, or a sick person in seeing ugly dreams. But the Greeks never have ugly dreams. They cannot draw anything ugly when they try. Sometimes they put themselves to their wits'-end to draw an ugly thing,—the Medusa's head, for instance,—but they can't do it,—not they,—because nothing frightens them. They widen the mouth, and grind the teeth, and puff the cheeks, and set the eyes a-goggling; and the thing is only ridiculous after all, not the least dreadful, for there is no dread in their hearts. Pensiveness; amazement; often deepest grief and desolateness. All these; but terror never. Everlasting calm in the presence of all fate; and joy such as they could win, not indeed in a perfect beauty, but in beauty at perfect rest! A kind of art this, surely, to be looked at, and thought upon sometimes with profit, even in these latter days.

176. To be looked at sometimes. Not continually, and never as a model for imitation. For you are not Greeks; but, for better or worse, English creatures; and cannot do, even if it were a thousand times better worth doing, anything well, except what your English hearts shall prompt, and your English skies teach you. For all good art is the natural utterance of its own people in its own day.

But also, your own art is a better and brighter one than ever this Greek art was. Many motives, powers, and insights have been added to those elder ones. The very corruptions into which we have fallen are signs of a subtle life, higher than theirs was, and therefore more fearful in its faults and death. Christianity has neither superseded, nor, by itself, excelled heathenism; but it has added its own good, won also by many a Nemean contest in dark valleys, to all that was good and noble in heathenism: and our present thoughts and work, when they are right, are nobler than the heathen's. And we are not reverent enough to them, because we possess too much of them.

That sketch of four cherub heads from an English girl, by Sir Joshua Reynolds, at Kensington, is an incomparably finer thing than ever the Greeks did. Ineffably tender in the touch, yet Herculean in power; innocent, yet exalted in feeling; pure in colour as a pearl: reserved and decisive in design, as this Lion crest;—if *it* alone existed of such, if it were a picture by Zeuxis, the only one left in the world, and you built a shrine for it, and were allowed to see it only seven days in a year, it alone would teach you all of art that you ever needed to know. But you do not learn from this or any other such work, because you have not reverence enough for them, and are trying to learn from all at once, and from a hundred other masters besides.

177. Here, then, is the practical advice which I would venture to deduce from what I have tried to show you. Use Greek art as a first, not a final, teacher. Learn to draw carefully from Greek work; above all, to place forms correctly, and to use light and shade tenderly. Never allow yourselves black shadows. It is easy to make things look round and projecting; but the things to exercise yourselves in are the placing of the masses, and the modelling of the lights. It is an admirable exercise to take a pale wash of colour for all the shadows, never reinforcing it everywhere, but drawing the statue as if it were in far distance, making all the darks one flat pale tint. Then model from those into the lights, rounding as well as you can, on those subtle conditions. In your chalk drawings, separate the lights from the darks at once all over; then reinforce the darks slightly where absolutely necessary, and put your whole strength on the lights and their limits. Then, when you have learned to draw thoroughly, take one master for your painting, as you would have done necessarily in old times by being put into his school (were I to choose for you, it should be among six men only,—Titian, Correggio, Paul Veronese, Velasquez, Reynolds, or Holbein. If you are a landscapist, Turner must be your only guide, for no other great landscape painter has yet lived); and having chosen, do your best to understand your own chosen

master, and obey *him,* and no one else, till you have strength to deal with the nature itself round you, and then, be your own master and see with your own eyes. If you have got masterhood or sight in you, that is the way to make the most of them; and if you have neither, you will at least be sound in your work, prevented from immodest and useless effort, and protected from vulgar and fantastic error.

And so I wish you all, good speed, and the favour of Hercules and the Muses; and to those who shall best deserve them, the crown of Parsley[9] first, and then of the Laurel.

[9] For another reference to the Parsley crown—the reward of Victor in the Nemean games—see above, § 77.

THE MORALITY OF STYLE

There is one strange, but quite essential, character in us—ever since the Conquest, if not earlier—a delight in the forms of burlesque which are connected in some degree with the foulness of evil. I think the most perfect type of a true English mind in its best possible temper, is that of Chaucer; and you will find that, while it is for the most part full of thoughts of beauty, pure and wild like that of an April morning, there are, even in the midst of this, sometimes momentarily jesting passages which stoop to play with evil—while the power of listening to and enjoying the jesting of entirely gross persons, whatever the feeling may be which permits it, afterwards degenerates into forms of humour which render some of quite the greatest, wisest, and most moral of English writers now almost useless for our youth. And yet you will find that whenever Englishmen are wholly without this instinct, their genius is comparatively weak and restricted.

Lectures on Art, par. 14.

Nor is it possible, therefore—observe the necessary reflected action—that any tongue should be a noble one, of which the words are not so many trumpet-calls to action. All great languages invariably utter great things, and command them; they cannot be mimicked but by obedience; the breath of them is inspiration because it is not only vocal, but vital; and you can only learn to speak as these men spoke, by becoming what these men were.

Now for direct confirmation of this, I want you to think over the relation of expression to character in two great masters of the absolute art of language, Virgil and Pope. You are perhaps surprised at the last name; and indeed you have in English much higher grasp and melody of language from more passionate minds, but you have nothing else, in its range, so perfect. I name, therefore, these two men, because they are the two most accomplished *Artists*, merely as such, whom I know in literature; and because I think you will be afterwards interested in investigating how the infinite grace in the words of the one, and the severity in those of the other, and the precision in those of both, arise wholly out of the moral elements of their minds:—out of the deep tenderness in Virgil which enabled him to write the stories of Nisus and Lausus; and the serene and just benevolence which placed Pope, in his theology, two centuries in advance of his time, and enabled him to sum the law of noble life in two lines which, so far as I know, are the most complete, the most concise, and the most lofty expression of moral temper existing in English words:—

> Never elated, while one man's oppress'd;
> Never dejected, while another's bless'd.[1]

I wish you also to remember these lines of Pope, and to make yourselves entirely masters of his system of ethics; because, putting Shakespeare aside as rather the world's than ours, I hold Pope to be the most perfect representative we have, since Chaucer, of the true English mind; and I think the *Dunciad* is the most absolutely chiselled and monumental work "exacted" in our country. You will find, as you study Pope, that he has expressed for you, in the strictest language and within the briefest limits, every law of art, of criticism, of economy, of policy, and, finally, of a benevolence, humble, rational, and resigned, contented with its allotted share of life, and trusting the problem of its salvation to Him in whose hands lies that of the universe.

Lectures on Art, pars. 67–70.

[1] *Essay on Man*, Ep. IV, 323.

DICKENS

Do you think you could tolerantly receive the opinion of a moderately and popularly wise man—such an one as Charles Dickens, for example? Have you ever considered seriously what *his* opinion was, about "Dependants" and "Menials"? He did not perhaps quite know what it was himself;—it needs wisdom of stronger make than his to be sure of what it *does* think. He would talk, in his moral passages, about Independence, and Self-dependence, and making one's way in the world, just like any hack of the *Eatanswill Independent.* But which of the people of his imagination, of his own true children, did he love and honour most? Who are your favourites in his books—as they have been his? Menials, it strikes me, many of them. Sam, Mark, Kit, Peggotty, Mary-my-dear,—even the poor little Marchioness! I don't think Dickens intended you to look upon any of them disrespectfully. Or going one grade higher in his society, Tom Pinch, Newman Noggs, Tim Linkinwater, Oliver Twist—how independent, all of them! Very nearly menial, in soul, if they chance on a good master; none of them brilliant in fortune, nor vigorous in action. Is not the entire testimony of Dickens, traced in its true force, that no position is so *good* for men and women, none so likely to bring out their best human character, as that of a dependant, or menial? And yet with your supreme modern logic, instead of enthusiastically concluding from his works "let us all be servants", one would think the notion he put in your heads was quite the other, "let us all be masters", and that you understood his ideal of heroic English character to be given in Mr Pecksniff or Sir Mulberry Hawk!

Fors Clavigera, vol. II, letter XXVIII.

SCOTT'S INFLUENCE

Of the four great English tale-tellers whose dynasties have set or risen within my own memory—Miss Edgeworth, Scott, Dickens, and Thackeray—I find myself greatly at pause in conjecturing, however dimly, what essential good has been effected by them, though they all had the best intentions. Of the essential mischief done by them, there is, unhappily, no doubt whatever. Miss Edgeworth made her morality so impertinent that, since her time, it has only been with fear and trembling that any good novelist has ventured to show the slightest bias in favour of the Ten Commandments. Scott made his romance so ridiculous, that, since his day, one can't help fancying helmets were always pasteboard, and horses were always hobby. Dickens made everybody laugh, or cry, so that they could not go about their business till they had got their faces in wrinkles; and Thackeray settled like a meatfly on whatever one had got for dinner, and made one sick of it.

That, on the other hand, at least Miss Edgeworth and Scott have indeed some inevitable influence for good, I am the more disposed to think, because nobody now will read them. Dickens is said to have made people good-natured. If he did, I wonder what sort of natures they had before! Thackeray is similarly asserted to have chastised and repressed flunkeydom,—which it greatly puzzles me to hear, because, as far as I can see, there isn't a carriage now left in all the Row with anybody sitting inside it: the people who ought to have been in it are, every one, hanging on behind the carriage in front.

What good these writers have done, is therefore, to me, I repeat, extremely doubtful. But what good Scott has in him to do, I find no words full enough to tell. His ideal of honour in men and women is inbred, indisputable; fresh as the air of his mountains; firm as their rocks. His conception of purity in woman is even higher than Dante's; his reverence for the filial relation, as deep as Virgil's; his sympathy universal;—there is no rank or condition of men of which he has not shown the loveliest aspect; his code of moral principle is entirely defined, yet taught with a reserved subtlety like Nature's own, so that none but the most earnest readers perceive the intention: and his opinions on all practical subjects are final; the consummate decisions of accurate and inevitable common sense, tempered by the most graceful kindness.

Fors Clavigera, vol. II, letter XXXI.

SCOTT'S LIFE

First, note these three great divisions—essentially those of all men's lives, but singularly separate in his,—the days of youth, of labour, and of death.

Youth is properly the forming time—that in which a man makes himself, or is made, what he is for ever to be. Then comes the time of labour, when, having become the best he can be, he does the best he can do. Then the time of death, which, in happy lives, is very short: but always a *time.* The ceasing to breathe is only the end of death.

He was fifty-four on the 15th August, 1825, and spoke his last words—"God bless you all",—on the 21st September, 1832: so ending seven years of death.

His youth, like the youth of all the greatest men, had been long, and rich in peace, and altogether accumulative and crescent. I count it to end with that pain which you see he remembers to his dying day, given him by—Lilias Redgauntlet, in October, 1796. Whereon he sets himself to his work, which goes on nobly for thirty years lapping over a little into the death-time (*Woodstock* showing scarcely a trace of diminution of power).

Count, therefore, thus:—

Youth, twenty-five years	...	1771–1796.
Labour-time, thirty years	...	1796–1826.
Death-time, seven years	...	1825–1832.

Fors Clavigera, vol. II, letter XXXII.

FANCY AND FAITH

1. ESSENTIAL KINDS OF POETRY

Do you know, in the first place, what a play is? or what a poem is? or what a novel is? That is to say, do you know the perpetual and necessary distinctions in literary aim which have brought these distinctive names into use? You had better first, for clearness' sake, call all the three "poems", for all the three are so, when they are good, whether written in verse or prose. All truly imaginative account of man is poetic; but there are three essential kinds of poetry—one dramatic, one lyric, and one epic.

Dramatic poetry is the expression by the poet of other people's feelings, his own not being told.

Lyric poetry is the expression by the poet of his own feelings.

Epic poetry is account given by the poet of other people's external circumstances, and of events happening to them, with only such expression either of their feelings, or his own, as he thinks may be conveniently added.

The business of Dramatic poetry is therefore with the heart essentially; it despises external circumstance.

Lyric poetry may speak of anything that excites emotion in the speaker; while Epic poetry insists on external circumstances, and no more exhibits the heart-feeling than as it may be gathered from these.

For instance, the fight between the Prince of Wales and Hotspur, in *Henry the Fourth*,[1] corresponds closely, in the

[1] 1 *Henry IV*, v, 4.

character of the event itself, to the fight of Fitz-James with Roderick, in *The Lady of the Lake.*[2] But Shakespeare's treatment of his subject is strictly dramatic; Scott's, strictly epic.

Shakespeare gives you no account whatever of any blow or wound: his stage direction is, briefly, "Hotspur is wounded, and falls". Scott gives you accurate account of every external circumstance, and the finishing touch of botanical accuracy—

> Down came the blow; but in the *heath*
> The erring blade found bloodless sheath,—

makes his work perfect, as epic poetry. And Scott's work is always epic, and it is contrary to his very nature to treat any subject dramatically.

That is the technical distinction, then, between the three modes of work. But the gradation of power in all three depends on the degree of imagination with which the writer can enter into the feelings of other people. Whether in expressing theirs or his own, and whether in expressing their feelings only, or also the circumstances surrounding them, his power depends on his being able to feel as they do; in other words, on his being able to conceive character. And the literature which is not poetry at all, which is essentially unsentimental, or anti-poetic, is that which is produced by persons who have no imagination; and whose merit (for of course I am not speaking of bad literature) is in their wit or sense, instead of their imagination.

Fors Clavigera, vol. II, letter XXXIV.

2. *"FIMETIC LITERATURE"*

The imaginative power always purifies; the want of it therefore as essentially defiles; and as the wit-power is apt to develop itself through absence of imagination, it seems

[2] Canto v, 14–16.

as if wit itself had a defiling tendency. In Pindar, Homer, Virgil, Dante, and Scott, the colossal powers of imagination result in absolute virginal purity of thought. The defect of imagination and the splendid rational power in Pope and Horace associate themselves—it is difficult to say in what decided measures—with foulness of thought. The *Candide* of Voltaire, in its gratuitous filth, its acute reasoning, and its entire vacuity of imagination, is a standard of what may perhaps be generally and fitly termed "fimetic literature," still capable, by its wit, and partial truth, of a certain service in its way. But lower forms of modern literature and art—Gustave Doré's paintings, for instance,—are the corruption, in national decrepitude, of this pessimist method of thought; and of these, the final condemnation is true—they are neither fit for the land, nor *yet* for the dunghill.

It is one of the most curious problems respecting mental government to determine how far this fimetic taint must necessarily affect intellects in which the reasoning and imaginative powers are equally balanced, and both of them at high level,—as in Aristophanes, Shakespeare, Chaucer, Molière, Cervantes, and Fielding; but it always indicates the side of character which is unsympathetic, and therefore unkind; (thus Shakespeare makes Iago the foulest in thought, as cruelest in design, of all his villains), but which, in men of noble nature, is their safeguard against weak enthusiasms and ideals. It is impossible, however, that the highest conditions of tenderness in affectionate conception can be reached except by the absolutely virginal intellect. Shakespeare and Chaucer throw off, at noble work, the lower part of their natures as they would a rough dress; and you may also notice this, that the power of conceiving personal, as opposed to general, character, depends on this purity of heart and sentiment. The men who cannot quit themselves of the impure taint, never invent character, properly so called; they only invent symbols of common humanity. Even Fielding's Allworthy is not a character, but a type of a simple English gentleman; and Squire Western is not a character, but a type of the rude English squire. But Sir Roger de Coverley is a character, as well as a type; there is no one else like him; and the masters of Tullyveolan, Ellangowan, Monkbarns, and Osbaldistone Hall, are all, whether slightly or completely drawn, portraits, not mere symbols.

Fors Clavigera, vol. II, letter XXXIV.

3. *THE MORAL LAW*

One farther great, and greatest, sign of the Divinity in this enchanted work of the classic masters, I did not then assert—for, indeed, I had not then myself discerned it,—namely, that this power of noble composition is never given but with accompanying instinct of moral law; and that so severe, that the apparently too complete and ideal justice which it proclaims has received universally the name of "poetical" justice—the justice conceived only by the men of consummate imaginative power. So that to say of any man that he has power of design, is at once to say of him that he is using it on God's side; for it can only have been taught him by that Master, and cannot be taught by the use of it against Him. And therefore every great composition in the world, every great piece of painting or literature—without any exception, from the birth of Man to this hour—is an assertion of moral law, as strict, when we examine it, as the Eumenides or the *Divina Commedia;* while the total collapse of all power of artistic design in Italy at this day has been signalized and sealed by the production of an epic poem in praise of the Devil, and in declaration that God is a malignant "larva".

And this so-called poetical justice, asserted by the great designers, consists not only in the gracing of virtue with her own proper rewards of mental peace and spiritual victory; but in the proportioning also of worldly prosperity to visible virtue; and the manifestation, therefore, of the presence of the Father in this world, no less than in that which is to come. So that, if the life-work of any man of unquestioned genius does not assert this visible justice, but, on the contrary, exhibits good and gentle persons in unredeemed distress or destruction—that work will invariably be found to show no power of design; but to be merely the consecutive collection of interesting circumstances well described, as continually the best work of Balzac, George Sand, and other good novelists of the second order. In some separate pieces, the great masters will indeed exhibit the darkest mystery of human fate, but never without showing, even then, that the catastrophe is owing in the root of it to the violation of some moral law: "*She hath deceived her father,*—and may thee."[3] The root of the entire tragedy is marked by the mighty master in that one line—the double sin, namely, of daughter and father; of the first in too lawlessly forgetting her own people, and her father's house; and of the second, in allowing his pride and selfishness to conquer his paternal love, and harden him, not only in abandonment of his paternal duty, but in calumnious insult to his child. Nor, even thus, is Shakespeare content without marking, in the name of the victim of Evil Fortune, his purpose in the tragedy, of showing that there *is* such a thing as Destiny, permitted to veil the otherwise clear Providence, and to leave it only to be found by noble Will, and proved by noble Faith.

Although always, in reading Scott, one thinks the story one has last finished, the best, there can be little question that the one which has right of pre-eminence is the *Heart of Midlothian,* being devoted to the portraiture of the purest life, and most vital religion, of his native country.

It is also the most distinct in its assertion of the moral law; the assignment of earthly reward and punishment being, in this story, as accurately proportioned to the degrees of virtue and vice as the lights and shades of a photograph to the force of the rays. The absolute truth and faith of Jeanie make the suffering through which she has to pass the ultimate cause of an entirely prosperous and peaceful life for herself, her father, and her lover: the

[3] *Othello,* I, iii.

falsehood and vanity of Effie prepare for her a life of falsehood and vanity: the pride of David Deans is made the chief instrument of his humiliation; and the self-confidence which separated him from true fellowship with his brother-Christians, becomes the cause of his eternal separation from his child.

Also, there is no other analysis of the good and evil of the pure Protestant faith which can be for a moment compared to that in the *Heart of Midlothian,* showing that in an entirely simple, strong, and modest soul, it brings forth fruit of all good works and kindly thoughts; but that, when it meets with innate pride, and the unconquerable selfishness which comes from want of sympathy, it leads into ludicrous and fatal self-worship, mercilessness to the errors, whether in thought or conduct, of others; and blindness to the teaching of God Himself, where it is contrary to the devotee's own habits of thought. There is no other form of the Christian religion which so insolently ignores all Scripture that makes against it, or gathers with so passionate and irrational embrace all Scripture that makes for it.

And the entire course of the tragic story in the *Heart of Midlothian* comes of the "Museless" hardness of nature, brought upon David Deans by the persecution in his early life, which changed healthy and innocent passion into religious pride,—

> "I bless God, (with that singular worthy, Peter Walker, the packman at Bristo port), that ordered my lot in my dancing days, so that fear of my head and throat, dread of bloody rope and swift bullet, cauld and hunger, wetness and weariness, stopped the lightness of my head, and the wantonness of my feet. And now, if I hear ye, quean lassies, sae muckle as name dancing, or think there's such a thing in the world as flinging to fiddlers' sounds and pipers' springs, as sure as my father's spirit is with the just, ye shall be no more either charge or concern of mine."

Over the bronze sculpture of this insolent pride, Scott instantly casts, in the following sentence ("Gang in then, hinnies", etc.) the redeeming glow of paternal love; but he makes it, nevertheless, the cause of all the misery that follows, to the end of the old man's life:—

> "The objurgation of David Deans, however well meant, was unhappily timed. It created a division of feeling in Effie's bosom, and deterred her from her intended confidence in her sister. 'She wad haud me nae better than the dirt below her feet', said Effie to herself, 'were I to confess that I hae danced wi' him four times on the green down by, and ance at Maggie Macqueen's.'"

Such, and no more than such, the little sin that day concealed—sin only *in* concealment. And the fate of her life turns on the Fear and the Silence of a moment.

Fors Clavigera, vol. IV, letter LXXXIII.

BLAKE

You must have nearly all heard of, many must have seen, the singular paintings; some also may have read the poems, of William Blake. The impression that his drawings once made is fast, and justly, fading away, though they are not without noble merit. But his poems have much more than merit; they are written with absolute sincerity, with infinite tenderness, and, though in the manner of them diseased and wild, are in verity the words of a great and wise mind, disturbed, but not deceived, by its sickness; nay, partly exalted by it, and sometimes giving forth in fiery aphorism some of the most precious words of existing literature. One of these passages I will ask you to remember; it will often be serviceable to you—

> Doth the Eagle know what is in the pit,
> Or wilt thou go ask the Mole?[1]

It would be impossible to express to you in briefer terms the great truth that there is a different kind of knowledge good for every different creature, and that the glory of the higher creatures, is in ignorance of what is known to the lower.

Eagle's Nest, par. 21.

SHAKESPEARE AND SHADOWS

"The best, in this kind, are but shadows."

That is Shakespeare's judgment of his own art. And by strange coincidence, he has put the words into the mouth of the hero whose shadow, or semblance in marble, is ad-

[1] Lines prefixed to *The Book of Thel.*

mittedly the most ideal and heroic we possess, of man; yet, I need not ask you, whether of the two, if it were granted you to see the statue by Phidias, or the hero Theseus himself, you would choose rather to see the carved stone, or the living King. Do you recollect how Shakespeare's Theseus concludes his sentence, spoken of the poor tradesmen's kindly offered art, in the *Midsummer Night's Dream?*

"The best in this kind are but shadows: and the worst are no worse, if imagination amend them."[1]

It will not burden your memories painfully, I hope, though it may not advance you materially in the class list, if you will learn this entire sentence by heart, being, as it is, a faultless and complete epitome of the laws of mimetic art.

"BUT SHADOWS!" Make them as beautiful as you can; use them only to enable you to remember and love what they are cast by. If ever you prefer the skill of them to the simplicity of the truth, or the pleasure of them to the power of the truth, you have fallen into that vice of folly, (whether you call her κακία or μωρία), which concludes the subtle description of her given by Prodicus, that she might be seen continually εἰς τὴν ἑαυτῆς σκιὰν ἀποβλέπειν[2]—to look with love, and exclusive wonder, at *her own* shadow.

There is nothing that I tell you with more eager desire that you should believe—nothing with wider ground in my experience for requiring you to believe, than this, that you never will love art well, till you love what she mirrors better.

Eagle's Nest, pars. 39–41.

[1] Act v, Sc. i, line 213.
[2] Xenophon, *Memorabilia,* II, i, 22.

CLASSIC AND ROMANTIC

The difference which I have pointed out to you as existing between these great nations, exists also between two orders of intelligence among men, of which the one is usually called Classic, the other Romantic. Without entering into any of the fine distinctions between these two sects, this broad one is to be observed as constant: that the writers and painters of the Classic school set down nothing but what is known to be true, and set it down in the perfectest manner possible in their way, and are thenceforward authorities from whom there is no appeal. Romantic writers and painters, on the contrary, express themselves under the impulse of passions which may indeed lead them to the discovery of new truths, or to the more delightful arrangement or presentment of things already known: but their work, however brilliant or lovely, remains imperfect, and without authority. It is not possible, of course, to separate these two orders of men trenchantly: a classic writer may sometimes, whatever his care, admit an error, and a romantic one may reach perfection through enthusiasm. But, practically, you may separate the two for your study and your education; and, during your youth, the business of us your masters is to enforce on you the reading, for school work, only of classical books; and to see that your minds are both informed of the indisputable facts they contain, and accustomed to act with the infallible accuracy of which they set the example.

Val D'Arno, par. 206.

THE PENTAMETRE

Upon adding the fifth foot to our gradually lengthening line, we find ourselves fallen suddenly under hitherto unfelt limitation. The verses we have hitherto examined may be constructed at pleasure of any kind of metre—dactyl, troche, iamb, or anapæst. But all at once, we now find this liberty of choice refused. We may write a pentametre verse in iambs only.

A most notable phenomenon, significant of much more than I can at present understand,—how much less explain; —conditions, indeed, first of breathing, which are merely physical, and as such explicable enough, only not worth explaining; but, beyond these, feelings, and instincts of speech, full of complex interest, and introducing us, in spite of ourselves, to all the grammatical questions of punctuation, and logical ones of clause, and division, which I must not attempt to deal with at present; the historical fact being quite indubitable and unalterable, that no poet has ever attempted to write pentametre in any foot but the iamb, and that the addition of another choreus to a choreic tetrametre—or of another dactyl to a dactylic one, will instantly make them helplessly prosaic and unreadable.

Leaving the reader to try such experiment at his leisure, and to meditate on the causes of it at his liking, I shall content myself with stating the principal laws affecting the manner and construction of the iambic pentametre, the most important, and that by far, of all accepted divisions of sentence in the English language.

Pentametre verse divides itself essentially into three kinds:—

(A.) Sententious.
(B.) Personally emotional.
(C.) Dramatic.

(A.) Sententious pentametre.

In this kind of verse, the structure and rhyme (if rhyme be admitted) are used merely to give precision and weight to a prose sentence, otherwise sifted, abstracted, and corrected into extremest possible value. Such verse professes always to be the result of the writer's utmost wisdom and utmost care; it admits therefore of no careless or imperfect construction, but allows any intelligible degree of inversion; because it has been considered to the end, before a word is written, and the placing of the words may afterwards be adjusted according to their importance. Thus, "Sir Plume, of amber snuff-box justly vain,"[1] is not only more rhythmic, but more elegant and accurate than "Sir Plume, justly vain of his amber snuff-box": first, because the emphasis of rhyme is laid on his vanity, not his box; secondly, because the "his," seen on full consideration to be unnecessary, is omitted, to concentrate the sentence; and with a farther and more subtle reason, which, unless the reader knows my *Munera Pulveris,* I cannot explain to him here,—namely, that a coxcomb cannot, properly speaking, *possess* anything, but is possessed by everything, so that in the next line Pope does not say, "And the nice conduct of *his* clouded cane," but of *a* clouded cane.

The sententious epic* may, however, become spoken instead of written language, if the speech be deliberate and of well-considered matter; but this kind of verse never represents precisely what the speaker is supposed to have said, but the *contents* of his speech, arranged so as to make it more impressive or memorable, as continually in Wordsworth's *Excursion.*

On the contrary, if the speech be dramatic,—that is to say, representing what the speaker actually would have

* I believe the word "epic" is usually understood by English readers to mean merely a long and grand poem instead of a short slight one—at least, I know that as a boy I remained long under that impression myself. It really means a poem in which story-telling, and philosophical reflection as its accompaniment, take the place of dramatic action, and impulsive song.

---

[1] Pope: *Rape of the Lock,* iv. 123.

said,—no forced inversion or artificial arrangement is allowable; and

"We are glad the dauphin is so pleasant with us,"[2]

must for no cause and under no pretence become,

"We are glad the dauphin is with us so pleasant."

All the work of Pope, Goldsmith, and Johnson is in sententious pentametre; in which emotion, however on sufferance admitted, never leads or disturbs the verse, nor refuses to be illustrated by ingenious metaphor. In this manner some of the wisest, and many of the acutest, things ever said by man, have been put into perfect syllables by Pope and Goldsmith. Johnson is of quite viler metal, and has neither ear nor imagination; yet the weight of his common-sense gave him such favour with both Scott and Byron, that they alike regard him as one of their masters.[3] I fancy neither of them ever tried to read *Irene.*

(B.) Emotional pentametre.

The measure of Gray's *Elegy, Lycidas,* and the *Corsair,* —sentiment always guiding and deepening the melody, while a lyric sweetness binds the verses into unbroken flow.

It always implies an affectionate and earnest personality in the writer; never admits satire; and rarely blame, unless, as in *Lycidas,* with the voice of an accusing angel. The forms of its music, always governed by feeling, are not to be analyzed by any cunning, nor represented by

[2] *King Henry V.,* Act i. sc. 2, line 259.

[3] " 'He (Sir Walter) often said to me,' continues Ballantyne, 'that neither his own nor any modern popular style of composition was that from which he derived most pleasure. I asked him what it was. He answered—Johnson's; and that he had more pleasure in reading *London,* and *The Vanity of Human Wishes,* than any other poetical composition he could mention' " (Lockhart's *Life of Scott,* 1837, vol. ii. p. 307). And so Byron, of *The Vanity of Human Wishes,*—"all the examples, and mode of giving them, sublime. . . . 'Tis a grand poem" (*Letters and Journals,* 1901, vol. v. p. 162).

any signs; but the normal divisions of the verse are studiously accurate, and all artificial inversions forbidden.

Thus—

"He asked no questions; all were answered now"[4]

is a perfect line of emotional pentametre; but would be an entirely unendurable one if, in order to rhyme to "call" or "fall," it had been written,

"No questions asked he; answered now were all."

(C.) Dramatic pentametre.

On the contrary, in noble dramatic verse, the divisions are purposefully *in*accurate;—the accepted cadence of the metre being allowed only at intervals, and the prosody of every passionate line thrown into a disorder which is more lovely than any normal order, as the leaves of a living tree are more lovely than a formal honeysuckle ornament on a cornice;—the inner laws and native grace being all the more perfect in that they are less manifest. But the study of dramatic melody is the study also of dramatic truth, and entirely beyond the scope of these pages.

Elements of English Prosody, pars. 39–43.

[4] *The Corsair,* canto iii. stanza xxi.

MODERN FICTION AND SCOTT

On the first mild—or, at least, the first bright—day of March,[1] in this year, I walked through what was once a country lane, between the hostelry of the Half-moon at the bottom of Herne Hill, and the secluded College of Dulwich.

In my young days, Croxted Lane was a green bye-road traversable for some distance by carts; but rarely so traversed, and, for the most part, little else than a narrow strip of untilled field, separated by blackberry hedges from the better-cared-for meadows on each side of it: growing more weeds, therefore, than they, and perhaps in spring a primrose or two—white archangel—daisies plenty, and purple thistles in autumn. A slender rivulet, boasting little of its brightness, for there are no springs at Dulwich, yet fed purely enough by the rain and morning dew, here trickled—there loitered—through the long grass beneath the hedges, and expanded itself, where it might, into moderately clear and deep pools, in which, under their veils of duck-weed, a fresh-water shell or two, sundry curious little skipping shrimps, any quantity of tadpoles in their time, and even sometimes a tittlebat, offered themselves to my boyhood's pleased, and not inaccurate, observation. There, my mother and I used to gather the first buds of the hawthorn; and there, in after years, I used to walk in the summer shadows, as in a place wilder and sweeter than our garden, to think over any passage I wanted to make better than usual in *Modern Painters*.

So, as aforesaid, on the first kindly day of this year, being thoughtful more than usual of those old times, I went to look again at the place.

Often, both in those days, and since, I have put myself hard to it, vainly, to find words wherewith to tell of beautiful things; but beauty has been in the world since the

[1] Wordsworth's "To my Sister."

world was made, and human language can make a shift, somehow, to give account of it, whereas the peculiar forces of devastation induced by modern city life have only entered the world lately; and no existing terms of language known to me are enough to describe the forms of filth, and modes of ruin, that varied themselves along the course of Croxted Lane. The fields on each side of it are now mostly dug up for building, or cut through into gaunt corners and nooks of blind ground by the wild crossings and concurrencies of three railroads. Half a dozen handfuls of new cottages, with Doric doors, are dropped about here and there among the gashed ground: the lane itself, now entirely grassless, is a deep-rutted, heavy-hillocked cart-road, diverging gatelessly into various brick-fields or pieces of waste; and bordered on each side by heaps of—Hades only knows what!—mixed dust of every unclean thing that can crumble in drought, and mildew of every unclean thing that can rot or rust in damp: ashes and rags, beer-bottles and old shoes, battered pans, smashed crockery, shreds of nameless clothes, door-sweepings, floor-sweepings, kitchen garbage, back-garden sewage, old iron, rotten timber jagged with out-torn nails, cigar-ends, pipe-bowls, cinders, bones, and ordure, indescribable; and, variously kneaded into, sticking to, or fluttering foully here and there over all these, remnants, broadcast, of every manner of newspaper, advertisement or big-lettered bill, festering and flaunting out their last publicity in the pits of stinking dust and mortal slime.

The lane ends now where its prettiest windings once began; being cut off by a cross-road leading out of Dulwich to a minor railway station: and on the other side of this road, what was of old the daintiest intricacy of its solitude is changed into a straight, and evenly macadamised carriage drive between new houses of extreme respectability, with good attached gardens and offices—most of these tenements being larger—all more pretentious, and many, I imagine, held at greatly higher rent than my father's, tenanted for twenty years at Herne Hill. And it became matter of curious meditation to me what must here become of children resembling my poor little dreamy quondam self in temper, and thus brought up at the same distance from London, and in the same or better circumstances of worldly fortune; but with only Croxted Lane in its present condition for their country walk. The trimly kept road before their doors, such as one used to see in the fashionable suburbs of Cheltenham or Leamington, presents nothing to their study but gravel, and gas-lamp posts; the modern addition of a vermilion letter-pillar contributing indeed to the splendour, but scarcely to the interest of the scene; and a child of any sense or fancy would hastily contrive escape from such a barren desert of politeness, and betake itself to investigation, such as might be feasible, of the natural history of Croxted Lane.

But, for its sense or fancy, what food, or stimulus, can it find, in that foul causeway of its youthful pilgrimage? What would have happened to myself, so directed, I cannot clearly imagine. Possibly, I might have got interested in the old iron and wood-shavings; and become an engineer or a carpenter: but for the children of to-day, accustomed, from the instant they are out of their cradles, to the sight of this infinite nastiness, prevailing as a fixed condition of the universe, over the face of nature, and accompanying all the operations of industrious man, what is to be the scholastic issue? unless, indeed, the thrill of scientific vanity in the primary analysis of some unheard-of process of corruption—or the reward of microscopic research in the sight of worms with more legs, and acari of more curious generation than ever vivified the more simply smelling plasma of antiquity.

One result of such elementary education is, however, already certain; namely, that the pleasure which we may conceive taken by the children of the coming time, in the analysis of physical corruption, guides, into fields more dangerous and desolate, the expatiation of an imaginative literature: and that the reactions of moral disease upon itself, and the conditions of languidly monstrous character developed in an atmosphere of low vitality, have become the most valued material of modern fiction, and the most eagerly discussed texts of modern philosophy.

The many concurrent reasons for this mischief may, I believe, be massed under a few general heads.

(I.) There is first the hot fermentation and unwholesome secrecy of the population crowded into large cities, each mote in the misery lighter, as an individual soul, than a dead leaf, but becoming oppressive and infectious each to his neighbour, in the smoking mass of decay. The resulting modes of mental ruin and distress are continually new; and in a certain sense, worth study in their monstrosity: they have accordingly developed a corresponding science of fiction, concerned mainly with the description of such forms of disease, like the botany of leaf-lichens.

In De Balzac's story of *Father Goriot,* a grocer makes a large fortune, of which he spends on himself as much as may keep him alive; and on his two daughters, all that can promote their pleasures or their pride. He marries them to men of rank, supplies their secret expenses, and provides for his favourite a separate and clandestine establishment with her lover. On his deathbed, he sends for this favourite daughter, who wishes to come, and hesitates for a quarter of an hour between doing so, and going to a ball at which it has been for the last month her chief ambition to be seen. She finally goes to the ball.

The story is, of course, one of which the violent contrasts and spectral catastrophe could only take place, or be conceived, in a large city. A village grocer cannot make a large fortune, cannot marry his daughters to titled squires, and cannot die without having his children brought to him, if in the neighbourhood, by fear of village gossip, if for no better cause.

(II.) But a much more profound feeling than this mere curiosity of science in morbid phenomena is concerned in the production of the carefullest forms of modern fiction. The disgrace and grief resulting from the mere trampling pressure and electric friction of town life, become to the sufferers peculiarly mysterious in their undeservedness, and frightful in their inevitableness. The power of all surroundings over them for evil; the incapacity of their own minds to refuse the pollution, and of their own wills to oppose the weight, of the staggering mass that chokes and crushes them into perdition, brings every law of healthy existence into question with them, and every alleged method of help and hope into doubt. Indignation, without any calming faith in justice, and self-contempt, without any curative self-reproach, dull the intelligence, and degrade the conscience, into sullen incredulity of all sunshine outside the dunghill, or breeze beyond the wafting of its impurity; and at last a philosophy develops itself, partly satiric, partly consolatory, concerned only with the regenerative vigour of manure, and the necessary obscurities of fimetic Providence; showing how everybody's fault is somebody else's, how infection has no law, digestion no will, and profitable dirt no dishonour.

And thus an elaborate and ingenious scholasticism, in what may be called the Divinity of Decomposition, has established itself in connection with the more recent forms of romance, giving them at once a complacent tone of clerical dignity, and an agreeable dash of heretical impudence; while the inculcated doctrine has the double advantage of needing no laborious scholarship for its foundation, and no painful self-denial for its practice.

(III.) The monotony of life in the central streets of any great modern city, but especially in those of London, where every emotion intended to be derived by men from the sight of nature, or the sense of art, is forbidden for ever, leaves the craving of the heart for a sincere, yet changeful, interest, to be fed from one source only. Under natural conditions the degree of mental excitement necessary to bodily health is provided by the course of the seasons, and the various skill and fortune of agriculture. In the country every morning of the year brings with it a new aspect of springing or fading nature; a new duty to be fulfilled upon earth, and a new promise or warning in heaven. No day is without its innocent hope, its special prudence, its kindly gift, and its sublime danger; and in every process of wise husbandry, and every effort of contending or remedial courage, the wholesome passions, pride, and bodily power of the labourer are excited and exerted in happiest unison. The companionship of domestic, the care of serviceable, animals, soften and enlarge his life with lowly charities, and discipline him in familiar wisdoms and unboastful fortitudes; while the divine laws of seed-time which cannot be recalled, harvest which cannot be hastened, and winter in which no man can work, compel the impatiences and coveting of his heart into labour too submissive to be anxious, and rest too sweet to be wanton. What thought can enough comprehend the contrast between such life, and that in streets where summer and winter are only alternations of heat and cold; where snow never fell white, nor sunshine clear; where the ground is only a pavement, and the sky no more than the glass roof of an arcade; where the utmost power of a storm is to choke the gutters, and the finest magic of spring, to change mud into dust: where—chief and most fatal difference in state—there is no interest of occupation for any of the inhabitants but the routine of counter or desk within doors, and the effort to pass each other without collision outside; so that from morning to evening the only possible variation of the monotony of the hours, and lightening of the penalty of existence, must be some kind of mischief, limited, unless by more than ordinary godsend of fatality, to the fall of a horse, or the slitting of a pocket?

I said that under these laws of inanition, the craving of the human heart for some kind of excitement could be supplied from *one* source only. It might have been thought by any other than a sternly tentative philosopher, that the denial of their natural food to human feelings would have provoked a reactionary desire for it; and that the dreariness of the street would have been gilded by dreams of pastoral felicity. Experience has shown the fact to be otherwise; the thoroughly trained Londoner can enjoy no other excitement than that to which he has been accustomed, but asks for *that* in continually more ardent or more virulent concentration; and the ultimate power of fiction to entertain him is by varying to his fancy the modes, and defining for his dulness the horrors, of Death. In the single novel of *Bleak House* there are nine deaths (or left for death's, in the drop scene) carefully wrought out or led up to, either by way of pleasing surprise, as the baby's at the brickmaker's, or finished in their threatenings and sufferings, with as much enjoyment as can be contrived in the anticipation, and as much pathology as can be concentrated in the description. Under the following varieties of method:—

One by assassination	Mr. Tulkinghorn.
One by starvation, with phthisis . .	Joe.
One by chagrin.	Richard.
One by spontaneous combustion . .	Mr. Krook.
One by sorrow	Lady Dedlock's lover.
One by remorse	Lady Dedlock.
One by insanity	Miss Flite.
One by paralysis	Sir Leicester.

Besides the baby, by fever, and a lively young Frenchwoman left to be hanged.[2]

And all this, observe, not in a tragic, adventurous, or military story, but merely as the further enlivenment of a narrative intended to be amusing; and as a properly representative average of the statistics of civilian mortality in the centre of London.

Observe further, and chiefly. It is not the mere number of deaths (which, if we count the odd troopers in the last scene, is exceeded in *Old Mortality*, and reached, within one or two, both in *Waverley* and *Guy Mannering*[3]) that

[2] For the arrest of Mademoiselle Hortense, murderess of Mr. Tulkinghorn, see ch. liv.

[3] In *Waverley* there are five deaths—viz., those of the Laird of Balmawhapple and Colonel Gardner (ch. xlvii.), Richard Waverley (ch. lxi.), Donald Bean Lean (ch. lxii.), and Fergus MacIvor (ch. lxix.). In *Guy Mannering* there are seven or eight deaths—viz., the murder of Kennedy, whose cruel function was that of "riding officer" (ch. ix.); the death from shock of Mrs. Bertram (*ibid.*), and of her husband (ch. xiii.); one or two smugglers, including Brown (ch. xxx.); Meg Merrilies, the

marks the peculiar tone of the modern novel. It is the fact that all these deaths, but one, are of inoffensive, or at least in the world's estimate, respectable persons; and that they are all grotesquely either violent or miserable, purporting thus to illustrate the modern theology that the appointed destiny of a large average of our population is to die like rats in a drain, either by trap or poison. Not, indeed, that a lawyer in full practice can be usually supposed as faultless in the eye of Heaven as a dove or a woodcock; but it is not, in former divinities, thought the will of Providence that he should be dropped by a shot from a client behind his fire-screen, and retrieved in the morning by his housemaid under the chandelier. Neither is Lady Dedlock less reprehensible in her conduct than many women of fashion have been and will be: but it would not therefore have been thought poetically just, in old-fashioned morality, that she should be found by her daughter lying dead, with her face in the mud of a St. Giles's churchyard.

In the work of the great masters death is always either heroic, deserved, or quiet and natural (unless their purpose be totally and deeply tragic, when collateral meaner death is permitted, like that of Polonius or Roderigo[4]). In *Old Mortality*, four of the deaths, Bothwell's, Ensign Grahame's, Macbriar's, and Evandale's, are magnificently heroic; Burley's and Olifant's long deserved, and swift; the troopers', met in the discharge of their military duty; and the old miser's, as gentle as the passing of a cloud, and almost beautiful in its last words of—now unselfish—care:—

> "'Ailie' (he aye ca'd me Ailie, we were auld acquaintance), 'Ailie, take ye care and haud the gear weel thegither; for the name of Morton of Milnwood's gane out like the last sough of an auld sang.' And sae he fell out o' ae dwam into another, and

heroine, shot by Dirk Hatteraick (ch. liv.), Glossin, killed in his struggle with him (ch. lvii.), with finally the suicide of Hatteraick himself (*ibid.*).

[4] *Hamlet*, Act iii. sc. 4; *Othello*, Act v. sc. 2.

ne'er spak a word mair, unless it were something we cou'dna mak out, about a dipped candle being gude eneugh to see to dee wi'. He cou'd ne'er bide to see a moulded ane, and there was ane, by ill luck, on the table."[5]

In *Guy Mannering*, the murder, though unpremeditated, of a single person, (himself not entirely innocent, but at least by heartlessness in a cruel function earning his fate,) is avenged to the uttermost on all the men conscious of the crime; Mr. Bertram's death, like that of his wife, brief in pain, and each told in the space of half-a-dozen lines; and that of the heroine of the tale, self-devoted, heroic in the highest, and happy.

Nor is it ever to be forgotten, in the comparison of Scott's with inferior work, that his own splendid powers were, even in early life, tainted, and in his latter years destroyed, by modern conditions of commercial excitement, then first, but rapidly, developing themselves. There are parts even in his best novels coloured to meet tastes which he despised; and many pages written in his later ones to lengthen his article for the indiscriminate market.

But there was one weakness of which his healthy mind remained incapable to the last. In modern stories prepared for more refined or fastidious audiences than those of Dickens, the funereal excitement is obtained, for the most part, not by the infliction of violent or disgusting death; but in the suspense, the pathos, and the more or less by all felt, and recognized, mortal phenomena of the sick-room. The temptation, to weak writers, of this order of subject is especially great, because the study of it from the living—or dying—model is so easy, and to many has been the most impressive part of their own personal ex-

[5] Ch. xxxix. of *Old Mortality*. For the other deaths, see ch. xvi. for Bothwell's and Grahame's; ch. xxxvi. for those of Macbriar, Evandale, Burley, and Olifant. For numerous deaths both of troopers and insurgents, in battle and otherwise, see chaps. xvi., xxv., xxxiii.–iv., and xliv. Ruskin omits to mention the death of Habakkuk Mucklewrath, the mad preacher, in ch. xxxiv.

perience; while, if the description be given even with mediocre accuracy, a very large section of readers will admire its truth, and cherish its melancholy. Few authors of second or third rate genius can either record or invent a probable conversation in ordinary life; but few, on the other hand, are so destitute of observant faculty as to be unable to chronicle the broken syllables and languid movements of an invalid. The easily rendered, and too surely recognized, image of familiar suffering is felt at once to be real where all else had been false; and the historian of the gestures of fever and words of delirium can count on the applause of a gratified audience as surely as the dramatist who introduces on the stage of his flagging action a carriage that can be driven or a fountain that will flow. But the masters of strong imagination disdain such work, and those of deep sensibility shrink from it.* Only under conditions of personal weakness, presently to be noted, would Scott comply with the cravings of his lower audience in scenes of terror like the death of Front-de-Bœuf.[8] But he never once withdrew the sacred curtain of the sick-chamber, nor permitted the disgrace of wanton tears round the humiliation of strength, or the wreck of beauty.

Fiction, Fair and Foul, pars. 1–11.

* Nell, in *The Old Curiosity Shop*, was simply killed for the market, as a butcher kills a lamb (see Forster's *Life*),[6] and Paul was written under the same conditions of illness which affected Scott—a part of the ominous palsies, grasping alike author and subject both in *Dombey* and *Little Dorrit*.[7]

---

[6] *The Life of Charles Dickens*, ch. xii. (vol. i. p. 188), where Forster explains that the tragic ending was his suggestion, Dickens himself not having thought of killing little Nell.

[7] *Dombey and Son* was written during the latter part of 1846, the whole of 1847, and the early part of 1848. During most of this time Dickens was on the Continent, subject, as he said, to "extraordinary nervousness it would be hardly possible to describe," and constantly haunted with the dread of "a race against time" (Forster's *Life*, vol. iii. pp. 221, 259–260). *Little Dorrit* came out between December 1855 to June 1857; for Dickens's restless and morbid condition at the time, see *ibid.*, pp. 156–157.

[8] See *Ivanhoe*, ch. xxx.

WORDSWORTH

Wordsworth's rank and scale among poets were determined by himself, in a single exclamation:

> What was the great Parnassus' self to thee,
> Mount Skiddaw?[1]

Answer his question faithfully, and you have the relation between the great masters of the Muse's teaching and the pleasant fingerer of his pastoral flute among the reeds of Rydal.

Wordsworth is simply a Westmoreland peasant, with considerably less shrewdness than most border Englishmen or Scotsmen inherit; and no sense of humour: but gifted (in this singularly) with vivid sense of natural beauty, and a pretty turn for reflections, not always acute, but, as far as they reach, medicinal to the fever of the restless and corrupted life around him. Water to parched lips may be better than Samian wine, but do not let us therefore confuse the qualities of wine and water. I much doubt there being many inglorious Miltons in our country churchyards; but I am very sure there are many Wordsworths resting there, who were inferior to the renowned one only in caring less to hear themselves talk.

With an honest and kindly heart, a stimulating egoism, a wholesome contentment in modest circumstances, and such sufficient ease, in that accepted state, as permitted the passing of a good deal of time in wishing that daisies could see the beauty of their own shadows,[2] and other such profitable mental exercises, Wordsworth has left us a series of studies of the graceful and happy shepherd life of our lake country, which to me personally, for one, are entirely sweet and precious; but they are only so as

[1] "Pelion and Ossa flourish. . . ."
[2] Vide Wordsworth's "So fair, so sweet. . . ."

the mirror of an existent reality in many ways more beautiful than its picture.

But the other day I went for an afternoon's rest into the cottage of one of our country people of old statesman class; cottage lying nearly midway between two village churches, but more conveniently for downhill walk towards one than the other. I found, as the good housewife made tea for me, that nevertheless she went up the hill to church. "Why do not you go to the nearer church?" I asked. "Don't you like the clergyman?" "Oh no, Sir", she answered, "it isn't that; but you know I couldn't leave my mother." "Your mother! she is buried at H— then?" "Yes, sir; and you know I couldn't go to church anywhere else."

That feelings such as these existed among the peasants, not of Cumberland only, but of all the tender earth that gives forth her fruit for the living, and receives her dead to peace, might perhaps have been, to our great and endless comfort, discovered before now, if Wordsworth had been content to tell us what he knew of his own villages and people, not as the leader of a new and only correct school of poetry, but simply as a country gentleman of sense and feeling, fond of primroses, kind to the parish children, and reverent of the spade with which Wilkinson had tilled his lands: and I am by no means sure that his influence on the stronger minds of his time was anywise hastened or extended by the spirit of tunefulness under whose guidance he discovered that heaven rhymed to seven, and Foy to boy.

Tuneful nevertheless at heart, and of the heavenly choir, I gladly and frankly acknowledge him; and our English literature enriched with a new and a singular virtue in the aerial purity and healthful rightness of his quiet song;—but *aerial* only,—not ethereal; and lowly in its privacy of light.

A measured mind, and calm; innocent, unrepentant; helpful to sinless creatures and scatheless, such of the flock as do not stray. Hopeful at least, if not faithful: content with intimations of immortality such as may be in skipping of lambs, and laughter of children—incurious to see in the hands the print of the Nails.

A gracious and constant mind; as the herbage of its native hills, fragrant and pure;—yet, to the sweep and the shadow, the stress and distress, of the greater souls of men, as the tufted thyme to the laurel wilderness of Tempe,—as the gleaming euphrasy to the dark branches of Dodona.

Fiction, Fair and Foul, pars. 50–52.

BYRON AND STYLE

"Parching summer hath no warrant
To consume this crystal well;
Rains, that make each brook a torrent,
Neither sully it, nor swell."[1]

So was it year by year, among the unthought-of hills. Little Duddon and child Rotha[2] ran clear and glad; and laughed from ledge to pool, and opened from pool to mere, translucent, through endless days of peace.

But eastward, between her orchard plains, Loire locked her embracing dead in silent sands; dark with blood rolled Isar; glacial-pale, Beresina-Lethe,[3] by whose shore the

[1] Wordsworth: *Inscriptions,* 1828 (iv. "Near the spring of the Hermitage").

[2] See Wordsworth's *To Rotha Quillinan,* his granddaughter, named after the stream that flows into Windermere from Grasmere and Rydal.

[3] The allusions are here to—(1) The *Noyades* at Nantes on the Loire (1793): "Women and men are tied together, feet and feet, hands and hands; and flung in: this they call *Mariage Republicain*" (Carlyle's *French Revolution,* Book v. ch. iii.). (2) The battle of Hohenlinden (Bavaria), December 1800, in which the French under Moreau defeated the Austrians with heavy loss. Ruskin doubtless was thinking of Campbell's poem on the battle—quoted in Vol. XXXI. p. 360—

"And bloodier yet the torrent flow
Of Isar, rolling rapidly"

weary hearts forgot their people, and their father's house.[4]

Nor unsullied, Tiber; nor unswoln, Arno and Aufidus;[5] and Euroclydon high on Helle's wave;[6] meantime, let our happy piety glorify the garden rocks with snowdrop circlet, and breathe the spirit of Paradise, where life is wise and innocent.[7]

Maps many have we, now-a-days clear in display of earth constituent, air current, and ocean tide. Shall we ever engrave the map of meaner research, whose shadings shall content themselves in the task of showing the depth, or drought,—the calm, or trouble, of Human Compassion?

For this is indeed all that is noble in the life of Man, and the source of all that is noble in the speech of Man.

—the Isar (twenty miles distant) being by poetic licence brought in sight of the field. The reference would, however, also fit the battle near Landshut on the Isar, where the French under Davoust defeated the Austrians (April 1809). (3) The battle on the banks of the Beresina (November 1812), in which the "grand army" of Napoleon was overwhelmed on the retreat from Moscow. Byron refers to the Retreat in the first stanza of *Mazeppa.*

[4] Psalms xlv. 10.

[5] The allusions here seem less precise, referring generally to the bloodshed in Napoleon's campaigns in Italy; Ruskin continuing his comparison by mentioning two of its most famous rivers, and then the Aufidus (Ofanto), famous in classical poetry for its swift and violent course (Horace, *Odes,* iii. 30, 10; iv. 9, 2). Next he passes to the Dardanelles, where the British fleet (as the ally of Russia against Napoleon) was threatening Constantinople.

[6] See the beginning of canto ii. of Byron's *Bride of Abydos* (1813): "The winds were high on Helle's wave," etc.

[7] See Wordsworth's piece of 1803:—

"Who fancied what a pretty sight
This Rock would be if edged around
With living snow-drops? circlet bright! . . .
It is the Spirit of Paradise
That prompts such work, a Spirit strong,
That gives to all the self-same bent
When life is wise and innocent"—

often referred to by Ruskin.

Had it narrowed itself then, in those days, out of all the world, into this peninsula between Cockermouth and Shap?

Not altogether so; but indeed the *Vocal* piety seemed conclusively to have retired (or excursed?) into that mossy hermitage, above Little Langdale.[8] The *Un*vocal piety, with the uncomplaining sorrow, of Man, may have a somewhat wider range, for aught we know: but history disregards those items; and of firmly proclaimed and sweetly canorous religion, there really seemed at that juncture none to be reckoned upon, east of Ingleborough, or north of Criffel.[9] Only under Furness Fells, or by Bolton Priory, it seems we can still write Ecclesiastical Sonnets, stanzas on the force of Prayer, Odes to Duty, and complimentary addresses to the Deity upon His endurance for adoration.[10] Far otherwise, over yonder, by Spezzia Bay, and Ravenna Pineta, and in ravines of Hartz.[11] There, the softest voices speak the wildest words; and Keats discourses of Endymion, Shelley of Demogorgon, Goethe of Lucifer, and Bürger of the Resurrection of Death unto Death[12]—while even Puritan Scotland and Episcopal Anglia produce for

[8] The reference is to Wordsworth's "Inscriptions supposed to be found in and near a Hermit's Cell."

[9] Ruskin takes the mountain Criffel, because it is just south of Burns's home (Dumfries).

[10] Here the references are to the *Ecclesiastical Sonnets; The Force of Prayer, or The Founding of Bolton Priory;* the *Ode to Duty;* and the following passage in the *Excursion,* Book iv.:—

"Thou, Thou alone
Art everlasting, and the blessed spirits,
Which Thou includest, as the sea her waves:
For adoration Thou endur'st."

[11] The references here must not be pressed too literally; for Keats wrote *Endymion* before leaving England for Italy; Shelley's *Prometheus Unbound* was written at Rome, and not, like several of his pieces, at Spezzia.

[12] In the ballad of Lenore, whose dead lover takes horse and rides with her to Death.

us only these three minstrels[13] of doubtful tone, who show but small respect for the "unco guid," put but limited faith in gifted Gilfillan, and translate with unflinching frankness the *Morgante Maggiore*.*

Dismal the aspect of the spiritual world, or at least the sound of it, might well seem to the eyes and ears of Saints (such as we had) of the period—dismal in angels' eyes also assuredly! Yet is it possible that the dismalness in angelic sight may be otherwise quartered, as it were, from the way of mortal heraldry; and that seen, and heard, of angels,[14]—again I say—hesitatingly—*is* it possible that the goodness of the Unco Guid, and the gift of Gilfillan, and the word of Mr. Blattergowl, may severally not have been the goodness of God, the gift of God, nor the word of God: but that in the much blotted and broken efforts at goodness, and in the careless gift which they themselves despised,† and in the sweet ryme and murmur of their unpurposed words, the Spirit of the Lord had, indeed, wandering, as in chaos days on lightless waters, gone forth in the hearts and from the lips of those other three strange

* "It must be put by the original, stanza for stanza, and verse for verse; and you will see what was permitted in a Catholic country and a bigoted age to Churchmen, on the score of Religion—and so tell those buffoons who accuse me of attacking the Liturgy.

"I write in the greatest haste, it being the hour of the Corso, and I must go and buffoon with the rest. My daughter Allegra is just gone with the Countess G. in Count G.'s coach and six. Our old Cardinal is dead, and the new one not appointed yet—but the masquing goes on the same." (Letter to Murray, 355th in Moore, dated Ravenna, Feb. 7, 1820.) "A dreadfully moral place, for you must not look at anybody's wife, except your neighbour's."

† See the mock, by Byron, of himself and all other modern poets, *Juan*, canto iii. stanza 80, and compare canto xiv. stanza 8.

---

[13] The reference is to Burns and his *Address to the Unco Guid;* Scott, for whose "gifted Gilfillan" (in *Waverley*, ch. xxxiv.), see below, §§ 113, 119; and Byron (whose translation of the first canto of *The Morgante Maggiore di Messer Luigi Pulci* was written at Ravenna in 1820).

[14] Timothy iii. 16.

prophets, even though they ate forbidden bread by the altar of the poured-out ashes, and even though the wild beast of the desert found them, and slew.[15]

This, at least, I know, that it had been well for England, though all her other prophets, of the Press, the Parliament, the Doctor's chair, and the Bishop's throne, had fallen silent; so only that she had been able to understand with her heart here and there the simplest line of these, her despised.

I take one at mere chance:

> "Who thinks of self, when gazing on the sky?"*

Well, I don't know; Mr. Wordsworth certainly did, and observed, with truth, that its clouds took a sober colouring in consequence of his experiences.[16] It is much if, indeed, this sadness be unselfish, and our eyes *have* kept loving watch o'er Man's Mortality. I have found it difficult to make any one now-a-days believe that such sobriety can be; and that Turner saw deeper crimson than others in the clouds of Goldau. But that any should yet think the clouds brightened by Man's *Im*mortality instead of dulled by his death,—and, gazing on the sky, look for the day when every eye must gaze also—for behold, He cometh with clouds[17]—this it is no more possible for Christian England to apprehend, however exhorted by her gifted and guid.

"But Byron was not thinking of such things!"—He, the reprobate! how should such as he think of Christ?

Perhaps not wholly as you or I think of Him. Take, at chance, another line or two, to try:

* *Island*, ii. 16, where see context.

---

[15] For the Bible words and allusions in this sentence, see Genesis i. 2; 1 Kings xiii. 3, 9, 19, 24.

[16] Again a reference to the *Ode on Intimations of Immortality*:—

> "The clouds that gather round the setting sun
> Do take a sober colouring from an eye
> That hath kept watch o'er man's mortality."

[17] Revelation i. 7.

"Carnage (so Wordsworth tells you) is God's daughter;*
If *he* speak truth, she is Christ's sister, and
Just now, behaved as in the Holy Land."

Blasphemy, cry you, good reader? Are you sure you understand it? The first line I gave you was easy Byron—almost shallow Byron; these are of the man in his depth, and you will not fathom them, like a tarn—nor in a hurry.

"Just now behaved as in the Holy Land." How *did* Carnage behave in the Holy Land then? You have all been greatly questioning, of late, whether the sun, which you find to be now going out, ever stood still. Did you in any lagging minute, on those scientific occasions, chance to reflect what he was bid stand still *for*? or if not—will you please look—and what also, going forth again as a strong man to run his course,[19] he saw, rejoicing?

"Then Joshua passed from Makkedah unto Libnah —and fought against Libnah. And the Lord delivered

* *Juan*, viii. 9; but, by your Lordship's quotation, Wordsworth says "instrument,"—not "daughter."[18] Your Lordship had better have said "Infant" and taken the Woolwich authorities to witness: only Infant would not have rymed.

---

[18] Byron, however, was quite correct, Ruskin being misled by Wordsworth's subsequent revision. Byron's note on the passage in *Don Juan* was as follows:—

"(*Thanksgiving Ode*, January 18, 1816, stanza xii. 20–23)
"But Thy[1] most dreaded instrument,
In working out a pure intent,
Is Man—arrayed for mutual slaughter,—
Yea, Carnage is Thy daughter."

[1] "To wit, the Deity's: this is perhaps as pretty a pedigree for murder as ever was found out by Garter King at Arms. What would have been said, had any free-spoken people discovered such a lineage?"

Byron's criticism went home, and Wordsworth, in the latest edition of his poems, revised by himself (1845), altered the lines thus:—

"But Man is Thy most awful instrument,
In working out a pure intent;
Thou cloth'st the wicked in their dazzling mail,
And for Thy righteous purpose they prevail."

[19] Psalms xix. 5.

> it and the king thereof into the hand of Israel, and he smote it with the edge of the sword, and all the souls that were therein."

And from Lachish to Eglon, and from Eglon to Kirjath-Arba, and Sarah's grave in the Amorites' land,

> "and Joshua smote all the country of the hills and of the south—and of the vale and of the springs, and all their kings: he left none remaining, but utterly destroyed all that breathed—as the Lord God of Israel commanded."[20]

Thus, "it is written":[21] though you perhaps do not so often hear *these* texts preached from, as certain others about taking away the sins of the world.[22] I wonder how the world would like to part with them! hitherto it has always preferred parting first with its life—and God has taken it at its word. But Death is not *His* Begotten Son,[23] for all that; nor is the death of the innocent in battle carnage His "instrument for working out a pure intent," as Mr. Wordsworth puts it; but Man's instrument for working

[20] Joshua x. 29, 30, 40.
[21] Matthew ii. 5, etc.
[22] For instance, John i. 29; iii. 17.
[23] The MS. here reads differently:—

"But Death is not His daughter, for all that; not even the death of the innocent in battle carnage—how much less that

'whose *threatened* sting
Turns Life to terror—even though in its sheath.'

A very notable piece of theology, you will please observe, and a sound; instead of the blasphemy you took it for.

"The real blasphemy is in picking out the texts of the Bible that please yourself—and saying that God couldn't have meant the others, or really, he is not the God you took Him for; and you must evolve a better one out of *your* moral consciousness, forsooth. 'Thou shalt not make unto thee any *graven* Image. No;—but perhaps an *Un*graven one, always on æsthetic principles, maybe—an improvement on the Unideal God. It was not, however . . ."

out an impure one, as Byron would have you to know. Theology perhaps less orthodox, but certainly more reverent;—neither is the Woolwich Infant a Child of God; neither does the iron-clad *Thunderer* utter thunders of God—which facts if you had had the grace or sense to learn from Byron, instead of accusing him of blasphemy, it had been better at this day for *you,* and for many a savage soul also, by Euxine shore, and in Zulu and Afghan lands.

It was neither, however, for the theology, nor the use, of these lines that I quoted them; but to note this main point of Byron's own character. He was the first great Englishman who felt the cruelty of war, and, in its cruelty, the shame. Its guilt had been known to George Fox—its folly shown practically by Penn. But the *compassion* of the pious world had still for the most part been shown only in keeping its stock of Barabbases unhanged if possible: and, till Byron came, neither Kunersdorf, Eylau, nor Waterloo, had taught the pity and the pride of men that

"The drying up a single tear has more
Of honest fame than shedding seas of gore."*

Such pacific verse would not indeed have been acceptable to the Edinburgh volunteers on Portobello sands. But Byron can write a battle song too, when it is *his* cue to fight. If you look at the introduction to the "Isles of Greece," namely the 85th and 86th stanzas of the 3rd canto of *Don Juan,* you will find—what will you *not* find, if only you understand them! "He" in the first line, remember, means the typical modern poet.

"Thus usually, when he was asked to sing,
He gave the different nations something national.
'Twas all the same to him—'God save the King'

* *Juan,* viii. 3; compare 14, and 63, with all its lovely context 61–68: then 82, and afterwards slowly and with thorough attention, the Devil's speech, beginning, "Yes, Sir, you forget" in scene 2 of "The Deformed Transformed": then Sardanapalus's, Act i. scene 2, beginning, "He is gone, and on his finger bears my signet," and finally the "Vision of Judgment," stanzas 3 to 5.

> Or 'Ça ira' according to the fashion all;
> His muse made increment of anything
> From the high lyric down to the low rational:
> If Pindar sang horse-races, what should hinder
> Himself from being as pliable as Pindar?
>
> In France, for instance, he would write a chanson;
> In England a six-canto quarto tale;
> In Spain, he'd make a ballad or romance on
> The last war—much the same in Portugal;
> In Germany, the Pegasus he'd prance on
> Would be old Goethe's—(see what says de Staël)
> In Italy, he'd ape the 'Trecentisti';
> In Greece, he'd sing some sort of hymn like this t' ye."

Note first here, as we did in Scott, the concentrating and foretelling power. The "God save the Queen" in England, fallen hollow now, as the "Ça ira" in France—not a man in France knowing where either France or "that" (whatever "that" may be) is going to; nor the Queen of England daring, for her life, to ask the tiniest Englishman to do a single thing he doesn't like;—nor any salvation, either of Queen or Realm, being any more possible to God, unless under the direction of the Royal Society: then, note the estimate of height and depth in poetry, swept in an instant, "high lyric to low rational." Pindar to Pope (knowing Pope's height, too, all the while, no man better);[24] then, the poetic power of France—resumed in a word—Béranger; then the cut at *Marmion*, entirely deserved, as we shall see, yet kindly given, for everything he names in these two stanzas is the best of its kind; then Romance in Spain on—the *last* war, (*present* war not being to Spanish poetical taste); then, Goethe the real heart of all Germany, and last, the aping of the Trecentisti which has since consummated itself in Pre-Raphaelitism! that also being the best thing Italy has done through England, whether in Rossetti's "blessed damozels" or Burne-Jones's

[24] See Byron's vindication of Pope in his "Reply to *Blackwood's Edinburgh Magazine*," vol. iv. p. 489 in his *Letters and Journals*, ed. 1900.

"days of creation." Lastly comes the mock at himself—the modern English Greek—(followed up by the "degenerate into hands like mine" in the song itself); and then—to amazement, forth he thunders in his Achilles-voice. We have had one line of him in his clearness—five of him in his depth—sixteen of him in his play. Hear now but these, out of his whole heart:—

"What,—silent yet? and silent *all*?
  Ah no, the voices of the dead
Sound like a distant torrent's fall,
  And answer, 'Let *one* living head,
But one, arise—we come—we come:'
—'Tis but the living who are dumb."

Resurrection, this, you see like Bürger's; but not of death unto death.

"Sound like a distant torrent's fall." I said the *whole* heart of Byron was in this passage. First its compassion, then its indignation, and the third element, not yet examined, that love of the beauty of this world in which the three—unholy—children, of its Fiery Furnace[25] were like to each other; but Byron the widest-hearted. Scott and Burns love Scotland more than Nature itself: for Burns the moon must rise over Cumnock Hills,[26]—for Scott, the Rymer's glen divide the Eildons;[27] but, for Byron, Loch-na-Gar *with Ida,* looks o'er Troy, and the soft murmurs of the Dee and the Bruar change into voices of the dead on distant Marathon.[28]

[25] Daniel iii.

[26] See Burns's *Death and Doctor Hornbook.*

[27] It was Michael Scott, the wizard, who "cleft Eildon Hills in three": see *Lay of the Last Minstrel,* canto ii. stanza 13, and Scott's note there. Among the Eildons is Scott's "The Rymer's Glen," the traditional scene of Thomas of Ercildoune's interview with the Queen of Faerie.

[28] Here Ruskin first quotes from Byron himself:—
"He who first met the Highland's swelling blue
Will love each peak that shows a kindred hue,
Hail in each crag a friend's familiar face,
And clasp the mountain in his mind's embrace . . .
The infant rapture still survived the boy,
And Loch na Garr with Ida looked o'er Troy."

Yet take the parallel from Scott, by a field of homelier rest:—

"And silence aids—though the steep hills
Send to the lake a thousand rills;
In summer tide, so soft they weep,
The sound but lulls the ear asleep;
Your horse's hoof-tread sounds too rude,
So stilly is the solitude.

Nought living meets the eye or ear,
But well I ween the dead are near;
For though, in feudal strife, a foe
Hath laid our Lady's Chapel low,
Yet still beneath the hallowed soil,
The peasant rests him from his toil,
And, dying, bids his bones be laid
Where erst his simple fathers prayed."[29]

And last take the same note of sorrow—with Burns's finger on the fall of it:

"Mourn, ilka grove the cushat kens,
Ye hazly shaws and briery dens,
Ye burnies, wimplin' down your glens
Wi' toddlin' din,
Or foamin' strang wi' hasty stens
Frae lin to lin."[30]

As you read, one after another, these fragments of chant by the great masters, does not a sense come upon you of some element in their passion, no less than in their sound, different, specifically, from that of "Parching summer hath

(*The Island,* 1823, canto ii. stanza 12.) He then applies the sentiment of the lines to the pathos which Byron puts into his descriptions of Marathon (*Childe Harold,* canto ii. 88 *seq.,* and *Don Juan,* canto iii.: "The mountains look on Marathon," etc.). For Byron's love of Lachin y Gair (or Loch na Garr), see the poem in *Hours of Idleness.*

[29] Introduction to canto ii. of *Marmion.*

[30] *Elegy on Captain Matthew Henderson.*

no warrant"? Is it more profane, think you—or more tender —nay, perhaps, in the core of it, more true?

For instance, when we are told that

> "Wharfe, as he moved along,
> To matins joined a mournful voice,"[31]

is this disposition of the river's mind to pensive psalmody quite logically accounted for by the previous statement, (itself by no means rhythmically dulcet,) that

> "The boy is in the arms of Wharfe,
> And strangled by a merciless force"?

Or, when we are led into the improving reflection,

> "How sweet were leisure, could it yield no more
> Than 'mid this wave-washed churchyard to recline,
> From pastoral graves extracting thoughts divine!"[32]

—is the divinity of the extract assured to us by its being made at leisure, and in a reclining attitude—as compared with the meditations of otherwise active men, in an erect one? Or are we perchance, many of us, still erring somewhat in our notions alike of Divinity and Humanity, poetical extraction, and moral position?

On the chance of its being so, might I ask hearing for just a few words more of the school of Belial?

Their occasion, it must be confessed, is a quite unjustifiable one. Some very wicked people—mutineers, in fact —have retired, misanthropically, into an unfrequented part of the country, and there find themselves safe indeed, but extremely thirsty. Whereupon Byron thus gives them to drink:—

> "A little stream came tumbling from the height
> And straggling into ocean as it might.

[31] Wordsworth, *The Force of Prayer*.

[32] No. 31 of *The River Duddon: a Series of Sonnets*. In the second of the lines here quoted, Wordsworth wrote "that," not "this."

Its bounding crystal frolicked in the ray
And gushed from cliff to crag with saltless spray,
Close on the wild wide ocean,—yet as pure
And fresh as Innocence; and more secure.
Its silver torrent glittered o'er the deep
As the shy chamois' eye o'erlooks the steep,
While, far below, the vast and sullen swell
Of ocean's Alpine azure rose and fell."*

Now, I beg, with such authority as an old workman may take concerning his trade, having also looked at a waterfall or two in my time, and not unfrequently at a wave, to assure the reader that here *is* entirely first-rate literary work. Though Lucifer himself had written it, the thing is itself good, and not only so, but unsurpassably good, the closing line being probably the best concerning the sea yet written by the race of the sea-kings.

64. But Lucifer himself *could* not have written it; neither any servant of Lucifer.[33] I do not doubt but that most readers were surprised at my saying, in the close of my first paper, that Byron's "style" depended in any wise on his views respecting the Ten Commandments. That so all-important a thing as "style" should depend in the least upon so ridiculous a thing as moral sense: or that Allegra's father, watching her drive by in Count G.'s coach and six, had any remnant of so ridiculous a thing to guide, —or check,—his poetical passion, may seem more than questionable to the liberal and chaste philosophy of the

* *Island,* iii. 3, and compare, of shore surf, the "slings its high flakes, shivered into sleet" of stanza 7.

[33] In place of this brief sentence, the MS. has:—

"I tell you this, mind you, in my old name and faculty of 'author of *Modern Painters*'—having looked at a waterfall or two in my time, and not unfrequently at a wave, and got some things fairly well said, though I say it, concerning both; and on such standing, or reclination, do farther certify you that neither I in my weakness, nor Byron in his might, could either of us have said one right word of these lovely and mighty things, but that we both of us had in our hearts reverence for the Laws of God and pity for the creatures of earth."

existing British public. But, first of all, putting the question of who writes or speaks aside, do you, good reader, *know* good "style" when you get it? Can you say, of half-a-dozen given lines taken anywhere out of a novel, or poem, or play, That is good, essentially, in style, or bad, essentially? and can you say why such half-dozen lines are good, or bad?

I imagine that in most cases, the reply would be given with hesitation; yet if you will give me a little patience, and take some accurate pains, I can show you the main tests of style in the space of a couple of pages.

I take two examples of absolutely perfect, and in manner highest, i.e. kingly, and heroic, style: the first example in expression of anger, the second of love.

(1) We are glad the Dauphin is so pleasant with us,
His present, and your pains, we thank you for.
When we have match'd our rackets to these balls,
We will in France, by God's grace, play a set
Shall strike his father's crown into the hazard.[34]

(2) My gracious Silence, hail!
Wouldst thou have laughed, had I come coffin'd home
That weep'st to see me triumph? Ah, my dear,
Such eyes the widows in Corioli wear
And mothers that lack sons.[35]

Let us note, point by point, the conditions of greatness common to both these passages, so opposite in temper.

(*A*) Absolute command over all passion, however intense; this the first-of-first conditions, (see the King's own sentence just before, "We are no tyrant, but a Christian King, Unto *whose grace* our passion is as subject As are our wretches fettered in our prisons"); and with this self-command, the supremely surveying grasp of every thought that is to be uttered, before its utterance; so that each may come in its exact place, time, and connection. The slightest hurry, the misplacing of a word, or the unneces-

[34] *Henry V*, I, 2.
[35] *Coriolanus*, II, 1.

sary accent on a syllable, would destroy the "style" in an instant.

(*B*) Choice of the fewest and simplest words that can be found in the compass of the language, to express the thing meant: these few words being also arranged in the most straightforward and intelligible way; allowing inversion only when the subject can be made primary without obscurity: thus, "his present, and your pains, we thank you for" is better than "we thank you for his present and your pains", because the Dauphin's gift is by courtesy put before the Ambassador's pains; but "when to these balls our rackets we have matched" would have spoiled the style in a moment, because—I was going to have said, ball and racket are of equal rank, and therefore only the natural order proper; but also here the natural order is the desired one, the English racket to have precedence of the French ball. In the fourth line the "in France" comes first, as announcing the most important resolution of action; the "by God's grace" next, as the only condition rendering resolution possible; the detail of issue follows with the strictest limit in the final word. The King does not say "danger", far less "dishonour", but "hazard" only; of *that* he is, humanly speaking, sure.

(*C*) Perfectly emphatic and clear utterance of the chosen words; slowly in the degree of their importance, with omission however of every word not absolutely required; and natural use of the familiar contractions of final dissyllable. Thus "play a set shall strike" is better than "play a set *that* shall strike", and "match'd" is kingly short—no necessity of metre could have excused "matched" instead. On the contrary, the first three words, "We are glad", would have been spoken by the king more slowly and fully than any other syllables in the whole passage, first pronouncing the kingly "we" at its proudest, and then the "are" as a continuous state, and then the "glad", as the exact contrary of what the ambassadors expected him to be.

(*D*) Absolute spontaneity in doing all this, easily and necessarily as the heart beats. The king *cannot* speak otherwise than he does—nor the hero. The words not merely come to them, but are compelled to them. Even lisping numbers "come", but mighty numbers are ordained, and inspired.

(*E*) Melody in the words, changeable with their passion, fitted to it exactly, and the utmost of which the language is capable—the melody in prose being Eolian and variable—in verse, nobler by submitting itself to stricter law.

(*F*) Utmost spiritual contents in the words; so that each carries not only its instant meaning, but a cloudy companionship of higher or darker meaning according to the passion—nearly always indicated by metaphor: "play a set" —sometimes by abstraction—(thus in the second passage "silence" for silent one) sometimes by description instead of direct epithet ("coffined" for dead) but always indicative of there being more in the speaker's mind than he has said, or than he can say, full though his saying be. On the quantity of this attendant fulness depends the majesty of style; that is to say, virtually, on the quantity of contained thought in briefest words, such thought being primarily loving and true: and this the sum of all—that nothing can well be said, but with truth, nor beautifully, but by love.

These are the essential conditions of noble speech in prose and verse alike, but the adoption of the form of verse, and especially rimed verse, means the addition to all these qualities of one more; of music, that is to say, not Eolian merely, but Apolline; a construction or architecture of words fitted and befitting, under external laws of time and harmony.

When Byron says "rhyme is of the rude", he means that Burns needs it,—while Henry the Fifth does not, nor Plato, nor Isaiah—yet in this need of it by the simple, it becomes all the more religious: and thus the loveliest pieces of Christian language are all in rime—the best of Dante, Chaucer, Douglas, Shakespeare, Spenser, and Sidney.

Fiction, Fair and Foul, pars. 53–68.

BYRON'S SENSIBILITY

If now, with the echo of these perfect verses in your mind,[1] you turn to Byron, and glance over, or recall to memory, enough of him to give means of exact comparison, you will, or should, recognize these following kinds of mischief in him. First, if any one offends him—as for instance Mr Southey, or Lord Elgin[2]—"his manners have not that repose that marks the caste",[3] etc. *This* defect in his Lordship's style, being myself scrupulously and even painfully reserved in the use of vituperative language, I need not say how deeply I deplore.

Secondly. In the best and most violet-bedded bits of his work there is yet, as compared with Elizabethan and earlier verse, a strange taint; and indefinable—evening flavour of Covent Garden, as it were;—not to say, escape of gas in the Strand. That is simply what it proclaims itself—London air. If he had lived all his life in Greenhead Ghyll, things would of course have been different. But it was his fate to come to town—modern town—like Michael's son; and modern London (and Venice) are answerable for the state of their drains, not Byron.

Thirdly. His melancholy is without any relief whatsoever; his jest sadder than his earnest; while, in Elizabethan work, all lament is full of hope, and all pain of balsam.

Of this evil he has himself told you the cause in a single line, prophetic of all things since and now. "Where *he* gazed, a gloom pervaded space."[4]

So that, for instance, while Mr Wordsworth, on a visit to town, being an exemplary early riser, could walk, felicitous, on Westminster Bridge, remarking how the city now did like a garment wear the beauty of the morning;

[1] Herrick: *Dirge for Jephthah's Daughter.*
[2] Vide: *Don Juan,* I, 222; X, 13; and *Curse of Minerva.*
[3] Tennyson: *Lady Clara Vere de Vere.*
[4] *Vision of Judgment,* 24.

Byron, rising somewhat later, contemplated only the garment which the beauty of the morning had by that time received for wear from the city: and again, while Mr Wordsworth, in irrepressible religious rapture, calls God to witness that the houses seem asleep, Byron, lame demon as he was, flying smoke-drifted, unroofs the houses at a glance, and sees what the mighty cockney heart of them contains in the still lying of it, and will stir up to purpose in the waking business of it,

> The sordor of civilization, mixed
> With all the savage which Man's fall hath fixed.[5]

Fourthly, with this steadiness of bitter melancholy, there is joined a sense of the material beauty, both of inanimate nature, the lower animals, and human beings, which in the iridescence, colour-depth, and morbid (I use the word deliberately) mystery and softness of it,—with other qualities indescribable by any single words, and only to be analysed by extreme care,—is found, to the full, only in five men that I know of in modern times: namely, Rousseau, Shelley, Byron, Turner, and myself,—differing totally and throughout the entire group of us, from the delight in clear-struck beauty of Angelico and the Trecentisti; and separated, much more singularly, from the cheerful joys of Chaucer, Shakespeare, and Scott, by its unaccountable affection for "Rokkes blak"[6] and other forms of terror and power, such as those of the ice-oceans, which to Shakespeare were only Alpine rheum;[7] and the Via Malas and Diabolic Bridges which Dante would have condemned none but lost souls to climb, or cross;—all this love of impending mountains, coiled thunder-clouds, and dangerous sea, being joined in us with a sulky, almost ferine, love of retreat in valleys of Charmettes, gulphs of Spezzia, ravines of Olympus, low lodgings in Chelsea, and close brushwood at Coniston.

[5] *Island,* II, 4.
[6] Chaucer: *Franklin's Tale.*
[7] *Henry V,* III, 5.

And, lastly, also in the whole group of us, glows volcanic instinct of Astraean justice returning not to, but up out of, the earth, which will not at all suffer us to rest any more in Pope's serene "whatever is, is right"[8]; but holds, on the contrary, profound conviction that about ninety-nine hundredths of whatever at present is, is wrong: conviction making four of us, according to our several manners, leaders of revolution for the poor, and declarers of political doctrine monstrous to the ears of mercenary mankind; and driving the fifth, less sanguine, into mere painted-melody of lament over the fallacy of Hope and the implacableness of Fate.

In Byron the indignation, the sorrow, and the effort are joined to the death: and they are the parts of his nature (as of mine also in its feebler terms), which the selfishly comfortable public have, literally, no conception of whatever; and from which the piously sentimental public, offering up daily the pure oblation of divine tranquillity, shrink with anathema not unembittered by alarm.

Fiction, Fair and Foul, pars. 72–74.

GEORGE ELIOT

All healthy and helpful literature sets simple bars between right and wrong; assumes the possibility, in men and women, of having healthy minds in healthy bodies, and loses no time in the diagnosis of fever or dyspepsia in either; least of all in the particular kind of fever which signifies the ungoverned excess of any appetite or passion. The "dulness" which many modern readers inevitably feel, and some modern blockheads think it creditable to allege, in Scott, consists not a little in his absolute purity from every loathsome element or excitement of the lower passions; so that people who live habitually in Satyric or

[8] *Essay on Man,* Ep. 1, last line.

hircine conditions of thought find him as insipid as they would a picture of Angelico's. The accurate and trenchant separation between him and the common railroad-station novelist is that, in his total method of conception, only lofty character is worth describing at all; and it becomes interesting, not by its faults, but by the difficulties and accidents of the fortune through which it passes, while, in the railway novel, interest is obtained with the vulgar reader for the vilest character, because the author describes carefully to his recognition the blotches, burrs and pimples in which the paltry nature resembles his own. *The Mill on the Floss* is perhaps the most striking instance extant of this study of cutaneous disease. There is not a single person in the book of the smallest importance to anybody in the world but themselves, or whose qualities deserved so much as a line of printer's type in their description. There is no girl alive, fairly clever, half educated, and unluckily related, whose life has not at least as much in it as Maggie's, to be described and to be pitied. Tom is a clumsy and cruel lout, with the making of better things in him (and the same may be said of nearly every Englishman at present smoking and elbowing his way through the ugly world his blunders have contributed to the making of); while the rest of the characters are simply the sweepings out of a Pentonville omnibus.

Fiction, Fair and Foul, par. 108.

BYRON AND TRUTH

Neither the force and precision, nor the rhythm, of Byron's language, were at all the central reasons for my taking him for master. Knowing the Song of Moses and the Sermon on the Mount by heart, and half the Apocalypse besides, I was in no need of tutorship either in the majesty or simplicity of English words; and for their logical arrangement, I had Byron's own master, Pope, since I could lisp. But the thing wholly new and precious to me in Byron was his measured and living *truth*—measured, as compared with Homer; and living, as compared with everybody else. My own inexorable measuring wand,—not enchanter's, but cloth-worker's and builder's,—reduced to mere incredibility all the statements of the poets usually called sublime. It was of no use for Homer to tell me that Pelion was put on the top of Ossa.[1] I knew perfectly well it wouldn't go on the top of Ossa. Of no use for Pope to tell me that trees where his mistress looked would crowd into a shade,[2] because I was satisfied that they would do nothing of the sort. Nay, the whole world, as it was described to me either by poetry or theology, was every hour becoming more and more shadowy and impossible. I rejoiced in all stories of Pallas and Venus, of Achilles and Aeneas, of Elijah and St John: but, without doubting in my heart that there were real spirits of wisdom and beauty, nor that there had been invincible heroes and inspired prophets, I felt already, with fatal and increasing sadness, that there was no clear utterance about any of them—that there were for *me* neither Goddess guides nor prophetic teachers; and that the poetical histories, whether of this world or the next, were to me as the words

[1] *Odyssey*, XI, 315.
[2] *Pastorals*, II, 74.

of Peter to the shut up disciples—"as idle tales; and they believed them not".[3]

But here at last I had found a man who spoke only of what he had seen, and known; and spoke without exaggeration, without mystery, without enmity, and without mercy. "That *is* so;—make what you will of it!" Shakespeare said the Alps voided their rheum on the valleys, which indeed is precisely true,—but it was told in a mythic manner, and with an unpleasant British bias to the nasty. But Byron, saying that "the glacier's cold and restless mass moves onward day by day",[4] said plainly what he saw and knew,—no more. So also, *Arabian Nights* had told me of thieves who lived in enchanted caves, and beauties who fought with genii in the air; but Byron told me of thieves with whom he had ridden on their own hills, and of the fair Persians or Greeks who lived and died under the very sun that rose over my visible Norwood hills.

And in this narrow, but sure, truth, to Byron, as already to me, it appeared that Love was a transient thing, and Death a dreadful one. He did not attempt to console me for Jessie's death, by saying she was happier in Heaven; or for Charles's, by saying it was a Providential dispensation to me on Earth. He did not tell me that war was a just price for the glory of captains, or that the National command of murder diminished its guilt. Of all things within range of human thought he felt the facts, and discerned the natures with accurate justice.

But even all this he might have done, and yet been no master of mine, had not he sympathized with me in reverent love of beauty, and indignant recoil from ugliness. The witch of the Staubbach in her rainbow was a greatly more pleasant vision than Shakespeare's, like a rat without a tail, or Burns's, in her cutty sark.[5] The sea-king Conrad had an immediate advantage with me over Cole-

[3] Vide *Luke*, xxiv, 11.
[4] *Manfred*, I, 1.
[5] *Manfred*, II, 2; *Macbeth*, I, 3; *Tam o' Shanter*.

ridge's long, lank, brown, and ancient, mariner; and whatever Pope might have gracefully said, or honestly felt of Windsor woods and streams, was mere tinkling cymbal to me, compared with Byron's love of Lachin-y-Gair.

I must pause here, in tracing the sources of his influence over me, lest the reader should mistake the analysis which I am now able to give them, for a description of the feelings possible to me at fifteen. Most of these, however, were assuredly within the knot of my unfolding mind—as the saffron of the crocus yet beneath the earth; and Byron —though he could not teach me to love mountains or sea more than I did in childhood, first animated them for me with the sense of real human nobleness and grief. He taught me the meaning of Chillon and of Meillerie, and bade me seek first in Venice—the ruined homes of Foscari and Falier.

And observe, the force with which he struck depended again on there being unquestionable reality of person in his stories, as of principle in his thoughts. Romance, enough and to spare, I had learnt from Scott—but his Lady of the Lake was as openly fictitious as his White Maid of Avenel: while Rogers was a mere dilettante, who felt no difference between landing "where Tell leaped ashore", or standing where "St Preux has stood". Even Shakespeare's Venice was visionary; and Portia as impossible as Miranda. But Byron told me of, and reanimated for me, the real people whose feet had worn the marble I trod on.

One word only, though it trenches on a future subject, I must permit myself about his rhythm. Its natural flow in almost prosaic simplicity and tranquillity interested me extremely, in opposition alike to the symmetrical clauses of Pope's logical metre, and to the balanced strophes of classic and Hebrew verse. But though I followed his manner instantly in what verses I wrote for my own amusement, my respect for the structural, as opposed to fluent, force of the classic measures, supported as it was partly by Byron's contempt for his own work, and, partly by my own architect's instinct for "the principle of the pyramid", made me long endeavour, in forming my prose style, to keep the cadences of Pope and Johnson for all serious statement.

Praeterita, vol. I, pars. 172–175.

DR JOHNSON

I have said that had it not been for constant reading of the Bible, I might probably have taken Johnson for my model of English. To a useful extent I have always done so; in these first essays, partly because I could not help it, partly of set, and well-set purpose.

On our foreign journeys, it being of course desirable to keep the luggage as light as possible, my father had judged that four little volumes of Johnson—the *Idler* and the *Rambler*—did, under names wholly appropriate to the circumstances, contain more substantial literary nourishment than could be, from any other author, packed into so portable compass. And accordingly, in spare hours, and on wet days, the turns and returns of reiterated *Rambler* and iterated *Idler* fastened themselves in my ears and mind; nor was it possible for me, till long afterwards, to quit myself of Johnsonian symmetry and balance in sentences intended, either with swordsman's or paviour's blow, to cleave an enemy's crest, or drive down the oaken pile of a principle. I never for an instant compared Johnson to Scott, Pope, Byron, or any of the really great writers whom I loved. But I at once and for ever recognized in him a man entirely sincere, and infallibly wise in the view and estimate he gave of the common questions, business, and ways of the world. I valued his sentences not primarily because they were symmetrical, but because they were just, and clear; it is a method of judgment rarely used by the average public, who ask from an author always, in the first place, arguments in favour of their own opinions, in elegant terms; and are just as ready with their applause for a sentence of Macaulay's, which may have no more sense in it than a blot pinched between double paper, as to reject one of Johnson's, telling against their own prejudice,—though its symmetry be as of thunder answering from two horizons.

I hold it more than happy that, during those continent journeys, in which the vivid excitement of the greater part of the day left me glad to give spare half hours to the study of a thoughtful book, Johnson was the one author accessible to me. No other writer could have secured me, as he did, against all chance of being misled by my own sanguine and metaphysical temperament. He taught me carefully to measure life, and distrust fortune; and he secured me, by his adamantine common-sense, for ever, from being caught in the cobwebs of German metaphysics, or sloughed in the English drainage of them.

I open at this moment, the larger of the volumes of the *Idler* to which I owe so much. After turning over a few leaves, I chance on the closing sentence of No. 65; which transcribing, I may show the reader in sum what it taught me,—in words which, writing this account of myself, I conclusively obey:—

> Of these learned men, let those who aspire to the same praise imitate the diligence, and avoid the scrupulosity. Let it always be remembered that life is short, that knowledge is endless, and that many doubts deserve not to be cleared. Let those whom nature and study have qualified to teach mankind, tell us what they have learned while they are yet able to tell it, and trust their reputation only to themselves.

It is impossible for me now to know how far my own honest desire for truth, and compassionate sense of what is instantly helpful to creatures who are every instant perishing, might have brought me, in their own time, to think and judge as Johnson thought and measured,—even had I never learned of him. He at least set me in the straight path from the beginning, and, whatever time I might waste in vain pleasure, or weak effort, he saved me for ever from false thoughts and futile speculations.

Praeterita, vol. I, pars. 251–252.

SCOTT AND HISTORY

It is strange to me, even now, on reflection—to find how great the influence of this double ocean coast and Cheviot mountain border was upon Scott's imagination; and how salutary they were in withdrawing him from the morbid German fancies which proved so fatal to Carlyle; but there was this grand original difference between the two, that, with Scott, his story-telling and singing were all in the joyful admiration of that past with which he could re-people the scenery he gave the working part of his day to traverse, and all the sensibility of his soul to love; while Carlyle's mind, fixed anxiously on the future, and besides embarrassed by the practical pinching, as well as the unconfessed shame, of poverty, saw and felt from his earliest childhood nothing but the faultfulness and gloom of the Present.

It has been impossible, hitherto, to make the modern reader understand the vastness of Scott's true historical knowledge, underneath its romantic colouring, nor the concentration of it in the production of his eternally great poems and romances. English ignorance of the Scottish dialect is at present nearly total; nor can it be without very earnest effort, that the melody of Scott's verse, or the meaning of his dialogue, can ever again be estimated. He must now be read with the care which we give to Chaucer; but with the greater reward, that what is only a dream in Chaucer, becomes to us, understood from Scott, a consummate historical morality and truth.

The first two of his great poems, *The Lay of the Last*

Minstrel and *Marmion,* are the re-animation of the Border legends, closing with the truest and grandest battle-piece that, so far as I know, exists in the whole compass of literature;—the absolutely fairest in justice to both contending nations, the absolutely most beautiful in its conceptions of both. And that the palm in that conception remains with the Scotch, through the sorrow of their defeat, is no more than accurate justice to the national character, which rose from the fraternal branches of the Douglas of Tantallon and the Douglas of Dunkeld. But,—between Tantallon and Dunkeld,—what moor or mountain is there over which the purple cloud of Scott's imagination has not wrapt its light, in those two great poems?—followed by the entirely heroic enchantment of *The Lady of the Lake,* dwelling on the highland virtue which gives the strength of clanship, and the Lowland honour of knighthood, founded on the Catholic religion. Then came the series of novels, in which, as I have stated elsewhere, those which dealt with the history of other nations, such as *Ivanhoe, Kenilworth, Woodstock, Quentin Durward, Peveril of the Peak, The Betrothed,* and *The Crusaders,* however attractive to the general world, were continually weak in fancy, and false in prejudice; but the literally Scotch novels, *Waverley, Guy Mannering, The Antiquary, Old Mortality, The Heart of Midlothian, The Abbot, Redgauntlet,* and *The Fortunes of Nigel* are, whatever the modern world may think of them, as faultless, throughout, as human work can be: and eternal examples of the ineffable art which is taught by the loveliest nature to her truest children.

Praeterita, vol. III, pars. 71–72.

INDEX